Here Comes the Bride

D0111538

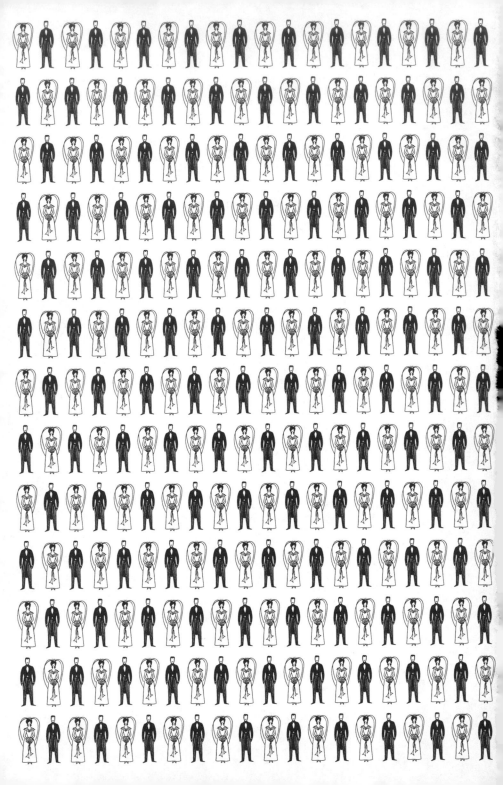

Here Comes the Bride

Women, Weddings, and the Marriage Mystique

Jaclyn Geller

FOUR WALLS EIGHT WINDOWS

NEW YORK / LONDON

PUBLISHED IN THE UNITED STATES BY

Four Walls Eight Windows

39 West 14th Street

New York, NY 10011

http://www.4w8w.com

UK OFFICES:

Four Walls Eight Windows / Turnaround

Unit 3 Olympia Trading Estate

Coburg Road, Wood Green

London N22 6TZ

First printing June 2001

LIBRARY OF CONGRESS CATALOGING-IN-PUBLICATION DATA:

Geller, Jaclyn.

    Here comes the bride : women, weddings, and the marriage mystique / Jaclyn Geller.

p. cm.

    Includes index

    ISBN: 1-56858-193-9

      1. Weddings—United States—Planning. 2. Weddings—United States—Psychological aspects. 3. Marriage customs and rites—United States. 4. United States—Attitudes. 5. Courtship—United States. 6. Mate selection—United States. I. Title.

HQ745.G45 2001

395.2'2—dc21   2001 023161

Printed in Canada

Interior design by Sara E. Stemen

10 9 8 7 6 5 4 3 2 1

In memory of Joan Goldstein

Contents

Acknowledgments

BECAUSE OUR SOCIETY values romantic relationships above all others, there exists no public ritual for affirming commitment and expressing gratitude to friends. It is therefore both a pleasure and a relief to formally thank the people who have sustained me emotionally and shaped my thinking over the years—the people who created the person who created this book.

To begin with, my twenty-year conversation with Barbara Seaman has been an education in itself. Thirty years ago Barbara followed her nose and ventured into what was then uncharted territory. She began investigating the medical and pharmaceutical industries' treatment of women and uncovered a set of dangerous assumptions and double standards. Her findings launched the modern women's health movement in this country. Her work also cleared a path for writers like myself. I began this project with the benefit of her experience, able to approach the wedding industry with skepticism and a sense of which questions to ask. I want to thank Barbara for going first and for dedicating her life to the health and reproductive freedom of women everywhere. I also want to thank her for encouraging me over the years and listening to my rantings and ravings with that superfocus that is her specialty.

The idea for this book emerged from a series of conversations with Miriam Bronstein, a friend for better or worse. Professor Pat Hoy of New York University, whose brilliant pedagogy of writing can unblock even the most self-conscious author, enabled me to develop the idea. Blanford Parker provided useful resistance and encouragement at every stage. A person of unbounded generosity of spirit, he put the resources of his capacious intellect at my disposal and helped me to keep going. He continues to offer an example of scholarly excellence that I will always strive to emulate. Daniel Harris, that Achilles of the English language, inspired me with the example of his work and took time from his own busy writing schedule to read and comment on the original draft of my manuscript. Amy Zalman and Frances Guerin supported this project with characteristic zeal. Anything of value in this volume can be attributed directly to these two great minds, wedded to two excellent hearts. Matthew Zuss was always there for me. Bruce Bromley was also on hand to give intellectual and emotional support; he is a friend for richer or poorer, but as graduate students together we have shared the anxiety of living on the poorer end of the spectrum. My deepest intellectual debt is to Joaquín Martínez-Pizarro. Joaquín has the gratitude of thousands of students who have passed through his graduate and undergraduate classes, but most of them have not enjoyed the privilege of his ongoing friendship. I am grateful for the attention he lavished on portions of the manuscript and for the intellectual guidance he has given me since the days when he was my professor at Oberlin College. He must have felt, during these past sixteen years, that he was teaching an unpaid seminar in world literature, history, philosophy, and religion, in which I was the only student, but he has never once complained.

Others disagreed with my ideas but supported me unconditionally. From this group, my deepest personal debt is to Marcia Geller, who showed her true character by throwing herself behind the book with frenzied enthusiasm despite the fact that it challenges everything she holds most dear. This project could have had no stronger advocate; neither could I. Daniel Fingeroth guarded my solitude for six years, so that I could read and think in preparation for the actual writing process. Jessica Berman, Elana Seaman, and Jeffrey Stern and Frances Rodriguez-Stern have been friends in sickness and in health. Life would not be the same without them. And it was Alvin Geller who began the process of my radicalization by explaining to me, when I was six years old, that it is absurd for any self-respecting adult to relinquish his or her name. George Gottlieb offered good practical advice at an early stage. Paul Schiff Berman turned up valuable legal sources and guided me through them; with characteristic efficacy, he also crafted a wonderful title. Leora Tanenbaum was always on the lookout for useful source material. Rita Schwartz motivated me with her gusto for the project and was willing to share her memories of a time that was very different—or maybe not very different at all. Ernest Gilman patiently answered my questions about marriage during antiquity and the Renaissance. He diverted time from his demanding schedule as a scholar, teacher, and college administrator to critique several portions of the manuscript, and his insights were incredibly useful. Danielle Insalaco helped by proofreading and researching publications, and Jane Ziegelman provided valuable information on wedding cakes. Merle Hoffman enabled me to first break into print. Kathryn Belden has been a remarkable editor and friend throughout. To all I am more grateful than I can say.

Finally, I must acknowledge Alvin Goldstein, my friend and patron and the best uncle anyone could have. My dedication memorializes his wife, Joan Goldstein, who convinced me to start this project but did not live to see me finish. Joan would have hated this book, but she also would have loved it. She died tragically at the age of sixty-seven, but I believe that her intelligence and trenchant sense of humor live on in these pages. Her granddaughter, the unfazable Ms. Rebecca Goldstein, was very important to the composition of this work. She helped me with research and organization; during periods when I was especially exhausted, she inspired me with the depth of her commitment to the written word. I hope that, when she is older, the book is useful to her in some small way. I hope that for her the unprecedented is ordinary.

Introduction

> My own sex, I hope, will excuse me, if I treat them like rational crea-
> tures, instead of flattering their *fascinating* graces, and viewing them as
> if they were in a state of perpetual childhood, unable to stand alone.
> —Mary Wollstonecraft, Author's Introduction,
> *Vindication of the Rights of Woman*

LIKE MANY BORN at the tail end of America's postwar baby boom I grew
up in an affluent suburb. Located forty minutes from midtown
Manhattan, Scarsdale, New York, was an upscale commuter town with
quiet tree-lined streets containing rows of large residential homes, a public high school, and a small cluster of shops and restaurants adjacent to
the train station from which male professionals traveled to the metropolis each day to generate the income that supported this tranquil little
haven. For a suburb of its kind Scarsdale had an unusually active publicity machine. It promoted itself as a utopia; the ultimate suburban
enclave, the community in which America's postwar dreams of prosperity, social stability, and assimilationism had reached a kind of glorious
apex. Its schools were said to be the finest schools, its students the most
successful college applicants, its sports teams the most competitive, and
its wives the prettiest and most highly educated of all female under-
achievers. Those of us instructed by Scarsdale's cadre of teachers were
inculcated with the town's sense of its own excellence; we were continually reminded of our good fortune in having the opportunity to grow up
in America's El Dorado, a virtual heaven on earth in which self-assured
corporate men supported privileged women and children, prosperous

households coexisted peacefully, crime was a distant rumor, and financial duress was unheard of.

Like other towns of its ilk Scarsdale upheld the ideals of two historical moments; the twentieth-century postwar economic boom and the Victorian age of sentimentalized domesticity. Throughout the 1950s and 1960s, access to education and the professions had enabled American immigrant groups to enter the upper middle class; with financial security came home ownership in the protective enclaves of suburbia; the future was bright, money was plentiful, and social roles were determined by gender. Adrienne Rich has written of this period, "in reaction to the earlier wave of feminism, middle-class women were making careers of domestic perfection, working to send their husbands through professional schools, then retiring to raise large families. . . . Life was extremely private; women were isolated from each other by the loyalties of marriage."[1] For Jewish women coming of age in New York in the 1950s, women like my mother, my aunt, and their friends, the goal of upward social mobility had been all consuming and unstated. The route from the tenements of the Bronx to the leafy streets of Westchester was clear; one made the journey armed with a wedding band and a college diploma. One attended a city university, met a man, and became engaged during senior year. Having attained that primary emblem of female achievement, a heterosexual marriage, in which economic solvency, personal fulfillment, and social prestige were neatly compressed, one taught elementary school while one's husband prepared for a career in law, medicine, or accounting. Teaching children prefigured one's own work in child care and domestic management, and the next step was retiring and bearing children; generating a nuclear family that would function as an autonomous social and economic unit held together by a sense of its own primacy. Home management, the upkeep of one's physical appearance, and the appropriate degree of conspicuous idleness advertised one's husband's professional success through those two chief indicators of bourgeois well being: the well appointed home and the leisured wife. Domestic supervision and marital self-promotion were the central occupations of the 1970s Scarsdale housewife, whose schedule was a virtual round of physical maintenance activities at the hair salon, the nail salon, the cosmetologist, the health club, the Weight Watcher's meeting, and, ultimately, the plastic surgeon's office.

The architecture and topography of the suburban household is perhaps the most powerful social document of this period. Houses lined each street, but they were not the homes of a farming village or a nineteenth-century city; there were no barns indicative of a domestic economy, no great room in which a community could dine together, no front porches lined with rocking chairs that beckoned visitors. The domestic and economic spheres were now disparate. The household no longer produced goods; it was a private arena of female leisure and childhood play sustained by an income earned in a distant urban office. The Victorian ideology of separate gender-based spheres had been perfectly realized in American's postwar experiment; the husband operated in a public, professional capacity, and the wife maintained a private, self-contained household, a neutral zone intended to serve as a refuge for her weary male commuter, insulating him from the stress and competition of corporate life. The world-at-large was comprised of a vague mass of secondary relationships: social acquaintances, colleagues, neighbors were at best benignly diverting and at worst hostile. In aspiring to the lifestyles of wealthy American Protestants, second generation immigrant women had absorbed the radical Protestant model of family; man and wife would function as complementary but unequal partners; their household would serve as a moral center in which the socialization of children by mothers was sacrosanct. For Jewish women of Eastern European descent the assimilation process was especially dramatic. The aggressive female entrepreneur of the Polish shtetl who had worked as a manufacturer, a saleswoman, or a shopkeeper to support her scholar husband[2] had been transformed within two or three generations into a full-time housewife and mother, an attractive domestic isolate. In the wealthier communities such as ours she resembled a glamorous, anesthetized doll.

Fortified against intruders, the suburban home was a fortress constructed to protect its denizens from a series of vaguely articulated external threats. Even as a child, I sensed that the suburbanite's fear of crime—home burglaries, muggings during occasional cultural expeditions into Manhattan—symbolized a deeper xenophobia. What historian Lawrence Stone has called "intensified affective bonding of the nuclear core at the expense of neighbors and kin"[3] had become so powerful that all outsiders were seen as potentially divisive to the family. To insulate each couple within its own domicile, postwar architects had eschewed the front porches of Victorian homes for the privacy of backyard decks. The standard house had a large eat-in kitchen with a washer-dryer set and a telephone that enabled communication without leaving home. It was here that a wife would spend most of her time, involved in food preparation. An adjoining playroom with toys and a television ensured close proximity to her children. The first floor living room was typically filled with family photos that chronicled the development of each child from infancy through college graduation. Upstairs were bedrooms and a guest room for the occasional visitor. The garage housed a car in which the wife did errands alone or with her children. Ian Watt has pointed out that suburbanization is indistinguishable from the modern belief in female delicacy: "The privacy of a suburb is essentially feminine because it reflects the increasing tendency... to regard the modesty of woman-hood as highly vulnerable and in need of defensive seclusion."[4] American postwar culture extended this protectiveness to the family itself. What had probably once been, in Europe, a fluid, loosely defined grouping of individuals bound together by economic ties was now a small, autonomous, emotionally based unit, consisting only of children and parents and undergirded by a companionate marriage. It was this precious, fragile structure that needed cloistering. The American suburban household of the 1970s did not merely protect female modesty; it enshrined and sheltered the nuclear family itself.

For many of us the suburbs were a dystopia whose social code seemed anything but natural. As a child I watched our town empty itself of its male population each day, when hordes of men boarded the commuter trains bound for Manhattan. I envied these men and wished I could follow them, leaving behind the women who glided through each week, food shopping, carpooling, picking up dry cleaning, playing the occasional game of tennis. These ladies sent holiday greeting cards with photographs of their children, managed the family's social calendar, and supervised the manual labor of the poor, immigrant women employed in their homes. In retrospect I realize that they occupied the social role historian Gerda Lerner claims to be the lot of upper-class women in the West throughout recorded history: while male status has rested on property ownership, success in military or business ventures, or intellectual achievements, class standing for women of the elite has always been defined in terms of sexual relationships.[5] My female neighbors were affluent, and the quality of life wealth afforded them was real. Their influence over children and domestic employees was equally real. But their power and economic ability derived from a single amorous relationship with a man on whom they were entirely dependent. More than three decades earlier, Virginia Woolf had issued a challenge to the young women of her generation, writing, "When I ask you to earn money and have a room of your own, I am asking you to live in the presence of reality, an invigorating life...."[6] The lives of the homemakers whom I scrutinized with amazement seemed to take place apart from the reality that I imagined adult life to be. They lacked the physical privacy that Woolf thought requisite to the emergence of genius. Their large abodes contained no offices, no discrete spaces in which to work, read, or think alone, as if a wife's psychic life was inseparable from the house itself and her mental reach need not extend beyond the physical horizons of her home. Postwar women eschewed the economic autonomy that Woolf championed, perhaps because in that reactionary historical moment female professional advancement seemed impossible. "This is," Gerda Lerner writes, "the female world of the social contract: women denied autonomy depend on protection and struggle to make the best deal possible for themselves and their children."[7]

But the Scarsdale wives who provided me with my first glimpses of adult femininity seemed content to mortgage their futures on the good will and good luck of male counterparts. If, as Simone de Beauvoir has written, the housewife's work is to transform the "prison" of her home into a "realm,"[8] these ladies did not appear to mind the task or to even notice their own domestic captivity. Apparently untroubled by the restraints placed on their mobility, they were content to symbolically relinquish their adult identities by eschewing their names in marriage, glad to speak in the first person plural, expressing corporate, marital status. ("We decided that I would give up teaching when I became pregnant," explained a neighbor to me. "We felt that, while I was replaceable as a teacher, I was irreplaceable as a mother, and we feel good about our choice.") As wives and mothers, these women enjoyed such immense social approbation that they were blinded to their own sacrifices and risks, propelled through each day by a reflexive belief that in the "good life" of wedlock, the primacy of the family, and the inevitability of a gendered division of labor.

Exiting the suburbs and entering a small, private college in 1980, I felt a surge of excitement. It seemed like an exodus from a sterile alien world predicated on fictional notions of inherent gender difference. For the first time, I felt, I would be able to indulge my feverish love of poetry, fiction, and philosophy; obsessions that had always seemed to me to be faintly criminal. I was not disappointed. The intellectualism of Oberlin College's student body, the communal living and eating arrangements, and the campus' physical isolation, in an underdeveloped semirural section of Ohio, facilitated intense debate and enabled me to forge a series of close friendships. In crowded dormitory rooms and cafeterias and on the front porches of professors' homes, I spent hours with friends, discussing the succession of literary texts with which I became rapidly and ridiculously obsessed: the Bible, the treatises of Aristotle, the great medieval romances, the poems of Emily Dickinson, the novels of Dostoyevski and Melville, and the feminist treatises of, among others, Simone de Beauvoir and Virginia Woolf.

This was the era of early academic gender studies. Perhaps in reaction to the repressiveness of postwar culture, women spoke of redrawing the social contract that had confined their mothers and grandmothers; of forgoing marriage, maintaining their own names, creating alternative structures for raising children, finding meaning in professional and intellectual pursuits and in the alliance of friendship. Women's studies programs burgeoned on campuses throughout the country, including ours; there was an influx of driven female professors whose lives attested to a different vision of selfhood than that of middle-class, postwar America. And the early rumblings of gay liberation problematized the idea of heterosexual partnership as a natural unassailable truth. Several years earlier, in the 1973 *Roe v. Wade* case, the Supreme Court had made motherhood a matter of choice, upholding pregnancy termination as a constitutional right. Having attained, in principle at least, this most basic form of health care, it seemed that women could embark upon the formidable task of analyzing their own historical condition. We could dissect the cultural myths in which our female ancestors had been drenched.

During my undergraduate years, battered copies of three books passed from hand to hand. The great manifesto of academic feminism, Virginia Woolf's *A Room of One's Own,* argued that achievement always emerges from a historical tradition and that women did not have one; Woolf urged women to collectively create the legacy that would facilitate female genius. Mary Daly's *Beyond God the Father* indicted sexist liturgical language, claiming that as long as God is envisioned as male, males will be seen as gods. And Adrienne Rich's *Of Women Born: Motherhood as Experience and Institution* praised parts of the event of childrearing while calling for the destruction of motherhood as a social institution. In subjecting the West's main cultural inheritances to stringent interrogations, academic feminism sought to deflate patriarchy's most enduring myths, enabling a new generation of women to look beyond the confines of the nuclear family and see themselves not as wives or mothers but as members of a historical continuum of women who could progress from dependence to autonomy, from obscurity to distinction. With a new awareness of history, we could begin to think independently and make rational choices. I felt, during these years, as many people, at many times, in many places, have felt, that I was living on the cusp of an epistemological shift. Nothing would ever be the same—or so I thought.

The change that occurred, in the social lives of those I knew, during the postcollege years was subtle, insidious, at first almost imperceptible. I had always heard that friends drifted apart after school when the pressures of adult life took over. I was prepared to endure a lower emotional voltage in the relationships that I had nurtured. What I was not ready for was a widespread devaluation of friendship and community in favor of the privileged isolation of amorous love. And nothing could have prepared me for the marriage mania that I witnessed among my contemporaries—for their adherence to the very social patterns that they had themselves scorned just a few years before.

During my twenties, after spending a year in Israel, I lived in New York City and worked for a nonprofit Jewish organization; at the age of thirty-one I applied to graduate school and, the next year, began pursuing a doctorate in English literature. A resident of Manhattan, I was, during this entire period, first exposed to the culture of formal dating. Ritualized courtship, I quickly came to understand, was predicated on two assumptions: each individual was a fragmentary being awaiting completion in a romantic partner of the opposite sex, and, accordingly, amorous relationships were paramount and must always take precedence over platonic friendships. In addition, dating had a distinct narrative shape. Heterosexual courtship was not open-ended; it was teleological. It aimed at marriage; in this quest, each woman was assigned the role of the husband hunter, while the man was the object of hot pursuit. Popular magazines, which warned women of the narrowing pool of matrimonial candidates as their ages progressed, made the race toward wedlock all the more frantic and competitive.[9] Despite recent social criticism, eighteenth-century constructs of femininity were, it seemed, still all-powerful. And the marriage market depicted ironically in the novels of the greatest satirist of domestic life in English, Jane Austen, was thriving on Manhattan's upper west side. Women were still divided into two opposing camps: spinsters and wives. The former were unpopular. The latter were popular—extolled, rewarded with the celebratory praise, money, and gifts that were withheld from the husbandless girl. To avoid the opprobrium of spinsterhood, one strategized as to how to obtain that most essential prize from one's male companion—a "commitment." Once this was secured, it was time to enter sanctioned coupledom.

I was stunned to see my female contemporaries don diamond engagement rings, displaying these jewels as tangible symbols of social victory. Women I knew who had just a few years earlier mocked the iconography of wedding literature now pored over bridal magazines, selecting their wedding dresses, invitation formats, and china patterns with great earnestness. The flurry of social engagements, showers, bachelor parties, and the great ceremonial wedding day itself, were attended by extraordinary pomp and circumstance. The married couple would forge a legal bond, placing its sex life under the mandates of the civil government. The pair would register for expensive gifts; household goods that the community was expected to provide. Once ensconced in their own domicile, the partners would enter life in the plural, assigning previous friendships a secondary status, enjoying the domestic arrangement to which our mothers had been taught to aspire. "Have I converted wholesale to an ideology that I despise?" a graduate school friend wondered out loud to me, after announcing her engagement. "Yes, I guess I have."

"Marriage is the norm," an old friend from my teenage years admitted to me, "and I've just decided not to fight it anymore."

I soon came to understand that as a young woman living with roommates I was an object of concern for those who knew me. I was defined as "single," a label that seemed nonsensical to me, since it did not resonate in any way with the reality of my life. The adjective *single* implies a person who is solitary, alone, incomplete. By contrast, I was, especially after entering graduate school, connected to a loving community of friends. I felt lucky to spend afternoons in libraries, glutting myself on novels, plays, and poems, and luxuriating in my own solitude. I was equally happy to spend nights in animated conversation with colleagues. After a childhood in which I had felt stranded in a shallow, anti-intellectual suburb, each day of adult life seemed like a new adventure, and the social validation of marriage was the last thing on my mind. In relationships with men, however, I found myself thrust into a repugnant role—that of the husband chaser. "I cannot give you—or anyone—a commitment," a man I was involved with after college ceremoniously confessed, displaying bizarre obliviousness to the fact that I had not asked for one. When I had moved into an apartment with my next boyfriend—my companion of two years—I was showered with anxious inquiries by relatives and friends who seemed dazzled by the possibility of my social completion through wedlock. Was this "it"? Was "it" finally going to happen?

My reply was consistently negative. I explained that I did not need the public sanction of matrimony, that I did not wish to celebrate a single relationship when so many relationships were important to me, that I did not want to place my sex life under civil governmental control, and that I could not in good conscience uphold a tradition that had originated in the barter of women as property. My response was always a disappointment to those who cared about me, and my lack of superstitious reverence for marriage continues to irritate friends to this day.

Then, as now, there was no word in English for what I was. There is no word in English for a woman who has chosen herself, her books, and her friends above sanctioned coupledom. There is no word in English for a woman whose erotic energies are directed toward men but who does not long to officialize a relationship with a single man. There is no word in English for a woman who does not perceive her social role in terms of men and romance. There is no word in English for a woman whose lover is one of many valued friends. Our language does not conceive of such a person. So entrenched is the notion of marital femininity that we can only envision women in terms of wedlock or its opposite. Our existing nouns and noun phrases—wife, divorcee, old maid, single girl—all emerge from our culture's marital economy. Even popular advice literature that cautiously validates the "single" life for women operates on the either-or premise that a woman is married or "single" and that no other options for self-definition exist.

By the late 1990s my only two old friends who had not married were an older, gay male professor and a lesbian social worker. My heterosexual male friends from college had stopped calling; they had retreated into conjugal isolation. For the most part, my closest female friends wore wedding rings and had begun to speak in the plural. This rhetorical habit intensified with the arrival of children, who in each case were cared for, primarily, by their biological mothers. There were of course differences between my generation of maturing women and that of our mothers. We worked, planned careers, pursued advanced degrees, and enjoyed unapologetic sex. We did not retire immediately to the suburbs after college. Perhaps most importantly, my circle of educated, middle-class female friends and colleagues had the legal right to terminate a pregnancy. Whether we exercised this right or not, the ability to decide whether and when to bear children gave us a sense of self-determination in other areas of our lives, a feeling that our immediate female ancestors had sorely lacked. Yet despite these advances, the great heterosexual myth of pairing and bearing remained the same. Dating habits had changed, but the assumptions underlying the courtship process had not, and the period's books reflected widespread marriage mania. The 1983 reprint of Helen Gurley Brown's seminal husband-hunting manual, *Sex and the Single Girl*, was accompanied by a plethora of dating handbooks authored by and written for women: Margaret Kent's 1984 *How to Marry the Man of Your Dreams*, Rusty Rothman's 1985 *How to Find Another Husband: By Someone Who Did*, Bonnie Barnes' 1986 *How to Get a Man to Make a Commitment or Know When He Never Will*, Jane Carpineto's 1986 *Husband Hunting: How to Win at the Mating Game*, Susan Page's 1988 *If*

I'm So Wonderful Why Am I Still Single? Ten Strategies That Will Change Your Love Life Forever, Patricia Curtis' 1988 *Why Isn't My Daughter Married? Daughters Tell Mothers the Real Reason They're Single,* Susan Deity's 1989 *Single File: How to Live Happily Forever with or without Prince Charming,* Ellen Lederman's 1991 *The Best Places to Meet Good Men,* Helen Andelin's 1993 *The Secrets of Winning Men,* Tina Santi-Flaherty's 1997 *The Savvy Woman's Success Bible: How to Find the Right Job, the Right Man, and the Right Life,* Barbara De Angelis' 1997 *The Real Rules: How to Find the Right Man for the Real You,* Nancy Fagan's 1997 *Desirable Men: How to Find Them,* Helena Hacker Rosenberg's 1998 *How to Get Married After Thirty-five: A Game Plan for Love,* and Dr. Gilda Carle's 2000 *He's Not All That: How to Attract the Good Guys.* These are only some of the titles that continue to crowd bookstore shelves. The wedding's dominance as a social institution is clear from the mass publication of books like these, which couch practical advice in the jargon of the self-help industry, urging women to "find themselves," "be themselves," and "assert themselves" in order to snare a spouse.

The relative paucity of husband hunting guidebooks prior to the 1970s and their prominence in American bookstores throughout the 1980s and 1990s reflects something more than a surge in the self-help segment of the book publishing industry. It points to an intensification of our culture's marriage mystique. The matrimonial fetish is everywhere in American popular culture: from the plots of cinema's romantic comedies to the professional matchmakers and online dating services that promise to match up "singles," from the bookstore wedding sections jammed with primers on how to plan and implement the perfect nuptial celebration to the fashion designers whose sole business is the production of bridal gowns and bridesmaids' dresses, from the bridal magazines whose circulation is steadily increasing, to the fashion and celebrity oriented glossies that promote highly successful special wedding issues.[10] In her 1922 novel *Jacob's Room,* Virginia Woolf ironically described marriage as a fortress, claiming that single women "stray solitary in the open fields, picking up stones, gleaning a few golden straws, lonely, unprotected, poor creatures."[11] Overwhelming cultural evidence attests to the contemporary woman's straightforward belief in wedlock's sheltering sanctions despite the fact that organized American feminism

11

is experiencing its third wave. There is a plethora of information available to us that our mothers and grandmothers did not have. Historical scholarship of the 1970s has enabled us to survey marriage as a changing institution; we can understand it as, traditionally, a social contract between men in which a woman's transfer solidified dynastic alliances, and we can perceive our current romantic view of wedlock as quite modern, dating to the early eighteenth century. Feminist analysis has suggested the extent to which socialization determines male-female behaviors in the home, the workplace, and especially, in sexual relationships. And ever-escalating divorce statistics reveal that, even in its own terms, romance-based matrimony usually does not work. Yet, despite this growing reservoir of data, women continue to mythologize marriage, embracing its rewards and dreading its punishments. It is an institution that has resisted all attempts at demystification. It seems that we would rather blindly uphold a familiar standard than work to generate a new one. For the woman who perceives herself as "single," friendship, intellectual life, and professional success are not enough. Unsanctioned sexual relationships, those unclassified affections that Virginia Woolf celebrated, are insufficient. A wedding ring is still the primary indispensable symbol of external validation. Surprisingly, this reverence for matrimony is especially powerful in educated accomplished women—those among us who lead the most independent lives.

A spinster herself, an outsider peering in at the rituals of the married, Jane Austen exposed matrimony's contradictions and incongruities in her 1813 novel, *Pride and Prejudice*. The social forces mediating the desires of one of the novel's minor characters, Charlotte Lucas, are shown to be inseparable from her decision to marry an imbecilic clergyman:

> The whole family in short were properly overjoyed on the occasion. The younger girls formed hopes of *coming out* a year or two sooner than they might otherwise have done; and the boys were relieved from their apprehension of Charlotte's dying an old maid. Charlotte herself was tolerably composed. She had gained her point, and had time to consider of it. . . . Mr. Collins to be sure was neither sensible nor agreeable, and his attachment to her must be imaginary. But still he would be her husband. Without thinking highly either of men or matrimony, mar-

riage had always been her object; it was the only honorable provision for well-educated young women of small fortune....[12]

A young woman of small fortune in England in 1813 had few options. She was barred from the professions and could exercise no voting rights to alter this state of affairs. In marriage she ceased to exist as a legal entity; outside of wedlock, she was destined to a life of grinding poverty and shameful spinsterhood. Domestic law itself effected the legal oppression of women by making it virtually impossible to exist outside of marriage. Today, when we embrace wedlock, we align ourselves with this cruel history, perpetuating an institution that randomly dispenses and withholds privilege according to the haphazardness of romantic attraction. The luster of Victorian wedlock becomes comprehensible when we acknowledge this century's social constraints. Matrimony's continuing allure, in the twenty-first century, when women have achieved reproductive choice and the actuality of political representation, educational inclusion, and professional mobility, is something of a mystery. It is a mystery that I will explore in the following chapters, as I follow the marital narrative from beginning to end, studying the wedding industry's prescribed etiquettes and examining how the marriage mystique is expressed in popular culture.

CHAPTER ONE

Courtship and the Marriage Quest

We live in a conjugal age, when the couple has become the standard for all intimate relationships, the unmarried and the married, the homo-sexual as well as the heterosexual. Commerce panders to the conjugal ideal, and municipalities zone in its favor. Children play at it. Marriage has become a form of serial conjugality, a sequence of partnerships taken up and abandoned with bewildering rapidity, as men and women seek the perfect mate. Most of us will spend at least two-thirds of our lives in couples, much longer than any previous generation. Of course, there are moments when couplehood is broken by death or divorce, but these are perceived as intervals of loss and deprivation, when the sense of wholeness can best be restored by finding a new partner.
—John Gillis, *For Better, For Worse: British Marriages, 1600 to the Present*

The clustering of women writers occurs in direct relationship to the development of a female reading public.... The relationship is com-plex: the existence of a female reading public enabled some female writers at last to make an independent living. Some of those who did also developed an independent lifestyle, which may have led them to an increasingly feminist consciousness.... On the other hand there are countless examples of female writers with vast female audiences who never developed any feminist consciousness; on the contrary many made their living by celebrating women's traditional nurturant and maternal functions or by fostering women's traditional focus on love and marriage.

—Gerda Lerner, *The Creation of Feminist Consciousness*

I. The Marriage Mystique

The late historian John Boswell has written that the most salient feature of the modern West's psychological landscape is its widespread obsession with romance and its assumption that amorous love should be the basis for marriage. Those immersed in what Boswell calls the "sea of love" mentality tend to take it for granted: "even many scholars of the subject fail to notice how remarkable is the degree of its prominence in the cultures in which they grew up. Very few premodern or nonindustrialized contemporary cultures would agree with the contention—uncontroversial in the West—that 'the purpose of a man is to love a woman, and the purpose of a woman is to love a man.' Most human beings in most times and places would find this a very meager measure of human value."[1]

The belief in erotic love as the wellspring of personal happiness and the equation of long-term amorous relationships with maturity and mental health are ideas that now saturate every corner of American culture. But a cursory glance at popular advice literature reveals that these subjects are not assumed to be the equal obsession of men and women. Magazines, self-help books, and radio talk shows aimed at men cover issues ranging from health to consumer guidance to recreation to career management, but popular advice to contemporary American women is single-minded in its concern with obtaining and sustaining a monogamous sexual partnership. The dominant theme of virtually every current American woman's magazine is the romantic relationship. Other frequently discussed subjects in magazines such as *Cosmopolitan*, *Mirabella*, *Self*, *Marie Claire*, and *Glamour* are fashion, fitness, home management, and career strategies. It could be argued, however, that such topics are subsumed within or at least directly related to the culturally mandated quest for officialized love. When a woman colors her hair, tones her body, redesigns her apartment, or even augments her resume, she builds cultural capital that will recommend her on what relationship experts call "the dating scene," helping her to attract a male partner. Magazine articles, newspaper columns, how-to dating manuals, and call-in radio shows ready the female consumer for the hunt, instructing her to fortify herself physically, psychologically, and financially. (Similarly, as we will see in Chapter Nine, advice columns to wives that feature get-to-know-your-partner quizzes and sexual bromides propagandize on wedlock's behalf, reinforcing in women the linked ideas that wedlock is their central project and marital commitment is a precious commodity to be reified and guarded. The myriad celebrity couples profiled in popular magazines praise conjugal life, enhancing the marriage mystique with domestic anecdotes and bits of romantic folk wisdom through which they present themselves to the population at large as emulative role models.) Televised daytime talk shows have become venues for husband-hunting advisors, and the popular psychology branch of the publishing industry panders increasingly to "single" women, offering a range of strategies for snagging a male partner.

Relationship experts focus on immediate romantic goals, appealing to the emotions rather than the intelligence of their female readers and urging women to use their analytical capacities solely as amorous strategists—operatives who secure male commitment through the clever deployment of tactical game plans. Self-scrutiny, and analysis of one's aspirations for an erotic relationship, the type of man one hopes to attract, and areas of compromise necessary to secure marital commitment are de rigueur in dating literature. But inquiry, through analysis and contextualiztion, of the institution of marriage itself, is taboo. Relationship pundits operate in an ahistorical void, a vacuum in which male-female partnership is a perpetual unassailable truth. Representatives of a media that provide easy ready-made solutions to female distress and assume such distress to always be personal, these advisors treat human relationships with a short-range approach that lacks the depth of historical perspective. Their twofold project—instructing the masses of American women presumed to be "single" and therefore love starved in the arts of winning male devotion and the follow-up task of helping frustrated wives jump-start their faltering marriages with techniques of erotic ignition—are short-term. The modern advice-giver's frame of reference is limited to the immediate, the quotidian, and the romantic.

What one scholar has described as a "present-minded" approach to reality[2] is necessary for these contemporary dating experts and essential to the cult of matrimony. Historical myopia on the part of both advisors and advice recipients is the fundamental requirement of today's marriage mania, a fetish for conjugality that demands each woman view herself as potentially or actually part of a marital unit—the female half of a couple—rather than a link between past and future generations of women. Viewing ourselves on a historical continuum of women who have been subordinate within male-dominated institutions such as wedlock would cloud the matrimonial mystique and problematize the all-important quest for conjugal commitment. Because marriage as an institution has been inextricably connected to the most potent forms of female oppression, its proponents cannot survey it from a detached perspective but must instead transform its inherently public, political nature into something magically personal, private, and inevitable. When a dating expert helps a female client determine whether her current beau is capable of "commitment," he assumes the permanent domestic contract to be a basic and universal female desire. He also naturalizes that desire. When a radio therapist advises a husband and wife to spend more private time away from the children—to reserve a part of each day solely for each other or to take romantic weekends away—she presumes the marital relationship to be sacrosanct and in need of unique kinds of maintenance. She also, perhaps without consciously intending to do so, projects romance-based marriage as a cultural ideal.

Matrimony is not, however, a set of raw, untempered, universal experiences. It is a humanly shaped institution that has its origins in the inception of western civilization itself. It is a political arrangement that merits a political critique rather than a personal impulse that deserves automatic complacent respect. When we remember the extent to which culture is cumulative, with each generation transferring economic conditions as well as social norms, precedents, laws, and interpretive metaphors to the next, we can begin to understand the fusion between contemporary women and the marriage ideal, a collaboration that has spawned and continues to sustain America's expanding relationship industry as well as its virtually recession-proof wedding industry. Marriage mania in modern American women did not arise sui generis. It is the result of millennia of law and social custom that have valued women solely in terms of their relationship to men, predicating female respectability on male stewardship. To understand the female obsession with romance-based domestic partnership we must preface our examination of popular culture with a brief foray into more complex and challenging sources: the history books that reveal to us our own past.

Simone de Beauvoir wrote famously in 1949 that women have no past and no history.[3] She was wrong. Women have a history, which, for the most part, appears unglamorous to modern female intellectuals, a history of private unpaid service within the family, a history in which marriage has been the central and defining act of most individual's lives, a history of absorption within an institution that has offered certain protections in exchange for the imposition of rigid restrictions. Wedlock has tended to offer women immediate social and psychological rewards while obstructing long-term female progress. Its traditional securities have come at a high price: the containment of female sexuality and the limiting of female agency. Yet this contract has been central and desirable to most women in most times and places. As Olwen Hufton has written of private life in early modern Europe:

> Marriage was seen not merely as women's natural destiny but also as a metaphoric agent, transforming her into a different social being as part of a new household, the primary unit upon which all society was based. The husband's role was that of provider of shelter and sustenance.... The role of the wife was that of helpmate and mother. At the highest levels of society, women became mistresses of houses with servants to organize, estates to manage with the help of stewards and agents, and hospitality to offer on their husband's behalf. The appearance and dignity of the wife confirmed the status of the husband.[4]

A helpmate, a domestic partner/subordinate/manager, and a visible index of male prestige, the wife traditionally received, and continues to garner, powerful social approbation. When we consider the primacy that the marital experience has had for western women, the current female obsession with wedlock as reflected in popular culture becomes comprehensible as yet another historical chapter in which matrimony has been mandated as a natural and laudable female good.

Glancing back in time, though, we can perceive the facts of female subjugation in the West to be inseparable from the evolution of marriage law. In prehistory inchoate attitudes, tribal customs, and legal dogma ossified over centuries in the process Gerda Lerner calls "the creation of patriarchy": a legitimized system of male dominance that culminated in the first western law codes, the Hammurabic Law Codes of 1750 B.C.E. and the subsequent Middle Assyrian Law Codes of the fifteenth through the eleventh centuries B.C.E. These bodies of law institutionalized monogamous marriage arranged by men, with household assets transferred to male offspring; the custom that has, until very recently, dominated the West. Both corpi of law are based on assumptions that bear repetition. Ancient near eastern culture assumed the strength and superior rationality of men and the status of males as political citizens and women as contingent beings destined to exist outside of political life. While men through their rational faculties were equipped to order and interpret experience, women were intended to nurture and sustain life, overseeing the continuity of the species in a kind of perpetual service position. From the earliest marriage regulations on record this role entailed male controls of female sexuality and reproductivity with no parallel female controls of male sexual and reproductive functions. It as well contained the belief in marriage as an asymmetrical partnership and the married couple as a unit whose stability was essential to the integrity of the public domain. The contractually united couple was, in Lerner's words, "the basic building block" of the healthy organism that was the state,[5] a belief echoed by marriage propagandists to this day. While historians disagree as to whether the ancient wife was a piece of property transferred from father to groom or a legally disenfranchised individual who garnered the symbolic gift of a bride price, it is clear that, from her beginnings as a historical entity, the wife occupied a subordinate position that was also, ironically, her sole option for respectability.

In ancient Greece marriage was, once again, a process of transfer by which a woman's *kyrios* ("lord" or "controller") gave her to another man for the purpose of procreating children. Normally the woman's father, but if he was deceased, her nearest male relative, the *kyrios* acted for her in all legal and economic transactions, as female judgment was thought to be impaired. A marriage in Athens was valid only if it began with a formal statement by the *kyrios* granting the bride-to-be to her husband.[6] In the Roman Republic matrimony was, again, "essentially the transfer of power over a woman, who had been under the control of her father (or brother, or uncle, or some adult male), to that of her new husband (or his father, if the husband was not head of his own household), who then stood in this role of her controller/protector."[7] Roman betrothal in fact entailed a ceremony between two men in which pledges were exchanged to cement the deal: the groom-to-be would ask his future father-in-law, "Do you promise to give your daughter to me to be my wedded wife?" "The gods bring luck! I betroth her!" the latter would reply.[8] While this concept of marriage, in which all persons in a household were subservient to a single adult male, changed in the later empire, imperial Roman marriage was by no means egalitarian. Roman law maintained mutual consent to be the basis of legal marriage, but the bride's consent was assumed unless she lodged an official protest, an objection taken seriously only if her fiance was proven base or unworthy.[9] And although she was legally defined as an adult in her own right, the imperial wife was subject to the rampant sexual double standard prevalent throughout the ancient world. Her husband might well have married her for financial or dynastic reasons; this would not prevent his finding erotic fulfillment in concubines, slaves, and prostitutes with no fear of public recrimination, while, in order to ensure the "legitimacy" of his heirs, her chastity was requisite. "If your slave, your freedman, your woman, or your client dares answer you, get angry," wrote the Roman author Seneca.[10]

Early medieval marriage among the Barbarian tribes who migrated westward, penetrating and ultimately supplanting the waning Roman empire, was even more male dominated than Roman marriage had been, granting women few rights but imposing upon them many obligations. Betrothal was arranged by male relatives of the bride, whose consent was not required, and who, once married, could not seek divorce. It consisted of an agreement between two fathers sealed by a feast at which the groom-to-be's family paid a sum of money—a bride-price—for her. Barbarian men commonly had concubines, but a Barbarian woman's adultery was, according to the Roman author Tacitus, punished immediately by her husband, who stripped her clothes off, cut her hair, ejected her from his home, and flogged her publicly throughout the village. Tacitus appreciated these firm measures to curtail female sexual autonomy. "No feature of their morality deserves higher praise," he wrote of Barbarian marriage.[11]

Medieval men were theoretically free to choose their marriage partners as soon as they attained majority—between the ages of twelve to fifteen according to various law codes. The Lombard Code, written down in the seventh century, enabled a woman's father or brother to choose for her without her consent, even after she had reached her twenties.[12] The ninth century archbishop, Hincmar of Reims, who defined legal marriage as *mutually* consenting (with the exception that a woman must be given and financially endowed by her father) presents an unsavory picture of medieval marriage. His writings depict men using various stratagems to rid themselves of their wives, ploys that include murder as well as legal deception: "They seized any pretext to suspend conjugal relations after a few years of married life, took mistresses, slandered their spouses to the clergy, forced them to tolerate concubines and to testify that their husbands were impotent or to pretend that they themselves longed to retire to a convent."[13]

Hincmar may have been exaggerating in order to justify his own reforms, but medieval marriage law, which operated from the premise that a woman's sexuality was not her own but her husband's, did give men overwhelming power over their wives. Anglo-Saxon legal codes in fact contained a scale of compensatory payments to husbands for the seduction of their wives. According to the eleventh-century laws of Cnut, a woman who committed adultery was a public disgrace, "and her lawful husband is to have all that she owns, and she is to lose her nose and ears."[14] According to feudal law in the high Middle Ages a wife could not plead in court without her husband's consent or make a will without his permission. His authority over her property was total; only when she reached widowhood did she acquire any degree of economic independence, and even then she was often subjected to powerful family pressures to remarry.[15]

Despite its brutal strictures marriage was, for medieval women, the universal objective. This was especially true for peasant women, to whom convents were closed.[16] Aristocratic women were pawns in the game of establishing dynastic households. According to the historian of marriage Georges Duby, the late medieval landholder did his best to marry off all available young women in order to distribute the blood of his ancestors, forging alliances that would last into the next generation.[17]

Medievalist Christopher N. L. Brooke writes, "The kings sought marriage above all to provide themselves with male heirs and for personal satisfaction; if the wife was unsatisfactory she was changed."[18] This changed in the twelfth century, when the Church took control of marriage, worked to stamp out concubinage, and imposed rules of permanence and monogamy upon both women and men. Succumbing to Church pressure, heads of aristocratic households came to center their aspirations on inheritance, which necessitated monogamy and demanded the chastity of women.[19] Because it ensured the purity of blood lines and the orderly transmission of property from one generation of "legitimate" male heirs to the next, wifely fidelity was the bedrock on which the new family rested.

Embedded in both medieval and Renaissance notions of marriage was the belief that the sexes were unequal. The biblical story of Adam's creation in God's image and Eve's emergence as a secondary figure taken from his rib reinforced the notion of inherent, timeless gender inequality. Male and female were merged into one unit, but that unit contained a hierarchy. Woman, who had caused humanity's fall from grace and exile from edenic paradise, was naturally inferior,[20] a notion supported by Paul's letter to the Ephesians, which stated that the husband was head of the wife as Christ was head of the Church.[21] In 1439 marriage was officially proclaimed a sacrament of the Catholic Church. Renaissance marriage was arranged, as medieval marriage had been, with negotiations between families centering on the dowry contributed by the bride's side. Once the couple married the husband assumed total control of both the dowry and all of his wife's effects. Renaissance wives were prohibited from acting for themselves in legal or commercial matters;[22] yet, as in previous centuries, they were socially mandated to desire and hopefully await their own legal subordination in wedlock. Those without husbands had no hope of obtaining a prestigious position in society. In Italy and elsewhere a favorite form of charity was the dowry fund, established by communities to help poor young girls attract husbands.[23]

Protestant reformers rejected the notion of marriage as a Christian sacrament as they likewise discarded the Catholic idea of clerical celibacy as a superior way of life. Martin Luther contended that marriage existed in order to satisfy the natural urge to procreate, effecting the salvation of souls by allowing men and women to act sinlessly in accordance with their physical natures. Sexuality, in this view, was the reason for marriage, and matrimony was thus the ideal state for all human beings. Subsequent theologians developed this idea, delineating the urgency of qualitative marital relations and, ultimately, allowing for divorce. (If individuals were compelled to marry by sexual drives they must be permitted to separate and remarry when their unions failed.) The Protestant notion of holy matrimony, probably the distant wellspring of our own culture's obsession with the caliber and tenor of marital relations, was still absolutely patriarchal. Husbands were mandated to love and protect their wives; wives were expected to obey their husbands.[24]

The historian Lawrence Stone argued that the Protestant sanctification of marriage resulted in the further domination of wives.[25] With its emphasis on the couple, Protestant morality isolated the family from the larger kinship and community network, stressing the household as a moral center for the socialization of children in which "power flowed increasingly to the husband over the wife and to the father over the children"[26] and in which husbands were less hampered by interference from relatives, neighbors, and clergy. Early modernity also gave rise to the romance-based "companionate" marriage. In the seventeenth century the idea that two people could find fulfillment in a partnership based on unsupervised personal choice and mutual affection was still so radical that it was considered dangerously subversive. One century later marriage based on personal and erotic attraction had become a popular norm. A growing, Protestant middle class re-envisioned wedlock as a complementary but unequal friendship. A stream of conduct books and novels— similar publications continue to the present day—suggested that women were naturally suited for this new model of wedlock, instructing them in the domestic arts and celebrating their wifely capacities.

These primers were, effectively, guidebooks on how to enjoy one's own subordination, since eigtheenth-century domestic law incorporated previous gender biases. In his 1765 *Commentaries on the Laws of England*, the jurist William Blackstone codified preexisting regulations with the definition of coverture: "By marriage, the husband and wife are one person in law, that is, the very being or legal existence of the woman is suspended during the marriage, or at least incorporated and consolidated into that of her husband, under whose wing, protection, and cover, she performs everything.[27] As a *femme covert* a woman could not initiate independent lawsuits, and any income or property not protected by a prior marriage agreement was automatically her husband's. Family law dictated that children belonged exclusively to the husband; in the event of his death his widow had rights over them only if such rights were stipulated in his will. Wives who left their husbands could take neither children nor property and could be forced to return, regardless of the cause of the abandonment. In eighteenth-century England a husband who killed his wife was tried for murder (punishable by hanging), while a wife who killed her husband was tried for "petite treason," a crime punishable by drawing and burning alive.[28] In France things weren't much better. The 1804 Code Napoleon, influential throughout Europe, recapitulated the old terms of the marriage contract, proclaiming a husband head of his household and dictating the arrangement as one of male protection in return for female obedience. Under this code women were classified with children and mental defectives as legal incompetents. Again, a married woman's only possible source of legal protection lay in the marriage contract drawn up by her parents, but these contracts tended to subordinate wives to their husbands, making it impossible for women to manage their own assets without their husbands' consent.[29]

Bolstered by custom and law, the patriarchal family was the source of heated polemics in England throughout the nineteenth century. Supporters saw it as a sacrosanct institution, a tranquil haven in a rapidly changing world. Sanctified by the Victorian's brand of evangelical Protestantism, marriage was said to be an ethereal state in which men and women complemented each other by operating in separate spheres. The husband was protector and breadwinner to a domestic, submissive, and self-abnegating wife whom one poet referred to as "the angel in the house."[30] Victorian culture seemed to have perfected the marital ideal set forth two centuries earlier by a Dorsetshire clergyman that "A good wife should be like a Mirrour which hath no image of its own, but receives its stamp from the face that looks into it."[31] With its beatification of woman's role within marriage, the nineteenth century gave rise to the event that is the subject of this book: the big white wedding featuring elaborate pageantry and lavish displays of spending and sentiment.

Victorians touted the components of the wedding—the gown and veil, the bridal procession, the throwing of rice, and the romantic honeymoon—as British traditions despite the fact that not one of these rites predated their own century. "The popularizing of the big white wedding as *the* British nuptial" was, according to scholar John Gillis, "an act of self-veneration by those seeking to legitimate and impose their own social standards."[32] Giving away a bride adorned in virginal white, hosting a family reception, and sending the couple off on an exclusive honeymoon enshrined the Victorian's romantic notions of female purity, conjugal love, and the nuclear family. This was the era in which marriage reached its apotheosis as an ideal. Despite the fact that it was, once again, legal subordination, with a husband controlling his wife's property and earnings,[33] wedlock continued to be the central aspiration of most women. ("Being married gives one one's position, which nothing else can," wrote Queen Victoria to her daughter in 1858.[34]) With its extraordinary profusion of images sentimentalizing wedlock and its rigid code of marital gender relations, the nineteenth century was, also, not coincidentally, the era in which women organized and began, overtly, to fight, coming together with an agenda of specific demands and ultimately achieving a series of sweeping reforms that included not just the vote but the protection of matrimonial property (in 1882) and equal access to divorce (in 1923).[35]

Our own century has absorbed the Victorian's complex inheritance: a reformed legal model of marriage as well as the ideology of the private family based on the powerful belief that marriage is a relationship unlike any other—a sacrosanct bond that takes precedence over all other emotional ties. Matrimony now entails a more equal contract between men and women than has ever existed. It also has a sentimental luster that most of our ancestors would have found bizarre if not laughable. The obsessive romantic mystique surrounding wedlock creates other kinds of inequity. The state-sanctioned, monogamous heterosexual partnership is now touted as *the* pivotal adult relationship for most men and women—a liaison so momentous that it necessitates celebration via a costly extravaganza that no mere friendship would justify. Despite wedlock's sexist legacy, the American relationship industry encourages men and women, and women in particular, to strive for marital commitment in a way that they would never pursue same-sex friendships, intimacy with biological relatives, or closeness with colleagues, teachers, and mentors. Once married, women's loyalty to and love for their husbands is supposed to take precedence over obligations to all other partners.

Given wedlock's history, the sanctimoniousness with which self-help experts praise marriage and promote conjugal commitment, the doggedness with which "single" women pursue such commitment, and the enthusiasm with which engaged women plan and orchestrate their nuptial celebrations is deeply ironic. Certainly, the emotional reality of marriage has always been varied. Even in the most rigidly patriarchal settings there have always been women who stood on equal footing with or even dominated their husbands. But despite the daily realities that have moderated matrimony's sexist doctrines, the institution has always been powerfully biased against women. Marriage is not merely stained with the notion of gender inequality; it has been the West's central vehicle for enforcing that inequality, as it has simultaneously offered women their primary work and main source of identification. But given the degree to which it has dominated female experience for over three millennia, it is perhaps not surprising that matrimony remains the state to which the majority of contemporary women aspire. In every era history has affirmed marriage as woman's natural state; in what are perhaps the two most influential ancient languages, Hebrew and Greek, the word for *woman* is also the word for *wife*. Western history records the names of male philosophers, generals, politicians, jurists, artists, and scientists. With few exceptions it has until recently recorded women only as wives of distinguished men or biological mothers, especially of prominent sons. With marriage as woman's chief occupation and sole honorable destination, the names of the great spinsters in western history are unfortunately lost to us. Thousands of exceptional unmarried women must have made contributions to the culture of the West but they have died anonymously, their achievements obscured by societal prescriptions for conjugal femininity.[36] With the weight of tradition mandating marriage as a woman's sole occupation, it is not surprising that American conduct literature written for females still traffics so heavily in the subject, especially by contrast with advice aimed at men. To be someone, to be like other important women, to prove oneself as a desirable person and a mature adult, to maintain a very basic kind of social dignity, a woman must be a wife. American relationship experts capitalize on this assumption, and in so doing, perpetuate it. Despite their often frantic protestations to the contrary, such pundits presume that the healthy woman's deepest innate drive is toward wedlock and then toward motherhood. Their advice blends description with prescription, naturalizing conjugality as female destiny.

It would be easy to disregard matrimony's origins as those of a distant, primitive, and irrelevant past. American history and contemporary American politics however demonstrate irrefutably our society's powerful links to this past. Throughout much of the seventeenth century in Virginia and New England adultery was technically punishable by execution. Defined as intercourse with a married or engaged woman, the colonial criminalization of extramarital sex perpetuated the old double standard and protected a husband's sexual control of his wife; a married man could not commit adultery with a "single" female.[37] Adultery is still a crime in many states, although the laws are rarely enacted and are considered "moribund." However, as recently as 1990 a twenty-six-year-old Wisconsin resident was charged with having an adulterous affair. (In order to avoid a trial, the defendant, Donna E. Carroll, agreed to forty hours of community service.)[38] Measures such as the 1872 Comstock Act prohibiting the use of mail to transport birth control, contraceptive information, or any other "indecent" or "immoral" material[39] may seem far away, but their premises are echoed in the 1996 Defense of Marriage Act invalidating same-sex partnership and protecting the traditional marital bond.[40] These measures attest to an ongoing societal interest in bolstering heterosexual partnership and controlling female sexuality. The 1998 feeding frenzy in which media analysts endlessly debated the state of the first marriage after President Clinton's sex life became public knowledge, vilifying the president's sexual partner, Monica Lewinsky, shows the degree to which marital fidelity and virtue are irrationally linked in the popular consciousness.[41]

The marriage mystique permeates American politics. The 2000 national conventions of both the Democratic and the Republican parties were not forums for policy discussion but prescriptions for heteronormativity in which male candidates vied for office by advertising their conjugal piety, and beaming political wives—both full-time homemak-ers who, in the words of one approving pollster, have "chosen to take on marriage, mortgage, and munchkins"[42]—gushed over their husbands, recounted their courtships, showed home movies chronicling their domestic lives, and smooched proudly with their consorts to demon-strate the health and happiness of their marriages. ("One's reserved, the other's outspoken, but Laura Bush and Tipper Gore have one thing in common: a commitment to family and their husbands' ambitions,"[43] a typically celebratory postcovention magazine headline proclaimed.) All indicators point to our culture's enshrinement of the couple as well as the continued presence of the age-old, marriage-based sexual double standard validating female sexual activity solely within marriage and distinguishing sharply between respectable and nonrespectable women. When an elected official like Governor Frank Keating of Oklahoma appears on television as he did on June 24, 1999, and announces as part of his platform the goal of reducing the divorce rate by one-third by the year 2000,[44] it is clear that he, like most politicians, shares the timeless and irrational belief that families are best served by traditional sex roles, that women are best protected by the institution of marriage, and that conjugal households somehow strengthen the state.

This promarriage bias cuts across the public and private domains, shaping policy in areas as diverse as immigration, health care, personal finance, and employment. It is so pervasive as to be practically invisible. In her 1999 study, *White Weddings,* Chrys Ingraham provides a general list of state-controlled marital entitlements. Such privileges vary from region to region but tend to include automatic inheritance, automatic housing lease transfers, bereavement leave, burial determination, child custody, exemption of property tax upon either partner's death, immunity from testimony against one's spouse, crime victim recovery benefits, medical insurance privileges, sick leave to care for one's partner, reduced rate membership, visitation of one's partner in the hospital or in prison, and wrongful death benefits.[45] Because our culture celebrates only amorous love and distinguishes rigorously between romantic couples and all other species of relationship, no such privileges exist for platonic friends. In spite of escalating divorce statistics,[46] the widespread belief in wedlock and the state-sanctioned couple appears to be stronger than ever.

In the past five years myriad periodicals have featured articles hailing the resurgence of early marriage as a widespread cultural trend. One such piece, Sarah Bernard's June 1997 *New York* magazine feature "Early to Wed" explains early marriage as a laudable return to traditional values, a way for precocious, sexually experienced, professionally mobile women in their twenties to achieve stability, calm, and balance. Drawing on the anecdotes of New York women from the "Wasp and preppy circuit" and the merchants (buyers for bridal shops, wedding gown designers, and wedding planners) who service these women, Bernard concludes happily that early marriage is back. Strolling across manicured lawns clad in white Vera Wang gowns and clasping white bouquets or beaming placidly from their Manhattan apartments, the women featured in her article express a shockingly nostalgic view of wedlock as the return to an earlier, simpler time. Twenty-four-year-old editor Cherise Grant explains, "My dream is to have a wonderful dining room perfectly set for eight people. I have all my glasses, all my silver.... The world is so unstable.... I think dating is emotional abuse. I think if you find a man you love you should marry him. There's something so grounding about being married, saying you'll be my mate for life."[47] Twenty-three-year-old author Katherine Davis concurs, admitting that she's often offended when people assume she's unmarried: "I do pride myself on being a good married person, a good wife."[48] "I found the person I had the most fun with, the best sex with, love more than anyone else," explains recent Barnard graduate and self-proclaimed former "wild child," Kira von Eichel, whom Bernard calls a "princess bride." "Every time we pictured the rest of our lives, we saw each other together."[49] "I wouldn't want to be thirty-five and looking for a husband," confesses an anonymous young woman.[50] Of this new breed of conservative, privileged, and matrimonially oriented women, Bernard concludes admiringly, "At twenty-three, they're no longer interested in a wild youth. If anything, they're tired of it."[51]

Such sentimental nostalgia displays profound ignorance of matrimony's history, but historical myopia is only one of the problem's intrinsic to the modern woman's marriage mania. When a young woman like Cherise Grant equates marriage with stability, and when a twenty-five-year-old publishing assistant like Willow Wycoff describes her decision to marry young as a "leap of faith,"[52] both women assume that only heterosexual marriage offers women emotional intimacy and socioeconomic security. When a journalist like Sarah Bernard applauds young women's willingness to commit early to monogamous relationships, quoting author Katie Roiphe, who explains that today's young women want "someone on their team,"[53] she reinforces this belief. Writer Lois Brody Smith, who covers weddings for the *New York Times,* proclaims that she is no longer "a wedding skeptic." She drenches her notebook with tears at every assignment, because she is so moved by details of each bridal ensemble, nuances that reveal that a woman is "getting married, changing her life for the good, making a huge promise, a gamble against divorce statistics, an ocean crossing."[54] In doing so she expresses the belief that matrimony entails some kind of ultimate virtue, that it has magically transformative powers for women and also represents the optimal arrangement for the care and socialization of children.

"The historian of marriage will have to explain how a period that witnessed unprecedented divorce rates and a determined assault on the whole concept by many of the younger generation, and especially by the freed female slaves of our era, should yet have been presented at many levels and from many sources with an ideal of marriage unknown to most of our ancestors,"[55] remarks historian Christopher N. L. Brooke. The popular enshrinement of marriage, the growth of the wedding industry, and the various hymns of praise to domestic monogamy sung by media representatives are indeed ironic corollaries to the political gains that women have made during the past two centuries. Perhaps an institution so drenched in sexist cruelty demands the support of a strong sentimentalizing ideology. Or perhaps the current marriage craze is in part a reaction to both the conjugal impermanence of modern times and the critique of wedlock launched by a small but vocal feminist minority. Whatever the reason, it is clear that America's marital publicity machine is currently in high gear.

From the burgeoning of classical literature in ancient Greece to seventeenth century England's early rumblings of feminism, there has been an antimarriage tradition among western intellectuals. Individual philosophers have critiqued nuptial life, putting forth various antimarriage polemics. An overview of such writings is beyond the scope of this book and is not of primary interest to me here. I wish to understand the psychological and commercial underpinnings of today's marriage process, a narrative that originates in dating, culminates in exchanged wedding vows, and concludes with the establishment of a companionate household and a series of culturally scripted domestic activities. Toward this end it would be pointless to provide lengthy explications of St. Augustine, Francis Bacon, Mary Astell, William Godwin, or Mary Daly, although these thinkers' critiques resonate throughout my consciousness and inform this analysis. These authors are read seriously by a dedicated but tiny elite. Marriage-oriented self-improvement books, ladies' magazines, and dating handbooks are consumed by millions of American women. To understand the female preoccupation with wedlock—what I call the marriage mystique—it is necessary to turn first to these sources.

II. Advice to Husband Hunters: The Relationship Expert

When addressing young American women the discrete media of television, film, books, and magazines coalesce into a formidable body of husband-hunting literature in which four themes recur: the value of intimacy, the importance of maintaining a positive attitude in courtship, the imperative of evaluating one's partner to learn if he is capable of "commitment," and the legitimacy of being "single."

The contemporary dating expert is an odd hybrid. She is at once a newfangled preacher, a nurturing psychologist, a gypsy fortune teller, an overbearing Jewish mother, a sorority chaperone, a corporate consultant, and an old world village matchmaker. A prominent figure in the relationship industry, the New Age dating expert functions as a perennially optimistic soothsayer, a man or (more typically) a woman who urges her female clients to reach past the artificial fraudulent self that "society" has constructed for them and find a realm beyond—a zone of inner spirituality that is frequently described as a "life force," a "higher self," or an "inner goddess." The New Age advisor appears to de-emphasize love's institutional trappings—formal engagement and marriage. He or she in fact claims that empty symbols of societal validation have caused women to lose touch with their essential selves and quest fruitlessly after that which seems always to elude them. The resulting sense of emptiness and failure can be alleviated through practices that combine the techniques of ancient pagan and eastern religions (chanting, meditation, prayer, the burning of incense) with those of modern psychology (retreats, workshops, breathing exercises, therapeutic movement, memory exercises, the keeping of journals). According to the New Age dating expert, once a woman achieves emotional enlightenment—once her false ego has dissolved and she has attained primordial energy, wisdom, serenity, and peace—she will find her optimal male partner, or, rather, he will find her. Once internal spiritual perfection has been attained, external romance will occur effortlessly and magically. The New Age relationship expert's message is twofold and convoluted; she argues that the locus of authority dwells at the center of each person, waiting to be released, and that female socialization has generally caused women to overvalue marital symbols of external validation—the engagement ring, the wedding invitation, the bridal gown. She then promises that by shifting her focus to the internal (and presumably authentic) experience of love, each woman will obtain these symbols, securing the marital tie through a set of karmic laws as invisible and compelling as the rules of physics. Although she appears to disdain matrimony's surface trappings, the New Age advisor actually embraces wedlock as woman's primary desire—the goal to which a magical life force can propel each woman.

"Empowerment specialist" Iyanla Vanzant is one of America's premiere soothsayers, a high profile relationship guru who frequently appears on television, often on the *Oprah Winfrey Show*. Vanzant's 1998 *New York Times* best-seller, *In the Meantime: Finding Yourself and the Love You Want*, instructs female readers in the art of marriage-oriented spiritual healing. Vanzant mixes two primary metaphors. The first is that of time: the female life span is divided into discrete periods: real time, during which a woman accepts and disseminates love, and "the meantime," a period of unfocused depression when one awaits the perfect romantic partner or languishes in an uncommitted relationship. The second metaphor is architectural: Vanzant describes the advancing stages of amorous awareness as a dwelling; the basement is the dirty region cluttered by negative emotional patterns, the second floor is "the place that you learn about the most important relationship you will ever have, the relationship you have with yourself,"[56] the third floor is a zone of increased self-awareness, etc. Vanzant envisions the final stage of love as an attic boudoir called the "Love is sweet suite" and explains that it is a zone in which major figures from various world religions congregate— the place where Christ, the Buddha, Krishna, and the archangels Michael, Ariel, Uriel, and Gabriel live.[57]

Through "housecleaning," "taking out the trash," "scrubbing the tub," and "rearranging the furniture," the modern woman can cleanse herself emotionally in readiness for amorous partnership. These are not of course actual housecleaning activities but rituals of self-improvement. "It's time to pick up our mops, brooms, and dust cloths and do some spring cleaning,"[58] Vanzant announces jubilantly. Her program of reducing emotional clutter includes such activities as asking oneself, "what am I feeling?" and "what do I want?"[59] writing letters to God, requesting the ability to love,[60] meditating on the question, "where am I?"[61] and visualizing oneself in optimal amorous circumstances.[62] When a woman has used Vanzant's methods to dissolve her own spurious ego and become "the light of the world,"[63] romantic love will magically find her. By accessing the powers of the female self to disseminate unconditional love, by abandoning the surface fantasies of marriage and family and performing healing rituals of self-acceptance, the modern woman can and will attract her man (and thereby obtain marriage and family). Like most dating advisors Vanzant presents herself as an emulative role model, a woman from humble origins who has lived through difficult times and propelled herself to emotional and economic heights, finally obtaining that all-important symbol of successful femininity: a marital relationship. *In the Meantime* is dedicated to, among others, Vanzant's husband: "*and to my husband,*/Ifayemi Adeyemi Bandele," the dedication reads, "who helped me realize that/the meantime does pay off!"[64]

Typically, the relationship expert who voices this schizophrenic message places wackily disingenuous emphasis on the validity of the "single" life. A spunky black lady who whoops cliches like a New Age football coach, Vanzant appeared on the *Oprah Winfrey Show* on August 10, 1999, leading women in the audience with the chant, "I'm Single, and it's okay." "I'm Single, and it's okay" female audience members intoned repeatedly, appearing titillated and shocked by the novel concept that

unmarried existence is acceptable. Two minutes later Vanzant was counseling individual audience members, reminding them that all romantic
obstacles can be conquered with the power of positive thought. She
addressed a beleaguered looking "single" mother who was feeling less
than optimistic about her chances on the dating scene. "Do you believe
there is a man out there who will love you and your children?" Vanzant
queried. The woman appeared uncertain, but Vanzant assuaged her with
the truism, "You cannot love yourself unless you are in total truth with
yourself." These strong if baffling words appeared to do the trick. In a
later appearance this woman seemed cautiously optimistic about her
prospects for romance and informed a supportive audience that she had
begun visiting museums and attending swing-dancing classes in the
hopes of meeting men. In the New Age dating expert's world view, ready
self-acceptance of the label "single" occurs as a necessary spiritual preparation for marriage.

While the New Age dating advisor urges women to unleash a putatively authentic, unfettered self in order to attract love, the hyperconventional relationship expert takes the opposite approach. Her goal—
obtaining permanent, exclusive, male commitment—is the same, but
her method is antithetical. She advises readers and clients to engage in an
elaborate charade of femininity. She instructs modern women to heed
the call of an earlier generation and construct a demure, sexually apa
thetic, ladylike self tailored to impress men. The female husband hunter
must scrupulously obey rules of sexual restraint that many consider outdated in order to win her man. Ellen Fein and Sherrie Schneider, authors
of another *New York Times* best-seller entitled *The Rules,* urge their
female readers to don a rigid, impervious social mask that conceals all
desire. Artifice rather than inner healing, ostentatious displays of reserve
rather than cleansing meditation, characterize their program. In the
absence of the protective mothers, grandmothers and aunts, female
chaperones and sorority supervisors who once safeguarded female
chastity and enforced the sexual double standard, the contemporary
woman is urged to act as her own policeman, monitoring herself with
steely self-will, reining in her own sexual appetite, concealing her emotional needs from the world at large and from men in particular. By
assuming an air of cool nonchalance and affecting disinterest in both

sexual and emotional intercourse, the "rules girl" bewitches her man and causes him to stumble, head over heels in love with her, into a marriage proposal. The trick, according to this wildly successful 1995 primer, is to always leave one's male companion feeling hungry. A woman must not sleep with her beau too quickly and must end each telephone call and dinner first, signaling that she has other more important things to do, other more interesting places to be. "Ending the date first is not so easy when you really like him and want to marry him," Fein and Schneider concede: "But it must be done, because you must leave him wanting more of you, not less."[65]

Like many advisors in the relationship industry Fein and Schneider possess no credentials or expertise. According to their bios, Schneider is a freelance magazine writer, Fein a Long Island-based mother. That both are married is a piece of information included to inspire awe and envy in female readers.[66] Dispensers of 1950s folk wisdom, these ladies clearly believe that a marriage certificate is the ultimate diploma, the consummate female achievement, and the only degree necessary to qualify one as an expert in human relations. Fein and Schneider appear to be unfamiliar with the pleasures afforded by solitude. They tantalize readers with images of institutionalized togetherness: "Think about never having to be alone on Saturday nights or having to ask your married friends to fix you up. Think about being a couple!"[67] Achieving life in the plural is simple if painful. It involves constantly attending "singles" events at which one circulates, wears a ladylike smile, shakes hands demurely, and affects a pose of casual disinterest. Once a "rules girl" has attracted a few suitors she secures her engagement ring by following a regimen of rigid self-denial and deceptive allure, a program intended to elicit the aggression that Fein and Schneider claim is a natural male trait, while highlighting a woman's own passive, mysteriously feminine nature. In 1950's fashion the "rules girl" never splits the bill for a dinner, never calls her beaus and rarely returns their telephone calls, does not accept dates for Saturday night after Wednesday, does not see a man more than once a week, does not reveal facts about herself too quickly, does not live with a man or leave personal items at his home, and ends a relationship with any man who does not purchase a romantic gift for Valentine's Day. By maintaining her distance, withholding sexual favors, and projecting an enigmatic aura, she procures a husband. But the key to her amorous triumph is never betraying her own marital agenda: "On a date, you never show that getting married is foremost on your mind. You're cool. He may think you've turned down several marriage proposals. You sip—never slurp—your drink and let him find out all about you, instead of the other way around. Your answers are short, light, and flirtatious. Your gestures are soft and feminine."[68] By appearing disinterested in her own primary goal, by moving with subtlety and grace, and by maintaining a genteel silence ("most men find chatty women annoying"),[69] the "rules girl," Fein and Schneider promise, will soon find herself a triumphantly married woman.

"The old rules our grandmothers followed to get a man don't work today (and, in fact, they never did)"[70] objects Barbara De Angelis in her 1997 *The Real Rules*. This affable, shiny-haired motivational speaker purports to offer a formula for finding marriages that are honest and fulfilling. She is neither New Age nor prurient but wholesome—a counselor focused on helping clients achieve what she considers to be nurturing healthy relationships. She repudiates Schneider and Fein's jaded approach to courtship, and, like a conscientious mother adding fiber to the family diet, urges female readers to build sturdy relationships comprised of emotional honesty and mutual support. In De Angelis' regimen women are allowed to act assertively with men whom they like but are advised to judge men by their practical and emotional availability, maintaining vigilant suspicion of the man who is married, bogged down by psychological baggage, or afraid of intimacy. For De Angelis love is neither a mythopoetical experience nor a delicately balanced game of power. Rather, it is a kind of ongoing encounter session in which partners take turns sharing, caring, and offering emotional validation. But even amidst this therapeutic love festival, the sexual double standard prevails. While she admonishes her readers to be themselves, practicing honesty and emotional generosity with their male partners, De Angelis does demand sexual self-restraint: "Don't lower yourself to behaving like a sex object."[71] She advises: "If you dress like a slut, a man will think you're a slut."[72]

De Angelis blends Puritanical sexual conservatism with the the values of modern psychology. Stressing the importance of positive thinking, she trumpets self-awareness, communication, openness, and mutual caring—those staples of the healthy long-term relationship touted by modern therapists. She eschews meditation and voodoo for plain talk ("The more natural and relaxed you are, the more natural and relaxed the right man will feel around you."),[73] relinquishes wily feminine manipulation for honesty ("If it's being yourself to spend half an hour on the phone with a guy you're beginning to see as he opens up and shares about his parents' divorce, even though he'll realize you really like him, DO IT.").[74] The first of her "Four Laws of Love" entails relinquishing marriage as a paramount goal: "The purpose of your life isn't to get married. The purpose of your life is to grow into the most loving, fulfilled, *real* woman you can be."[75]

Having affirmed this politically correct bit of feminist dogma, De Angelis then defines female happiness in terms of romantic success, substituting the troubling word *marriage* with the more neutral word *commitment*. In her view, happiness and emotional health hinge on partnership; romantic partnership based on long-term, exclusive togetherness in which each man and woman form a dyad. This equation, which sounds suspiciously like the marriage contract that she has just flouted, is presented as the bedrock of the good life, the natural and primary goal of women everywhere. De Angelis urges her readers to assess their relationships, and she even provides an optimal time frame for love. There are four stages in the courtship process: the agreement to be sexually and emotionally monogamous (up to three months), the contract to work toward a partnership (three to six months), the decision to spend the future together (six months or longer), and the commitment to spend a lifetime together. "I don't think there's any one word in our language that can cause more tension between men and women than the 'C' word: Commitment,"[76] she concedes. But with emotional openness, maturity and responsibility, high self-esteem, and a positive attitude toward life, today's independent yet loving woman can achieve romantic happiness. Finally, like so many in the human potential industry, De Angelis presents herself as a paradigm of mental health and marital success, reminding readers that she is married and emphasizing the fact that she is happily conjoined—a woman of quality who values the authentic man rather than the the the status he affords. "I love the beautiful ring my husband gave me when he asked me to marry him," she gushes, "but compared to the emotional promises he made and kept, that ring means nothing."[77]

While these three types of relationship advisors—the guru, the disciplinarian, and the therapist—seem to espouse divergent philosophies, their programs are actually based on a set of common assumptions. Each assumes that togetherness is superior to solitude. Romantic evenings out and cozy weekends spent burrowing at home with one's consort always take precedence over extended stretches of time alone. In this relationship-biased perspective, the conjugal activities of sex, affection, and conversation are inherently superior to reading, writing, thinking, and prayer, activities that require solitude and can only be done properly in the quiet of one's own room, the silence of a library, or the peace of a sanctuary. Each advisor as well presumes that sexual activity is superior to celibacy and that sexual normalcy, for women, entails an ongoing relationship with a single partner who has pledged fidelity to her. Carnality is assumed superior to the discipline of sexual asceticism that many religious traditions claim to sharpen spiritual and mental faculties. And for women sex must occur with a single steady, loving, attentive partner, because women are presumed monogamous and emotionally needy by nature. The excitement of multiple or alternating relationships or physical intimacy with anonymous strangers or paid professionals receives no acknowledgment. Finally, each pundit assumes that romantic partnership takes precedence over all other forms of attachment. Each sees the ultimate goal of such partnership as the establishment of a reciprocal identity in which man and woman no longer use the singular pronoun *I* but instead begin each sentence with *we*. Each takes for granted that the natural outcome of this corporate identity will be a marriage license— the modern state's seal of approval.

Anti-intellectual, mindlessly romantic, sexist, and sexually reactionary, these assumptions are enormous and problematic. They play themselves out, not just in dating advice, but in the real life narrative of marriage-oriented courtship. They are embedded in the literature of the entire wedding industry and the rituals, documents, and adornments of matrimony. The popularity of authors like Iyanla Vanzant, Ellen Fein and Sherrie Schneider, and Barbara De Angelis demonstrates that

American women have swallowed and digested these myths wholesale and are as fetishitically obsessed with marriage as they have ever been. Men, such authors presume, constitute a different genus of being, a group naturally averse to romantic partnership. The New Age consultant's man is a spiritual soul mate, a preordained partner who is guided toward the enlightened woman by forces that neither can harness or understand. The hyperconventional advisor's man is a featureless blank, a cipher who provides the all-important social validation of marriage. The psychologist's man is a therapy partner, a good-hearted but insecure fellow who can be brought around to the act of commitment through support and open loving communication. The quality that each of these cardboard figures share is elusiveness. The modern man is assumed to be skittish about what experts purport as the natural progression of love; the long-term relationship that is finally officialized as a permanent partnership. Whatever her bent, the modern dating expert believes courtship to be teleological rather than open-ended. The heterosexual relationship must always move forward, expanding, intensifying, changing to become, finally, that totemic foundation, a *marriage*. Toward this all-important end, men must be coaxed, coddled, finessed, handled, or outright tricked.

The figure who tacitly lurks behind so much of today's modern dating literature is this evasive would-be husband. The diametrical opposite of the uxorious modern woman, this problematic figure is often referred to as a "commitment phobe" or a "Peter Pan." Portrayed as a callow youth who selfishly refuses to yield to matrimony's mandates, he is anatomized in book after book and article after article. "If men didn't have to marry, we wouldn't"[78] confess Bradley Gerstman, Christopher Pizzo, and Rich Seldes, the authors of *What Men Want*. Respectively an attorney, an accountant, and a physician, these unmarried men and self-professed "regular guys" have written a primer on how to lure male professionals into marriage. They typify the corporate model of relationship expert; their manual describes dating, cohabitation, and wedlock using modern capitalism's jargon. They advise women to approach relationships like effective business strategists—firm-minded managers or savvy headhunters who evaluate marriage candidates with the understanding that men are reluctant monogamists. "A man feels very nervous about committing to marriage," Gerstman, Pizzo, and Seldes explain. "He may love you, he may even think he wants to spend the rest of your life with you, but he really hates signing on the dotted line."[79] Like most in the relationship industry, these authors consider the sexes' different responses to commitment to be a symptom of inherent gender difference: "One of our Maker's little tricks was to make women love commitment and love talking about it. Men are made of different stuff. We need commitment, but fear it.... Relationships pass through different levels of commitment, but whether it is committing to monogamy or to marriage, we still hate to pin ourselves down."[80]

Faced with such dauntingly essential gender difference, how does today's woman clinch the deal? According to Gerstman, Pizzo, and Seldes, she steers clear of obvious "Mr. Wrongs," avoiding men who are distant, on the rebound, or too sexually aggressive too soon. Once she has weeded out these bad seeds, she zeros in on those males who are real marriage material. Then, with the energy and finesse of a corporate self-starter, she nurtures the relationship in a "proactive" fashion, calling her guy to say hello or thank him for dinner, bestowing small gifts upon him, making him the occasional home-cooked meal, and sprucing up his apartment. She does not play hard to get but projects an aura of confidence enhanced by kindness, vocalizing her appreciation of him and showing her enthusiasm without appearing desperate. Using the techniques graphically described in the eighth chapter of *What Men Want*, she becomes adept at administering fellatio. If she's uncertain about the status of the relationship, like a star manager, she confronts the problem head on: "When in doubt, ask him."[81] And since she's striving for respectable middle-class coupledom, she keeps her sexual past to herself: "No man wants to think the woman of his dreams is promiscuous,"[82] these three lotharios point out, echoing the prurience of female relationship experts. Eventually, this smooth operator reels in her man.

According to some relationship experts, however, the deck is hopelessly stacked against women, and a good husband has become increasingly hard to find. Advice-givers commonly claim that male commitment phobia has reached epidemic proportions. "Men have always been wary of commitment," Steven Carter and Julia Sokol, the authors of yet another *New York Times* best-seller, *Men Who Can't Love*, proclaim, "But today there is a difference. Today, unlike any other period in our history, the fear of commitment is destroying the fabric of our society."[83] Providing no statistical evidence to back up this sweeping claim, Carter and Sokol sketch a portrait of the ubiquitous male commitment phobe. He's everywhere—the guy who wants sex but won't agree to perpetual togetherness, who demands companionship without the accompanying documentation. In courtship he's charming at first, coming on strong. Then he begins to pull back, sending out a baffling array of mixed messages and double signals that the contemporary husband hunter must decipher as if it were Morse code. Just as he gets emotionally close, the commitment phobe withdraws sexually; just as he reveals secrets about his past, he stops calling and begins to break dates. What's the cause of his behavior? Fear, according to Carter and Sokol, who, without a single statistic or research-based fact, diagnose male anxiety about marriage as a clinical phobia akin to agoraphobia or claustrophobia. The commitment phobe is warm one moment and chilly the next, because when he's in an extended relationship he experiences physical panic attacks that prevent long-term love. "Although I am not asking you to pity this man, I am asking you to recognize that his personal demons make him a truly pathetic character,"[84] the authors explain. The levelheaded, mature, marriage-oriented gal must finally steer clear of this pariah. His pathology is her misery, his irrational fear of "forever after" the obstacle to her happy social completion.

While authors like Carter and Sokol use psychiatric jargon, isolating the marriage-shy male as a disturbed loner, an extreme pathological type, dating experts tend to concur that there is a touch of commitment phobia in all men. The offensive courtship narrative scripted by the relationship industry (and accepted and enacted by American women) is one of female pursuit and male retreat, female enticement and male seduction, female single-mindedness and male submission. This narrative rests on a prejudice so popular that its ludicrous extremism often escapes notice: that wedlock is the endpoint to which all worthwhile erotic relationships progress. Accordingly, women must be constantly on the lookout for matrimonially available men and must eschew or reform those suitors whose plans do not include permanent coupledom. The quandary is described in column after column of women's magazines.

First, the "single" woman must survey the playing field, assessing the seriousness of her suitors. "Is he mate material?"[85] query the editors of *Mode*, a fashion magazine for plus-size women. (He is apparently, if at age twenty-five he does his own laundry and pays his rent, at thirty-five sends his laundry out and has a mortgage, and at forty-five pays the hotel bills for romantic rendezvous and owns his own company.) "Is he relationship ready?"[86] asks Suzanne Murray of *Cosmopolitan* magazine. Her assess-your-partner quiz includes a series of small litmus tests: when one's boyfriend has exciting news, how long does he wait before calling? Does he ogle other women? Is it permissible to answer his telephone when it rings? "Does his definition of 'space' put you somewhere north of Pluto?"[87] quips Peter Jon Lindberg in the November 2000 issue of *Glamour* magazine. Lindberg advises women on how to interpret the "midrelationship freakout," a crisis point at which many men apparently express the desire to enhance their live-in relationships with a modicum of solitary time. "Worry if . . . he needs space all the time, but can't say for how long. . . . If he can't or won't give you a timetable and some mutually agreeable guidelines, he's simply being selfish. . . . Move on."[88]

Experts agree that the marriage-minded female must take action and either truncate the open-ended relationship or rehabilitate her partner, transforming him into a would-be husband. *Cosmopolitan*'s Murray quotes Jane Greer's *Gridlock: Finding the Courage to Move on in Love and Work*, which advises, "If you've been together for more than six months with no progress, it's time to break this bad-boyfriend habit. . . . Go out with the girls or sign up for a night course at your local college."[89] *Glamour* magazine's July 1999 issue features advice from Suzanne Lopez author of the primer *Get Smart With Your Heart*. Lopez instructs women to assess their liaisons with the penetrating question, "Is he a commitment phobe?"[90] The man apathetic to marriage is just such a fiend; Lopez terms him a "knight," because his intentions are ephemeral and fantastic and don't include the nuts and bolts business of matrimony. "If you want a band of gold in the future, move on," she cautions.[91] *Mademoiselle* magazine sums up the problem neatly in its January 2000 issue: "He won't commit. When you've got a white picket fence fantasy and he's just signed a ten-year lease on his studio apartment, you're clearly not on the same romantic page."[92] Like most periodicals of this sort, *Mademoiselle* suggests eschewing such men in order to protect one's mental health: "If he's a seasoned soloist with no interest in having a copilot, it's best to get out while you still have a shred of self-esteem."[93] "My guy of six months is worried that in a year I'll want to get married and have kids and he won't be ready. What should I do?"[94] an anxious female correspondent queries in this magazine's "Q & A Love" column. "If your respective inventories don't jibe...I'm afraid you'll have to take a deep breath and move on,"[95] is columnist Ellen Tien's somber reply.

When the dating advisor is not urging women to abandon their marriage-phobic lovers she's instructing them in the fine art of matrimonial seduction, explaining just how to ensnare these reluctant Peter Pans. In November 1999 *Marie Claire* magazine commissioned four separate advertising agencies to design campaigns that would make wedlock appealing to men. The results, published in an article entitled, "How to Get a Man to Marry You," feature mock pornographic advertisements ("Live, SEXY woman in your own home!!!...24-Hr. advice and support...GIGANTIC HUGS!") alongside images that stress the intergenerational continuity of marriage. In one poster three sets of wedding cake figurines are accompanied by the captions: "Your great grandfather did it, your grandfather did it, your father did it....If this isn't reason enough for you to marry the woman you love, you must be a bastard."[96] "Heat Up His Cold Feet," advises the May 1999 issue of *Cosmopolitan*, which locates fear at the root of male commitment phobia. "Men don't know if they can handle the risk of becoming vulnerable to you," the column explains. "That's when they start acting standoffish and wanting more friend time."[97] The solution is to play it cool, appearing nonchalant about the issue of matrimony. "Take Your Love to the Next Level,"[98] suggests Julie Taylor in the November 2000 issue of *Cosmopolitan*; her program for facilitating amorous commitment includes stretching sexual boundaries ("The erotic activities should range from swinging-from-the-chandelier sexcapades to barely R-rated romps"),[99] creating private relationship rituals (cooking omelettes every Sunday morning, taking monthly camping trips), and becoming "his personal cheerleader" (hinting publicly that one's partner is sexually skillful, expressing an interest in his career).[100] *Glamour* magazine's December 2000 issue urges female readers to pray for a husband. "Ask God to bring you a partner who will fit into all areas of your life. But be open, because he may come in a package you're not expecting."[101] "I think it's okay to change for a man,"[102] declares Clare Naylor, the author of *Love: A User's Guide,* who suggests expanding one's horizons and often altering or relinquishing professional plans to secure male commitment: "Rachel, who used to be a stressed-out, power-lunching babe whose cell phone rang twenty-four-seven while she was wedded to her Hollywood career, fell in love with a farmer. Now she lives on his ranch and paints and landscapes—the only ringing she hears these days is cowbells."[103]

This happily married woman who has, with relief, stepped off the professional treadmill and settled into comfy-cozy rural isolation, is the dating expert's icon of female success. The relationship industry presents a retrograde and insulting model of femininity. According to its spokespeople the modern woman is clingy by nature, desiring institutionalized togetherness above all else, craving emotional intimacy as well as the baubles and trinkets that signal love. She feels terror in the pit of her stomach when her man expresses the desire for solitude, because it's a longing with which she is unfamiliar. She is born for the institutionalized togetherness of matrimony but lives in a baffling modern world in which wedlock's traditional structures—the marriage broker, the arranged nuptial, the formal spousal agreement, the church-enforced partnership—have eroded. Accordingly, she must negotiate her way through a confusing, amorous wilderness populated by seducers and deadbeats. Ever present is the willful, obstinate "Peter Pan," that problematic figure who refuses to submit to her marital desires, who will not let go of his independence, who values his friends, his work, his privacy, all aspects of life that she is presumably willing to sacrifice for the sake of matrimonial validation. This woman's deepest fear is growing old without the companionship and validation of a spouse. Her anxiety is encapsulated in a recent *New Yorker* magazine cartoon in which a group of cranky-looking senior citizens sit in a row of rocking chairs on the porch of what appears to be a retirement home. One of the elderly gentlemen is turning toward the bespectacled grandmotherly woman sitting next to him and shouting, "I said I'm ready to make a commitment."[104]

Since the dating experts, empowerment specialists, psychologists, "love coaches," psychics, advice columnists, and lifestyle consultants who populate the relationship industry rely solely on anecdote and folk wisdom, offering no hard data to substantiate their belief that modern men fear marital commitment, it is impossible to say whether such widespread anxiety is real or a fantasy concocted by marriage propagandists. If amorous skittishness is rampant among American men, it may, however, represent reasonable apprehension rather than trauma-based pathology. Psychologists and pundits, columnists and authors have become so preoccupied with diagnosing and finding antidotes to the alleged Peter Pan syndrome that they have overlooked this possibility. Perhaps American men avoid marriage because it is inherently undesirable. Perhaps they perceive wedlock as a trap, because it is a trap. Perhaps the reluctance to relinquish one's social independence and physical space is not a disturbance but a healthy response to the claustrophobic ideal of intimacy championed by the human potential movement. I am not claiming that men have superior insight into erotic relationships. I am merely pointing out that, because their socialization process is different than women's, male responses to marriage are different in a way that is not necessarily evidence of an emotional pathology.

For modern men, marital commitment has often entailed shouldering long-term financial responsibility for several other people—a prospect that is daunting at best. In addition, wedlock now involves a much lengthier and more focused commitment than it ever has. Greatly increased longevity, the ready availability of divorce, and access to reliable contraception have radically altered relationships between men and women. It is no longer institutional bonds that yoke us together but the purely emotional ties of affection and personal attraction. Sex and procreation have been separated, and our relationships have to a great extent been severed from their traditional moorings in the state and the family. Until approximately 1940 the average marriage was devoted to childbearing; each couple had less than a year of marriage after the last child left home before one or the other partner died. Figures in the second half of the century have increased this period to twenty years.[105] These technological and demographic changes have occurred recently in our own century, and it is in the second half of our century that an industry has arisen that prescribes lifelong, ecstatic love between two free agents whose relationship exists primarily for their own mutual enjoyment, fulfillment, and improvement. Women have tended to blindly accept this prescription, absorbing the mythology of the committed long-term relationship like an emotional narcotic. Male hesitance to succumb so completely to an unrealistic romance ideal that demands over forty years of adulation and erotic fulfillment in a single individual probably represents healthy skepticism rather than emotional puerility. "Commitment phobia," to the extent that it exists, seems to me to be the sound emotional response of me—whose social worth has not been traditionally valued in erotic terms and who therefore are better equipped to relish their own privacy—to a new set of conjugal conditions in which death no longer grants the ultimate form of divorce.

III. The "Single" Girl in the Contemporary Imagination

I married for the first time at thirty-seven. I got the man I wanted. It *could* be construed as something of a miracle considering how old *I* was and how eligible *he* was.

David is a motion picture producer, forty-four, brainy, charming, and sexy. He was sought after by many a Hollywood starlet as well as some less flamboyant but more deadly types. And *I* got him! We have two Mercedes-Benzes, one hundred acres of virgin forest near San Francisco, a Mediterranean house overlooking the Pacific, a full-time maid, and a good life.

I am not beautiful, or even pretty. I once had the world's worst case of acne. I am not bosomy or brilliant. I grew up in a small town. I didn't go to college. My family was, and is, desperately poor and I have always helped support them. I'm an introvert and I am sometimes mean and cranky.

But *I* don't think it's a miracle that I married my husband. I think I deserved him! For seventeen years I worked hard to become the kind of woman who might interest him. And when he finally walked into my life I was just worldly enough, relaxed enough, financially secure enough (for I also worked hard at my job), and adorned with enough glitter to attract him. He wouldn't have looked at me when I was twenty, and I wouldn't have known what to do with *him*.[106]

47

These are the opening paragraphs of Helen Gurley Brown's 1962 dating primer, *Sex and the Single Girl,* a book that advertises the glory of the "single" life while carefully advising women on how to fashion just the kind of self that attracts a husband. Gurley Brown describes how to be sexy (smile, sit very still, wear clothing that fits well, lower your telephone voice to a husky, Lauren Bacall growl, tuck a perfume-doused cotton ball in your bra), where to meet men (bars, parties, sales conventions, the men's section of department stores, alcoholics anonymous meetings), and how to prepare romantic dinners (crabmeat puffs and escalopes of veal, stuffed mushrooms and lobster en brochette) for that potential special someone, that iconic male whom she refers to merely as "him."

Like many blockbuster authors, Gurley Brown tapped into what was at one time an overlooked segment of the consumer population: unmarried women. Like most successful pundits she possessed an uncanny sense of the way in which her readers wished to see themselves, and her manifesto shrewdly played to their fantasies of glamour, autonomy, and joie de vivre. She addressed the myriad young women in American cities who, in the 1960s, shared cramped apartments, scraped by on low wages, and felt, as the years passed, increasingly self-conscious about their unmarried status. Understanding their dilemma, she reversed the marital equation. She did not merely express tolerance for unmarried women: she assured "single" secretaries, receptionists, salesgirls, and flight attendants that they were *superior* to their married suburban counterparts. Rather than living as parasitic dependents, they were economic free agents for whom no professional dream was unattainable. Rather than confining themselves to full time motherhood's grinding routine, they enjoyed lives of urban sophistication. In Gurley Brown's cosmos there is no glass ceiling, no male network that officially/unofficially excludes women from the boardroom or pushes them off of the partnership or tenure track. The single girl is an untrammeled success—a leggy Horatio Alger wearing false eyelashes and a miniskirt who can take any industry by storm. Constantly upbeat and on the move, her schedule is a whirlwind of parties, dinner dates, concerts, and exciting professional events at which men, frustrated by their own dull, sheltered, homebody wives, gaze at her longingly.

Herein lies the magical formula that made *Sex and the Single Girl* such a landmark success: it cloaked the old prince charming fantasy in a narrative of American individualism. Gurley Brown told her readers that by succeeding at their jobs, maintaining their physical appearances, learning to cook, decorating their apartments nicely, attending various social functions, and assuming the confident swagger of the male competitor they would ultimately—in their thirties or forties—find a husband. Her message was not "don't marry": it was "marry a little bit later, after you've had some fun." While preparing her readers for the matrimonial hunt, she simultaneously allowed them to perceive their own unmarried lives as stupendous rather than marginal, enviable rather than paltry. It did not matter if they were not wealthy, highly educated, or exceptionally beautiful. They were independent and upbeat, and their work ethic would find its just, conjugal reward. A stenographer was no longer just a stenographer: she was a "career girl." A secretary forced to fetch coffee, answer telephones, and take dictation at her company's weekend conference was not a servant harnessed to a menial job by dire financial need. She was an employee attending an important professional function at which she could bask in the company of eligible men. (Married men were fair game in Gurley Brown's view.) The most desirable males would, in fact, ultimately, recognize their true counterparts in these hardworking, vibrant, sexually uninhibited creatures. Instead of offering up chastity, passivity, and sexual modesty to attain a male partner, the "single" girl deployed sensuality, assertiveness, and professional confidence to attract the male gaze. The time frame and the strategy had changed, but the final reward had not. A hillbilly turned secretary who worked her way to the top of the publishing world, a chic Californian with a wealthy husband, two luxury cars, a maid, and an ocean view, Gurley Brown offered her own story up as reassuring proof that the "single" girl would not stay "single" forever.

Cosmopolitan, the magazine which Gurley Brown took over in 1965 and stewarded for several decades, and through which she made her imprimatur on American culture, remains a wellspring of folk wisdom on how to snag a man. It is a primal source for doublespeak around the issue of "single" women; a periodical dedicated to extolling the glories of the unmarried life that simultaneously coaches its female readers in

alluring, seducing, and entrapping men into permanent erotic partnership. *Cosmopolitan* popularized Gurley Brown's philosophy and continues to confirm her shrewdness in marketing the myth of the glamorous
"single." The magazine's very title conjures up images of urban elan and
feminine decadence; its glossy pages feature photographs of models
striking sultry poses and convey this fantasy to America's female, working class population—those women stranded in small towns, yoked to
menial jobs, and yearning for an illusory Prince Charming to enter their
lives and effect a full scale socioeconomic transformation. In the pages of
Cosmopolitan, female "single" existence is not a life but a "lifestyle," and a
glamorous fun-filled one at that. The *Cosmo* girl is wildly social. A typical month for her entails late-night forays to discotheques, sun-soaked
weekends in the Bahamas, Saturday night dinner dates at exclusive
French restaurants, and Sunday champagne brunches with "the girls."

But at the heart of this nonstop recreation lies the marriage quest.
Articles on the optimal "Man Meeting Methods" (e.g. whitewater rafting,
jet skiing, hospital visits to scope out eligible doctors, pumping one's
own gas at service stations, visits to cybercafes and the science fiction
sections of local bookstores, outdoor music festivals), which include
"Go-get-him hints,"[107] prepare the "single" girl for her presumably all-
important task of husband hunting. While she is advised to enjoy sex
during the dating process, the "single" girl is clearly on a marriage mis-
sion. In its advice columns *Cosmopolitan* echoes the sentiments of psychologically oriented dating experts, urging its readers to evaluate their
partners' intentions. Through articles that scrutinize the hidden subtext
of male behavior—gift-giving habits, facial expressions, body language,
and taste in clothing and food—the magazine guides women in the eval-
uation of their amorous partners' seriousness; the proverbial willingness
to "commit." "How Deep Is His Love?" queries the title of a March 2000
article. "You hope your man is ready to be steady, but maybe his heart is
here and now. Take this quiz to measure his commitment temperature
and learn our tricks for upping his love level,"[108] advises Megan
Fitzmorris McCafferty, who proceeds to instruct the female reader on
how to crack her male partner's "commitment code" (examine his role in
the planning of your upcoming birthday celebration, think about
whether he holds you or not after sex, assess whether he would miss a tel-

evised sports event to accompany you to a professional function). "Guys in a coupledom state of mind will put aside their schedule to make *you* the priority," concludes McCafferty.[109] That twentieth-century concoction, the male commitment phobe is a steady fixture in the *Cosmopolitan* universe; female readers are advised to minimize their efforts on behalf of men who won't deliver our culture's marital promise. "Its a classic commitment conundrum: You think he's husband material, he thinks you're definitely bedable and possibly wedable. He may have this on-again, off-again attitude simply because you allow it. . . . So stop giving him your total attention—both in and out of the bedroom."[110]

Cosmopolitan often uses the New Age dating expert's voodoo techniques for assessing male marriageability. It offers customized tarot cards to enable readers to "tap into the secret forces of the cosmos"[111] in order to glimpse their romantic futures and advises women to scope men out according to their astrological signs. "Get inside his head with this cosmic star guide," the September 1999 issue enjoins,[112] and the column instructs readers in the art of sexually ensnaring the entire range of astrological males, providing a list of especially felicitous "lust days" (the fifth, the thirteenth, and the twenty-eighth for Cancer, the tenth, the sixteenth, and the twenty-fifth for Sagittarius). Readers are urged to erotically email the uninhibited Virgo, play the dominatrix with the inherently passive Pisces, bestow a gift of fingerpaints on the creative Aries (to encourage his artistic side), and perform a striptease for the randy Leo. The same issue instructs female readers to interpret the facial features of their male companions in order to see which ones are husband material. Relying on the insights of Rose Rosetree of Women's Intuition Worldwide and Beverly Hills "face reader" George Roman, the magazine applies this method of interpretation—apparently a contemporary version of the quackish nineteenth-century practice of phrenology (analyzing personality according to bumps in the human head). "*Cosmo* shows you how to tell his love style by the shape of his eyes, nose, and lips," the title proclaims, and the article proceeds to explain that in men wide irises indicate the capacity for doting loving companionship while small irises suggest coldheartedness, that males with large lower lips are emotionally open and generous and those with thin lips tend toward shyness, and that an angular chin suggests contentiousness while a round one signals a cooperative mate.[113]

Cosmopolitan balances its occultism with simple anecdote, often employing men as advisors in the dating game. The September 1999 issue also features an article by J.D. Heiman entitled "How She Hooked Me," in which "guys reveal the five signs that say you're his forever woman."[114] This piece contains no particular revelations: trustworthiness, good looks, a strong sex drive, toleration of occasional nights out with "the guys," and the rather vague attribute of "coolness" make a woman a desirable long-term partner. What's significant is the bias built into the article: that women are engaged in the active project of entrapping men. "In spite of what you may think, men *aren't* allergic to the concept of settling down with Ms. Right," assures Heiman, placating female readers with the standard *Cosmo* credo that if they bubble over with enthusiasm and sexual adventurousness, they will obtain the all-important sanction of a male commitment, capturing that elusive butterfly, the potential husband. In the August 1999 issue Steve Johnson instructs readers in the art of transforming an apparent one-night stand into a meaningful L.T.R., urging women to act gracefully disinterested the morning after, sipping a cup of coffee, and saying goodbye quickly. "Whatever you do, don't discuss the two of you as a couple,"[115] he impugns. (Despite her sexual bravado, *Cosmo's* "single" girl bears an eerie resemblance to Fein and Schneider's "rules girl"; both must erect facades of cool self-reliance, cloaking their desperation for marriage by appearing apathetic to the institution.) The women on *Cosmopolitan's* pages likewise share their own success stories, recalling the means by which they transformed casual sexual affairs into solvent relationships,[116] and advising on "super sneaky ways to snag him."[117] The magazine's editors offer a time frame for marital commitment, explaining that women who want ecstatic sex and several children should marry in their twenties, and those who value high-powered careers, monogamy, and financial stability should marry in their thirties.[118] That women may wish to relinquish sex or enjoy it with multiple partners, that childrearing might optimally occur in a structure other than the marriage-based nuclear family, and that male fidelity is perhaps not the world's most precious commodity, are ideas that never enter the picture.

According to *Cosmopolitan*, domestic partnership is a woman's birthright and penultimate desire, so men who aren't invested in coupledom don't merit time or attention. The magazine's August 2000 issue contains one of its signature formats: anecdotes from actual women recalling the precise moment they snagged their men. "I Knew He'd Fallen When..."[119] reads the title, and the feature contains a predictable list of stories from putatively real-life women whose angelic boyfriends opened their homes and hearts, sacrificed prized football playoff tickets for romantic weekends in Vermont, accompanied their girlfriends to the hospital for medical tests, relocated, had their cherished tattoos removed, got rid of their dogs to accommodate pet allergies, and, finally, proposed marriage. "My period was more than two weeks late one month, and I thought for sure I was pregnant," one woman recalls. "I called my boyfriend, Damon, right away, and asked him to come over.... But instead of freaking out like I expected, Damon simply dropped to one knee and asked me to marry him. It turns out that the pregnancy was a scare, but Damon and I are planning a June wedding next year."[120] This is Gurley Brown's "single" girl's happy ending.

Some forty years after Gurley Brown proudly inaugurated the "single" girl in the popular consciousness, the unmarried woman is a significant cultural icon. With female encroachment into the professions such women are now a powerful segment of the consumer population; a force to which commerce panders increasingly. Retailers shape their advertising campaigns to appeal to unmarried women, psychologists build practices that focus on the concerns of unmarried female clients, travel agents coordinate women-only vacations, and bed-and-breakfasts throughout the country cater to female business travelers. Roughly one-fifth of 1999 home sales were to unmarried women, up from ten percent in 1985.[121] Journalists report that there are currently 43 million "single" American women—more than 40 percent of all adult females as compared to the 30 percent who were unmarried in 1960.[122] The publishing industry has boasted a recent string of popular female-authored novels about unmarried women,[123] and television has several hit series that center on the dilemmas of unmarried women in their thirties and forties.

But while the "single" woman has become a prominent figure in popular entertainment, the plots she enacts betray the same deeply divided consciousness about her that Gurley Brown's primer expressed. In fiction, film, and television, the "single" woman is now a hipster—a freewheeling sexual agent who enjoys her space, revels in the company of friends, and has sex with abandon. She lives in an urban center and works in a glamorous field that is often related to the arts. She is a gallery owner, a book editor, a magazine columnist, a designer, an actress, or an agent. Or, she's a high-powered professional: an attorney, a judge, a television producer, or a marketing executive. She's Ivy League educated, and her fashion sense is impeccable. With a master's degree from Princeton and a six-figure salary, she walks with the hip-swinging slouch of a runway model. But she is still quietly sentimental, yearning for the right man, pining silently for Prince Charming, hoping for the big white wedding that will signal her social completion. At night, when she removes her makeup, she encounters her reflection in the bathroom mirror, contemplates the tiny lines forming around her eyes, and hears the tick-tock, tick-tock of her biological clock. In public she cracks sarcastic jokes to conceal her aching heart and downs shots of tequila to numb her inner marriage pangs. She may appear to have it all, but she doesn't, according to the popular media. Its protagonists are women, and women, in every age, long to return to the loving bosom of the patriarchal family.

Television images of "single" women extend Gurley Brown's myth and elaborate her version of the marriage mystique. They rest on an imaginary binary: the wild, enjoyable, sexually charged, casual, and ultimately empty "single" nightlife versus the stable, centered, monogamous, and loving homelife of the married woman. A prime example of this spurious dichotomy is the current Home Box Office hit series, *Sex and the City*, which purports to weigh the pros and cons of "single" versus married existence. A situation comedy about four female friends living the high life in Manhattan, this series has generated media images galore. Its four stars, Sarah Jessica Parker, Cynthia Nixon, Kristen Davis, and Kim Cattrall have appeared on numerous magazine covers throughout the country as emblems of alleged female sexual emancipation. "Who Needs a Husband?" the August 2000 cover of *Time* magazine queried provocatively as it ran a photograph of the four actresses. The series' star, Sarah Jessica Parker, stares from the cover solemnly, pensively, as if challenging readers to come to terms with her tough, modern woman's sensibility. She's flanked by her three immaculately coiffed and airbrushed costars, each of whom looks intense and reflective, as if ruminating on the cover's subsequent question, "More women are saying no to marriage and embracing the single life. Are they happy?"[124] The August 1999 issue of *Newsweek* features the four actresses clad in skin tight black dresses, looking like economically independent women of the twenty-first century. "*Sex and the City* shows us single women are anything but desperate," the copy reads. "They're looking for men, sure, but it's just shopping, not survival."[125] Candace Bushnell, the *New York Observer* columnist on whose book the series is based, has frequently been interviewed as a pundit on the "single" life and the state of modern women. The September 2000 issue of *Talk* magazine features the blonde Bushnell in a sultry pose, fielding questions about the series, explaining that her characters are composites of people whom she knows rather than real individuals, and reporting on her own love life. Currently living with a venture capitalist in London, Bushnell claims that she's "technically still single." "I don't know if I'll ever get married," she remarks nonchalantly.[126] In a November 2000 interview with Fox 5 News, Bushnell had changed her tune. While the anchorwoman conducting the interview claimed that *Sex and the City* has legitimized—even popularized— "single" life for women, Bushnell herself was apparently feeling matrimonial. "Who wouldn't want to be in a great relationship?" she asked mournfully, finally admitting, "I'd love to be married." [127]

It's a major question for her four characters, each of whom embodies a different aspect of the female psyche. Introspective Carrie Bradshaw (Parker), the center of the program's consciousness, is supposed to balance skepticism about marriage with healthy romantic yearnings for coupledom and motherhood. A self-styled "sexual anthropologist," she fills her weekly column with her friends' amorous adventures, speculating on the sexual mores and trends of the early twenty-first century and offering wry witty observations as she pines away for a man. The program's most amusing episodes center on Carrie's horror at the labeling of people as "singles" or "couples." On the street with her gay friend, Stanford (Willie Garson), she listens to his complaints that gays are succumbing to marriage mania and taking wedding vows. When they meet her friend Joe, accompanied by his "life partner," Lou, the two men look happily sanctimonious and proudly display their matching gold wedding bands. "Where are you registered?" Stanford inquires nastily. "Barneys" replies Joe in earnest. "I was only kidding," says Stanford, looking stunned as his voice trails off. When Joe and Lou ask Carrie to consider donating an egg to aid their fertility efforts, she concludes that she has experienced the ultimate form of single bashing: "I was no longer even considered a person. I was an egg farm."

With its satire of couple fascism, *Sex and the City* is in one sense a truly innovative program. In a sequence from the first season an anonymous woman stares directly at the camera and justifies her own choices in devastatingly conventional terms, explaining, "It's all about what you want out of life. Some people like me choose to grow up, face reality, and get married, and others, choose to, what? Live an empty, haunted life of stunted adolescence." Viewers witness the self-flattery built into the mindlessly promarriage rhetoric that permeates our culture. "It's fabulous," says Brooke, Carrie's acquaintance who has just married a man she doesn't care for. "I feel like an enormous weight has been lifted," and we are cued into the pathos of women envisioning their lives in terms of the marital trajectory, equating the beginning of life with procurement of a marriage license.

To its credit, *Sex and the City* also critiques the current system of marital entitlement, which, while it accords intangible accolades, also bestows monetary rewards on married couples. Carrie notes that after the wedding day Brooke is all business—"the business of marriage," as she watches this new bride exchange and return expensive gifts. When Stanford asks Carrie to marry him so that he can receive his inheritance from a wealthy homophobic grandmother, she plays along, consenting to a fake union so that she might register for china and housewares and rake in some of wedlock's tangible rewards—the bounty to which her married friends feel reflexively entitled. During her meeting with Stanford's grandmother, however, Carrie succumbs to conventional marriage longing, gazes hungrily at the wedding photographs, baby pictures, and other memorabilia on the mantle piece, and admits that she wants to marry and start a family. ("I love my Stanford; he's a very sweet boy, but you know he's a fruit," croaks the old lady.)

Unfortunately, the program balances its brand of nasty, highly effective satire with this romantic counterplot in which Carrie searches for Prince Charming, dating and enjoying sex with various men but hoping to find *the* man, the one with whom she can couple and procreate. Carrie's keen social observation and verbal facility do not prevent her seduction by the marriage mystique. She defines herself incorrectly as a sexual anthropologist; an anthropolgist is not part of the society he or she studies and therefore has the requisite detachment to survey its denizens objectively. Carrie is herself immersed in dating culture, and her emotional mood swings respond to the ups and downs of her amorous relationships. As clingy as the female protagonists of daytime soap operas, she panics when her divorced, real estate mogul lover (Chris Noth) tells her he will never marry again. She follows him to church on Sundays to precipitate a meeting with his mother ("Getting on his mother's good side is like closing the deal," her friend Charlotte explains), dresses and alters her behavior to please him, barges in on him watching a boxing match on television and attempts to seduce him, and pleads with him to tell her she's "the one." When he doesn't, she ends the relationship, and the writers and director elicit sympathy for her: "After he left I cried for a week. And then I realized I do have faith; faith in myself. Faith that I would one day meet someone who would be sure that I was the one."

Like many actual "single" women, Carrie Bradshaw doesn't question the power of her own consuming need for "the one." Actually, she's done better than that, having found "the three." Far from being alone, she enjoys the companionship and support of three other women. This group is a family—a small community whose members are intertwined, committed to each other, and joined for life by shared experiences and the bonds of unconditional love. But like many popular entertainments about "single" women, *Sex and the City* presumes that family is a noun reserved for biological relatives, and that the only exception to this rule is one's spouse, who becomes a chosen family member. Author Karen Lindsey refers to this belief as the destructive myth "of the spouse as chosen relative"[128] and explains that its power rests in the notion that marriage is an atypical adoption in which a nonrelative becomes a permanent family member. But, as Lindsey compellingly argues, there is no reason this act should be reserved for sexual partners. Women are inculcated to believe that family is biological, largely because women have been the biological bedrock of kinship systems, providing men with a sense of continuity through the production of children who carry the male patronym. Women thus tend to feel that they cannot choose their friends as relatives, because there is neither historical validation nor institutional machinery behind such a choice. When campaigning politicians announce that they will support working families with tax cuts and social programs they do not refer to clusters of unmarried friends. When hotels and restaurants promote themselves as family venues, and when communities describe themselves as "family oriented," they allude only to the restricted nuclear unit rather than the nonbiological family. No officializing rhetoric exists to sanction fictional Carrie Bradshaw's love for her three best friends, and so she feels fragmentary, alone, without family.

Sex and the City accepts this distinction. Its creator, Darren Star, has explained that the program puts forth the idea that "it's okay to be single."[129] Toward this end it extends Gurley Brown's philosophy of "single" female life, demonstrating the claim made explicitly in Cosmopolitan's June 1999 issue, that "Single Girls Have More Fun."[130] But with its underlying romantic imperative, Sex and the City depicts this mad, bed hopping as a prelude, a warm-up for the main act, which is matrimony. The show's four writers add some class and some good campy humor to the Cosmopolitan equation, but their guiding narrative framework is a hackneyed plot about jaded young women sowing their wild oats in the big city before tiring of the bar scene and leaving the decadent metropolis for domestic stability. And the episodes recur to the problematic binary between "single" and "married" life and in so doing, perpetuate this division and the oppressive definitions of family that accompany it. The program does not ultimately indict the marriage myth, allowing its characters (and female viewers with loving communities of friends) to realize that they already possess families and should therefore stop worrying about precisely when real life will commence. The realization that families are not biological and are optimally a matter of gender-blind choice would enable a character like Carrie Bradshaw to abandon her quixotic search for the ideal male partner.

The idea that "single" life is enjoyable but solitary and marriage dull but intimate permeates the program. "There are thousands, maybe tens of thousands of women like this in the city," Sarah Jessica Parker says in voice-over, as the camera shows a series of well-dressed professional women walking briskly along midtown Manhattan streets at midday: "They travel, they pay their taxes, and they're alone." The imagined solitude of the female professional is best exemplified by the burnt-out, overworked corporate lawyer Miranda Hobbes (Nixon), a fiery redhead who expresses continual irritation about the souring prospects of aging professional women. Miranda scorns domestic partnership but yearns for it at the same time. "The ones who don't fear you pity you," she says of married women. Dressed defiantly in black, she brings a gift of condoms to a Connecticut baby shower in which a gaggle of suburban mommies clad in delicate pastels stare at her in horror. She admits that she has given herself carpal tunnel syndrome from excessive masturbation. But beneath her mask of sullen contempt is the typical fear of becoming an old maid. "I have a friend who'd always gone out with extremely sexy guys," she says in the show's first episode, as she waits in line at a salad bar: "One day she woke up, and she was forty-one. She couldn't get anymore dates. She had a complete physical breakdown, couldn't hold onto her job, and had to move back to Wisconsin to live with her mother. Trust me; this is not a story that makes men feel bad."

Outliving one's shelf life on the marriage market is a major fear for the conventional, not-too-bright brunette gallery owner Charlotte York (Davis), who, in Carrie's words, treats marriage "as a sorority" she is "desperately hoping to pledge." Charlotte embodies the spirit of matrimonial romanticism; she dates man after man in the hopes of landing a wealthy handsome partner and even uses *Cosmo*'s New Age techniques for charting her amorous future. When a hearty Jewish psychic and tarot reader tells Charlotte that she will never find a husband, she is traumatized and travels alone to an unsavory part of town to try for a different result. In a shabby room lit only by candles, a voodoo-practicing con artist chants and cracks an egg into a bowl, finally announcing that there is an unfortunate curse that will prevent marriage. He offers to remove it for a mere one hundred dollars. (In spite of the curse Charlotte finds a wealthy handsome physician-husband in the persona of Trey MacDougal (Kyle MacLachlan) only to discover that he's impotent—a good joke on the 1950s imperative of premarital chastity that Charlotte has decided to practice.)

Only public relations executive Samantha Jones, the program's sexual renegade, has truly relinquished the marriage fantasy. Played by the brilliant comedic actress Kim Cattrall, who makes everything she says sound smutty, accusatory, and funny, Samantha enjoys multiple sexual partners without guilt and scoffs at the idea of long-term romance ("Who needs it?"). Sitting with the friends in a restaurant staffed by drag queens, she explains her credo that sex is for pleasure and pleasure only, and that women's new economic mobility entitles them to turn the tables, using males as sex objects. Glaring at credulous Charlotte, Samantha declares, "The right guy is an illusion...you understand that...start living your life."

Samantha is not an intellectual. Her philosophy is based on hard-boiled folk wisdom rather than political or historical critque, but her insights have a certain pungent accuracy. "I don't understand why women are so obsessed with getting married," she observes. "Married people just want to be single again." Samantha practices what she preaches too, enjoying sexual intercourse with real estate agents, doormen, and firemen, sleeping with the young and old alike, and throwing a celebratory "I don't have a baby shower." When Charlotte ponders a beau's request for anal sex, and the other ladies express disdain, Samantha advises, "Don't be so judgmental. You could use a little backdoor." When one of Samantha's married guys phones to declare his love and announce that he's leaving his wife, she responds with bewilderment: "Who is this?" When Carrie admits that she's dating a man who lives with his parents, Samantha doesn't miss a beat; "Oh, honey, dump him immediately. Here, use my cell phone."

Darren Star has explained that he initially imagined Samantha as a woman in her forties who has made the decision to live life on her own terms,[131] and one journalist has recently termed the character "a symbol of fuck-you feminist freedom."[132] Cattrall herself appeared recently in *New York* magazine, her arms and legs discreetly crossed, wearing nothing but high heeled shoes and a knowing lascivious smile. But this same issue, which praises her character as a new model of aggressively sexual femininity, stresses the actress' own proper domestic life as a married woman. Journalist Lisa DePaulo admiringly describes Cattrall and her husband, stereo designer Mark Levinson, cooing at each other and cuddling on the sofa of their New York apartment as they watch the romantic classic, *Casablanca*. According to this piece, Levinson is a dotingly attentive husband who does all the cooking for the pair, preparing meals of fish and tofu. In classic "single"-girl doublespeak, Cattrall protests that she wasn't looking for a husband when she hit the jazz club at which she met Levinson but concedes that she moved in with him five days later and adds that it's time for her t.v. character to "have a real relationship,"[133] as if Samantha's bonds to her three best friends are synthetic.

This compensatory rhetoric characterizes the media's approach to *Sex and the City*. "Loose Ladies? Not on Your Life,"[134] declares a headline in *People* magazine, which explains that Cynthia Nixon lives with her lover Danny Moses and dotes on their child, placing maternity above career; "motherhood is the role she takes most seriously."[135] It also reports that while Kristen Davis is in no rush to marry, she is not promiscuous or even comfortable with the sexually explicit aspect of the series that has catapulted her to fame: she was embarrassed during her debut as Charlotte, and turned "bright, bright red."[136] *People* assures troubled fans that the married, monogamous Cattrall is nothing like her character. The assumption seems to be that viewers who feel guilty about enjoying the sexual escapades of four women need reassurance that behind these stylized fictional personas, lie simple, domestic, good-hearted girls; girls who don't sleep around, who blush at the mention of sex, and who put the traditional family first.

The cover of this issue celebrates Sarah Jessica Parker in the classic langauge of matrimony, as a fairy tale princess who captured the heart of a real life Prince Charming, her husband, actor Matthew Broderick: "Real life Cinderella: from a hardscrabble childhood to fame, a great marriage and *Sex and the City*," the copy reads.[137] As if reassuring viewers that their favorite television bad girl is safely contained within matrimony, the article describes Parker as "squeaky clean, happily married, and ready for kids,"[138] shows her nestled in the arms of her husband, and informs readers that Parker, who is "nothing like Carrie,"[139] gave up the F-word as a New Year's resolution. The couple wed in a civil ceremony, but "not before Parker had spent considerable time cooling her four-inch heels waiting for a proposal. And she wasn't alone."[140] A friend admits that those who cared about Parker wondered if Broderick would step up to the plate and make her an honest woman: "It's as if all her friends were standing beside her, their arms crossed, thinking, 'What are you gonna do, Bud?'"[141] Describing the couple, *People*'s copy reads like the depictions of married life found in the smarmy personal advertisements of major magazines and newspapers. "Parker has found what Carrie and her clique seem to have been seeking since the series began in 1998; a partner for flea market jaunts and bike rides through Central Park who also shares her devotion to the Yankees and makes her laugh."[142] *Time* depicts Parker as someone worried about being "a good traditional wife"[143] to Broderick. "I know he doesn't have his laundry done, that he hasn't had a hot meal in days.... That stuff weighs on my mind."[144]

If we are to believe such annoyingly conventional accounts, this emblem for female independence is, in her real life, closer to the "rules girl" of reactionary dating experts than the savvy author she portrays. She's a nice young lady with a clean mouth who passively awaited the male request that would complete her emotionally and define her socially. Smugly married, her priority is her husband, and her life a round of wholesome connubial activities that range from day trips to flea markets to bicycle jaunts in the park to that all-American pastime, baseball. Reporters use sanitizing rhetoric to describe *Sex and the City*'s star, depicting Parker's wholesomeness with a sense of happy relief. Their characterizations of her as a cheery homebody wife are tailored to ideological ends. They serve to justify the commercial and critical success of a salacious series and to assure readers that female sexuality is still circumsribed by the old marital boundaries—that one of America's favorite television actresses has the key marker of female virtue: a solid marriage.

Viewers who enjoy *Sex and the City* might do well not to focus too closely on its accuracy of sociological observation. Those of us who live in New York would not be able to suspend the requisite disbelief if we reflected on the fact that Carrie Bradshaw, a writer who might earn six hundred dollars per week, rents a splendid Upper East Side apartment that would cost twice her salary, decks herself out in designer clothing, and, with her friends, enjoys a full round of cultural activities, splurging on nightly dinners at upscale restaurants. When they are not sampling the entrees at fashionable eateries, attending gallery openings, museums, ballet performances, fashion shows, and night clubs, the members of this foursome are in their respective homes, munching on candy and cake and downing cartons of greasy Chinese food. This steady diet of junk combined with nightly cosmopolitans and entire bottles of chardonnay over lunch seems to have no adverse effect on any of them. All are energetic and alert, high functioning at work, fit and never even slightly puffy or red eyed. And despite their nightly escapades, none contract sexually transmitted diseases. Although its frank presentation of female sexuality is new for television, in many ways this program represents a very old-fashioned, Hollywood fantasy of what women's lives are like—glamorous female existence as imagined by a female impersonator. There's never a dull moment—never an evening spent at home paying bills or an obligatory weekend visiting relatives. These lovely, pleasure-driven urban vixens are constantly slipping in and out of their designer gowns, changing their jewelry and their Gucci and Manolo Blahnik pumps, reapplying their lipstick, stuffing condoms into their Prada bags as they rush out the door, and throwing impromptu shindigs at their Manhattan pads where they sip champagne, engage in bitchy repartee, and smoke languidly while regaling each other with the physical details of their various lovers. (Some critics have noted that Samantha's character seems more like a drag queen than an actual woman, in the way that Mae West's 1930s characters did.) After a wild night out, Carrie Bradshaw can be found teetering on high heels and clutching a beaded bag on a lower Manhattan street corner at dawn, when, suddenly, a chauffeured limousine containing a handsome, Armani-clad New York power broker pulls up and whisks her away to her next rendezvous.

While actual "single" women have less frenetically sexual and less consumerist lives, and while they may no longer perceive themselves as economically resourceless pariahs, they still appear to indulge in the divided rhetoric of the "single" girl—on the one hand validating their own social independence, on the other reserving a space for the potential Mr. Right who could alter their social status. Magazines like *New York* and *Time*—the same periodicals that gleefully celebrate *Sex and the City*—proffer a list of impressive, successful, classy women who are unattached to male partners. All talk the same game. Thirty-two-year-old bank manager Jodie Hannaman, who takes solo vacations and enjoys the "social whirl of the Junior League volunteer circuit" in Texas, says that she "would love a great romance that would lead to marriage," but "no longer feels that she has to apologize for being single."[145] Fifty-two-year-old, Washington D.C.-based, nonprofit director Debra Lee asserts that she is reluctant to change her life for her male companion: "We talk about getting married, but this is so good right now."[146] Describing unmarried television reporter Kristin Whiting, journalist Rebecca Johnson reassures readers that "Whiting is no loser,"[147] and depicts her subject as an urban sophisticate with a house in the Hamptons and a "network of similarly bright, ambitious friends."[148] New York City accountant Pam Henneberry says that she's unwilling to accept someone who will make her unhappy, while another New Yorker, thirty-three-year-old documentary producer Pam Wolfe, indicates that marriage will transpire only with a partner capable of unconditional love: "I'm not going to do anything to attract a person that means changing. I've worked long and hard to be myself."[149]

Even the most defiantly "single" women tend to describe their marital status in subjective terms, representing their lives in the human potential movement's vocabulary of personal growth and fulfillment. While they affirm, and affirm, and reaffirm the validity of being unmarried, none of them appear to rule out matrimony, and none appear to be aware of wedlock's chillingly oppressive past. None interrogate the category "single" itself. To say that one is "single" is to define oneself through absence, to concede that one is lacking, to conjure up images of a lone fragmentary existence. This has been the stigma attached to unmarried women throughout western history. Rather than assuming the disingenuously nonchalant pose of the freewheeling "single" girl who, like Candace Bushnell, says she may or may not marry, who can take or leave the matrimonial package as she might a pair of designer shoes, women now need to approach the issue with a more precise vocabulary. Even those who define themselves positively as "single" accept marriage culture's traditional and sexist valuation of human relationships. They unwittingly further the marriage mystique.

Since my teenage years I've scoured the annals of the past for women who recoiled against matrimony's smug mandates and rejected its privileging distinctions—unusual women who sought social definition outside of the standard male-female social contract. I've found inspiration in a handful who, at various times and in different places, did recoil against matrimony. In correspondence with her former teacher and lover, the twelfth-century French scholastic philosopher Peter Abelard, for instance, the nun Heloise wrote, "God knows I never sought anything in you except yourself; I looked for no marriage bond, no marriage portion, and it was not my pleasures and wishes I sought to gratify, as you well know, but yours. The name of *wife* may seem more sacred or more binding, but sweeter for me will always be the word *mistress*, or, if you will permit me, that of *concubine* or *whore*."[150] Heloise was in her thirties when she penned these words; the abbess of a convent and clearly still tortured by the tragic love affair that had ended in Abelard's public disgrace and castration. Her antimarriage invective is so intense that some modern scholars claim the epistle to be spurious, finding it impossible that such sentiments could have been uttered by a twelfth-century woman.[151]

Equally compelling is the story of Caterina of Siena, the Tuscan saint who lived for a little over thirty years in the middle of the fourteenth century. Her biographer, the monk, Raymond of Capua, describes Caterina's upbringing as one of the survivors of twenty-five children born to a prosperous Tuscan and his wife, Lapa. Caterina apparently knew from the age of seven that she was destined for a life of spiritual rather than domestic substance and decided, early on, to become a hermit. As a child she set out one day with a loaf of bread, traversed the countryside near her home on foot, and finally ensconced herself in a cave in which she intended to take up lifelong residence. Perhaps it was inclement weather or imminent nightfall that changed her plans, but she returned home a few hours later: no one in the household had noticed her absence. But Caterina's determination for a life of asceticism and celibacy did not abate. Reared in the domestic arts in which she had no interest and pressured to marry when she reached puberty, she flatly refused, cutting her hair off and wearing an unflattering cap on her head. Her parents resorted to the standard method with intractable girls in the late Middle Ages; they locked her in her room and told her that she was their prisoner until she conceded to marry the suitor of their choice. She did not capitulate. Ultimately she joined the Dominican Sisters of Penitence, an order that refused any woman who was not a widow but made a concession for Caterina. Living among them she learned, for the first time, to read and write.[152]

Often the most inspiring role models for me have been fictional, such as Olive Chancellor, the protagonist of Henry James' 1886 novel, *The Bostonians;* a mannered, eccentric suffragette who may have been based on the nineteenth-cenutry feminist reformer Susan B. Anthony. "There are women who are unmarried by accident, and others who are unmarried by option; but Olive Chancellor was unmarried by every implication of her being. She was a spinster as Shelley was a lyric poet, or as the month of August is sultry,"[153] wrote James lovingly of his creation. Olive's heart is broken when Verena Tarrent, the protege whom she has nurtured in the cause of female emancipation and who has taken a vow to never marry, fails to debut at an important suffragist meeting. Verena instead opts to elope with the charming, southern misogynist Basil Ransom, a man who finds the suffragette cause alternately amusing and contemptible. Perhaps more than any other novel in English, *The Bostonians* demonstrates the kind of cold dismissal that the very subject of female equality can elicit in a man and the ways in which sexual attraction and social convention compel women lacking analytical capacities toward such men. But the novel also vindicates those who consciously break free of marital constraints. Crushed by the sense of personal loss and demoralized by the conventionality of her young friend's choice, Olive, in the novel's final scene, nevertheless summons the strength to take Verena's place at the podium.

When she demonstrates that obtaining the female vote is more important than her own private grievances, Olive shows the tangible strengths of an independent female existence buttressed by community and a strong sense of social purpose. Her character, explicitly described as a spinster, hearkens back to the traditional premodern notion of spinsterhood—a denotation of women who spun cloth and textiles,[154] producing valuable commodities and contributing economically to their households. The modern image of a spinster—an aging woman rendered ridiculous, pathetic, and useless, by her unmarried status—onset in the early eighteenth century, when the romantic marriage ethos penetrated popular culture. Its first use as a derogatory word occurs in the

Oxford English Dictionary in 1719. Prior to the period that gave rise to the companionate marriage ideal, the word referred simply to "the laudable 'industry of female manufacturers.'"[155] James' Olive Chancellor lives in the heyday of modernity's etherealization of marriage, the late Victorian period in which full-scale industrialization had caused women's spinning, weaving, and other economic tasks to fall into disuse. Wives were mandated to live as superfluous dependents or low-earning manual laborers and governesses. James re-envisions spinsterhood: Olive's tireless efforts on behalf of female equality represent a new kind of industry that entails spinning a vision of the future in which the sexes are equal; an era without marriage, which she imagines as "the greatest change the world had seen . . . a new era for the human family."[156]

Literary models are in some ways as powerful as real-life biographies, because they transpire in a fictional realm that liberates the imagination, enabling us to envision social realities radically different from our own. The novel, in particular, is a genre that often highlights social injustice in illuminating ways. A major antimarriage feminist of the twentieth century, dancer/choreographer Isadora Duncan has described her emotional response to an initial reading of George Eliot's novel *Adam Bede*, in which an unwed mother is publicly disgraced. Distressed by the sexual double standard represented in this novel, the twelve-year-old Duncan pursued an investigation into marital history and was alarmed by the facts she unearthed:

> I was deeply impressed by the injustice of this state of things for women, and putting it together with the story of my father and mother, I decided, then and there, that I would live to fight against marriage and for the emancipation of women. . . . These may seem strange ideas for a little girl of twelve years old to reason out, but circumstances of my life had made me very precocious. I enquired in to the marriage laws and was indignant to learn of the slavish condition of women.[157]

According to what may be a piece of feminist apocrypha, Duncan then burned her parents' marriage certificate, so that she might never enter wedlock's prison.

It is ironic and sad that in 1927 this remarkable woman asserted, with certainty, that the social tide had turned against marriage. "Things have changed and there has been so great a revolution in our ideas that I think today every intelligent woman will agree with me that the ethics of the marriage code are an impossible proposition for a free-spirited woman to accede to," Duncan wrote.[158] Dying in 1927, at the age of forty-nine, she did not live to see the postwar cult of wedlock in which women retreated to the home in droves, and psychoanalytically trained "experts" and ladies' magazine columnists promoted marriage as a full-time female career.[159] In the decade in which Duncan lived women comprised 34 percent of the American undergraduate student body; after the Second World War this proportion fell to just under 20 percent; the number of women who never married fell from close to 20 percent in the late nineteenth century to roughly 5 percent in the postwar years; and by 1962 over one-third of all brides in the United States were nineteen years old or younger (as compared to one-fourth in the United Kingdom).[160]

Duncan perhaps could not have imagined that such retrograde social patterns would succeed the period of artistic and intellectual ferment in which she lived. She could likewise not have foreseen the growth of America's wedding industry in our own time. When Emily Post published her first edition of *Etiquette* in 1922 she devoted scant space to the subject of weddings, advising couples to set a date and order invitations. Today the wedding sections of American bookstores are crowded with wedding planners that delineate every aspect of the event, establishing guidelines for bridal showers and bachelor parties, invitations, registration, dress selection, makeup, hair, and skin care for the bride, floral arrangements, catering, cakes, musical accompaniment, and honeymoons. There are numerous books devoted to individual aspects of the nuptial celebration, entire volumes that explicate such specifics as the purchase of engagement rings, the authoring of one's wedding vows, and delivery of the wedding toast. Conde Nast's *Bride's*, which first appeared in 1934 as a free handout, is now a glossy magazine as thick as the telephone book which enjoys a circulation of roughly 327,595. Estimates indicate that in the mid 1990s Americans spent as much as $32 billion per year on weddings,[161] and $18 billion a year on wedding gifts.[162] The wedding coordinator has recently emerged as a new kind of entrepreneur: a consultant who can single-handedly plan and stage manage the block-buster wedding, leaving the bride and groom free to bask in the adulation of their big day. Entering this field requires a minimal amount of startup capital and a connection to the Association of Bridal Consultants or the National Bridal Service, which offer workshops on wedding planning: A.B.C. claims over one thousand members and N.B.S. boasts a membership of eight hundred.[163]

The intelligent woman who Isadora Duncan predicted would repudiate matrimony and demand her social freedom did not emerge in the late twentieth century or the early twenty-first century; it is women who work as bridal consultants and wedding coordinators, women who patronize the ever expanding wedding industry, women who visiting theme-wedding web sites on the internet, employ bridal consultants, meet with florists, hire caterers, interview photographers, design brides-maids' outfits, custom order wedding cakes, and select china patterns. What cultural critic Mark Caldwell calls the "bridal buying binge"[164] is an integral part of the segue from "single" to married life. Perhaps this should not be surprising, considering the powerful seductions that wedlock offers women and the fact that until recently marriage did constitute the only prestigious female social role. A compelling historical legacy that values women only as wives combined with an industry that dazzles with lustrous images, promising bliss to each bride, is a lethal combination and one that is understandably hard for most women to resist.

Those women who have sensed fundamental rottenness at the heart of the marital contract have always been in the minority. Those who have recoiled against their culture's prescriptions for conjugality have done so for various reasons, but all have shared a discomfort with the brutal history of marriage as well as a need for a social definition outside of the marital economy—something that was neither "married" nor "single." Some who refused to marry felt that their love for an individual man was sacrosanct and would be besmirched by a utilitarian bond. Others felt married to God. Others were repulsed by the notion of perpetuating an institution that originates in the barter of women as property. Others, like the early twentieth-century aviatrix Amelia Earheart, did finally marry, but with grave reservations about the choice. In 1931 Earheart wrote to George Palmer Putnam, the publisher who had repeatedly proposed to her and finally obtained her consent to marry. She expressed reluctance to enter the institution that she considered to be a "an attractive cage":

> You must know of my reluctance to marry, my feeling that I shatter thereby chances in work which means so much to me. I feel the move as foolish as anything I could do. I know there are compensations, but I have no heart to look ahead.
>
> In our life together I shall not hold you to any code of medieval faithfulness to me, nor shall I consider myself bound to you similarly. If we can be honest, I think the differences which arise may be avoided.
>
> Please let us not interfere with each other's work or play, nor let the world see private joys or disagreements.[165]

In my research for this book I have waded through hundreds of romantic marriage narratives and have stumbled upon bits of startling antimarriage sentiment expressd by women like Earheart, who assessed matrimony in harshly realistic terms. I have also spoken with many intelligent women, some of whom are married and many of whom hope to be married someday. In conversation some have observed that I judge the institution of marriage and thereby indict the woman whose personal taste or private inclination leads her to marry. This is true. Although it is not cost free, easy, or safe, although it is not smooth and conciliatory as is the "to each her own" doctrine, *judgment* is the right and the obligation of every thinking person. I deviate from popular rhetoric in my belief that not all choices are "valid" merely because sane individuals make them. I believe that marriage is destructive, because it perpetuates negative hierarchical divisions such as the celebration of wives and the accompanying denigration of spinsters, the artificial distinction between good (sexually monogamous) and bad (sexually experimental) girls, the exaltation of conjugal love over platonic friendship, and the privileging of institutionalized togetherness over solitude. Wedlock is tainted by the historical residue of female subordination; an overwhelming, oppressive social history that many modern brides and grooms are simply not aware of. I think that each woman who pursues marital commitment and dons a diamond engagement ring and then a

white lace dress, believing that she is operating from a personal, spontaneous, or romantic impulse, should reflect more closely on her own
behavior. While it is much touted in contemporary psychological parl-
ance, individual "choice" is rarely neutral, unbiased, or individualistic.
Major life choices are the result of multiple influences, most of which are
unstated or stated in complicated, indirect ways. Marriage, in particular,
is a decision unlike any other—a decision with an elaborate social context. It is overdetermined by family pressure, legal sanction, and the deluge of consumer images linking wedlock to female happiness and
self-worth. I hope, in the following chapters, to substantiate these beliefs
and dissuade many would-be wives from draping themselves in white
and walking down the aisle.

When a woman like Gloria Steinem—for decades a popular icon of
female independence—describes her recent decision to marry by stating
that "feminism is about the ability to choose what's right at each time in
our lives,"[166] she recurs to the morally relativistic language of popular
psychology, in which everything is "valid." I would argue that choosing to
uphold an institution rooted in the barter of women as property, an institution that devalues friendship and envisions female existence in terms of
a romantic narrative of male redemption, is not valid, not right at any
age. I wonder if there were a time when Steinem would have agreed with
me. The inaugural issue of *Ms.* magazine, the periodical she launched in
1972, featured a brilliantly savage piece of antimarriage satire, Judy
Brady's essay, "I Want a Wife." "I want a wife who will work and send me
to school," the anonymous female narrator asserts. "And while I am going
to school I want a wife to take care of my children."[167] The narrator continues to list her desires: an altruistic helpmate who will perform grind-
ingly repetitive household chores without complaint, manage the social
calendar, offer emotional support, and remain sexually faithful without
demanding fidelity in return. "If, by chance, I find another person more
suitable as a wife than the wife I already have, I want the liberty to replace
my present wife with another one. Naturally, I expect a fresh, new life. My
wife will take the children and be solely responsible for them,"[168] the piece
concludes. This is pure Swiftian irony aimed at exploding the myth of
happily-ever-after and revealing the matrimonial contract, as it has
existed for many women. There are no disclaimers in Brady's piece, no

comforting platitudes about personal choice, no soothing aphorisms about the equal validity of being "single" and married. The essay treats matrimony as an inherently political subject deserving of satirical critique. The fact that Steinem, thirty years later and now herself a newly-wed, describes wedlock in such depoliticized language, attests to the increasing power of America's marriage mystique.

For women to exert real influence commensurate with our numbers we must break with the matrimonial narrative that has defined us for four thousand years. Toward this end, we must stop psychologizing our own choices and must relinquish the comfortingly neutral, "everything is valid" credo and part with the the relationship industry's "I'm okay, you're okay" relativism. We must stop repeating the absurd mantra, "it's okay to be single," and adopt the more aggressive stance that, "it's not okay to be married." Until now no word has existed to denote the woman who is neither married nor "single," because female worth has been measured and valued solely in terms of the marital standing. A word does exist in our gender's etymological history, though. The word is *spinster* in its traditional sense: one who produces, one who manufactures, one who spins. Because independent women are anathema to marriage culture—because internalized spinsterphobia is so powerful—it is a word from which most women and men recoil. But *spinster by choice* better than any other term designates women who refuse a social definition that denotes marriage or its opposite. When we reclaim and reinvent this term, modulating it to our own social and economic circumstances and imbuing it with the dignity of a new kind of female productivity, we will have come a long way. But to accomplish this we need first to part with the seductive cultural script of marriage-oriented courtship, which has many pivotal moments for dramatic self-display. It is to the first of these key moments—the wedding proposal—that we now turn.

CHAPTER TWO

"Will You Marry Me?" The Proposal Scene in the Contemporary Imagination

...it is always incomprehensible to a man that a woman should ever refuse an offer of marriage.

—Jane Austen, *Emma*

The shift of the setting for courtship from the domestic world to the commercial sphere created a whole new consciousness of the watching public and radically altered both the economics and the aesthetics of seduction, creating an atmosphere of intense competition in which suitors were forced to prove their worth through ostentatious displays of purchasing power.

—Daniel Harris, "The Romantic"

I. Dramatizing Masculinity

"A man proposes marriage to a woman, he should kneel down!" These words are spoken sharply, accusingly by Loretta Castorini, the character portrayed by Cher in the wildly popular 1987 film, *Moonstruck*. Loretta is a thirty-seven-year-old widow and bookkeeper living with her parents in an Italian enclave of Brooklyn. A pragmatist and a traditionalist, she has decided to seize her only option for social prestige, accepting the advances of a man for whom she has no feelings, the befuddled Johnny Camareri, played by Danny Aiello. The viewer knows instinctively that Johnny is wrong for her, because he cannot manage his proposal with the requisite flourish. Loretta choreographs the entire event early in the film in a scene that takes place in a cozy Italian restaurant. He has asked her to marry him cautiously, tentatively, and she has expressed dissatisfaction with his ignorance of romantic convention. To Johnny's chagrin ("This is a good suit!"), she instructs him to kneel down, at which point amused fellow diners become involved in the botched proposal. "Is that man praying?" a drunken professor several tables away asks a waiter, as Johnny drops to both knees and shuffles awkwardly around their table toward Loretta. "Where's the ring?" she demands impatiently as Johnny, who has not purchased the all important gem, looks increasingly morti- fied. "A ring!" shouts a gangster type sitting nearby. "That's right," jeers the gangster's companion, "I would've sprung for the ring if it was me. *Capice?*" "You propose marriage to a woman, you should offer her a ring of engagement," Loretta chides, finally instructing Johnny to use his pinky ring. Looking defeated, he reluctantly turns over the pinky ring, complaining, "I like this ring!" Finally, with all of the elements in place, he regains his composure and assumes the appropriately solemn tone of voice: "Loretta. Loretta Castorini Clark. On my knees, in front of all these people, will you marry me?" She replies promptly albeit unenthusiasti- cally: "Yes, Johnny. Yes, John Anthony Camareri, I will marry you. I will be your wife."

The restaurant staff and its patrons applaud, and Johnny kisses Loretta's hand. But the viewer is skeptical. Johnny, we have seen, is no match for the tough-minded, secretly passionate Loretta. This brief, ini- tial scene reveals him to be ridiculous, confused, asexual. He is, in the words of Loretta's plumber father (Vincent Gardenia), "a big baby," and this immaturity takes a very specific form. Johnny lacks the conventional male lead's romantic prowess. At the moment that most requires deci- siveness, grace, and self-confidence—the marriage proposal—he becomes awkward, confused, and embarrassed. In American cinema the proposal is a moment of masculine self-presentation in which speech, gestures, and the management of a central prop—the ring—must coor- dinate. In literature, scholars often focus on the narrative scene as an independent unit with its own rhetoric.[1] In fictional and historical prose, minute details such as comments, gestures, and objects are crucial to the expression of a scene's central idea. This is true in film as well, and it is especially clear in the proposal scene, a major component of the cine- matic marriage plot. In romantic comedies like *Moonstruck* the marriage proposal is a rhetorically complex moment. Each declaration, physical movement, and object is subordinated to the overall point of wedlock as a male initiative, an act of sexual pursuit bolstered by a display of financial success. Film reverses husband-hunting literature's view of marriage as a female quest. The cinematic proposal is a moment when two masculine impulses converge: laying claim to one's sexual territory and crystallizing the vision of a joint marital future. In accordance with today's marital ideal, this pursuit means claiming a single female partner for life, flattering her with chivalrous adoration, and marking her with a symbol of bourgeois ownership, the engagement ring. Only men who are their own agents—take charge guys—can master these initiatives, appealing to women who must recline, in Henry James words, "...in attitudes more or less gracefully passive, for a man to come their way and furnish them with a destiny."[2]

Moonstruck's Johnny Camareri is clearly not such a man. He appears unable to manage the details of his own life, let alone a woman's. His proposal lacks the necessary undertone of sexual conquest, so he seems incapable of mapping a marital trajectory for the future. His physical ineptness is our first clue. In the film and television versions of romance that saturate the popular imagination, real men kneel when proposing marriage. The suitor who approaches his intended on bended knee declares that she is royalty, symbolically deferring to her as commoners ingratiated themselves to monarchs in a bygone feudal era. The marriage proposal is assumed to elevate each woman to regal status, but the male lover's stance is also a reversal of sex roles. The hopeful suitor entices his bride by overturning gender hierarchies, prostrating himself before her in symbolic abnegation so she can momentarily enjoy a superior social position. The formulaic proposal is, like so much modern marriage ritual, an ersatz relic of love's past. Its erotic display hearkens back to medieval courtship literature that reversed actual social conditions, depicting males as supplicants before omnipotent females. Often a pawn in the game of arranged marriage, the legally disenfranchised woman of the eleventh century was, as Virginia Woolf once pointed out, "the slave of any boy whose parents forced a ring upon her finger."[3] But the period's literature transforms her into a figure of supreme power, the object of obsessive pursuit. She dictates the activities of obedient, worshipful knights and hears the amorous appeals of troubadour poets.[4]

The marriage proposal retains this courtly sentiment, demanding that a man feign powerlessness, bowing before his love object while simultaneously laying claim to her.

Moonstruck's Johnny Camareri can barely manage this complex maneuver; he kneels on command, miserably, and waddles toward Loretta, looking painfully aware of his own inadequacy. His lack of preparation with the ring hammers home his lack of masculinity. When a man produces the diamond ring he presents the conventional symbol of husbandly appropriation while suggesting his ability as a financial provider. The gesture announces that for him such purchases are easy, that he is capable of decorating his beloved with baubles and gems (and by implication, supporting her in high style). The proposal scene's central object—a glittering diamond mounted on a platinum band and presented by a kneeling lover—is always offered by a man to a woman, never vice versa. The gift combines romantic finesse, sexual prowess, and economic savvy in a streamlined package of middle-class masculinity, casting its female recipient in the role of a genteel coquette, an aristocratic lady in waiting. An unfit husband, Johnny Camareri comes without the magical gem that will dazzle Loretta into submission. In the postproposal scene, we see the source of his inadequacy: Mommy. Instead of whisking Loretta off to bed, Johnny sets off to visit the ailing Sicilian mother to whom he is neurotically attached. En route to the airport he and Loretta discuss possible wedding dates, but what's important in this scene is that she drives the car while he sits in the passenger seat ruminating on the schedule of their wedding. This big sissy, John Patrick Shanley's Freudian screenplay tells us, is too weak to occupy the driver's seat. He cannot disentangle himself from his mother's apron strings, cannot assert himself sexually, cannot project the image of adult masculinity, cannot manage the props or gestures of a romantic scene, cannot even get himself to the airport. Most importantly, he cannot bear the onus of the marital initiative.

But American cinema's rendition of the marriage plot provides each woman with her inevitable, romantic other, that man for whom she is intended. We do not doubt that *Moonstruck* will eventually send Loretta a fitting counterpart. When her appropriate love-match appears, it is in the form of Nicholas Cage, who plays Johnny's smoldering brother, Ronny. A hot-blooded bakery employee who loves opera, Ronny seizes Loretta in a passionate embrace not long after they meet, declaring his love for her. He is a man who knows what he wants and pursues it, a man driven by instinct, lacking self-consciousness. Estranged from his mother and brother, he is free of all Oedipal ties, and he appears to be free of any troublesome intellectual activity as well. Ronny is all primal energy, and the film sexualizes his anger, glorifying the irrational grudge he holds against his brother. Cage plays Ronny as a comically glamorous, sweaty loner, a Brandoesque baker who toils in his undershirt, stoking ovens in the cavernous basement beneath a Brooklyn bakery. In his own words, to do this hellish job is to "sweat and sweat and sweat, and shove this stinkin' dough in and out of this hot hole in the wall!" He is, of course, the stud to domesticate Loretta. Shortly after meeting him she's coloring her hair, plucking her eyebrows, swooning in sexual ecstasy, and traipsing through the early morning streets of Brooklyn in a postcoital haze. In the film's final scene, Ronny displaces his brother, barging into Loretta's home unannounced and figuratively taking her in a spontaneous proposal of marriage that requires no stage directions. As her parents toast the newly engaged pair, the camera pans to a turn-of-the-century, colorized photograph of an anonymous couple from the old country—probably Loretta's grandparents—which hangs in the Castorini's living room. This traditional husband and wife, the film suggests, who understood gender roles within marriage, had it right, and Ronny and Loretta will preserve their legacy.

In spite, or perhaps because, of its retrograde sexual politics, *Moonstruck* was the comedy of its year, garnering both commercial and critical success. It received three Academy Awards. The eminent and usually astute critic Pauline Kael lapsed into uncharacteristic sentimentality in her review, praising the film as "a giddy homage to our desire for grand passion."[5] As in many contemporary films that further the marriage mystique, *Moonstruck*'s parochialism is obscured by cartoonish ethnicity, a fact that partially explains its popularity. Director Norman Jewison has his principals behave the way Italians do only in American movies: honking their lines in exaggerated New York accents and gesticulating wildly. Loretta responds to the men in her life with slaps, stupefied double takes, rhetorical questions like "What are you talkin'?" and imperatives like "Snap out of it!" She appears strong in her hearty Italianness. But the film's ethnic banter is superficial, subordinate to a fairy-tale narrative in which boy meets and sweeps girl off her feet, giving her life meaning. *Moonstruck* is a reactionary celebration of wedlock, a paean to Loretta's homemaker mother Rose (Olympia Dukakis), who forgives her meandering husband and holds the family together. In this popular story's prescription for marital health, normal male sexuality requires antipathy for one's mother accompanied by displays of violence. The film's initial, incoherent proposal scene and its final successful betrothal prescribe masculine domination within matrimony.

Advice literature on how to propose marriage concurs. In the narrative of heterosexual romance, women yearn for commitment, but men formally initiate marriage in a clearly delineated ritual. As compared to the hundreds of bridal guidebooks that crowd the reference sections of American bookstores, there are very few marriage primers written for men. Those manuals aimed at the groom-to-be focus on the engagement ring and the proposal scene. The act of proposing is, in the minds of marriage advisors, the one really male part of the process, the point at which men invest themselves fully in the matrimonial ideal. Bridal literature covers a range of subjects, from the most graphically personal (e.g. avoiding a yeast infection on one's wedding day, optimal contraception for the honeymoon) to its most symbolic (selecting a maid of honor, overhauling one's mother's wedding dress). By contrast, advice to the modern groom-to-be focuses almost exclusively on the proposal, giving particular attention to the engagement ring. The aspiring husband must immerse himself in the world of gemology before broaching the subject of marriage with his partner. He must become adept at appraising gemstones, learning to assess a diamond's color (the ideal gem should be transparent), its cut (skillful chiseling allows the diamond to reflect light more perfectly), its clarity (a flawless stone has no internal cracks), and its carat (the diamond's weight determines its price).[6]

While providing its reader with nuts-and-bolts information on gem certification and insurance policies for jewelry, the groom's handbook also performs a psychological function: it flatters its male reader with notions of his own virility. Michael Perry's *The Groom's Survival Manual,* for instance, opens with the following assurance:

Fortunately you had the depth of character to realize that something so unbelievably good happens only once in a lifetime, and you should take some action to preserve the magic. You asked the woman of your dreams to marry you. . . . Unlike many men who don't know what they want, you have the wisdom and resolve to capture the initiative and start traveling the path toward real happiness.

Adjacent to this paragraph is a black-and-white photograph of a youngish man in a dark suit walking briskly along an urban street in a purposeful manner. He's handsome in a 1940s B-actor way. The caption beneath this photograph reads: "A man who chooses to get married is a man of action. A guy who knows what he wants and won't take no for an answer."[7]

Perry's prose blends fantasies of primitive machismo with psychobabble. He tells his readers that marriage for men is all about taking charge, being in control, and he equates male aggression with notions of self-realization lifted directly from modern films and pop-psychology primers. The man who becomes engaged possesses superior "character" in that he is driven: he takes action, has resolve, travels, chooses, knows what he wants . . . and won't accept rejection. But he is also sagacious: a man of wisdom and emotional depth. *The Groom's Survival Manual* unleashes a barrage of flattery to address its male readers' apprehensions about wedlock. Once again, the contemporary man is assumed to fear those very institutional trappings that the modern woman craves: a public declaration of devotion, the promise of monogamy, and legal sanctions on sexual activity. But male trepidation is assumed to be even more profound. The man perceives marriage as emasculation, the process of agreeing to one's own humiliating domestication. Perry therefore employs a plethora of action verbs to appease the male who fears he has lapsed into passivity, allowing a woman to rope him in. *The Groom's Survival Manual* addresses this anxious reader directly, assuring him that his autonomy will remain intact and promising that he has not been captured by a predatory husband hunter. His intelligence, savvy, and machismo would prevent such submission. The groom-to-be has in fact engineered the whole marital scenario, proving himself as that most cherished archetype of American maleness: the assertive, forward-looking self-starter, the corporate powerhouse.

Other male-oriented marriage handbooks operate from the same premise but proceed more subtly. A common means of flattering the groom-to-be entails snideness. Wedding manuals written for women are almost uniformly earnest, celebrating the entire nuptial process, from the proposal to the betrothal announcement to the bridal shower to the gala day itself. Popular handbooks like the *Bride's Book of Etiquette* and *1000 Questions About Your Wedding* are written by and for women. Their covers feature immaculately coiffed, glowing, young women decked out in full bridal regalia, and their chapters on compiling the guest list, designing invitations, selecting china, and planning a honeymoon are written in a tone so pious it borders on religiosity. Wedding guidebooks written for men, by contrast, employ a sardonic tone that betrays hostility to the entire engagement process. *Esquire's Things a Man Should Know About Marriage*, for instance, treats the proposal scene with facetious contempt: "Decent proposals: In private, on a starry night, preferably atop something tall—the Eiffel Tower, the Matterhorn, etc. On bended knee: Optional. Skip the bended knee thing if there are lots of other people around—you don't need applause. Besides, she might say no."[8] This primer suggests that, before popping the question, the groom-to-be should check his girlfriend's hope chest for "items of inordinate weirdness"[9] that would betray such quirks as heroin addiction or a predilection for taxidermy. The *Esquire* guide flatters its reader by treating him as a sarcastic hipster, an independent tough guy who doesn't really take these marital protocols seriously. The groom-to-be's masculinity is uncompromised, such handbooks promise, because rather than succumbing to sentimentality he is secretly guffawing at the whole matrimonial process, and his ironic detachment protects him from what could be perceived as a degrading concession to female whimsy. The celebrity groom-to-be sometimes adopts this pose, posturing as a hipster who plays by his own rules. Actor/comedian Howie Mandel claims that he proposed to his wife Terry at a delicatessen, dumping an unset diamond onto their table and remarking, "If you want you can make a ring out of this. I have to go to the men's room."[10] Mandel's narrative highlights his own apathy for the engagement process. The pedestrian location of the proposal, his lack of care in having the gem set, the contemptuous plunking of the diamond onto the table followed by an immediate jaunt to relieve himself in a public bathroom all display forced indifference to the conjugal ideal. But such conspicuous disinterest seems fraudulent.

There are many legitimate reasons for men to feel nervous when proposing marriage. Fear of rejection is only one factor. Other notables include enacting outdated gender roles through a hypermasculine cultural scene, promising lifelong monogamy when statistics demonstrate this commitment's probable failure, perpetuating an isolationist social arrangement, placing one's sex life under the control of the civil government, and shouldering possible financial responsibility for another person. These are not psychological phobias; they are real moral and intellectual quagmires. And because our culture provides no venue where such issues can be seriously discussed, men facing matrimony resort to facile snideness, mindless quipping, and conspicuously insincere yawns of boredom to avoid the sources of their own discomfort. All the while they cling to wedlock's comforting sanctions as tenaciously as their female counterparts do. When we peel back the thin layer of masculine disdain, we find a set of familiar, maudlin notions of wedlock. Another celebrity husband, baby boomer actor-turned-author Paul Reiser, recalls his self-conscious marriage proposal: "I remember officially proposing. Actually asking this woman to literally, legally, officially marry me. I couldn't get the words out. I couldn't stop laughing. It felt so dopey. So cliche. 'Asking for her hand in marriage.' I felt like I was in some bad Ronald Colman movie."[11]

Reiser's 1994 book, *Coupledom*, is an autobiographical memoir of married life. A smarmy valentine to his wife Paula, the book, like most pieces of glad-to-be-married propaganda, is an orgy of heterosexual self-congratulation. Admitting embarrassment at having taken his cues from hackneyed Hollywood films, Reiser nevertheless basks in the glow of the marital good life, its small frustrations and its larger rewards. He vacillates between discomfort with nuptial protocol and mawkish sentimentality ("When I met the woman of my dreams, I knew. I saw her, and I was immediately unable to speak. My throat locked up, my stomach was in knots, I was sweaty, clammy, and nauseous. I had learned years before that being nauseous means you're in love...").[12] He also provides a dose of psychobabblish folk wisdom ("Ask most guys why they marry the woman they do and they'll tell you, 'She's the first one who called me on everything. . . .'").[13] His primary message is stock issue celebrity self-promotion: the trappings of success are unimportant. It is marriage—home and hearth—that provides ultimate meaning. And it is this glib sentimentality that Reiser shares with his colleagues in the wedding industry, marriage propagandists like Arlene Hamilton Stewart, whose *A Bride's Book of Wedding Traditions* celebrates the typical woman's bliss as she is "transported from the ecstasy of proposal to the thrill of engagement."[14] The assumption that is shared by the most naively romantic bridal guidebook, the most ostentatiously jaded groom's manual, and the most syrupy ode to couplehood is that the marriage proposal initiates adulthood. The proposal is, in our romance-saturated culture, the pivotal moment of male self-determination and female social completion.

Five years after his success in *Moonstruck* Nicholas Cage starred in another marriage-oriented romantic comedy. This time he played that stock character familiar to all women who have watched afternoon talk shows, read ladies' magazines, or dipped into the self-help sections of their local bookstores: the commitment phobe. As Manhattan-based private detective Jack Singer, the protagonist of Andrew Bergman's 1992 *Honeymoon in Vegas*, Cage is a man with a dilemma. He loves his schoolteacher girlfriend Betsy Nolan (Sarah Jessica Parker), but her youth is waning, her biological clock is ticking, and the ring finger of her left hand is still bare. Early in the film, marriage-obsessed Betsy lays it on the line: "Jack, we have to go to the next step," she tells him over dinner. "I'm just telling you that I won't be a girlfriend forever. There's too much that I want. I want kids and a family. Jack, I've got to know what the deal is with us." "I'm in love with you," Jack responds. But that's not enough for this impatient "single" gal—where's the ring, the white dress, the invitations, the honeymoon? Most importantly, where is the security and social prestige? "I'm in love with you," Betsy replies matter of factly, "but I need a commitment. Life's too short. I want to be married." Jack looks rumpled and miserable.

Jack Singer has the syndrome concocted by marriage propagandists: wedding phobia. Bergman explains this private eye's Peter Pan complex in both practical and psychoanalytic terms. Jack spends his days tailing cheating spouses; he follows adulterous wives to the hotels where they meet their lovers and tails errant husbands and their paramours through the streets of Manhattan, documenting their every move. His firsthand knowledge of failed monogamy has resulted in a cynical view of wedlock. But once again, the marriage plot has misogynistic underpinnings. Jack's real fear of commitment can be traced to his deceased mother (Anne Bancroft), a possessive control freak who, on her deathbed, entreated her son never to marry, whispering, "No girl can love you like I did." Yet another Freudian plot, in which a male protagonist must wrench himself from the grasp of a haunting matriarch in order to develop sexually and emotionally, is set in motion. In Jack's recurrent dreams about her, his mother is naked, and it is clear that his ambivalence about what the film presents as normal male-female relationships stems from his early life with this castrating carnivore, the harridan with whom perky, petite Betsy is contrasted. In Freud's Oedipal drama, a male child must detach himself from his mother and identify with his father in order to activate his erotic instincts for another woman.[15] *Honeymoon in Vegas* presents matrimony as the endpoint of this laudable maturation process. It sympathizes with conventional Betsy, the girl who unselfconsciously mouths sexist cliches, announcing that "life is too short" to remain unwed, as if a meaningful existence commences at the altar. This commitment-hungry no-nonsense gal is the film's moral center, the one who is presumed to have her priorities in order and to speak from an adult point of view. To reach her emotional plateau, Jack must loosen his mother's stranglehold; a grip that is incredibly powerful even from the grave. Toward this end he must suffer a Freudian test of manhood, undergoing a series of emotional and physical ordeals.

Following Betsy's ultimatum, Jack proffers a lackluster proposal in the front seat of a car, and the two fly to Las Vegas to elope. When they arrive it's clear that Jack has a case of the jitters, and instead of whisking Betsy off to one of the city's many drive-in chapels, he temporarily abandons her to play poker. A contrived plot ensues; Jack is taken for $65,000 by gambler Tommy Corman (James Caan), a card shark who wears shiny suits and swaggers through the lobby of Las Vegas' Bally Hotel with a menacing facial expression. Compared to mild-mannered indecisive Jack, Tommy is a walking talking phallus. He's the primal father of Freudian mythology, the omnipotent figure of self-assertion, who, in

Freud's account of prehistory, ruled over a horde whose male members eventually challenged him.[16] Tommy is a fantasy of pure, prehistoric masculinity prior to its dilution by time and organized civilization. Like Freud's primal father, this gangster has a cadre of male attendants—lackeys, house boys, bodyguards, and servants—to do his bidding. They sublimate their desires by fulfilling his and aid his quest for sexual gratification. Soon Tommy has his eye on Betsy, and he lures her to Hawaii for the weekend as a means of settling Jack's debt. Shaken into action, Jack appeals to Betsy frantically before her departure. Kneeling in their hotel suite, his hands clasped together in a gesture of mock prayer, he pleads, "Okay, marry me tonight!" "No," she replies. Then, citing the film's underlying psychoanalytic theories, she continues, "I mean, Jack, if you really wanted to marry me you would have done it this afternoon. You were looking for a way to get out of this. I mean, you don't have to be Freud to figure that one out."

She's off to the big island with her gangster suitor, and soon he's wooing her with walks on the beach, romantic canoe rides, and a marquise-shaped diamond so enormous that it appears to outweigh her. "I want to marry you . . . like, tomorrow," Tommy confesses to Betsy, whom he has known for all of twenty-four hours. She is dazzled. Having found someone ready to take the mythical "next step" without ambivalence, someone unencumbered by mother love, she concurs and flies with him back to Las Vegas to make it legal. By this time Jack has shaped up. He's taken the reins, and, in the film's view, become a man, pursuing Betsy to Hawaii and then to Vegas, where he performs an act of flamboyant self-sacrifice, jumping from a plane with a troupe of sky-diving Elvis Presley imitators, landing at Betsy's feet, and confessing that he can't live without her. The film's final shot is of Jack and Betsy's wedding photo taken in a cheesy Las Vegas chapel, with the Elvises in their white suits and pompadour wigs seated as wedding attendants. Mr. and Mrs. Right are together, as fairy-tale love dictates they must be.

Honeymoon in Vegas is meant to be a lighthearted spoof of Las Vegas tackiness that freely mixes characters from opposing genres. The sexual neurotic with a Hamlet complex is a Woody Allen-style New Yorker. The film's central joke is his triumph over a threatening hood from the gangster world. It might be easy to laugh off a slight film like this as mere entertainment, without realizing that it is the kind of comedy that popularizes standards of courtship. Adrienne Rich has pointed out the degree to which vulgarized readings of Freud determine notions of parenting and sexual development. When considering the impact of Freudian sexism on the popular consciousness, she writes, "We should not underestimate the power of films, plays, and jokes."[17] In 1913 Freud wrote that "Sexual desires do not unite men but divide them."[18] Cinematic romances like *Honeymoon in Vegas* dramatize this competition, pitting primal son against primal father in a struggle for sexual supremacy that ends in marriage. Much contemporary American cinema spews similar Freudian ideology along with the self-help movement's most appalling ideas, stereotypes that are equally offensive to both sexes. Romantic comedies tend to present men as one of two polar opposites: either immature floundering man-children or virile stalwarts. Such films recapitulate popular psychology's biases, pathologizing male reservations about marriage as symptoms of immaturity or weakness. For the wishy-washy adolescent to achieve his swaggering counterpart's machismo, he must sever his ties to mother, grow up, take charge, and, finally, like an upstanding caveman, take a woman and make her his own. Accordingly, the marriage proposal constitutes a key moment of male self-realization. Women in cinematic marriage plots are likewise either ball-busting viragos who desexualize their male partners or females awaiting social completion through wedlock. An ugly duckling like *Moonstruck's* Loretta Castorini undergoes a Cinderellalike transformation after tumbling into bed with the man of her dreams, and this physical blossoming signals her readiness for the sublime state of marriage. An ingenue like *Honeymoon in Vegas'* Betsy Nolan is ready for marital action. In sanctioning these characters' marriage mania and naturalizing their view of themselves as incomplete without a wedding band, such films flagrantly promote the myth of wedlock as redemption, telling us that the independence of the "single" life is something we must outgrow for our own good—that for both men and women marriage is tantamount to self-actualization.

Honeymoon in Vegas' penultimate scene exemplifies an important trend in American courtship: the elaborately staged marriage proposal. The wedding industry dictates that today's proposal be overproduced, enhanced by gimmicks and theatrical props. A plane, a parachute, and a white suit are the items that accentuate Jack Singer's pursuit of Betsy Nolan. These props underscore one of the film's subjects: spontaneous Las Vegas marriages that result from this glittering aphrodisiacal city's assault on the senses. But in today's proposal scenario each suitor is advised to come prepared with his own set of romantic accouterments, objects that encode special messages to his sweetheart. A velvet box containing a ring is no longer enough. The ring must now be extravagantly outfitted, strategically placed in a champagne glass by a conspiring restaurant waiter,[19] inserted into a bouquet of flowers that arrives at the unsuspecting bride-to-be's office with a note that reads "Will you be my wife?"[20] or mounted on green velvet and placed in a sterling silver box engraved with the imperative, "Marry me."[21] Corporations encourage the frenzy for novelty proposals. *Bride's* magazine, with other companies, now cosponsors a Valentine's Day multimedia event for which lovers compete to write unique marriage proposals; on February 14, *Bride's* nationally televises the proposals of thirty-five winners from Times Square in New York City. (Although both men and women are eligible for this competition, the magazine's "Will You Marry Me?" Day advertisement features the photograph of a gushing young woman gratefully embracing a man who has clearly just popped the question.)[22] Beringer Vineyard in California sponsors an "Irresistible Proposals" contest in which the most creatively outrageous marriage proposal wins a "weekend Napa getaway" for two.[23] Gregory Godek's *1001 Ways to Be Romantic* advises grooms to perform costly, public marriage proposals, painting their requests on billboards, having them sky-written, inserting them inside Chinese fortune cookies, or custom ordering jigsaw puzzles. Godek praises the extravagance of a suitor whose bride-to-be "received an unexpected gift from Tiffany's. She opened it to find a sterling silver tray—engraved with, 'Sally, will you marry me?'"[24] For a wealthy duo or a high-profile celebrity couple, the ring is often just one in a series of lavish gifts bestowed by a groom-to-be on his bride. *In Style* magazine's 1999 special wedding issue praised the extravagance of actor Patrick Labyorteaux who proposed to television producer Tina Albanese in grand old-Hollywood style. After sending Albanese by limousine to the Burke Williams Spa in Santa Monica for a day of "pampering,"

Labyorteaux waited at an airstrip with a dozen red roses and a private jet, flying his beloved to Las Vegas and proposing marriage over lobsters and champagne. "The crowning touch? Tina was handed a valet parking ticket that led her to a Mercedes 560 SL, her dream car."[25]

Because the cult of marital femininity predates the industrial revolution, strict Marxist analysis, which views companionate wedlock as an outgrowth of capitalism, does not adequately explain the marriage mystique. But it is impossible not to notice the compatibility of romance-based matrimony and American corporate interests. With its high-priced amorous merchandise, Madison Avenue fuels fantasies of marital bliss. Advertisers encourage men to overspend wildly, relinquishing two to three months' salary on an engagement ring, emptying their bank accounts on complimentary jewelry, reserving tables at exclusive restaurants, booking lavish cruises, hiring bands, composing singing telegrams, contacting sky writers, and ordering custom-made gifts. The marriage proposal is now a consumeristic experience, as the entire dating process, which has taken place in the public venues of restaurants, theaters, coffee bars, discotheques, concert halls, hotels, and health clubs, has been, among other things, an exhibitionistic foray into capitalism. Because courtship is no longer private, the date offers each man an opportunity to advertise his earning capacity to the world, competing with other males in a Darwinian battle for romantic supremacy. The pièce de résistance of the entire process, the marriage proposal, is, in fact, the ultimate date, a moment of unabashed material excess in which each man must astound his bride-to-be while vanquishing his sexual competitors. The suitor who proposes with a sterling silver tray, the keys to a Mercedes, or an ostentatious diamond flaunts his sexual prowess and assumes the role that still defines American masculinity—that of married provider.[26]

Less costly proposals often involve gimmicks that capitalize on the element of surprise or technology that documents the moment. As is the case with so much marriage custom, celebrities set the trends. *People* magazine's 1999 "Weddings of the Year" issue documents a series of gimmick proposals, each of which has its own theme. Actor Barry Williams' proposal to Eila Mary Matt stressed the adorableness of being a couple; Williams' request was punctuated by the entrance of Matt's cocker spaniel "wearing a black velvet collar with a miniature Kelly bag attached to it, and inside was beautiful diamond ring."[27] Singer Fabian Forte proposed to talent agent Andrea Patrick with a romantic epistle that emphasized the myth of fated love; he inserted a handkerchief inscribed with the message, "My Maui princess, marry me," into a bottle and flung it into the ocean off Hawaii.[28] Actor Brendan Fraser played the part of the techno-geek, proposing to actress Afton Smith on a bridge in Paris and using a self-timing Polaroid camera that clicked as he opened his coat to reveal a note pinned inside that read, "Marry me."[29]

Noncelebrity grooms have now begun emulating their Hollywood role models, proposing through advertisements in their local newspapers or on specially printed invitations that read, "You are cordially invited to marry me. Party to follow for the rest of our lives."[30] Such contrived productions affirm the groom-to-be's masculinity by granting him control of the romantic process. Gimmick proposals also encourage the couple's self-veneration by providing the bride with what are intended to be heartwarming anecdotes. The wedding keepsake diaries sold in bookstores and gift shops all open with a special section, a lined page that reads, "How He Proposed." It is here that the modern wife can record for posterity the memory of her husband's proposal. She can read and reread her entry, basking in self-satisfaction and memorializing herself as the object of romantic pursuit.

The setting of the marriage proposal is equally important to wedding specialists. "Think New York and what comes to mind? Sophistication...Elegance...Romance?" The editors of *For the Bride* magazine ask readers to ponder this question while thrilling to the fairy-tale union of business manager Grace Karsos and restaurateur Costas Kossimis, whose proposal was "straight out of a Hollywood movie set." After dinner at Manhattan's Tavern on the Green, the groom took his bride-to-be on a hansom cab ride around Central Park. "Little did Grace know that within moments of boarding the horse drawn carriage, she would be saying 'yes' to Costas' marriage proposal."[31] While some suitors strive to enhance their images as urban sophisticates, others like to prove their closeness to nature. Pastoral settings often provide the scenery for proposals of marriage. An Afrocentric groom celebrated by Sally Kilbridge and Mallory Samson in their 1999 *Real Weddings: A*

Celebration of Personal Style, Elliot Blades "swept" Rhonda Reed to a Florida beach "where he led her up a huge sand dune, got down on one knee, and proposed."[32] *Bride's* magazine tells how Scottish groom-to-be Peter Prophit proposed to furniture store manager Jackie Reinhard on a beach, the location of which is not specified, but on which he constructed the sentence, "Will You Marry Me?" in pebbles.[33] "Eric took me to the state park where we had our first date," another bride, Jill Sewell, reminisces in *Bride's* magazine. "It was warm and beautiful on the Washington coast and we walked barefoot out on the sand and collected seashells. Then he stopped in the middle of a tide pool, took me in his arms, and asked me to marry him."[34]

Daniel Harris has pointed out that nature's elements are allegorical to the romantic scene; they are images that convince us of the permanence of our vows despite our experience of modern life's fleetingly transient love affairs. As divorce statistics multiply and male-female partnerships appear increasingly impermanent, the unchanging landscape of a windswept beach or an alpine canyon suggest that our relationships are immutably stable. The natural setting also celebrates each couple's romantic isolation in a "pastoral utopia in which all rivals have been ruthlessly liquidated through a type of aesthetic genocide. The greeting-card industry's favorite Valentine images of perennially itinerant couples forever walking over sand dunes and wading through snow drifts are based on a recurrent fantasy: lovers are portrayed as refugees from their own kind, ostracized and oppressed by society at large...."[35] This misanthropic romanticism of retreat, in which one's spouse is one's only ally, permeates contemporary wedding rhetoric and is especially important in advice literature on home management. It does not dominate the very public proposal scenario. But when marriage proposals do occur in rustic settings, the wilderness suggests not only matrimonial permanence and isolation but the "naturalness" of wedlock itself. The rural landscape transforms a synthetic cultural moment into a spontaneous, primitive encounter. The man who proposes at the seashore suggests that sanctioned heterosexuality is as elemental as the ocean. The suitor whose marriage request takes place in a field on a starlit night implies that matrimony's artifices are as physical as the rotation of the planets.

II. Redeeming the Woman

The proposal scene's male agent must project control and self-assurance, managing the event like a flamboyant Broadway producer or a perfectionistic Hollywood director, or enacting the role of the noble savage who abducts his bride-to-be to an Edenic wilderness. The scene's female protagonist is scripted to play a complementary role. She must appear disoriented, overwhelmed by shock and delight. Despite the hard work and perseverance that may have actually brought her to the moment of securing male commitment, she must seem to be caught off guard. She is cast in the role of a confused Marilyn Monroe type; a woman who doesn't quite know how she's managed to attract such a lavish form of male attention, or a Maureen O'Sullivan-style stowaway whose erotic feelings are suddenly aroused by the primitive isolation of the forest or mountaintop to which her Tarzanish groom-to-be has abducted her. First and foremost, the proposal formula demands surprise on the part of today's bride-to-be; she must seem joyously stunned despite the fact that in most cases she and her companion have discussed the possibility of marriage, and the request is hardly unexpected. Judith Martin's *Miss Manners on Weddings* describes the consummate proposal scene as a female performance:

> The gentleman secretly plans a special occasion and lures the lady to conform with his plans without her guessing the purpose. If she does, she is obliged to preserve the illusion by pretending to be bewildered. The setting he has chosen has sentimental associations, or luxurious or romantic characteristics, or as many and much of these as his imagination and resources allow. He is on his most courtly and attentive behavior, but he draws things out for maximum suspense. At the great moment, he brings out the engagement ring that he has chosen and bought by himself. Perhaps he hides it somewhere clever for her to find (food seems to be the hiding place of choice), or perhaps he just produces it dramatically as he pronounces the age old formula: "Will you marry me?" She appears to be overcome with confusion and emotion. After a suitable period of blushing and protesting her amazement, she agrees to allow him to slip the ring on her finger.[36]

Martin explains that this method of agreeing to marry has increased in popularity in recent years, despite the fact that "those who practice it are not generally in their first youth or first stages of courtship."[37] She suggests that the advanced ages at which many Americans become engaged, as well as their sexual experience prior to wedlock, may create the need for elaborate ceremonies that project an idealized view of the past. The extraordinary legal power that matrimony once held, particularly in the lives of women, has largely eroded due to female access to the professions, the availability of birth control and sexual information, the perceived normalcy of premarital sex for both women and men, the common practice of cohabitation, the ease with which adults formalize and dissolve marriages, and high divorce rates. As recently as 1835 a married woman in New England, for instance, was absolutely subordinate to her husband; she could not sue, contract, or even execute a will of her own, and her wages and estate were his the moment she took his name. Her public life was so severely circumscribed that access to divorce was all but impossible.[38] At the dawn of the twenty-first century, when women enjoy more mobility than ever before, they cling tenaciously to matrimonial ritual. As its legal strictures weaken, wedlock's cultural power intensifies; contemporary nuptial life demands increasingly elaborate celebrations: larger weddings, more complex prewedding parties, more costly food, more dramatic clothing. And the pomp and circumstance must begin with a full-scale, theatrical proposal of marriage in which the bride-to-be feigns shock followed by delirious happiness.

The modern bride-to-be's amazement must in fact appear so intense that in the standard proposal scenario she loses her capacity for speech. In today's commercialized romantic ethos, incoherence is a sign of true love; amorous desire, in film, television, and advertising renders men and women speechless.[39] This trend is nowhere more powerful than in the American woman's stock response to a marriage proposal. Commercial and cinematic images alike project a woman whose silence is evidence of emotional transcendence, whose erotic and social dreams have been realized in a single moment. But the bride-to-be's reverie is not generically romantic. The illusion of shock that she produces, as well as her inarticulate bliss, constitute a very specific element of the marriage proposal: female redemption. The reverie into which the contemporary woman must slip at the sight of an engagement ring betrays relief at her rescue from the shame of spinsterhood. The emotional response so powerful that it temporarily robs her of the faculties of reason and speech announces the experience of a woman who has been, in her own mind, liberated from the opprobrium of the "single" life.

An advertisement for Scott Kay platinum engagement rings features a single photograph: the face of a woman. She clasps her hands together in front of her mouth. She smiles broadly as tears stream down her cheeks. Beneath the photograph is a cluster of engagement rings: two round diamonds and an emerald-shaped diamond, all set in platinum. "The moment is unending... /captured in a single box/whose whispered promise/was beyond all expectations," the copy reads.[40] Without any narration, the reader recognizes the elements of a proposal: a ring, a smiling woman, tears, hushed silence. "How else could two month's salary last forever?" the advertisement for De Beers' diamond engagement rings asks. The accompanying photograph shows only the bottom half of a man and a woman's face. She smiles and holds her left index finger to his mouth as if to silence him. On her ring-finger glistens a round faceted gem in a silver and gold setting.[41]

Female love necessitates either utter silence or violent sobs, as in novelist Alex Prudhomme's proposal to Sarah Buffem on a rocky patch of coastal Maine, when he set the tone for what would be a rustic wedding by handing her a ring fashioned from "dandelions, daisies, and dried out lobster antenna" and waiting for her crying to abate before initiating a discussion of the wedding details.[42] "I said, 'Say it again,'" recalls makeup artist Tracy Warbin of her Valentine's Day proposal from actor Noah Wyle: "I was bawling."[43] (Approximately one year later, at their May 6, 2000, Los Olivos, California, wedding ceremony, Warbin and Wyle had guests reply, "We do," when the minister asked if those present supported the marriage.) "Our experience of love is so colored by advertising, so mediated by the aesthetics of consumerism, that we have only the faintest sense of where our own marital troubles end and the histrionics of narrative begin," Daniel Harris observes.[44] The contemporary American proposal scene's theatrics involve female displays of shock, disorientation, and, finally, violent emotion that betrays relief at one's new social status. The marriage proposal recipient is no longer a "single" girl; she is someone's fiancée. In accordance with stylized images of joyous engagements, she swoons at what she has been told is her paramount social victory.

In screenwriter/director Jonathan Darby's 1987 drama *Hush*, a Tennessee Williams-style gothic, the upstanding Manhattan yuppie Jackson Barry (Jonathan Schaech) proposes to his architect girlfriend Helen (Gwyneth Paltrow) upon learning of her accidental pregnancy. "I'm pregnant," she announces when he comes home from work one evening. "...It seems that, uh, my diaphragm is broken." "Marry me," is his immediate response. "Oh, Jackson," she whispers, "I think I lost my job today too...." His subsequent speech is the updated proposal that appears to present an enlightened view of marriage but actually falls back on reactionary beliefs about the need to legitimize children through wedlock: "Like you said, there's no other reason to get married, unless you were pregnant. You're pregnant, so..." He kneels down: "I love you. Marry me." Helen looks down demurely, shaking her head, overcome with ineffable feeling. He leans toward her and asks, "Is that a yes?" Looking up and smiling, she can only nod in silent acquiescence.

Two scenes later we see Helen draped in a clingy white wedding gown; she says "I do" at Kilronen, her husband's horse farm set in an unnamed southern state. But she's in for trouble, of course, and that trouble comes from Kilronen's sole occupant, Helen's menacing mother in-law, Martha (Jessica Lange), a psychopathic widow who languishes in her bedroom in a black negligee shooting hot insinuating glances into a mirror. Martha is a nightmarish image of maternity. She chain smokes, speaks in a soft southern drawl that's like the purr of an evil cat, confesses to her daughter-in-law that she once had an abortion (always a sign of female amorality in popular entertainment), and caresses her son a little too lingeringly, dancing with him seductively at a New Year's Eve party. In the film's hilariously campy Oedipal plot, Martha becomes so envious of her daughter-in-law that she attempts (unsuccessfully) to kill Helen by jabbing her with a poisoned needle.

Once again, a marriage plot reveals cultural fears of maternity's dark side. The much celebrated, altruistic woman who nurtures her biological children, attuning her life to their rhythms and living to meet their needs is shown to have a monstrously needy, violently possessive flip side. It is this doppelganger that the young married couple must battle in order to attain autonomy, and, ironically, it is this woman that the young female protagonist who opts for the self-enclosure of family life will eventually become. *Hush*'s Jackson Barry starts out on the path to sexual and emotional completion in his proposal scene, when he kneels before his partner and asks for her hand, promising to make an honest woman of her while legitimizing their unborn child with the marriage covenant. He achieves maturity when he rejects his mother completely after her crazed assault. In the film's view, he must repudiate the female source of his own biological origins in order to function as a proper husband and father. When she sees him drop to one knee, "single" Helen understands this; she intuits the depth of his commitment to her as the primary, all-purpose woman in his life. She knows that she is displacing his mother and obfuscating previous friendships in accordance with the hierarchic demands of the marital system. And, like the nonfictional bride-to-be, she realizes her own social success in having secured that which parents, friends, colleagues, therapists, practical advice handbooks, novels, and television programs have told her to value above all else: male commitment. For the woman living in a conjugally organized society the marriage bond is paramount, because it rescues her from imagined social desuetude: solitude, celibacy, financial instability, and most importantly, shame based on the inability to capture a man for life. The female proposal-recipient's tidal wave of feeling that renders only the most tentative gestures possible—a barely perceptible nod of acceptance or, if she can summon forth a single syllable, a whispered "yes"— is predominantly a moment of relief.

It is the diamond ring itself that produces paroxysms of emotion in the "single" woman, as it provides tangible evidence of her new social standing, announcing her redemption to the world at large and demonstrating her respectability as well as her desirability. Whatever gadgets or props accompany the proposal, the ring soon emerges as the scene's focal point as well as the centerpiece of later anecdote. Understanding its talismanic power, advertisers promote the ring as the endpoint of each woman's dreams. "This is the ring/she's dreamed about/since she was five years old," proclaims an advertisement for Keepsake, a diamond jewelry company. Behind the image of a diamond mounted on a gold band is a photograph of two children sitting on the front porch of a house. The girl, who appears to be five years old, wears a white wedding dress complete with veil and matching handbag and clasps a makeshift bouquet of daisies. She smiles at the camera, revealing two missing front teeth. The boy, in jeans, sneakers, and a top hat, grins mischievously.[45] Keepsake here celebrates the average American girl who, even in prepubescence, playacts fantasies in preparation for what she already anticipates as the most climactic day of her life. "Whenever you steal a glance at it,/at least 3,000 times a day,/you won't remember the time/before you and he became we," reads another De Beers ad, which features a woman wearing a pear-shaped diamond on a gold band.[46] The ad celebrates the ring's ability to obliterate all distasteful memories of unmarried existence. For many jewelers the ring is a symbol of unending love. Christian Bauer's advertisement superimposes images of several diamonds with platinum bands, enhanced by what appear to be gold racing stripes, onto the photograph of a newly married couple driving down a country road in a white convertible. "Timeless..." the caption reads.[47] Some advertisers go so far as to conflate the image of the ring with wedlock itself. "Your vow to spend the rest of your life together, cast in platinum and eighteen-karat gold and set with fiery diamonds" is how Gottlieb & Sons advertise its "eternity collection" of diamond engagement rings.[48] Here, the ring is no longer a figure of love; it is love. It has been transformed from a symbol into an object indistinguishable from the nuptial relationship itself.

The wedding industry's operatives have an uncanny sense of male and female insecurities. Its advertisers cynically pitch their campaigns to Americans' deepest anxieties, addressing the male need to demonstrate earning power and aggressive sexuality and the female need for popularity and sexual desirability. The industry cynically plays to the overriding desire on the part of both men and women to conform, especially in sexual matters. The thing that finally motivates a man to buy an expensive engagement ring is the desire to blend in with the married masses. The diamond ring is not his innovation; it's what everyone else purchases, and it establishes his identity as a normal heterosexual. The desire to appear no different from the woman on her left or the woman on her right is what ultimately motivates an American woman to wear matrimony's badges of honor: the diamond ring, the gold band, and the white dress.

Jewelers glamorize these mundane imperatives by emphasizing the engagement ring's traditional status with adjectives such as *timeless* and designs like that of the "eternity" collection. This pious rhetoric imbues the engaged couple with solemn dignity, including each bride and groom-to-be in a sacred historical continuum that extends back aeons.

In fact, the diamond engagement ring is a cultural artifact of early modernity; its popularity originated in European exploration as well as the growth of luxury industries in capitalism's early stages. One of its first recorded uses is in the 1477 proposal of Archduke Maximilian of Austria to Mary of Burgundy; the ring in question had a thin flat piece of diamond shaped into an *M* to signify the bride's first initial, and this "hogback" style diamond set the trend for aristocratic marriages of the period. One hundred years later diamond cutting and polishing techniques emerged in Europe, making possible the range of designs that would eventually emerge as the engagement ring's basic shapes: round, pear, oval, marquise (oval with pointed corners), emerald, and baguette (rectangular). Despite seventeenth-century Puritan objections to the opulent diamond ring, its popularity continued throughout the early modern period among the upper and nascent middle classes. In 1761, England's King George III set the trend of the "keeper ring," a diamond band worn by Queen Charlotte next to her engagement ring in order to protect it. The eighteenth century's discovery of diamonds in Brazil increased the gem supply to Europe, further popularizing the engagement ring, as did the nineteenth century's discovery of major diamond deposits in Africa. The most popular current engagement ring, and one that is often advertised as traditional, is actually a late nineteenth-century invention: the six-pronged open mount designed by Tiffany jewelers in New York. While previous settings had concealed most of the diamond's body, the Tiffany open mount exposes the stone, which is held up to light by six prongs, displaying the gem's cut, clarity, and color.[49] It is with this expensive, boldly designed ornament that the contemporary bride-to-be announces her engagement to passersby. Through this cherished bauble, the wedding industry promises, today's bride is "connected to men and women in love in both past and future generations," as "part of a tradition of love that has spanned centuries."[50]

Marriage-hungry women tend to accept such proclamations uncritically. The newly engaged woman's relationship to her diamond is obsessive, fetishistic. Michael R. Perry confides to fellow grooms-to-be that, "A pleasing feminine quirk is the way that a woman will walk around with her left hand extended for weeks after receiving an engagement ring, greeting old friends and strangers by waving her new bauble in their faces. This kind of appreciation can make any man feel like a righteous dude...."[51] "Just watch her after she gets her ring...." snickers John Mitchell. "Watch her. It's a constant hand-grabbing, oohing and aahing fest with her girlfriends. They will continue to grab each other's hands well after you're married to view this piece of compressed carbon."[52]

Unfortunately, these assessments are fairly accurate. Contemporary brides-to-be engage in the most ostentatious displays of what they sadly believe to be enhanced social status, using their rings to advertise their success on the marriage market. Writing for *Modern Bride*, thirty-six-year-old author Suzanne Finnamore recalls her postproposal state of mind as one of "exhilaration. Also something darker: a sense of triumph. It's primal, furtive; my ovaries cracking cheap champagne. I win. That's how I feel."[53] The diamond provides tangible evidence of this author's triumph over other women on the marriage-oriented dating scene, and in Finnamore's account, the gem actually speaks to her. "The ring twinkles madly. It seems to whisper, 'Hey girl, you really deserve me.'"[54] Marg Stark's *What No One Tells the Bride* opens with an autobiographical anecdote in which her husband, a naval officer with the amusingly macho name of "Duke," perpetrated a gag proposal, faking a leg cramp on a ski slope in Taos, New Mexico, falling to one knee, and asking for the author's hand.[55] Stark, whose book purports to expose the truths concealed by marriage propagandists (e.g. wedding plans are stressful, new brides aren't always happy, men don't like to do housework), confesses that thirty minutes later she found herself in a bathroom of the nearest ski lodge, "gawking at the ring. Holding it out in front of me. Holding it up to the light. Knowing someone would ask me if it was a full karat and wondering if there was any delicate way of asking Duke if it was."[56]

While it is the source of her glory, the engagement ring is often the focal point of the newly engaged woman's anxieties as well. So thorough is our culture's distaste for unmarried women that it is difficult for those who have recently become engaged to relinquish fears of abandonment and broken promises. "Must the groom present his bride with an engagement ring at the moment of the proposal of marriage?"[57] is an inquiry in Jaclyn C. Barrett-Hirschhaut's *1000 Questions About Your Wedding*. "Although many grooms-to-be take pleasure in slipping an engagement ring on their fiancee's finger along with offering a proposal, it is certainly not a requirement for a couple when pledging their love to each other,"[58] Barrett-Hirschhaut explains. Her words seem intended to soothe the anxious bride-to-be, assuring her that even without the physical evidence of a marriage proposal, the engagement is real. Having tasted social victory and achieved sexual respectability, newly engaged women often seem terrified that it will be wrenched from their grasp. A question asked frequently of marriage advice columnists is what constitutes an "official" engagement. An anonymous bride's query to Cele Goldsmith Lalli, the editor-in-chief of *Modern Bride* magazine, is typical. Because the woman's fiance proposed in an unusual manner, does this invalidate the engagement, make it less than binding? "The manner in which your fiance proposed may be unconventional...but that does not affect the validity of his intent to ask you to be his wife. If you accepted, you are officially engaged,"[59] replies Goldsmith Lalli, assuring the anxious woman that her future is one of social and material reward. Another anonymous bride confesses that she was reluctant to share information on her financial background with her new fiance: "I had so much debt from school loans and credit cards that I thought he'd rescind his proposal."[60] "I was engaged for a year," I recently heard a young woman in the locker room of my gym remark, "and then he broke it off." "Well," the older woman she was speaking to replied, "at least you can always say someone asked you. Did he make you give back the ring?"

The central object in today's proposal scene, the diamond engagement ring is central to modern female self-definition. The woman who gazes at her gem's brilliant surfaces is not materialistic in a simple vulgar way. She is riveted to the stone as a sign of both her male partner's prowess and her own social importance. She is titillated by the attention the gem commands and anticipates the wedding day itself, when all eyes will focus on her as she proceeds up the aisle. During a recent trip to a nail salon in Manhattan, I sat next to a perky blonde woman in her midthirties. During our manicures we struck up a conversation and she explained that she had never had her nails done before. Why the sudden bit of pampering, I wondered. "Oh," she explained excitedly, "I just got engaged. Suddenly everyone wants to look at my left hand! So I don't want my skin to be dry or my nails to be crooked, now that my hands are this big focal point of attention." She then removed her left hand from the plastic bowl of warm water it had been soaking in and extended it toward me to display three square-cut diamonds mounted on a gold band.

The newly engaged woman's demands for praise of her ring are exhorbitant, and frequently the "single" woman is subjected to interrogations that focus on her bare left ring-finger. "Will I live to see you wear a ring?" my late grandmother asked me mournfully in 1992, three years before her death. "Any inkling that, you know...a ring is on the way?" inquired an anxious coworker in 1994, as I was setting up an apartment with my then boyfriend.

Since it encompasses both male and female fantasies, the engagement ring is the perfect metonym for today's gendered marriage proposal described by Diane Ackerman in a tongue-in-cheek manner: "Carol and Jerry are getting married. He pops the question, she accepts, then they happily tell their families and friends that they're tying the knot. Jerry gives Carol an engagement ring and she shows it to her girlfriends and wears it proudly on the third finger of her left hand."[61] Ackerman's flippancy reveals her sense that generic courtship, with its rules of male pursuit and female submission, is silly and outdated. But this is the very template that current wedding primers operate from. Marriage, in the wedding industry's literature, is a female dream and a male initiative. Real men propose, and gracious women—ladies—accept gracefully. Real men provide, grateful women receive. Real men offer rings, flattered women are adorned. Real men redeem, "single" girls are rescued. The marriage proposal's iconography perfectly expresses these beliefs. "Gentlemen do not wear engagement rings," declares Judith Martin emphatically in response to a query from a woman who wishes to alter some of the proposal's rules of etiquette, "And the lady's giving herself an engagement ring tends to suggest that the gentleman's role in the relationship will be negligible."[62] John Mitchell, the author of *What the Hell Is a Groom and What's He Supposed to Do?*, concurs, "Don't let her ask you...."[63] Mitchell recommends classic male-initiated proposals over dinner at a fine restaurant or a candlelit table at home, during a stroll on the beach, or at a romantic bed-and-breakfast. He mandates the courtly proposal stance: "Yes, you have to get down on one knee and *ask* her to marry you. It's very important. Believe me, her mother and friends will ask her if you got down on your knee.... It's the whole Prince Charming rigamarole."[64] Like his male colleagues in the wedding industry, Mitchell mocks the myth of marital redemption for women while seeming to enjoy it. It is deeply pleasurable, no doubt, to imagine oneself as a regal prince; monarchs, after all, are wealthy and powerful, and they command respect. The perception of oneself as a knight in shining armor who can charge into a woman's life and infuse it with significance, offering her material comfort as well as sexual pleasure, remains one of the most potent and self-gratifying male fantasies. It is a dream bolstered by the woman who schemes to alleviate her "single" status, who turns to jelly when her suitor drops to one knee, and who "oohs" and "aahs" at the sight of a diamond. But as women we would do better to deflate the myth of wedlock as redemption, contemplating rationally rather than emotionally, asking questions rather than lapsing into an ecstatic reverie, investigating the history of marriage before perpetuating that history.

Such initiatives are difficult. They are difficult because film, advertising, and popular advice literature urge women to feel rather than think; the solitary female intellectual does not exist in American popular culture. They are difficult because the gratification of a beautiful gem and a shower of accolades is so immediate. They are difficult because it is tempting to flatter and indulge the men in our lives with the fantasy that they can redeem and support us. But such fantasies quickly blur into lethal social realities. The woman who abandons herself to the drama of the proposal scene embraces a self-condemning myth. She capitulates to a society that defines her partner's proposal as the turning point of her existence, relegating all that went before to insignificance.

When she gleefully acknowledges herself as a winner in the marriage competitions, the newly engaged woman tacitly suggests that unmarried women are losers. When she experiences paroxysms of emotion over a ring that marks her as the object of male desire, the bride-to-be accords her male partner godlike power. When she celebrates her transformation from a girlfriend to a would-be bride, the contemporary woman expresses the belief in marriage as a magical alchemizing agent of female improvement. These are the ideas built into the proposal scene—a custom which, more than any other in the courtship narrative, distinguishes between "single" and married life with its rituals of noblesse oblige. They are unacceptable ideas. Women may feel flattered when their suitors drop to one knee and ask the generic question, "Will you marry me?" But the appropriate response is, "Thank you so much for asking, but, no thank you."

Significantly, John Mitchell's chapter on how to propose marriage contains a bold-faced insert, a quotation attributed to Frank Klock's *Apes and Husbands*: "When a man elopes with a girl without her parents' approval he reverts to methods of the most primitive times, marriage by capture."[65] Klock seems to encapsulate Mitchell's domestic philosophy, which is the philosophy of American cinema and advertising as well. Popular culture tells us that men and women haven't changed since prehistoric times, when some believe abduction was the norm for male-female mating arrangements. Masculinity and femininity have remained static, in this view, for roughly three million years, since hominids developed from primates, bipedalism caused the female birth canal to narrow, human infants were born tiny, immature, and helpless, and their dependence on their biological mothers brought about widespread female reliance on males. The marriage industry, again and again, claims that the modern woman's natural stance is one of passive waiting and dependence; like her Neanderthal ancestor of 100,000 B.C.E., she remains subordinate. In this archaic view, the man who grasps inherent gender roles and enacts them symbolically in his marriage proposal is the ideal groom-to-be. With his fiancée at his side he embarks upon matrimony's second rite of passage, a ritual that links the engaged couple to a rigidly gendered past: the betrothal announcement.

CHAPTER THREE

Spreading the Word: The Betrothal Announcement as a Cultural Script

> Custom, then, is the great guide of human life.
> —David Hume, *An Enquiry Concerning Human Understanding*

I. Reifying the Conjugal

Having agreed to assume a reciprocal identity, the engaged couple customarily announces its merger verbally, first to biological relatives and then to friends. Lawrence Stone has described modern life's disruption of the once-conventional marriage sequence: "the chaste courtship, followed by the formal engagement announced in the newspapers, followed by the public wedding in a church, followed by consummation, followed by pregnancy, is now no longer the norm."[1] Twentieth-century life may indeed have unsettled the orderly progression of Victorian betrothal; now sexual activity permeates courtship, formal newspaper announcements occur less frequently, and weddings are often casual, intimate, and secular. But, as we have seen, courtship is by no means open-ended. It maintains a teleological pattern in which individuals, and women in particular, anticipate the endpoint of wedlock in a way that permeates the entire dating process, shaping what could be a series of random encounters into that tangible prize so valued by current self-help experts; the "serious relationship." Within the culturally determined movement from "single" to married status the moment at which a couple announces its engagement is one of single importance. Contemporary wedding advisors are extraordinarily pious about the rituals for sharing the news, mandating a specific order for those informed.

Whether they follow these guidelines or reveal their engagements improvisationally, modern couples advertising their intentions to marry participate in a unique ritual—a moment of disclosure unlike any other.

Given their vexed relationship to matrimony, women have a special part in this drama. For the modern woman redemption is the central motif of the proposal scene, and self-congratulation is the controlling idea of the betrothal announcement. In making public her engagement the contemporary bride-to-be projects her own self-image in three distinct ways, each of which resonates with the values of her romance-saturated culture. First and foremost she proclaims her own popularity and desirability evidenced in having secured a formal commitment from a man. While extolling her social victory she conveys her own sagacity, letting her community know that she is ready to assume the serious responsibilities of adult life that her engagement ring symbolizes. Here she echoes the values of a Puritanical culture that assumes that sexual experimentation is something we outgrow when we are mature enough to embrace monogamy; a culture that fetishizes the married couple and enshrines the nuclear family. The denizen of a society whose mental health industry equates marriage with psychological fitness, the woman announcing her engagement also lets friends and relatives know that the she is emotionally "together" and therefore capable of domestic stability. Each time she reveals her status as a fiancee, today's bride-to-be targets not just the parent, aunt, uncle, friend, or colleague to whom she speaks but an audience of anonymous, imaginary listeners whom she imagines to be overjoyed by her news. Her announcement anticipates widespread cultural applause, and recipients are scripted to provide her with enthusiastic validation.

The scenic betrothal announcement is a staple of American cinema's romantic comedies, especially those of recent years. Described by *Variety* magazine as "a thoroughly engaging matrimonial romp,"[2] the 1990 film *Betsy's Wedding* for instance opens with news of an engagement and proceeds through subplots overlaid with ethnic farce (e.g. the bride comes from a large, cloying Italian extended family affiliated vaguely with mobsters while the groom's parents are stiff blue blood WASPS) to the inevitable madcap wedding scene. The film opens in the Long Island home of the Hoppers, a middle-aged couple played by Alan

Alda and Madeline Kahn. The members of this down-to-earth Italian-Jewish family, warm and hearty despite their Anglicized name, are stunned when the oldest daughter Betsy (Molly Ringwald) breaks the news of her engagement to investment banker Jake Lovell (Dylan Walsh). As they sit down to dinner she begins coyly: "Well, I sort of have some news. Jake and I are getting married." The camera pans to the faces of her astonished parents. Soon, Betsy's mother, her aunt (Catherine O'Hara), and her sister (Ally Sheedy) are encircling her, hugging, kissing, cooing, and squealing with joy. "I am so happy for you," her mother expostulates. "I knew you were going to say that!" "My little sister married. I can't believe you guys are getting married, and I can't even find a guy to play cards with. I hate you!" exclaims Betsy's sister, as her father stares into space in what appears to be a melancholy, Oedipal daze. Finally, Dad leaps into action, kissing his daughter warmly: "This is so great! You're going to have a fantastic wedding. Fantastic!" Real estate mogul Uncle Oscar (Joe Pesci) offers "the first gift," a bargain rental in one of his buildings, and the couple appears to be on its happy way. Amid the general merriment of discussing wedding details is Betsy's forlorn sister. Her brown eyes are mournful. Her mane of auburn hair frames a face tilted downward in an expression of envious self-pity. In the scene's final shot, the camera lingers on the deliberately pathetic image of this "single" girl.

Written and directed by television sitcom veteran Alda himself, *Betsy's Wedding* is pitched to the middlebrow sensibilities of well-heeled, late 1980's viewers. It upholds this happy, nutty family as a mirror into which such viewers could gaze at their own softened reflections, seeing themselves as both ethnic and American, conventional and offbeat. It is one of many American films to express what journalist Susan Faludi refers to as the "backlash" sensibility of the 1980s; a powerful media reaffirmation of domestic femininity that vilified "single" and professional women, projecting cautionary images of miserable, burnt out female careerists and advertising false man shortages and bogus infertility statistics.[3] Backlash films and television programs, which continued to abound in the 1990s, do not overtly attack the women's rights platform, although its journalists and television and radio pundits do. Rather, such entertainments juxtapose contented female homebodies with dour, angry, female loners whose ambitions obstruct romantic fulfillment and who exemplify the myriad fictitious mental disorders ascribed by psychologists to "single" female professionals despite the fact that statistics proclaim unmarried women to be mentally and physically fitter than their married counterparts.[4] Writer/director Alda affirms the loving Hopper family; the bumbling contractor father struggling to finance a wedding he cannot afford, his homemaker wife, whose stupefied expression and comatose voice are intended to charm us, the leering heavy-drinking Italian grandmother and her sidekick, the chain-smoking aunt.

Betsy herself is depicted as an adorable kook, a charming oddball. A designer of outlandish fashions, she wears outfits described by her mother as "weird": a skirt with a waist so high it starts at the armpits, vampish black sunglasses, and a blue chiffon scarf draped over her head and neck. Her husband-to-be confesses that he loves her because she is "crazy" and "strange." But the film provides no evidence of genuine nonconformity; Ringwald's Betsy holds no independent points of view and expresses no convictions that differ from those around her. She is "weird" if weirdness is comprised of having bright red hair, pouting a lot, biting one's lip, and wearing unpleasant clothing. Ringwald's character is typical of contemporary cinema's kooky bride whose putative individuality consists of a few superficial quirks. She is actually a sexual and personal conformist, becoming engaged to her lover and following strict wedding protocol by breaking the news to her parents before spreading the word to those who are presumably less important: friends, teachers, colleagues. Like the zany bride of so many backlash films, she announces her social ascendance and personal maturity to those whom society has told her are paramount, those whose social roles she has chosen to emulate in the very act of getting married: Mom and Dad. In so doing, she validates the conjugal as society's ordering principal, and the film approves of her behavior; this nutty girl, it tells us, has real family values. Like her sweet, ditsy, housewife mother, she has a heart of gold.

The plot of Betsy's wedding is exhaustingly formulaic, hearkening back to the conventional marriage plots of MGM films of the 1950s that normalized the shuttered existence of well-heeled married suburbanites. Prewedding pressures and temperamental differences strain the betrothed couple's relationship; the two threaten to separate but of course do not, and the movie ends with a happy, messy chaotic wedding sequence in which all disagreements are resolved, all hard feelings forgotten. Of course, freewheeling Betsy can't bear to wear the traditional, long-sleeved, white wedding gown that Mom has talked her into. At the last minute she takes a pair of scissors to the frock and walks down the aisle in what is finally a sleeveless number, the front of which has been cut out and inserted with panels of flowing, multicolored lace. She also wears a top hat decorated with a pink chiffon bow and lace-up cowboy boots, and guests gasp at this breach of decorum as if it comprises a radical act of self-assertion rather than a mere display of bad taste. But Betsy proceeds up the aisle on the arm of both her parents. They deliver her to the hands of her admiring groom, and the rabbi officiating tells them that they no longer belong to their parents but to each other. Despite her wacky getup, Betsy is an advocate of tradition, prioritizing the nuclear family above all else and beaming beatifically as she is symbolically transferred from one conjugal household to the next.

In her choices, behaviors, and attitudes, this typical film heroine resembles the photograph of a sartorially conservative bride who beams from the cover of Perigree's 1999 *Brides' Book of Etiquette*. A brunette in her twenties, this anonymous bride wears a white gown with a close-fitting beaded bodice, diamond tiara, diamond earrings, and a white veil, Her white gloved hands clasp a delicate white bouquet. Her expression is one of happy tranquility combined with triumphant self-satisfaction. She emblematizes one of the most popular wedding books on the market today. Authored by the editors of *Bride's Magazine*, the *Bride's Book of Etiquette* insists on parental notification before all else in the "wedding checklist": "Tell your family. Tell your friends. Tell your boss/coworkers,"[5] the handbook intones. *The Engagement Journal,* a conduct book/diary that allots space for couples to jot down their thoughts and paste momentos, insists upon the same chronology; a lined section bordered by an illustration of sepia-toned flowers reads: "Breaking the News to Our Parents." The following page allots space for the bride and groom to reminisce on paper about sharing the news with friends.[6] Matrimonial consultants draw a rigorous distinction between relatives and friend—a division that permeates all aspects of the late twentieth-century wedding, from announcement protocol to invitations to seating arrangements.

This division is nowhere more powerful than in wedding primers' mandates for betrothal announcements. Such conduct books remind modern brides and grooms that they have selected not just a person but a conjugal package, not just a lover but a paradigm for love. The decision to marry and create one's own connubial household encodes a belief in the nuclear family as a natural primary unit of social organization, and readers are urged to remember this as they take their first tentative steps in public as official couples. They must observe the strict hierarchy of informees: the bride's parents, the groom's parents, more distant relatives, friends, coworkers. They must fan outward in concentric circles until their news reaches the outermost boundaries of their acquaintance.

Handbook after handbook admonishes engaged couples to first inform the bride's parents. Her mother and father are seen as the central beneficiaries of the stupendous news, although wedding consultants provide no real explanation as to why this is so. The *Bride's Book of Etiquette* for instance instructs the modern woman to speak initially to her parents with her fiance present: "choose a time when you're all together."[7] Second in the order of things, the groom should discuss the engagement with his parents privately, "so they can express their excitement and any possible reservations."[8] The meaning of such advice is tacit but plain: as opposed to the potentially ambiguous response of a man's parents, an engaged woman's parents are assumed to experience unmitigated joy. They will inevitably feel proud that their daughter is upholding social convention, happy that she is linked in amorous partnership, relieved that she is no longer an unclaimed sexual vessel. They will imagine for her a future of companionship and social and economic security in contrast with the loneliness, deprivation, and penury that they associate with the "single" female life. Because the wedding is at some level *for* the bride's mother and father, they must learn of it first. "Traditionally—if you must know—the bride's family get first dibs on the news," states Carley Roney, the author of *The Knot's Complete Guide to Weddings in the Real World*.[9] This is because traditionally, marriage has stripped women of their legal rights while providing them with their sole option for social respectability, an option that could only thrill and relieve their mothers and fathers. Whether a bride wears a pink top hat or a diamond tiara, she accepts this legacy when she follows conventional guidelines, basking with her parents in the news of her own betrothal.

Marriage handbooks' strenuous choreography of the betrothal announcement tells the female reader that her engagement is the most climactic news of her life, that the inner circle of close family must hear the news first, and that her parents' gratification at their daughter's success on the marriage market is reasonable and laudable. These related messages transmit a larger and more basic idea to the modern bride-to-be: "you're a whole person now; your identity is no longer fragmentary, because you're embarking upon the creation of your own family." Like most of the wedding industry's covert messages, this one is retrograde and insulting to women; it is far more demeaning than the images from popular pornography that feminists continue to lament. When a bride-to-be embarks upon marriage by announcing her engagement she is immediately swept up in a tidal wave of social convention, a swell of customs affirming the family as an institution that is a woman's natural place and primary destiny. The nuclear family remains the locus of modern female gender indoctrination. It is the realm in which women are purported to attain fulfillment in the dual service capacity of mother and wife, and the wedding industry's prescriptive marriage ideals are integral to this socialization process.

Although the family is a fluid institution that reconfigures in each period, adapting to social and economic change, it has certain stable features. Adrienne Rich lists the following characteristics as constants:

> . . . the supernaturalization of the penis, its division of labor by gender, its emotional, physical, and material possessiveness, its ideal of monogamous marriage until death (and its severe penalties for adultery by the wife), the "illegitimacy" of a child born outside of wedlock, the economic dependency of women, the unpaid domestic services of the wife . . . the imprinting and continuation of heterosexual roles.[10]

Rich argues convincingly that these attributes are transcultural, permeating even the most seemingly egalitarian families in which women are allotted a high degree of independence. The are certainly the values reflected perfectly in the glossy pages of *Town and Country* magazine's wedding announcement section, an upper echelon venue for formal wedding announcements. *Town and Country* features photographs of beaming newlyweds. The husbands are clad in generic black tuxedos, the wives draped in white lace and festooned with flowers. Their attire announces that these couples are complimentary opposites representing masculinity and femininity, strength and delicacy. A joint marital title adorns each image: Mr. and Mrs. Edward Charles Gardner, Mr. and Mrs. Kenneth L. Weingrod, Mr. and Mrs. Eric Charles Berkeley, and Mr. and Mrs. Clive Anthony Walcott, with the wife's name (respectively Paula Irene Bacardi, Justine Larissa Blanda, Christina Joy Rand, and Wanjuku Juanita Barrington) tucked discreetly in parentheses beneath.[11] Female independence, *Town and Country*'s "Weddings" section tells us, has been bracketed, subordinated to the family's imperatives. Like the bride who basks in parental joy over her engagement, the women in these photographs glow, relishing their entry into the seemingly protective enclave of the nuclear family.

Perhaps *Town and Country*'s brides believe, as many women do, that the late twentieth-century family has been reformed, altered into an egalitarian institution. I've often heard my contemporaries express this point of view, and I've been struck by their optimism about matrimony. Many educated women who have come of age in the 1990s feel that the women's liberation movement has achieved its goals and that marriage is now an even playing field in which the two sexes operate as equal partners. I have noticed my female friends and colleagues' tendency to take a condescending, almost mocking view of women of the past, perceiving their mothers and grandmothers' marriages as outmoded social arrangements that have no bearing on today's jazzy, egalitarian, two-income couples.

I think all brides-to-be should temper their feelings of self-congratulation with fact. They should refer to Susan Faludi's research, data that attests to the fact that married women do not live under conditions of equality in their own homes, "where they still shoulder 70 percent of household duties—and the only major change in the last fifteen years is that now middle-class men *think* they do more around the house...."[12] Surely these numbers bear quite directly on Faludi's female employment statistics that challenge popular notions of untrammeled female progress in the workplace: As recently as 1991 80 percent of all full-time working women earned less than twenty-thousand dollars per year and were employed in support positions such as secretaries and salesclerks.[13] Gerda Lerner reports that among the nine occupations with the highest mean earnings, ranging from physician to medical science teacher, women represent from 1 to 17 percent of the practitioners. Among the five occupations with the lowest mean earnings, ranging from childcare worker to domestic, women represent from 83 to 98 percent of the occupation. Time-use studies are equally disturbing, and show that whether or not they work outside the home, women still do most of the unpaid housework; the low figure for American women is 64 percent. Everywhere statistics are available, women are predominantly responsible for caring for children and the elderly.[14] In his 1997 study of American gender roles Michael A. Messner reported on the economics of marriage:

> In two-income families the husband is far more likely to have the higher income. Women are far more likely than men to have part-time jobs; among full-time workers, women still earn about $.69 to the male's dollar and are commonly relegated to lower-paid, lower status, dead end jobs. . . . As a result, most women are not in the structural position to be able to bargain with their husbands for more egalitarian divisions of labor in the home.[15]

According to Messner the family's biased domestic economy results in women silently shouldering the "second shift" job of housekeeper and parent.[16]

While the institution of marriage is not the sole culprit of such inequity, marriage iconography does reinforce the notion of wedlock as women's primary work, projecting an explicitly antiprofessional image of femininity. The modern bride's ensemble conjures up notions of aristocratic leisure. Her attire is confining and cumbersome; the bridal gown's tight bodice and flowing train restrict mobility, evoking the prefeminist Renaissance when women of means often wore elaborate clothing that obstructed their movements to the point that they often required cadres of attendants to help them move about their own homes. The bride's entourage of maids of honor, bridesmaids, junior bridesmaids, and flower girls suggests a fantasy of courtly female dependence; a feudal period of ladylike decadence and sexual segregation in which leisurely women reclined in their chambers primping cushions, embroidering, and braiding each other's hair. Marriage handbooks celebrate this bastion of femininity. In *A Bride's Book of Wedding Traditions* Arlene Hamilton Stewart glowingly describes the bridal party prior to a hypothetical wedding: "Tissue paper flies in the air and lingerie are unfurled. Combs, brushes, cosmetics—all weaponry for beauty—come to the fore. Bridesmaids reach out to fasten gowns and pin on veils as photographers capture every teardrop and embrace."[17] Hamilton Stewart reminds us that an important member of the entourage, the flower girl, originated in the Greek wedding, where she carried sheaves of freshly cut grain that symbolized hopes for the bride's fertility.[18] The contemporary bride as an emblem then condenses several retrograde fantasies of femininity: domesticity, physical delicacy, economic dependence, frivolity, vanity, female sorority, and maternity. And these are the qualities most directly antithetical to the prerequisites of professional life that might be listed as autonomy, stamina, confidence in facing new environments, the goal of economic independence, seriousness of purpose, and the ability to work side by side with both male and female colleagues. But marriage imagery continues to glamorize women's subsidiary role, naturalizing the kind of service jobs to which American women still gravitate, positions in which subservient employees develop and express themselves through the achievements of their superiors, much as conventional wives are urged to actuate themselves through their husbands and children.

II. Deferring to Paternal Authority

The modern American wedding industry's protocols for betrothal announcements glorify female submission in shockingly overt ways. Most wedding manuals, for instance, positively acknowledge the custom of obtaining paternal consent to marry a woman. *Wedding Bells* magazine, which establishes the verbal announcement first in the order of the "Wedding Countdown," is typical: "Your first responsibility as a newly engaged couple is to inform your families and close friends of your decision. Traditionally, the bride's parents are informed first (and the groom may or may not go through the formality of asking her father's permission), then the groom's parents."[19] Arlene Hamilton Stewart writes rhapsodically of the moment of announcing one's engagement:

> Soon after a couple decides to marry, a thrilling moment awaits them—telling their parents. In the not-so-distant past, it was the responsibility of the prospective groom to ask the bride's father for her hand in marriage. This gesture has nearly vanished in this country over the past twenty years. It has been replaced by a joint venture into breaking the news, most often to the bride's family first, a social nicety which may be appreciated—and remembered—by one's future in-laws. After squeals of delight and tears of happiness, it's time to arrange one of the oldest of engagement rites: introducing one set of parents to the other.... [20]

Like most wedding advisors, the anonymous *Wedding Bells* columnist and Hamilton Stewart condense two conflicting narratives. The moment of announcement must embrace conjugality while expressing patriarchal deference. In the first narrative, that of disclosure, the couple assumes its own independence in the area of marital choice. In so doing it expresses loyalty to the modern, companionate marriage ideal, extolling the values of autonomy, self-direction, and mutual attraction that underlie contemporary matrimony. Fulfillment through an individualized, erotic, and social partnership are the values undergirding this model of wedlock. In the second scenario the couple must bow in deference to the utilitarian past, a bygone era in which men "took" brides and the central dialogue was a contractual negotiation between a man and his wife's father. Obligation and familial honor—the sense of oneself as merely a link in a greater chain of social being—are the guiding assumptions of this premodern paradigm. Wedding advisors efface these irreconcilable sets of beliefs through language that depoliticizes its subject. Both authors mention the tradition of obtaining parental consent as if it were a quaint custom of a distant and irrelevant past; a charming mannerism that may or may not be dispensed with, a "formality," a "gesture," a "social nicety," or, in the words of the *Bride's Book of Etiquette*, "old fashioned courtesy."[21]

Actually, the custom extends four thousand years back into western history crossing regional boundaries and cultures, as all marital ritual does. It provides concrete evidence of marriage as a dialogue between men; an institution in which women were bartered, passing from one man's household to the next. The sex/gender system that underscores marriage expands beyond the law, back into history and into the consciousnesses of individuals undertaking the nuptial process.

In the ancient near east, male heads of households arranged marriages for their daughters and sons. While neither men nor women had autonomy in wedlock, the social and legal codes of ancient cultures were severely skewed against married women, assigning husbands control of financial assets and thereby ensuring female dependence. The 1750 B.C.E Mesopotaminan Code of Hammurabi protected patrilineal descent in families and the inheritance rights of sons. This gender division recurs in subsequent, ancient, near eastern legal codes, finding expression in such areas as rape law, which considered a woman's husband or father to be the injured party, divorce, which was easily obtained by a husband but difficult for a wife to secure, and abortion. Middle Assyrian law in fact allowed men to expose their infant children to die but punished the woman who self-aborted with impalement, a penalty also exacted on those found guilty of high treason.[22] The notion of a woman acting to shape her own destiny through the control of her bodily functions was perceived, early on, as a lethal threat to the family's stability, and current antichoice rhetoric reiterates this position.[23] Middle Assyrian law also dictated that a bride whose betrothed died prior to the marriage be given to one of his other sons, and that a widow without sons be transferred to her husband's brother or father. In its earliest codification, the marriage system is based on the belief in women as a subspecies under necessary sexual restraint for the good of the family, for which she must serve as a perpetuating, stabilizing force, and whose male operatives must determine her future. This conviction undergirds the western family in its earliest stages, when female subordination, marriage law, and social custom flowed into each other as into a feedback loop. As Gerda Lerner explains, "The customary right of male family members (fathers, brothers, uncles) to exchange female family members in marriage antedated the development of the patriarchal family and was one of the factors leading to its ascendancy."[24]

It is within this context that we should view the Hebrew Bible, the wellspring of so much western morality and gender imagery pertaining to marriage. Negotiations for the ancient Hebrew bride's personal, sexual, and financial future were undertaken with her father, her legal guardian until she married. "If the woman is young and still under her father's roof," writes Rachel Adler, "the husband or his agents give her father a bride-price, *mohar*, for her. Whether the bride must consent is unclear."[25] The biblical term in Hebrew for marriage is in fact *lakahat*, "to take," and the word for husband—still used in modern Hebrew—is *ba'al*, master. No equivalent relational term exists for the biblical (or modern) Hebrew wife; she is merely *isha*, woman, an etymology that flows naturally from the ancient belief in wedlock as the Hebrew woman's raison d'etat and the custom of her transfer from one male-dominated household to the next. In the Books of Genesis and Exodus the biblical matriarchs are the objects of formal negotiations; the details of their consent in wedlock constitutes a baffling omission.

Genesis' familiar tale of Jacob, for instance, is overtly a story of sibling rivalry, parental error, and the value of forgiveness, but it is also a prescriptive narrative of female subordination. Jacob's polygamous household generates the original twelve tribes of Israel, and his paternal favoritism causes his sons to do the unspeakable, selling their brother Joseph into slavery. This act has cataclysmic repercussions for the Israelites, leading to their eventual enslavement in Egypt. Early in the narrative, in Genesis 29:15–19, Jacob bargains for Rachel, the one woman he loves, with her male relative, Laban, who openly reviews the pros and cons of his kinswoman's betrothal. Addressing Jacob, Laban philosophizes, "Better that I give her to you than that I should give her to an outsider."[26] The biblical narrator later details the suffering of Jacob and Rachel's son Joseph as a prisoner and a slave; Joseph's agony foreshadows Israel's degrading confinement as a slave class. But the text does not so much as acknowledge the marital imprisonment of Rachel, her sister Leah, and their two concubines within Jacob's household. Later biblical passages reflect this casual view of women as property. Deuteronomy

22:16-17 for instance envisions the hypothetical scenario of a man defending his daughter against charges of sexual promiscuity from her husband: "I gave this man my daughter to wife, but he has taken an aversion to her; so he has made up charges, saying 'I did not find your daughter a virgin.'"[27] In narrative after marriage narrative and in law after law, the Bible curtails female agency with paternal authority, describing betrothal as the "giving" of a woman to another man. Subsequent rabbinic commentators grant women the right of conjugal consent, but the biblical view of marriage as the acquisition of women (through finance, a written contract, or sexual intercourse) persists in orthodox Jewish circles to this day.

While the histories, law codes, and instructional literatures of the ancient near east may present behavioral ideals rather than historical realities, these ideals reverberate throughout western history. They resonate in the passages of modern etiquette books on marriage, exerting a strangely powerful psychic influence—an undertow pulling each bride-to-be toward a past that is presented as quaint, charming, and chivalrous; a nonspecific era in which responsible authoritative fathers consented to the marriages of chaste dutiful daughters. But those who follow the wedding industry's matrimonial guidelines should acknowledge the four-thousand-year-old historical drama that they are enacting. It is a drama that hearkens back to the Roman Republic, in which matrimony entailed the transfer of legal power over a woman from her father, brother, or uncle to her husband.[28] It recalls the Lombard Code of the seventh century, which allowed a girl's father or brother to select her husband without her consent.[29] It brings to mind Tuscany in the fourteenth and fifteenth centuries, when young girls were married off at the average age of sixteen after their parents had spent years negotiating with future husbands and in-laws.[30] It evokes the Puritanism of seventeenth century New England, when young women's marriages were subject to stringent parental approval, parents generally timed marriages according to the ages rather than the desires of their daughters, and young women were "not encouraged to cultivate the general sentiment of heterosexual love."[31] It is, quite simply, the drama of paternalistic dominance of women.

It would be unrealistic to claim that the late twentieth-century American husband-to-be who calls on his fiancée's father is acting as the eleventh-century French nobleman did when he abducted the bride of his choice and then bargained with her father, who had promised her since her childhood to another man, for the right to keep her.[32] The contemporary American bride has the power of refusal, the right of matrimonial property, the right to vote, the right (if not always the necessary access) to contraception including abortion. But it would be equally naive to believe that the historical imperatives of the past do not exert powerful influence over the present. Wedlock itself is bound up in the notion of generational continuity and the preservation of tradition and social order. Marriage propagandists emphasize the deference of youthful caprice to mature stability, of "single" isolation to conjugal commitment, of (presumably destructive) sexual impulsiveness to virtuous if predictable monogamy. The ideology of wedlock is itself inseparable from the celebration of received social conventions as evidenced by the fact that many of the customs considered traditional were in fact invented in the nineteenth century, when the big white wedding gained cultural ascendance. But because weddings are always at some level celebrations of tradition, the most newfangled rituals must shine with the patina of history; they must appear to be old. When she dons a diamond ring, announces her engagement, registers for china, compiles an invitation list, walks down the aisle on her father's arm, and is showered with rice, the modern bride cements herself legally to one person, but just as powerfully, she ties herself to a past that normalizes female dependence. When she allows herself to feel flattered by her fiancé's request for paternal consent, today's bride succumbs to romanticized notions of male dominance.

A few wedding advisors admit the problematic nature of requesting paternal consent. In her *Unofficial Guide to Planning Your Own Wedding,* Eileen Livers for instance mentions that rare woman whose husband-hunger does not eclipse her judgment: "Some women find the custom of the man asking the woman's parents for her hand in marriage romantic. Others dislike its distinctly chauvinistic implications. And some don't care—as long as a marriage proposal is imminent."[33] But most marriage consultants seem charmed by the ritual. The authors of ethnic wedding primers are by far the most positive about the act of obtaining parental permission, presenting the custom in sentimental terms, as if it were a means of maintaining old world character. Shu Shu Costa's *Wild Geese and Tea: An Asian American Wedding Planner* advises grooms to initially defer to their bride's parents: "In China, families first reported a betrothal to the ancestors by offering incense, candles, wine, and fruit on the ancestral alters. While it is no longer mandatory for a man to ask his fiancée's father for her hand, his discussing his intentions with her family shows courtesy and respect—especially for Asian families."[34] Harriette Cole's *Jumping the Broom: The African American Wedding Planner* likewise praises the deference to patriarchy in African tribal culture:

> For the Akan of Ghana in West Africa, according to Dr. Kwasi Ohene-Bekoe...the proposal begins with the father of the young man handling all of the negotiations. "The man's father would go to the wife's father, talk to him, tell him what he wants," he explains. "Then the woman's father would say that he will get back in touch with him. In a couple of weeks, her family would respond saying 'It's okay. We give our blessings.'"...Although the actual steps to getting engaged may vary from region to region, Ohene-Bekoe assures us that parental involvement is a given throughout the continent....The way to organize your engagement announcement here in America should entail just as much respect, if less ceremony.[35]

Built into both Costa and Cole's account is the peculiar assumption that tribal cultures—often the most rigidly oppressive to women—are superior because they are nonwestern. According to this logic any demonstration of ethnic pride, even one that denigrates one's own social status, is somehow bold, unique, and empowering.

The editors of *Signature Bride Magazine* concur:

> Among the Koro people of Africa, the aspiring groom pays three ritual visits to the family of the girl he wishes to marry. On the first visit he gives them three shillings; on the second, four shillings; on the third, five shillings. He is then asked to bring three or four pounds and ten bundles of corn. If he cannot complete these payments in one year, he continues to make annual installments until he has given the full amount.[36]

Surely, we should not romanticize the custom of the bride-price, regardless of its regional origin. When a man of any nation, race, or ethnicity requests permission to marry a woman, he assumes—without stating— that the woman has no agency, that she is unwilling or unable to speak for herself, to articulate her own goals and desires. Whether he is African, Asian, or European, the man who trades foodstuffs for a female partner objectifies her through the process of barter. And when a future husband addresses his request to a woman's father, he approaches her with anything but the "respect" championed by marriage advisors. His "ceremony" conveys the tacit message that she is still a child. Yet ethnically oriented wedding primers urge brides and grooms to connect with their respective traditions, reveling in national rituals, even if these rituals are shamefully sexist. The *Signature Bride* staff juxtaposes its blurb on Koro African courtship with an admonition to contemporary black American women: "Your fiancé may have secured *your* 'yes' first and now wants to make the 'Traditional' gesture. There is no right or wrong way to proceed in these matters of the heart. If your parents know him and like him, it's perfectly appropriate for him to go to them for their blessing—alone if he wishes, or with his happy bride-to-be at his side."[37] Framed in quotation marks, the word tradition is here made anomalous; it is presented as something quirky and morally indeterminate. But since women are rational multidimensional creatures who have been *traditionally* categorized as members of a subspecies, and since the custom of bargaining for women in marriage stems from this degraded social position, it is deeply wrong to ask for one's fiancée's hand. It is not chivalrous, it is not quaint, and it is not morally or politically neutral. And the custom does not distinguish one ethnically, reviving lost national pride. Patriarchal deference in marriage is transcultural, common to western and nonwestern nations, European and non-European societies. The advice aimed at black readers is in fact echoed in that most white bread of all wedding guidebooks, *The Christian Wedding Planner*. Addressing the contemporary, Christian bride-to-be, this manual intones, "Encourage your fiancé and your father to have a word together. This could be done by making an appointment at your home or the office.... This is a Christian ceremony of respect and courtesy, and it will be appreciated by all involved."[38]

It is perhaps not surprising that those wedding authors who can most accurately be identified as zany concur with their minority and sectarian coauthors. John Mitchell's *What the Hell is a Groom and What's He Supposed to Do?* suggests obtaining permission from the bride's father and subsequently informing friends:

> You may be wondering about asking her father for her hand in marriage. I believe that asking her father is very admirable, and shows concern for tradition and for her family. But you better ask her first, and make sure she accepts the ring.... Okay it's done. You're engaged. You were smart and didn't tell too many people beforehand, just in case she said no. Now you must begin the tedious, all-day affair of telling people the big news. Happy! Make sure you "have a smile in your voice." Priority number one: Call her parents and any stepparents. (You may ask her father for her hand: "I've asked your daughter to marry me. I hope we have your blessing." More brownie points earned.) Next, call your parents; then let the chips fall where they may. Don't mix up the order... make sure her parents are the first ones to know.[39]

As we have seen, marriage handbooks written for husbands-to-be tend to flatter their readers, elevating men above the matrimonial scenario. Mitchell's planner is in this sense unexceptional. Its facetious title makes explicit the belief in marriage as a female affair, a venue for feminine self-display, a drawn out series of vaguely absurd rituals that the good-natured groom tolerates. While bridal primers urge women to enact their marital roles with pious earnestness, Mitchell encourages contemporary grooms to go through the motions of marital custom with a kind of patient restraint, indulging their fiancées as if these women were adorable, silly, slightly vicious pets. In encouraging the newly engaged man to attempt to sound happy, Mitchell tacitly conveys the idea that betrothal is a female victory in which the groom-to-be has been caught, ensnared, roped in. But Mitchell's sneering tone, which invites the male reader to laugh affectionately at these outdated nuptial rituals, also assures the contemporary groom that his engagement has not compromised his autonomy. Informing friends is for the bride-to-be a heightened drama, tantamount to announcing that she has become a complete person, but for her superior male partner it is a "tedious all-day affair" in which he must feign ecstasy. As in most wedding literature, when the noun *tradition* appears in regard to the betrothal request from one's future father-in-law, it does so insidiously. The notion of tradition—old things that are somehow made good by their oldness—is collapsed into the vague concept of familial respect. This imprecision and condensation have a palliating effect. Showing concern for one's partner's relatives while nodding deferentially in the direction of a nonspecific past seems harmless enough, a way to achieve popularity with one's fiancée's family, earning "brownie points." Omitting the tradition's origins, Mitchell transforms it from an act in which the bride is designated a piece of property to an amusingly benign, old world custom.

Otherwise diverse wedding primers describe the custom of approaching a woman's father and asking for her hand in similar terms. Whether the guidebook is blandly generic, ethnically oriented, religious, or secular, whether it is aimed at brides or at grooms, the treatment is consistent. The wedding announcement is mentioned in the same breath as the betrothal request, as if these antagonistic narratives blend into a seamlessly coherent whole. Among the planners, diction is consistent: *custom, ceremony, respect,* and *tradition* are the recurrent nouns. And these nouns are never qualified. The ritual of obtaining parental consent to marry a woman—a custom as old as western civilization itself—is glossed over with peculiar apathy.

Inquiries and reminiscences by grooms and brides themselves are as complacent as are the idealized standards projected by matrimonial consultants. Model Donovan Leitch recalls his botched proposal to fellow model Kirsty Hume—or rather, to her father: "I wanted to do it the old-fashioned way," he explains, in a recent issue of *Talk* magazine: "I went into the study where her dad was—an older, conservative Scot. Very intimidating guy. And I swear I sat there for, like, half an hour, talking about a bunch of shit that I didn't know about. Like soccer, football. Finally, Kirsty walked into the room and asked, 'Have you told him yet?'"[40] "I am twenty-five, divorced, and plan to be married again shortly. My fiancé is thirty and has been divorced for two years. Should he talk to my parents and ask their permission and tell them our plans, or should we tell them together?" queries an anxious bride in Elizabeth L. Post's

Emily Post on Second Weddings.[41] This anonymous divorcee does not consider the possibility of asking her fiancé's parents for their permission to "take" him in marriage, despite the fact that both are adults; adults with the sexual and practical experience of prior relationships behind them, adults who stand as equals before the American legal system. "In with the old and out with the new" is how *Modern Bride* magazine describes the recent nuptials of computer software consultants Michael Hunt and Ingrid Batiste, who were engaged nine months after meeting each other. But the couple's marital protocols were not new; they were old in the worst sense of the word. Before approaching his bride-to-be, Michael secured her father's approval. "I didn't know he had even talked to my Dad—I thought that was so old-fashioned and very special," Batiste rhapsodizes.[42]

III. Obscuring Motivation

Women who announce their engagements to friends inevitably do so in a tone of social victory that anticipates the regal production of the wedding procession in which the bride appears at center stage, bathed in ethereal light. While the modern couple approaching the bride's parents enacts a drama of filial piety, the contemporary bride announcing her engagement to other women flaunts her elevated social status. I had been out of college for three or four years when I began experiencing a repeated encounter. In the gym, in the supermarket, on the street, in synagogue, at the movies, or in the library I would meet an old female friend, colleague, fellow alumnus, or acquaintance, often someone I barely knew. We would acknowledge each other with the usual niceties, ask a few preliminary questions about work and future plans before she would announce her engagement, extending her left hand to display a diamond ring while anticipating an ecstatic response, an outburst of praise and envious congratulations.

This, I began to realize, was not a spontaneous encounter; it was a culturally scripted moment in which I was mandated to produce the "squeals of delight" described by Arlene Hamilton Stewart and other wedding propagandists. It was a stock moment of pulp novels, television soap operas, and cinematic romances. I was cast in the role of the excited recipient of stupendous news, and for a time I was willing to play this part, shrieking, congratulating, hugging, kissing, squeezing, admiring the ring, feigning a bit of envy, inquiring as to the date of the big day. As my readings in the history of wedlock progressed and my understanding of marital inequity broadened, I found it increasingly difficult to appear delighted about what seemed to me to be a disappointingly conventional choice. I became less enthusiastic in my replies, offering the stock response of, "all the best to you." And then at a certain point I relinquished altogether the role of the thrilled recipient of betrothal news. For the past two years, when I have met a woman who tells me that she is engaged to be married, advertising her new social standing with an extended, diamond-clad hand, I reply with the honest question, "Why?"

I have been repeatedly surprised by the total disorientation of brides-to-be in the face of this question. Women seem struck dumb by this simplest inquiry, perhaps because any departure from an exchange determined by rules of social decorum is jarring. But I also believe that in our marriage-obsessed culture the vast majority of engaged women have never seriously reflected upon this question.

The more composed women with whom I've spoken generally answer my question in one of two ways. They claim that they feel the need to make a commitment to their male partners, that, in the words of one acquaintance, "It's time to make a decision." Or they say that they want to have children. What continues to perplex me about these responses is that they totally evade the issue of matrimony. Although the impulse to "commit" to one's lover is not one that I am especially sympathetic to, it seems quite possible to undertake such an agreement privately, apart from the spectatorship of friends and relatives, without the elaborate legal and bureaucratic procedures of wedlock and certainly without the stupendous costs of a wedding.[43] Likewise, creating a child entails the private act of sexual intercourse between two adults; no jewelry, invitations, party favors, licenses, toasts, or vows are necessary. The sole requirement of this project is sex without contraception.

The standard answers given by brides are in fact incomplete. When a woman says that she is getting married to make a commitment and to receive one, she tells a partial truth. An accurate answer would be that she wishes to make a particular kind of commitment; a contract that has been presented to her as the only substantive commitment possible. It is an agreement between herself and her culture as much as it is a commitment between two lovers. It is rooted in historical custom and entails many privileges and apparent securities. I believe that American women take this step primarily in order to remain in sync with the world around them, because that is how most people are comfortable living. This is not a glamorous reason for undertaking any serious endeavor, and it is therefore most often left unsaid. But it is evidenced in the fact that when a contemporary woman yokes herself to one man she does so publicly, so that everyone knows she is a bride, a wife, a desirable woman, a popular woman, a good girl, all those things that we are supposed to want to be. With its personalized ceremonies, lengthy guest lists, photography sessions, elaborate speeches, toasts, and videotapes, current marriage is an act of exhibitionism as much as it is an act of contract. It transforms that which began privately into a public spectacle—a binge of self-congratulations that actually cheapens the sentiment between two people. It is worth remembering that this popular ritual is not the only way that a man and a woman can convey their feelings to each other, expressing hope for a long-term friendship, although it has conventionally been treated as such.

When women claim that they are marrying in order to become mothers they again obfuscate. A more complete statement would be that they are marrying to become mothers within patriarchy's definition of motherhood, in which all children born outside the sanctioned conjugal home are stigmatized. They are embracing the notion of state-controlled sexuality. They are committing to the idea of the enclosed nuclear family in which parents possess their progeny and motherhood is primary, elemental. "Institutionalized motherhood," writes Adrienne Rich, "demands of women maternal 'instinct' rather than intelligence, selflessness rather than self-realization, relation to others rather than the creation of self. Motherhood is 'sacred' so long as its offspring are 'legitimate'—that is, as long as the child bears the name of the father who legally controls its mother."[44] Indeed, it might be possible to create a different template for motherhood in which women were not subject to such taxing demands and children were not classified as either respectable or nonrespectable. Detaching the act of procreation from the social apparatus of wedlock would be a necessary first step in this enterprise.

A bride with whom I recently spoke explained that she was marrying as a means of ensuring lifelong sexual companionship. She told me that she likes sex on a regular basis and is unwilling to seek it out in bars, nightclubs, or parties, exposing herself to sexual diseases and/or abuse at the hands of strangers. She loves her fiancé and with him enjoys an active sex life as well as a close personal friendship. When I asked why she felt it necessary to involve ritual and law in her sexual partnership, she explained that societal intervention in the form of a license, a contract, and a public ceremony would keep them on their toes, forcing them to work at the relationship. "If we made our vows privately we wouldn't really take them seriously. Somehow, with all the people involved, there's more at stake."

More than any defense I've encountered, this explanation expresses the essence of contemporary marriage. Drained of religious content, the marital ideal has been psychologized, reoutfitted to the emotional and physical needs of men and women in the aftermath of the sexual revolution. In Jewish tradition, marriage is a *mitzvah*, a sanctifying commandment. Talmudic interpretations of the biblical injunction to procreate stress matrimony with such adages as "God waits impatiently for man to marry," and "One who does not marry dwells without blessing and without goodness."[45] In Catholic tradition marriage is one of the Church's seven sacraments and is integral to God's cosmology as represented in the Book of Genesis. The marriage bond is indissoluble and demanding of fidelity: "From a valid marriage arises a *bond* between the spouses, which by its very nature is perpetual and exclusive; furthermore, in a Christian marriage the spouses are strengthened . . . consecrated for the duties and the dignity of their state *by a special sacrament*," the catechism reads.[46] These religious models stress obedience, either to the survival needs of a people or the theology of a church. By contrast, current marriage invokes no authority but the self; it is a psychological boon, a positive development in the emotional and sexual health of both partners defined, centrally, by their support for each other.

Advocates of secular wedlock don't believe that the marriage vows should permanently bind unhappy couples. They tend to favor no-fault divorce and to oppose government sponsored "save the family" initiatives. Such modern brides and grooms praise matrimony as a health-inducing agent that is salutary to the individual but still very much a matter of personal choice. But they cannot relinquish the utilitarian model in which wedlock serves a divine plan and/or stabilizes a society. They therefore attempt to fuse two irreconcilable views of conjugality with a circular logic in which people must be socially pressured to adhere to that which they most want. Wedlock should somehow get us to continue desiring what's really good for us. This uneasy fusion of romantic and utilitarian matrimony produces the image of adults as overgrown children who need to be badgered and coaxed into taking the next bite of nutritious food, embracing that which is emotionally fortifying—and gratifying. But this common defense of marriage begs the fundamental question, if we stop wanting sex and companionship with a particular person, why shouldn't we be able to void our commitment to our partner? And once this right is granted, as it has been in the twentieth century, why drag the courts, the Church, and our friends into our bedrooms in the first place?

On the eve of the millennium the kooky bride resurfaced in popular cinematic comedy. An updated version of the backlash good girl appeared in the 1999 hit film *Notting Hill*, which featured the British actor Hugh Grant as William Thacker, the owner of a London bookstore, and Julia Roberts as Anna Scott, the Hollywood star who is his love interest. After mishaps and miscommunications, lapses of time during which she is absent and he cracks jokes to conceal his broken heart, these two finally come together, recycling a stale Hollywood plot in which the wealthy celebrity can only find real happiness with one of the "little people," a man who understands her true value. As is de riguer in such narratives, a romantic subplot features the pairing of two secondary characters, and it is here that the kooky bride emerges. Thacker's younger sister Honey (Emma Chambers) is, like her 1980's predecessor, a redhead given to sartorial excess. She wears garish thrift-shop dresses in tones of orange and pink and pins her hair in ragged strips on top of her head. This pint-sized, bug-eyed record store employee complains early in the film, "No one will marry me, because my buzzies have actually started shrinking." But as her staid brother closes in on romantic success, she too finds social completion in the figure of a moronic Welshman named Spike (Rhys Ifans), a gangling, uncoordinated buffoon who eats mayonnaise straight from the jar, masturbates to the British tabloids, and wears tee-shirts with slogans like "I Love Blood," and "Fancy A Fuck?" Honey proclaims her engagement to her brother and their group of friends: "Since it's an evening of announcements, I've also got one. I've decided to get engaged. I've found myself a nice, slightly odd-looking bloke, who I know is going to make me happy for the rest of my life." Fielding questions from the delighted group, she describes her fiancé as "an artist with brilliant prospects"; taken aback by the news, Spike gazes at her mooney eyed and whispers, "Groovy."

In this scene it is not the bride's parents who squeal with delight at the thought of their daughter's sexual containment. A surrogate family of friends congratulates the bride-to-be, but these friends play parental roles and operate from the same retrograde assumptions that parents might; they perceive Honey's future husband as a provider and inquire as to his financial prospects. They celebrate the fact that she will not languish as an old maid on the marriage market. They valorize her creation of a conjugal household. As in the 1980's cinematic engagement scene, the bride's unusual appearance is intended to distract viewers from a set of reactionary sentiments. Unconventional hair and clothing are used as substitutes for independent thought, enabling viewers to reassure themselves that Honey—and girls like her—don't lose their individuality in marriage. *Notting Hill*'s penultimate scene is a wedding of the two principals. Guests meander about a manicured English lawn; beneath a billowing tent, Julia Roberts undulates in a flowing bridal gown and diamond tiara. Amid the glamorous guests, grungy Spike and offbeat Honey slow dance, locked in an incongruous passionate embrace in which her feet do not touch the dance floor. He wears an electric blue, disco-style suit and she wears another orange thrift-shop frock. This Papageno, the film tells us, has found his Papagena, and all is right with the world. The myth of marital inevitability maintains its power; in a narrative of multiple weddings each person obtains earthly happiness by finding and joining with his or her other half.

Filmed versions of the marriage plot equate personal happiness with amorous stability, affirming the married couple as a cell in the larger societal body, the most basic building block for what we have been told is a healthy culture. In fact such couplings appear to me to be socially divisive, motivated by an ideology that demands exclusion and isolation, in which the love partner is envisioned as a paramount ally and the home is seen as a fortress to be guarded. I wish that monogamy was not so heavily prescribed in this culture, that people didn't feel the need to own each other sexually. I wish that men and women didn't succumb to the pressure to make unrealistic lifelong commitments to their lovers and to produce their amorous relationships with costumes, decorations, and music, as if such liaisons were Broadway shows. I wish that women without lovers and biological children were not made to feel that their lives were barren. I wish that children grew up in more fluid, open-ended living arrangements, because I believe the stiflingly intimate conditions of today's isolated nuclear family to be deeply unhealthy. But if two heterosexual partners yearn for the immediate security of promised permanence, they can exchange vows or letters privately. If they want to create children, they can do so. Popular culture equates institution with experience, telling women that wedlock is the natural outcome of love and inseparable from it and that matrimony is the sole precondition for parenting. But wedlock's laws and rituals are humanly shaped cultural artifacts that can be disposed of, replaced.

In the most famous passage of Plato's *Republic* a group of cave dwellers sits facing a wall onto which fire-lit images are projected. Never having stepped out of their cave to view the sun, the cave denizens do not know that these images are shadows and mistake them for substance, reality. And in the darkness what they see reflects only partial truth, a fleeting one-dimensional version of the world.[47] Most contemporary American women dwell in epistemological darkness, viewing matrimony as natural rather than artificial, timeless rather than historical, spontaneous rather than deliberate, benignly egalitarian rather than maliciously sexist. Such women are not dishonest when they cite commitment, sexual enjoyment, motherhood, and emotional companionship as motivations for wedlock. Our culture tells us that we cannot enjoy these pleasures without matrimony, so that to many wedlock is not an institution but a totality that encompasses all meaningful personal goals. But when we acknowledge that marriage is not love, friendship, sex, parenthood, or permanence but a set of particular social conditions under which to pursue these goals, we make an important perceptual leap.

With its admonitions to distinguish sharply between friends and nonrelatives and its predilection for filial piety, marital advice literature conveys the message that every woman who does not marry is an isolate who lacks a circle of primary people to emulate, defer to, please, be first with, reward and receive rewards from. The conventional wedding announcement is one detail of an enormous cultural projection that depicts the engaged woman glowingly as a fulfilled future wife, a loving daughter, a joyfully anticipating mother-to-be. Her cautionary shadow, the dark, flickering image of the "single" woman is by contrast empty, barren, lacking in life's emotional bounty, a fragment. Popular film bolsters these perceptions, setting the tone for what Susan Faludi refers to as a time of "isolation and crushing conformism,"[48] when "finding a safe harbor inevitably becomes a more important course than bucking social currents. Keeping peace with the particular man in one's life becomes more important than battling the mass male culture...."[49] Faludi asserts that, "To expect each woman, in such a time of isolation, to brave a solitary feminist stand is asking too much."[50] I disagree. When we as women summon the courage to step out of romantic patriarchy's cave and view wedlock in the illuminating light of historical fact, we can begin to perceive the difference between experience and social prescription. We can cast off oppressive definitions and view ourselves as neither wives nor old maids, neither married nor "single." And we can discover our own potential in new ways as we emerge from our gender's adolescence. But we must first become willing to view marriage realistically; to relinquish its conventional securities, to part with the pleasure of dramatic self-presentation that it affords. It is this pleasure that informs the engaged couple's first formal, written exercise as a social team: the wedding invitation, to which we shall now turn to explore how today's bride and groom publicize their wedding while managing their cultural anxieties about matrimony itself.

CHAPTER FOUR

"We Request the Pleasure of Your Company" The Crisis in Contemporary Wedding Invitations

> And one may as well be single if the wedding is not to be in print.
>
> —Jane Austen, letter to Anna LeFroy

WITH THE RARITY of printed newspaper announcements[1] most contemporary American couples proclaim their engagements to the world at large in a very specific way: through an invitation to friends, relatives, and colleagues to attend a wedding ceremony. Ostensibly the invitation is a functional document that beckons friends to a gathering, providing information as to the time, place, and location of the event while suggesting the standards of taste and decorum to which it will adhere; what wedding consultants frequently refer to as the wedding "theme." But today's wedding invitation is not a purely pragmatic text; it is a document of profound cultural significance. It provides the first glimpse of its authors in the act of self-presentation as a couple. We have all experienced the disorientation of receiving wedding invitations that seem to have been written in another era and posted from a faraway kingdom. Such documents often come from intimate friends with whom we've shared our most embarrassing moments, but our friends include their middle names, surnames, and titles, as if we might mistake them for someone else. They request "the honor" of our "presence" as well as "the favor of a reply," as if we were distant acquaintances or members of the aristocracy. And they enhance their proposals with lavish visual imagery.

131

Our engaged friend who writes to us on shimmering pearl-colored paper inscribed with black gothic lettering or on linen white stationery decorated with tendrils of green ivy, or on a cream-colored card embossed with the image of a heart comprised of pink seashells, does not do so simply as our friend. She writes in an elevated tone, as a bride who has ascended to a position of social supremacy. Her invitation, with its lofty, antiquated diction and ornate script expresses her new social standing. The odd sensation of reading epistles from those closest to us written in stilted patrician language is unique to the wedding invitee.

Contemporary wedding invitations are manufactured by printers adept at seducing brides and grooms with notions of elegance while simultaneously indulging these couple's most self-flattering fantasies. One such company, Invitations by Dawn, operates through a mail-order wedding invitation catalog whose cover features the photograph of a bride clad in white and clutching a bouquet. Above her the phrase, "He loves me...He loves me not...He loves me...He loves me not..." is printed in a serpentine line of green letters. This catalog alludes rhapsodically to the epiphanic process of opening a wedding invitation:

> Imagine...you open the mailbox and among the bills and magazines is...a large envelope of rich ecru paper elegantly addressed in calligraphy. Inside, a gold-lined inner envelope holds an embossed invitation card of thick ecru paper accented with gold foil. Wording in gold script invites you to a cathedral wedding at five o'clock in the afternoon. And the enclosure card invites you to a dinner and dance at an exclusive club.[2]

Elegance, opulence, and exclusivity are the standards praised by wedding invitation literature; like all pieces of wedding iconography, the invitation promotes matrimony's magical qualities. Wedding invitation authors are encouraged to cast a spell by beckoning to friends from the fairy-tale kingdom of matrimony, drawing a deliberate contrast between the recipient's drab quotidian existence of paying bills and discarding junk mail and the enchanted wedding day to which he or she has been summoned. The bride who sends Dawn's "embossed rosebud" invitation printed on "Forever Floral" paper does not merely announce the particulars of a party. She publicizes her success in securing a man, answering the question of marital commitment that reverberates throughout the dating process and hovers above the glowing countenance of Dawn's anonymous bride. Rexcraft, another popular catalog, narrates the awed anticipation of the wedding entourage:

> They've heard the news about your wedding...now your friends and relatives are just *waiting* to see what invitation they'll receive. Because your invitations not only announce the date, time, place, and hosts of your ceremony, they set the tone for your entire celebration! So whether your theme is classic or traditional, unique and new, bright and colorful, or absolutely YOU, Rexcraft will have an invitation—or several—to match the occasion![3]

Rexcraft's copy exemplifies the general trend on the part of such merchants to enshrine the invitation as a mimetic device—a mirror of each couple's wedding, which, like the nuptial itself, is determined by personal style. Toward this end the catalog features a baffling array of choices, from ecru taupe-tinted paper with a filigree border to sheer stationery, the text of which is framed by a wallpaperlike pattern of gray diamonds, to a translucent invitation with a swirling design across its front panel that reads, "From This Day Forward, to Have and to Hold." As is the case with most wedding literature, the catalog's copy is addressed only to brides, assuming the wedding production to be a female undertaking. Rexcraft explicates the nuances of paper color for the perplexed wife to be: "Many brides ask us 'What *IS* the difference between white, bright white, and ecru paper?' We've described each paper color below and throughout the catalog have listed each invitation's color after its size."[4] Typically, the authors mollify and flatter the anxious bride, assuring her that the conventional act of marriage does not detract in any way from her uniqueness. The wedding invitation can in fact showcase her individuality, Rexcraft promises. The contemporary printer asserts that every component of the invitation expresses the bride's distinct personality. Even the most seemingly banal portion of the invitation—the envelope for instance—makes a statement about her as an extraordinary person, conveying her essence, her style, the special joie de vivre that sets her apart from the crowd: "Envelopes—just for addressing and mailing your invitations, right? Wrong! With Rexcraft, even your envelopes can be an expression of your style and can coordinate with your wedding's theme, spirit, and color scheme!"[5]

Yet despite the frantic emphasis that manufacturers like Rexcraft place on individuality, the invitation remains uniform in terms of the cultural standards that it prescribes. When we acknowledge the tension in current wedding invitation literature—and in the invitations themselves—between the stated goal of individuation and the actual conformist message, we uncover one of the central paradoxes of today's marriage mystique. The wedding invitation is an ideological document. Without explicitly formulating ideas, the invitation suggests a body of assumptions that command immediate, inarticulate, emotional assent. Perhaps more than any other accouterment, the formal invitation belies the myth of marital privacy. The notion of love burgeoning between a man and a woman and flowing spontaneously into wedlock is contravened by the invitation, which features not just the couple but its family members. Invitations are rarely sent from the bride and groom independently. They generally include the names of one or both sets of parents, demonstrating, once again, the social forces that determine marital choice and the unspoken convictions to which betrothed couples adhere. Probably without awareness on the part of its authors, the invitation celebrates the conjugal as the ordering principal of society, much as the betrothal process has; it could be said, in fact, to codify beliefs expressed verbally in the engagement announcement. The wedding invitation announces the altered status of a relationship, joyously proclaiming the intention of two individuals to merge into a social unit; a "couple." And it depicts the bride and groom's primary affiliations—their familial ties—and their emulation of respective sets of parents through the act of marriage. Since weddings are generally sponsored by a parent or set of parents, the invitation as well projects a set of parental self-perceptions and goals for the young couple—a sort of abbreviated wish list for nuptial happiness. In the contemporary wedding invitation these overlapping functions are often at odds with each other. Conflicting pieces of self-advertisement and contradictory agendas create internal incoherence—a kind of confusion that gives the present-day invitation its incongruous tone.

Although current wedding invitations have great diversity in terms of layout, wording, and design, they consistently prescribe certain standards: companionate marriage as an expression of romantic love and the primacy of biological family. The wedding is inevitably described as "a celebration," "a day of joy," or "a sacrament" that will be enhanced by the "honor" (in the case of religious ceremonies) or "pleasure" (for secular events) of the recipient's company. The visual repetition of the names of a series of married couples enforces the idea of complementary heterosexual partnership as natural and inevitable. Etched on expensive marbled paper or on creamy stationery bordered with lace trim, wedding invitations as well suggest the pomp and circumstance of marriage, hinting at wealth or at least financial success. They advertise privilege and self-satisfaction, projecting an image of the bride and groom as people who have "arrived" and are comfortable with their place in society. The wedding invitation's very uniformity suggests a man and woman embracing, not just each other, but a set of conventions; a package of middle-class, heterosexual, and romantic privileges that reify each other.

Yet despite its self-venerating tone, the wedding invitation is a document that bears traces of cultural anxiety. Upon close inspection the facade of each invitation—its neutral colors, careful wording, and graceful calligraphy—cracks. The wedding invitation advertises uniformity in an age of affective individualism. It promotes female delicacy and dependence in an age of nascent egalitarianism. It reinforces the closed nuclear family in an age in which, some suggest, the eco-family has begun to replace the conjugal family; mobility has made it possible for people to live at great distances from their parents, and education, shared professional life, and spiritual fellowships such as twelve-step programs have fostered a set of significant relationships that threaten to gain on or in some cases even to eclipse familial ties. The wedding invitation declares the permanence of marriage at the very historical moment at which divorce rates are at their highest and no-fault divorces can be obtained through a simple administrative procedure. (The wedding's parental sponsors, often themselves the refugees of broken marriages, induce guests to witness a purportedly irrevocable union between a man and a woman.) The wedding invitation sanctions heterosexuality in the age of burgeoning gay liberation. Betrothed couples do not—cannot—

acknowledge these contradictions, and the formulaic wedding invitation obscures them beneath a veneer of uniformity that announces marriage to be laudable, permanent, and timelessly stable. But this very uniformity seems to generate further anxiety in the contemporary bride or groom afraid of being perceived as ordinary, so that it is now de rigueur for couples to depart from the standard invitation, embellishing the document with decorative ornamentation intended to express their personalities.

Like many wedding rituals, the invitation's origins are obscured by folklore and mythmaking, and its history is a narrative of emerging technologies and changing cultural attitudes. Prior to the printing press' invention, in England, when the nuptial celebration was a day of gaming and feasting for each rural village, weddings were announced verbally by bidders, men hired to promote each celebration to the inhabitants of its respective town. At an indeterminate point in the late Middle Ages wealthy families began purchasing wedding invitations, many of which were handwritten by monks, the church representatives who had maintained records of royal weddings. The early seventeenth century gave rise to the copper plate invitation, which, like the current thermographed invitation, simulates the appearance of calligraphy, using antique, roman and florid, gothic fonts.[6] By the eighteenth and nineteenth centuries, couple-oriented Puritan wedlock had become the standard and the ceremony's focus had shifted from the community to the couple itself. Invitations then became integral to what John Gillis has called the "big white wedding,"[7] an originally nineteenth-century ceremony that extolled matrimony as the ordering force of society and the mainstay of personal happiness, venerating each couple in a large costly celebration said to epitomize tradition. Victorians in fact considered a wedding of fifty or less small enough to merit handwritten invitations, and the parents of the bride hired and dispensed servants or couriers to deliver the documents.[8] Printed in black ink, on pale paper, the text of a standard nineteenth-century wedding invitation reads as follows:

Mr. and Mrs. G.W. Pierson
request the pleasure of your presence at the
marriage of their daughter
Wednesday, June 14th, 1876

at their residence
Clifton Springs, New York
Ceremony at 7:00 P.M.
Justin Bagley   Minnie Pierson[9]

The message of this document is clear. The primacy of heterosexual marriage is asserted via the centrality of the bride's parents within the invitation's schema. The bride and groom's adherence to a model upheld by the previous generation is affirmed. The bride's mother's first name is withheld, suggesting her assimilation within her husband's legal and social identity according to the previous decade's laws of coverture in which husband and wife are viewed as a single male-dominated entity. This ideal was represented by wedding invitations from such couples as "Mr. and Mrs. G.W. Pierson," "Mr. and Mrs. Stanley Ward," and "Mr. and Mrs. Robert Thorpe," which extend hospitality from a joint association in which one partner is all but submerged. Likewise, in the nineteenth-century invitation, the bride's name is absent from the main portion of the text, but her social role is announced; the phrase, "marriage of their daughter" ends dramatically with the word *daughter*, stressing the subservience of personal identity to the relational system in which each woman is embedded.

A sentimentalized transfer of property is about to occur, the invitation tells us. The woman who is a daughter will soon become a wife, shifting her primary loyalty and financial dependence from one male agent to another and assuming his surname as the logical extension of this process. In the nineteenth-century invitation, the groom's parents are omitted. The document features not the bride but her mother and father, who celebrate their daughter's absorption into another man's household as well as her desirability and social validation within marriage. They are the operatives in this intergenerational transition; fittingly, the wedding takes place "at their residence," the household which has sheltered their daughter and from which she is emerging. Again, such documents do not accurately mirror social reality. The emotional conditions surrounding the nineteenth-century wedding invitation must have varied immensely. Assertive women find ways to exert their influence, even in the most rigid patriarchies, and Victorian women were no exception to this rule. However, the symbolism of wedding invitations of the previous century is clear; it is that of two parents proudly handing the torch of female subordination to their betrothed daughter.

The nineteenth-century wedding invitation, then, reflects the principles that anthropologist Robin Fox claims to be indigenous to kinship-based societies:

> Principle 1. The women have the children.
>
> Principle 2. The men impregnate the women.
>
> Principle 3. The men usually exercise control.
>
> Principle 4. Primary kin do not mate with each other.[10]

With its celebration of the monogamous woman, the invitation as well expresses the fetish for female chastity that Jack Goody claims to be shared by most agriculturally based, class-stratified societies.[11] We have seen how these values, which interlock to form the foundation of what feminists call "patriarchy," permeate the institution of marriage from its inception. We should not be surprised then that patriarchal ideals inform the rhetoric of wedding invitations, influencing such seemingly incidental details as the cut of each line of text and the placement of participants' names on the page. These are beliefs with which most middle-class Victorians would have been comfortable. The invitation was merely one of a plethora of social documents that confirmed the social organization of nineteenth-century culture.

Yet, the format of this invitation has survived into the latter part of the twentieth century, in which it still dominates. Like most current wedding planners, Perigree's current *Bride's Book of Etiquette* asserts the following guidelines for invitations: the bride's parent's should announce the wedding, the bride's surname should be omitted, the groom's surname should be included, and, if the bride's mother is divorced, she should combine her maiden and married surname.[12] Published in 1986, Yetta Gruen's equally reactionary *Weddiquette*, concurs: "Traditionally, no matter who's paying for the wedding, the bride's parents are her sponsors and their names head the invitation."[13] (Gruen, however, advises the maternal divorcee to use the title *Ms.* in order to conceal her past, a suggestion that illustrates the marriage ethos' uncanny ability to coopt and exploit instruments of women's liberation.) Wedding manuals such as these phobically avoid the question of meaning within language, claiming that titles and name changes form a set of neutral apolitical customs—unanchored social mores. Such guidebooks sidestep the issue of historical origins, alluding, as Beverly Clark's *Weddings: A Celebration,* does, to an obscure past in which conventions emerged randomly and continued by force of accident: "Traditionally, the bride's parents host the wedding and are the ones who request either 'the honor of your presence' or 'the pleasure of your company' in the invitation."[14]

Once again it is the imprecise notion of tradition itself—a set of hallowed customs and universally accepted forms of cultural authority—that produces discomfort in the contemporary bride and/or groom; the present-day wedding invitation bears the mark of an individual wriggling nervously within a set of conventions that he or she can neither accept nor discard. In our current era of pop feminism and romantic individualism, the wedding invitation author must negotiate the precipitous path between the rock of tradition and the hard place of self-expression. Today's invitation represents frantic efforts to reconcile its male author's conformity to the code of marriage with his perception of himself as a daring individualist, an iconoclast whose free spirit cannot be tamed. Likewise, the invitation often demonstrates its female author's confused attempt to embrace a sexist tradition while maintaining her own treasured self-image as a politically correct feminist.

Current wedding planners address these anxieties by claiming the invitation to be a venue for individualistic self-expression. The *Bride's Book of Etiquette* for instance suggests inscribing invitations with personal features of each man and woman, details that suggest each couple's hobbies and interests: "The invitation might be shaped like a piano or a top hat, embellished with pearls or feathers, rolled like a scroll, sent inside a bottle. It might have a computer chip that will play a traditional wedding song."[15] Such invitations protest that the bride and groom are not anonymous drones mindlessly entering the realm of sanctioned domesticity; they are talented esthetes with highly refined sensibilities or scientists whose rare erudition cannot be captured by a blank white page inscribed with black letters. In *Real Weddings: A Celebration of Personal Style,* Sally Kilbridge and Mallory Samson repeatedly praise the initiatives of brides who create their own invitations. Among them is artsy Sarah Buffem, the bride who sobbed on the Maine beach where her fiancé asked for her hand in marriage. She crafted invitations "using an old photographic process called cyanotype, in which objects are placed on a piece of paper that's been hand coated with special chemicals and then exposed to sunlight. The objects she used were maidenhair and Himalayan ferns, the paper was heavy stock from Italy, the type was simple letterpress, the wording was traditional."[16] Equestrian Kristina Lloyd's February 28, 1998, wedding to golfer Robert Sample was announced with "one-of-a-kind" invitations created by the bride's sister Katy. Each invitation was a box containing objects that had personal meaning to the bride and groom: a golf ball, a horse ribbon, and loose lavender to stress the couple's "Provencal theme."[17] And magazine editor Holly Turchetta expressed her September 9, 1998, wedding's "beach theme" in invitations "that were in harmony with the sea. For the folded overlay she designed a picture of two intertwined fish and block-printed it on delicate, Tibetan paper, using blue ink for one fish, gold for the other. Inside went the semiformally worded invitation card, which was edged in blue."[18]

Madeline Barillo's *The Wedding Source Book* urges the modern bride to prove, through visually excessive invitations, that she is not merely one of the crowd. Barillo extols the contemporary invitation, whose "luxurious details now include moire bows, hand-painted flowers, watercolor effects, laser-cut designs, shimmery embossed designs... even envelopes dripping with lace, pearls, sprays, or netting."[19] But like most wedding planners, Barillo's book affirms sexist wedding rhetoric, diverting her readers' attention to superficial design details such as paper quality and font. Don Altman, the author of *201 Ways to Make Your Wedding Special*, instructs less artistic couples, urging them to operate within the framework of the traditional wedding invitation and utilize the document as a venue for self-expression:

> Create something unique that works within the more traditional wedding format. Do the bride and groom have a favorite short poem or song? Writer and poet Kahlil Gibran's books of poems are quite moving. Shakespeare mused about the power of love in many of his plays.

It could be quite a fun project finding a poem that expresses what the couple feels.

Whether the poem is original or found, a poem can easily be incorporated into the invitation. When thinking about which poem to use, remember the words of Ralph Waldo Emerson, who said, "The quality of the imagination is to flow and not to freeze." So have fun finding the words that express your feelings![20]

Altman praises an anonymous couple who created "a four-page fold-out, story book, or fairy-tale style invitation. Using both pictures and words, the brief story traced the story of a little boy and little girl who grew into adulthood, eventually met and fell in love. The fairy tale ended happily by telling guests where the wedding took place."[21] Altman does not, of course, note the irony in using an ostentatiously unique invitation to encode that most conventional message in which fairy-tale love provides life's happy ending. Like Altman, Richard Mitzer views the process of invitation authorship as creative and personal. In *The Longest Aisle: An Offbeat Guide to Planning Your Own Wedding,* he argues that the wedding invitation is an a priori indicator of each couple's individuality: "Ivory paper with black or dark blue ink: Traditional couple. Nothing out of the ordinary at this wedding; you can set your watch by it." But bold colors and dramatic patterning hint at daring nonconformity: "Red or orange paper with yellow or black ink: This couple is far from traditional. Expect the unexpected, and don't volunteer when the bandleader or D.J. asks for someone from the crowd to come on up."[22]

Nineteenth-century wedding invitations placed no value whatsoever on creativity. Their authors seem to have been comfortable with the generic invitation, as they were, at least publically, at ease with the uniformity of matrimony itself.[23] There is little if any evidence of the need to "express oneself" through the venue of a Victorian wedding invitation, asserting one's detachment from the marital norm. Wedding advisors of this era did not address a population *overtly* ambivalent about matrimony, so they did not need to contrive methods of creativity to prove each couple's distinctiveness. Such consultants did not blend iconoclasm with convention, as contemporary author Daphne Kingma does:

My suggestion is that you follow your heart and express what is true for you, rather than routinely following the customary form.... There's more than white vellum for a wedding invitation. One couple I know sent theirs in paper-covered mailing tubes, another in seed packets. Still others have used beautiful handmade papers, a photograph of themselves, or replicas of antique Valentines. Let yourself go![24]

Because many late twentieth-century brides and grooms have a subtly antagonistic relationship to the institution of marriage, their invitations must be decorated, gussied up, enhanced with photographs, finger painted, left to fade in the sun, printed on exotic paper, inserted into seed packets, or packaged with sentimental objets d'art. The authors of wedding guidebooks cater to their readers' anxious need to individuate, offering a highly defensive rhetoric. They appease such readers, insisting that rather than buckling to social convention in getting married, brides and grooms are actually expressing their individuality—setting themselves free. Accordingly, authors like Kilbridge and Samson, Barillo, Altman, Mitzer, and Kingma describe the open-ended quest for the perfect invitation mystically and psychotherapeutically, as a loss of self-consciousness, an unblocking of artistic energy, a wild foray into creativity, a letting go. Wedding invitation designer Marc Friedland concurs, but rather than unleashing each couple's primal creativity, he takes control of the process. Because the wedding invitation is "the first big event" in a married couple's life together it should, according to Friedland, constitute, "an expression of their combined styles and sensibilities." Before designing a wedding invitation Freidland holds an "intense consultation" with the couple. He investigates various aspects of their lives in order to unearth that special something, that strain of uniqueness in each bride and groom that will find expression in the final product: "Ink color, typefaces, papers, even the size of the piece all end up reflecting various aspects of that personality."[25]

Print companies operate according to the same premises, claiming to understand each betrothed pair's unique spirit and promising to capture that ineffable quality in print. Merchants urge couples to channel their pent up creativity when authoring invitations, but like their counterparts in the publishing branch of the wedding industry, printers advise brides and grooms to test without crossing conventional boundaries. Advertisements featured in current bridal magazines promote a kind of controlled independence—individualism contained within the larger structures of marital custom. The company Creations by Elaine advertises "classic designs" that are "elegantly you," promising that the traditional layout of the invitation will not obscure the bride's personality.[26] Now and Forever offers to craft invitations that will make each celebration "truly unique."[27] The advertisement's emphasis on singularity is belied by its photograph of a traditional place setting of bone china and silver flatware. Heart Thoughts challenges the contemporary couple with a rhetorical question: "Why send an ordinary wedding invitation?"[28] It features the image of a single-paneled invitation covered in white, textured, translucent paper. The company may express contempt for the commonplace, but the invitation's barely legible wording is hardly unorthodox: a doctor and his wife, whose first name is omitted, advertise the marriage of their daughter. Renaissance Writings appeals to the bride or groom who are both free spirited and environmentally conscious, promoting "one-of-a-kind" invitations made with "unique, handmade, tree free, cotton paper."[29] This company's product is unique, not in any thematic way, but in its method of tearing the edges of each invitation to create a rough "deckle" effect. Renaissance Writings' invitations are intended to look handmade and old world, as if they had not come off an assembly line or been cookie cut by a computer graphics program. But, once again, the veneer of craftsmanship does not conceal an ordinary conjugal philosophy. The advertisement features an invitation written in familiar, tired, sexist language: "Mr. and Mrs. Robert Woods/ request the pleasure of your company/ at the marriage of their daughter/ Miss Elizabeth Carol."

Print catalogs and wedding manuals alike allow each married pair to play at iconoclasm through cutting edge visuals, designing asymmetrical invitations in which the bride's parent's names hover at the top left corner of the page while the betrothed couple's names lurk at the bottom right, adjacent to a set of baffling, abstract geometrical shapes or utilizing letters that don't end but swirl across the page, overlapping, in a pink, spaghettilike scrawl. But the announcement that alternates Roman script and block lettering, or comes decorated with gold streamers, sprinkled with confetti, encumbered by a pompous silk tassel, or wrapped in a hilariously oversized white chiffon bow, echoes, finally, attitudes identical to those of the austere Victorian wedding invitation. The piano or top hat-shaped invitation or the one whose vellum panels open like the playbill to a Broadway show, announcing, "Brian and Megan!" in garish purple print, expresses an utterly conventional conjugal philosophy.

Contemporary brides and grooms employ a range of diverse rhetorical strategies to subtly protest their absorption into the marital conglomerate. Today's wedding invitations often display sensitivity and taste. The couple whose invitation quotes the opening line of Shakespeare's sonnet 18, "Shall I compare thee to a summer's day," or whose announcement is engraved with the Beatles lyric, "Images of broken light which dance before me like a million eyes/they call me on along across the universe," takes solace in its own estheticism, enjoying its illusions of uniqueness. These brides and grooms suggest that, as literary connoisseurs or hip rock aficionados, they marry as a nod in the direction of social convention rather than an act of all out submission to it. Similarly, engaged pairs who quote the platitudinous writings of Kahlil Gibran or the aphorisms of popular psychology ("As our marriage brings new meaning to love, so our love brings new meaning to life....")[30] advertise a mood of somber contemplation. These invitations suggest betrothal to be the result of profound meditation; the engaged couple presents itself as a pair of philosophers absorbed in quiet reasoning and introspection. Their amorous choices are, the invitation tells us, untouched by peer pressure. Such documents project the image of two, sober, inward-looking individuals who have made the autonomous choice to marry.

Similarly, the self-help industry's influence on wedding rhetoric is evident in an invitation like the one praised by Beverly Clark:

> We invite you to join us in celebrating our love.
> On this day, we will marry the one
> we laugh with, live for, dream with, love.
> We have chosen to continue our growth through marriage.
> Please join
> Donna Smith

and
Bill Crain
at four o'clock
Saturday, the fifth of July
First Presbyterian Church
Santa Barbara, California[31]

This invitation envisions marriage as an act of gentle self-affirmation—an extension of California couples therapy and encounter-style workshops. The bride and groom are "in process," working out their emotions under the gaze of admiring friends. Marriage, this invitation suggests, is evidence of the couple's superior degree of emotional advancement. They are communicating on the page itself—laughing, living, dreaming, loving, and growing before our very eyes. Their wedding is an act of self-improvement; another step in the journey toward mental health that seems to involve exhibitionistic displays of sentimentality. Anxiety about adhering to convention is obvious; the announcement claims that these two super-sensitive individuals have "chosen" wedlock, implicitly refuting the claim that anyone has selected for them. The invitation likewise omits the names of parental sponsors, suggesting the popular psychology movement's transformation of a legally binding contract between families into an act of cathartic self-expression. Yet, the residue of standard marriage ideology remains; the bride and groom announce their intentions to marry the one that they "live for," affirming the standard belief in the redemptive nature of love and the sense that wedlock is the mainstay of self-worth. Beneath the freewheeling sensitivity of popular psychology propaganda lies a set of commonplace bourgeois attitudes in which the self-sanctifying myth of marriage is central.

Another convenient and often prescribed method of pooh-poohing the dull conventionality of marriage while embracing its sanctions is to utilize zaniness. Current wedding planners suggest that the bride and groom unleash their madcap spirits, encoding clever "in-jokes" and using wedding invitations as slapstick props. The invitation that comes stuffed in a bottle or accompanied by a whoopie-cushion that guests are instructed to bring to the wedding "in preparation for the grand toast," convey the desperate spirit of forced merriment. In this scenario, the bride and groom are gleeful jokers, overgrown teenagers whose playfulness cannot be constrained by wedlock. Following this trend, Don Altman recommends caricature invitations in which the bride and groom are "portrayed with their arms outstretched and fingers pointing at the reader with the caption 'We Want YOU!!!...' Upon opening the card, the guests get the rest of the message: '...To attend our wedding and have a great time.'"[32]

Daniel Harris has observed that zaniness is a form of banal humor that creates the false impression of unruly autonomy: "In a society intolerant of unconventional behavior, we have devised a symbolic method of achieving the illusion of rebelliousness by practicing what might by called controlled nonconformity. Zaniness allows us to misbehave and yet minimizes our risk of being ostracized as eccentric. It is not based on real individuality but on the harmless iconoclasm of the typical prankster...."[33] Zaniness permeates a great deal of marriage ritual, from the invitation to the merry banter of wedding shower guests to the gag gifts with which they regale the bride (e.g. heart-covered condoms, matching his and her nightshirts that announce, "Hey, I'm a Nut!"). The sitcom jocularity of the wedding toast, in which friends depict the groom as a lovable oddball, a square peg who cannot really fit into the round hole of marriage and guests provide the equivalent of canned laughter, illustrates Harris' thesis that zaniness is a form of spurious nonconformity utilized on occasions that are particularly staid to allow its practitioners the illusion of rebelliousness. A corollary or subcategory of the zany invitation is the cute one recently employed by a fair number of high-profile celebrity couples. In 1999 actor David Arquette and actress Courtney Cox sent wedding invitations that featured "a photo of Arquette dressed like a giant squirrel and a blonde-wigged Cox." The caption read, "We're Nuts About Each Other."[34] A Rexcraft invitation shows the photograph of a little boy in an oversized tuxedo and top hat kissing a little girl sheathed in a bridal veil. The caption beneath reads, "I took his hand/to have and to hold/Our hearts embraced/and never let go."[35] These invitations employ earnest language that stresses the fusion of matrimonial permanence, but their puns and images suggest a bride and groom who are just fun-loving adorable youngsters—kids trapped in the bodies of adults, dreamy children for whom these elaborate nuptial ceremonies are faintly absurd.

Wedding manuals themselves deploy zaniness as a tactic, lampooning the very readership from which their authors reap profit. Judith Martin's *Miss Manners on Weddings* for instance provides the following example of a classic wedding invitation:

> Mr. and Mrs. Greatly Relieved
> request the honor of your presence
> at the marriage of their daughter
> Darling Airhead
> to
> Mr. Orville Suitable Right[36]

In this hypothetical invitation Martin pokes fun at the decorum of marriage, hooting at the idea of two parents getting their ditsy daughter off their hands. In order to suggest her own persona as a facetious hipster independent from the status quo of marriage she evokes the milieu of screwball farce, a world in which rakish lovers slip on banana peels and dumb blondes do astonished double takes. Like all venues for kooky humor, this jokey invitation elicits a mindless guffaw rather than a chuckle of genuine amusement. (A subtler, more observant humorist might note satire latent in the fact that current invitations featuring female military officers still emphasize feminine delicacy, adhering to the format in which the bride's parents give her away: "Mr. and Mrs. Jackson Formand request the honor of your presence at the marriage of their daughter, Janet Lesley Formand, Lieutenant, United States Air Force, to Frank Joseph Marlington.") Martin's madcap guidebook upholds each reactionary convention. Like Richard Mitzer, who gleefully suggests an invitation to the wedding of a visibly pregnant bride ("Mr. and Mrs. (name withheld due to embarrassment) request the honor of your presence at the rather hasty marriage of their stupid, stupid, stupid daughter, Jessica"),[37] Martin's humor is that of the puerile vulgarian who uses "naughty" jokes to advertise her deviance from normality. The advice of wedding consultants such as Martin and Mitzer have resulted in invitations that celebrate, with self-congratulatory wacky emphasis, their own liberation from traditional standards of taste: "Save the Date. . . . We're Doing It! Andrea and Daniel Are Getting Hitched!"

As is the case with all marriage iconography, a popular means of inscribing individuality onto wedding invitations is to advertise the betrothed couple's ethnicity. *Wedding Bells* magazine praises the Italian custom of sending invitations tied with ribbons to small boxes of cookies in the shape of love knots.[38] Delicate rice paper invitations on which graceful Japanese characters balance portions of English text express a longing for the order and integrity of Japanese ancestry. Addressing the Asian bride, author Shu Shu Costa suggests, "Asian looking borders or imprints, or perhaps your family's crest" to distinguish the wedding invitation.[39] Harriete Cole's *Jumping the Broom: The African American Wedding Planner* of course recommends reviving African customs: "Africans often deliver their good news by word-of-mouth through a trusted family member. The person travels from home to home, passing the word to loved ones and indicating the date of the big event."[40] Cole praises the invitations of California-based designer Margot Dashiell, who silk-screens sepia toned ink onto parchment paper, rolls each piece of parchment, and stuffs it with raffia, "to give the formally scripted message an Egyptian flavor."[41] The invitations are then hand delivered by friends serving as couriers. Announcements bordered with Hebrew lettering that reach out exuberantly, exclaiming, "Come dance at our *Simcha*! Celebrate at Shai Sussman and Lynn Genser's Wedding!" demonstrate an attempt to infuse a Protestant custom with the vitality of turn-of-the-century immigrant life. Invitations proclaiming, "*Do di Li, V'ani Lo*" ("My beloved is mine, and I am His") claim that the bride and groom have not assimilated, that their mating rituals are those of "the old country." Always anxious to demonstrate their ethnic flair, celebrity brides and grooms have now outfitted the invitation to suit their needs. The November 18, 2000, wedding of actor Michael Douglas and Welsh actress Catherine Zeta-Jones, which garnered the kind of media attention normally reserved for international summits, was preceded by an ethnic invitation. Two months prior to the New York City gala, guests received a cream-colored box containing a trifold card embossed with a ring formed by the word *love*, and its Welsh translation, *cariad*.[42]

Our current ideal of marriage—the man and woman as a tight nucleus, the household as a moral center—is a Puritan invention and one that would probably have met with little sympathy in premodern, nonindustrialized, and nonwestern cultures. It is not merely that such cultures would question romantic love as the basis of wedlock; they would reject such a belief outright. John Gillis reminds us that, "In the seventeenth century, the idea that two people could find fulfillment in their mutual affection was so new as to be regarded subversive; and even when it became thoroughly respectable during the Victorian age, it was largely confined to the educated classes."[43] Modern American brides and grooms tend to accept this marital paradigm uncritically, rarely questioning (or even acknowledging) their own convictions: that romance-based matrimony provides life's essential meaning, that conjugality is the best way to organize a society. However, these same couples like to pepper their wedding invitations with playful dashes of ethnicity to prove that they are not really part of the white Anglo-Saxon majority, that they have not deliquesced into the melting pot of American life but have retained independent cultural identities, which they will pass on to their children. Our present era of marital conformity has a contrivedly ethnic slant.

If, as many historians believe, the restricted family emerged within the chaotic fragmentation of the post-Reformation, assuming its insular character as Europe modernized between the ages of 1520 and 1800, it did so accidentally, because of the spread of Protestantism, the emergence of nation states, which weakened village networks, and the growth of capitalism. The result was the modern, gender-stratified family, an autonomous structure unified by a belief in its own primacy, with a marriage at its center. The Victorian wedding invitation expressed this ideal unapologetically, and most minority groups in the West have absorbed this notion of family life. Whether it is printed on Tibetan paper or enhanced with Gaelic love poetry or images of Himalayan ferns, whether it has frayed edges or includes a golf ball or cookies or a whoopie cushion or is hand delivered by a courier, the contemporary wedding invitation continues to advertise on behalf of companionate wedlock, even as its authors frantically advertise their deviation from this marital norm.

Contemporary American couples handle their cultural anxiety about matrimony in many ways. One method is to author invitations that seek to infuse individualism into an institution intended to impose uniformity and social control. Brides and grooms advertise themselves as tasteful aesthetes, healing inner-children, kooky protagonists starring in a nuptial farce, or unassimilated ethnic group members. But virtually all wedding invitations extol our era's belief in the primacy of sanctioned, heterosexual, romantic love, a force so powerful that it relegates the particular quirks of brides and grooms to virtual insignificance. After viewing hundreds of seemingly diverse invitations, one notices the dull sameness of these documents—the way in which they ultimately express an identical point of view. None of them scrutinizes our culture's glorification of matrimony. None of them challenges the assumption that amorous love is the sole source of earthly happiness and that female worth stems from erotic partnership. None of them questions the marriage mystique. These efforts would comprise real individuality, independent thought as opposed to the cherished illusion of nonconformity. But independent thought rarely garners the kind of lavish material rewards bestowed on sexual conformists, as we will see in our examination of the next stage in the today's marital drama: registering for wedding gifts.

CHAPTER FIVE

The Politics of Marital Entitlement

> Once we abandon the concept of women as historical victims, acted upon by violent men, inexplicable "forces," and societal institutions, we must explain the central puzzle—woman's participation in the construction of the system that subordinates her.
>
> —Gerda Lerner, *The Creation of Patriarchy*

> Yet, because short term advantages are often the only ones visible to the powerless, we too, have played our parts in continuing this subversion.
>
> —Adrienne Rich, *Of Woman Born:*
> *Motherhood as Experience and Institution*

I. Undercover at the Bloomingdale's Registry

Bloomingdale's on Fifty-ninth Street in Manhattan is a temple of mouthwatering capitalist decadence. The ten-story building has a dismal grey facade, but behind its revolving doors lies a cornucopia of temptations. I enter and walk briskly through the first floor where supple leather handbags line mahogany shelves, and silver, gold, and mesh watches gleam from glass display cases. Climbing the stairway to the second floor, I encounter coiffed women in vaguely medical looking black robes; they police cosmetics counters lined with bottles of astringent, stacks of makeup compacts, lipsticks, soaps wrapped in rice paper, sculpted glass jars of perfume, canisters of bath beads, and tubes of skin cream. The escalator takes me past the second, third, and fourth floors on which designer suits adorn faceless plastic mannequins, cashmere sweaters and wool pant suits hang on metal racks, and bins overflow with silk and lace lingerie. Gliding past the fifth and sixth floor I peer quickly at the sprawling displays of home furnishings: oversized leather sofas, glass coffee tables, pine armoires, Turkish rugs, and mountains of needlepoint cushions. On the sixth floor, tucked away behind lavish displays of crystal and china is my destination point, the Bloomingdales registry, an unassuming white room with a desk, three chairs, and a computer terminal.

In 1963 Gloria Steinem went undercover as a Playboy bunny, donning fishnet stockings, a strapless bathing suit, and rabbit ears to work for one month at the Playboy Club in New York City, where she could experience life as a Hefneresque sex symbol. The Smith College graduate, journalist, and activist assumed the persona of an anonymous sex toy, displaying her cleavage for tips so that she could debunk the glamorous image of Playboy women generated by Hugh Hefner's publicity machine. Published in *Show* magazaine, her subsequent two-part essay, "A Bunny's Tale" remains one of the most effective exposes of the merger of corporate interests and sexual liberation without women's liberation.[1] For two weeks in 1992 black attorney Lawrence Otis Graham endured a seven-dollar-an-hour job as a busboy in Connecticut, working at the Greenwich Country Club in order to detail the self-indulgence and casual racism and antisemitism of contemporary American suburbia in his article, "Invisible Man."[2] The Princeton graduate, corporate lawyer, and author of eleven books became a polyester-clad minimun-wage employee addressed as "busboy" by the patrons who barked orders at him. These writers temporarily eschewed their own trappings of social and professional status to taste commonplace humiliation firsthand. Today I'm utilizing their method to a different end. Rather than relinquishing social prestige, I'm assuming it. I'm stepping inside the world of the soon to be married. I plan to taste the rewards of wedlock firsthand. I plan to know the admiration and feel the self-satisfaction of the bride-to-be. I plan to experience, if only for one fictitious afternoon, the engaged woman's sense of material entitlement. Selecting one's own wedding gifts—household goods such as dishes and bed linen—is an integral part of the marriage process. At no other point in life does a middle-class person feel able to ask his or her community for what he or she needs and wants, and at no other moment does the community reach out with such magnanimity. I've studied the etiquette of registration in myriad wedding planners, but I feel that I need to undergo the process in order to truly understand it, so I've come to the Bloomingdale's registry undercover as a would-be bride.

It's late afternoon on a winter Sunday. The registry is sparsely populated. It's staffed by a single employee—an elegant West Indian woman wearing a grey blazer and skirt, a black turtleneck, and pearl earrings. She appears to be my age—midthirties. Sitting behind the desk, she speaks to the only other registrant in the office, a petite woman who is perhaps in her midtwenties and who wears a rumpled blue trench coat and nervously clutches a clipboard. The wedding consultant's tone is pious, insistent. "You'll want your champagne glasses to match your wine glasses and your water goblets," she intones. "Understand something, very often someone at the table will drink wine and someone else will have champagne. Or let's say you're serving both. Someone isn't ready for the champagne yet; they're still working on the wine. So you have both kinds of glasses on the table, and you want everything to match."

"I just like two different patterns," insists the woman. "The Calvin Klein goblets and champagne flutes and the Waterford wine glasses."

"No, no. It's not a good idea. Trust me. I've been doing this a long time. You're not gonna be happy, and you're gonna get into returns, which is a mess, and with everything else on your mind right now. Keep it simple."

"My husband—"

"Forget about him. Don't involve him. Keep it simple. Keep it uniform."

"Okay, but he told me to make sure to register for a full set of demitasse cups. That's the only thing he cares about in the whole business. He's European."

"Sure, European or not, you need demitasse cups. No question."

Sensing that this dialogue may continue for some time, I signal the wedding consultant to let her know that I'm waiting to register but will take a hiatus and be back shortly. I leave the registry and wander through the floor, soaking in the opulence. Everything in the displays that surround the Bloomingdale's registry conspires to make one feel that she has entered a magical world, a never never land of material splendor in which money is no obstacle. The beautifully set tables that glow with china, silver, and crystal, advertise a romantic myth, the gilded fortress in which the bride and groom set up home—the private sanctuary into which Mr. and Mrs. Right retreat from the world to revel in opulent connubial bliss. Delicate porcelain place settings adorn tables draped in white linen. Crystal decanters flank glass champagne buckets. Silver candlesticks line ceramic trays alongside stacks of lace napkins and place mats. These displays announce a mood of abundant self-satisfied domesticity. Bloomingdales does not merely offer products to shoppers; it demonstrates the tranquility, prestige, and financial comfort that middle-class marriage is supposed to entail. From what I can see, wedlock's social code still dictates female management of the domestic sphere. Wandering among the displays are two or three lone women holding clipboards, deliberating over their selections. There is also a handful of women shopping in pairs and three with older women, aunts or mothers. I do not see one male registrant or couple.

"Should I get the nonstick or the Cuisinart cookware?" I overhear a woman anxiously asking an older companion. "The Cuisinart," the older woman replies definitively. "The nonstick gets black after a few washings. The Cuisinart is stainless steel. Take good care of it, and it will shine like it does when you first buy it."

Nancy Armstrong has written that the eighteenth century, which saw the rise of a large middle class in England and then in the United States, also witnessed the emergence of a new archetype of femininity: the bourgeois domestic woman invested with the power of educating children, managing a household, and ensuring standards of domestic taste. As Europe industrialized and men established businesses outside of the home, the previously male-centered, medieval household was feminized. "Thus it was the new domestic woman rather than her counterpart, the new economic man, who first encroached upon aristocratic culture and seized authority from it.... She therefore had to lack competitive desires and worldly ambitions that consequently belonged—as if by some natural principle—to the male.... She was supposed to complement his role as an earner and producer with hers as a wise spender and tasteful consumer."[3]

Any skepticism about the sweeping nature of Armstrong's claims or her assertion that eighteenth-century domestic ideals have become more rather than less powerful in the last three hundred years, evaporates upon visiting the Bloomingdale's registry. Here, the domestic woman takes her first faltering steps toward wifely authority. Here, soothing maternal wedding consultants school female consumers in the art of purchasing. Here, women wander among display cases accompanied by uxorious aunts, mothers, and mothers-in-law, selecting items to personalize those shrines of coupledom, their homes. Although the store has veered toward egalitarianism in shortening its name from the "bridal registry" to the "registry," this is a service offered to and utilized by women, an arena in which men clearly have no place.

After wandering aimlessly among the displays for ten minutes, I find a china pattern that I do like and would purchase if I were financially able to. (I'm not.) I then return to take my place as a bridal registrant. I sit on one of the grey, upholstered chairs in the registry office and introduce myself.

"Hi, I'm Jackie. I'm getting married, and I'm here to register."

"Well, congratulations, Jackie. I'm Jackie too! I'm your wedding consultant." She smiles at me as if to say, "you've arrived," and then continues, "I'm here to help you. We'll work together throughout this whole process. Now, I want you to look over some material."

I don't feel entirely comfortable lying to this friendly stranger. But there's no other way to elicit that smooth knowing smile, that intimate congratulatory handshake, that admiring glance that tells me that I've achieved what is, in the final analysis, most important: the promise of permanent monogamy from a man.

She hands me a thick packet of paper, forms to fill out with my name and address, charts that list registration options: formal china, casual china, formal stemware, casual stemware, barware, formal flatware, casual flatware, giftware, serveware, table linens, cookware, bed linens, small electric appliances, towels, luggage, and decorative home items. I glance over the forms, and she anticipates my reaction:

"Listen, it's very overwhelming at first, setting up a home. I know that. And you can't do it all in one day. You'll want to make several trips to decide what you like and don't like. Don't commit if you're not certain, because as soon as you register for an item, it will be computerized in the system. And, your mother's friends who know that you're getting married, they may stop off here for some other reason and just end up buying, you know, since they're here anyway. And then we send it to you, and you have it, and if you don't like it, you get into returns and making corrections on the computer, which is a nightmare."

"Listen," I interrupt, "I think that I basically know what I want, the Ralph Lauren porcelain—the Academy platinum pattern. And the matching glasses—Glen Plaid I think it's called."

"Beautiful. Good choice. That goes with everything, no matter what your decor is."

"But," I continue, "my friends and relatives aren't wealthy. There are an awful lot of options here—towels, bedding, kitchen stuff. I thought that I would just do dishes and glasses—twelve place settings—and then leave it at that. . . ."

"Why when you can get everything for free?" she asks me earnestly. "This is your time."

"So I should just go for it?"

"Sure. A lot of my brides register for furniture, sofas, rugs. Everyone chips in. That's the point. This is your time to get what you need. And whatever they don't buy you we'll sell to you at a significant discount. Ten percent on the furniture, for instance."

"Are you married?" I ask.

"No, not yet. But I'll sure know exactly what to do when it's my turn."

I enter my hypothetical choices—twelve settings of china, twelve settings of crystal wine glasses and water goblets—on the selection sheet and hand it to her, promising to return next week after evaluating my flatware, cookware, and linen options. She shakes my hand and sends me off with a gift, a book entitled, *Inspirations: The Bloomingdale's Home Planner*.

"Any final advice?" I ask, as we both stand up to say goodbye.

"Yeah. I tell all of my brides to get the George Foreman grill. It's the one advertised on television that tilts down to let all of the fat drip off of whatever meat you're cooking. It's excellent. You don't want to be without it."

"I'll think about it."

I ride the escalator down two floors, sink into a cream-colored leather sofa, and peruse *The Bloomingdale's Home Planner*, a hardcover volume with a spiral binding that contains page after glossy page of advice to the newly married. The text is enhanced with photographs of domestic plenitude. Like most pieces of popular advice literature, this book combines the banal with the personal, the starkly utilitarian with the poetic. There is a recipe for mushroom frittata, "an easy-to-prepare, one-course meal that's perfect anytime"[4] alongside rhapsodic descriptions of the contemporary home ("Your sanctuary and your show-place.... Where you retreat for relaxing times alone.").[5] Directions on how to make a bed are juxtaposed with sentimental addresses to the soon to be married reader: "We wish you well on your journey. It is an exciting one."[6] The *Planner* is divided into seven sections, each of which offers a distinct component of the marital promise: "Dining In" (companionship), "Gourmet Kitchen" (hospitality), "Master Suite" (erotic fulfillment), "Personal Pleasures" (leisure time), "Interior Design" (domesticity), "Home Finance" (economic solvency), and "Travel Plans" (romantic isolation). At the bottom of each exquisitely designed page is a drawing of two interlocking, gold wedding bands adjacent to the imperative, "Call 1-899-888-2WED."

The *Planner* opens with a note from registry director MaryBeth Shea: "We may leave our home to got to work each day, to travel, to do the things that make our lives richer and more beautiful. But wherever we go and whatever we do, our hearts know where home is and can lead the way."[7] The *Planner* depicts the home in much the same way that eighteenth-century conduct books did, as a sanctuary, a self-enclosed world whose means of support were, in Nancy Armstrong's words, invisible, "elsewhere... removed from the scene."[8] Its utopian vision of the middle-class household prescribes uniformity enhanced by flourishes of individuality. Just as wedding manuals urge couples to use their invitations as exercises in controlled noncomformity, *The Planner* depicts home decoration as an opportunity for each bride and groom to exhibit their uniqueness, rising above the commonplace and amplifying their personalities through fabric, lighting, and furniture choices. Couples are urged to pamper themselves while striving toward individuation, bringing their own imprimaturs of taste to their domiciles, using Tiffany china that "transforms the ordinary table into a moment of extraordinary beauty,"[9] or appointing their tables with Calvin Klein flatware, which extends the designer's "philosophy of modern living."[10] Selecting a china pattern is "as easy as choosing the setting that complements your lifestyle."[11]

Lifestyle, the all important word in this handbook, connotes elegance, savoir faire. It suggests class distinction expressed through judicious taste and the enjoyment of such activities as "a day at the spa" or traveling "from St. Barts to Singapore."[12] In one photograph a bride and groom stand in a relaxed embrace on the beach at the Sea of Cortez in Mexico; the waves crash at their bare feet.[13] Another pair grins from a sailboat, the deck of which is stacked with several large pieces of Louis Vuitton luggage.[14] Despite the bland features of these models posing as married couples, *The Planner* consistently stresses uniqueness. Readers are urged to counterbalance the powerful statement of group conformity that marriage entails with the individuality of purchasing choices. MaryBeth Shea promises, "Our Home Planner will help you create a home that's all your own. . . . We'll help to surround you with an ambiance that's uniquely yours."[15] She suggests that couples dare to mix china patterns in order to "make table setting an imaginative adventure."[16] She prescribes selecting bed linens that are a "private collection of stage sets that are as personal as they are practical."[17] These prescriptions for individuality are interspersed among passages of advice on matters as mundane as selecting the optimal dust ruffle, sharpening knives, removing stains from duvet covers, assembling a household first-aid kit, packing for a vacation, and researching mortgage rates.

As I browse through the pages of *The Bloomingdale's Home Planner,* I begin to detect the phantom bride for whom this frothy concoction has been whipped up. She is the perennial, middle-class, "single" woman who yearns for the stable normalcy of married life. Having snagged a man, she must now master the domestic arts, learning how to brew the perfect pot of coffee, toss and dress the exemplary salad, and fold formal napkins. But she simultaneously feels anxious about submitting to wedlock's dicta and becoming part of a homogeneous heterosexual mass. She is the same woman whose wedding invitations—enhanced with Renaissance poetry, self-help cliches, or kitschy show tune lyrics—use a defensively individualistic rhetoric. *The Bloomingdale's Home Planner* is cunningly written to assuage this schizophrenic reader's fears. Each page assures the bride-to-be that while learning the art of home management —ordering wallpaper, sampling paint colors—she will not become a household drone. Her independent spirit, her essence, her personal style will burst through, finding expression in that shrine of self-advertising domesticity, her home. "We'll help to surround you with an ambiance that's uniquely yours," *The Planner* promises.[18]

Another distinct, equally powerful image emerges from the pages of this book: the stressed out, hardworking professional couple retreating from its daily corporate battles at the end of each day to the privacy of gourmet dinners, soothing milk baths, and restful naps on Stearns & Foster mattresses fitted with percale sheets. The wife is no longer envisioned as a full-time homemaker, vacuuming, cooking meat loafs, and fluffing pillows to ready the house for the return of her weary male commuter. Like her husband, she is a high-powered earner, a corporate warrior. Like him, she is vulnerable to the pressures of the external world, the professional and social realm outside the home that is subtly portrayed as hostile. Home is envisioned as a refuge for the overwrought modern couple, a fairy-tale retreat where each stressed out pair can find solace in each other, stirring martinis ("For a ten-to-one drink, use only two teaspoons of dry vermouth."),[19] roasting chicken ("The classic method is to baste the chicken with butter or oil every ten to twenty minutes."),[20] and sipping espresso ("Amazingly enough, cup for cup, espresso has less caffeine than regular coffee.").[21] *The Planner* prescribes marital togetherness as the panacea to modern woe, urging couples to cook, clean, eat, bathe, and sleep together and preaching the value of egalitarian symbiosis: "And remember, women are not the only ones doing the cooking any longer. As more men are discovering the joys of cooking.... they are preparing many a fine meal.... And couples are finding out that cooking as a team is time together well spent."[22]

In the midst of American feminism's third wave, advice literature prescribes complementary heterosexual partnership as the means by which each woman can achieve the good life. Because one's spouse provides ultimate meaning, time with him at home, even if it is spent chopping vegetables or washing dishes, facilitates intimacy and is therefore productive, useful, good. In this stabilizing social vision the conjugal household insulates each pair from worldly anxiety, offering a cornucopia of therapies for the body and mind. It is a zone of endless comfort in which "today's working couples" can enjoy dinner "from a well-set tray in the library or a warm, comfortable bed."[23] Appointed with Karastan rugs and distressed leather sofas, the urban bedroom is a modern day Garden of Eden in which today's Adam and Eve are instructed to recline ("your private corner of the world . . . an intimate room where you can relax, be alone, and be completely yourself").[24] Only at home can men and women shed their stern, adult masks and become themselves; playful kids who indulge in the "grown-up water toys" of hot tubs, jacuzzis, and hand-held shower heads.[25] Readers of *The Bloomingdale's Home Planner* are advised to soak in scented baths (". . . many a young couple has shared a drink and a bath to relax and steal an intimate hour at the end of a long, stressful day")[26] and, in a section entitled "Mastering a Massage," to rub each other's stress away.[27]

The Bloomingdale's Home Planner's glossy magazine version of marriage is, of course, no more realistic a presentation of wedlock than *Playboy* magazine is a reliable account of American male sexuality. This document presents an inflated fantasy, a bubble. But fantasies and myths have the power to seduce. Perusing *The Planner*'s pages, I begin to understand why so many highly educated women—independent thinkers in other areas—adhere to marital convention. Despite the recent flurry of articles validating the "single" life, no set of idealizing images exist for unmarried people. There are no equivalent domestic guidebooks for "single" women, no photographs that glamorize the celibate life, no images of a woman burrowing at home with a book and a glass of wine or sitting up with a friend talking. To walk away from the life justified in primers like *The Bloomingdale's Home Planner* is to resist a massive body of cultural propaganda on behalf of wedlock and jump into imaginative nothingness. Most of us are not willing to leap into a cultural void.

Before leaving Bloomingdale's I head back up to the sixth floor to browse one last time among the Limoges soup tureens, Spode tea sets, and Rosenthal dinner plates. The registry is closed, the floor all but deserted. I stroll past crystal pitchers, Nambe sauce bowls, silver fondue dishes, the famed words of Virginia Woolf's 1927 novel *To the Lighthouse* echoing in my mind: "an unmarried woman has missed the best of life."[28] But this is only because we withhold it from her.

Stepping onto the escalator to leave, I witness a telling vignette. A young blonde woman in jeans and a pea coat is speaking to an older female companion; the physical resemblance is too striking for them not to be mother and daughter. "It's really nice," the young woman gushes, "to be, you know, getting settled, all settled, all married, together, with the stuff we need...it just feels right." As I pass the pair I notice the mother nod approvingly, smiling in what appears to be a combination of empathy, admiration, and relief. This, I realize once again, is the myth of wedlock in a nutshell, its "rightness," its "naturalness." The marital ideal rests on its proponents' inability to differentiate emotion (e.g. sexual attraction, trust, love) from institutionalization (e.g. the wedding ceremony, the bridal shower, wedding invitations, the marriage contract, bridal registration). The journey from the initial tense date to the first blush of love to intensifying commitment to betrothal to the registry to the altar is purported to be one of seamless coherence. This is ideology's peculiar power, to alchemize cultural artifice into human experience.

During the subway ride home I'm in a crowded car surrounded by the usual, heterogeneous pack of New York commuters: Chinese mothers cradling infants, Wall Street commuters working even on Sunday, young black couples completing an afternoon of shopping, Hispanic men reading the sports pages, teenagers huddled in groups, orthodox Jews heading to the far reaches of Brooklyn. I'm especially aware of the women in the car, and I find myself glancing at their left hands to see which ones are wearing a wedding band. Even a group this eclectic is divided along lines of romantic affiliation; the married women on the train share a common set of experiences that separate them even from the "single" women of their own ethnic groups. The Chinese, black, and Hasidic women who wear gold wedding bands have received tangible validation from their respective cultures, no matter how different those cultures may be from each other.

I have a sudden thought; what if each of these cultures pooled its resources toward a different kind of celebration? What if each community established the practice of celebrating a woman's twenty-fifth birthday? Just before the big birthday, friends and relatives could chip in to provide her with some basics: furniture, cookware, linens, cash. A celebration might even occur in which she would walk down an aisle, alone or surrounded by the most important people in her life, one of whom might be a lover. If it was a religious ceremony, a cleric would bless her; a secular event might involve readings, reminiscences, toasts that expressed hopes for her future. The woman would be celebrated as a remarkable entity unto herself, apart from erotic partnership, apart from the fact of having attracted a man, apart from the service that her reproductive organs might render to her community.

She would look forward to this day, as contemporary teenage girls fantasize about their weddings. She would understand the event as a landmark—the day she became someone different, special, adult, in the eyes of others. But she would feel no pressure to find a man in order to secure this celebration. It would be in place, part of the trajectory of her life plan. She would not have to focus obsessively on male attention or ritualized courtship, with all of its snares and contrivances. She would not have to withhold or provide sex in order to secure the relationship that would advertise her validity to the world. Her intrinsic value would be assumed—and acknowledged materially. There is, after all, something touching about the custom of communal support for an individual coming of age. There is something admirable about the older generation's desire to help the younger generation get a start in life. These generous impulses are more expansive than the consumerist vision of domestic bliss offered by a store like Bloomingdale's. But reserving this kind of substantive support for couples is deeply problematic. All women—all people—deserve it, or no one does.

The idea of offering ritualized celebration and support to all adults, regardless of their sexual preference or romantic status, seems impossible, contrived, absurd. But this is only because the notion of wedlock as an unassailable truth is so deeply embedded in our consciousness. It is important to remember that marriage, like institutionalized male dominance itself, is not natural, timeless, or ahistorical, but that it is codified in a specific time (6000–600 B.C.E.) in the near east.[29] Archaic nation states maintained a controlling interest in women as reproductive agents and enforced female subordination through marriage law. Various means of achieving female compliance were used; among the most powerful were the bestowal of class privilege to conforming women and the "artificially created division of women into respectable and not respectable women."[30] After centuries of reform and counterreform and even in the aftermath of the twentieth-century West's mobilization of its female population, these remain wedlock's underlying categories. A woman attached to one man—a wife—is celebrated, applauded, rewarded, while a woman attached to many men or free of all men is still, very often, the subject of fear, ridicule, and contempt. To alter this state of affairs—to shift the balance in the politics of marital entitlement—we must therefore repudiate the delicious package of privilege that is modern middle-class marriage. We must eschew the short-term advantages of wedlock and instead create alternative structures that fulfill our need to ritually mark the passage into adulthood.

I return from the contrived opulence of the Bloomingdale's registry to my stark studio apartment in Brooklyn determined to do just this. I eye my shelves crammed with books and listen to answering-machine messages from friends anxious to hear about my adventures as an undercover bride. Recalling Virginia Woolf's words once again, I decide that as an unmarried woman, I do in fact have the best in life.

II. Rewards and Punishments: Reflections on the Marriage Ideal

The bridal registry as an institution is guided by a set of interlocking assumptions: life begins with marriage, home begins with marriage. Domestic pleasure begins with marriage. Hospitality begins with marriage. Monogamous male and female partners who are legally yoked together deserve and need well-appointed homes, as opposed to the stark, glorified dormitory rooms that are appropriate to house the "single" population. Such partners, having settled on a sole complementary love object, have, in some ineffable way, "arrived." ("This is your time.") Their life choice represents an undeniable truth. They form a structure that sustains a larger structure; a stable society comprised of male-female units of platonic wholeness, each of which has found its happy ending. The couple's orderly functioning is, at some preconscious figural level, equated with the stability of the public realm. Like other marriage venues, the registry promotes conjugality as an ideal; it presents each nuptial unit as a cell, a building block in the healthy organism that is the middle class. Each cell must be nurtured, fed, kept alive. Therefore, those who perform the ritual of becoming couples in the conventional way deserve a plethora of gifts. Household necessities should be bought for them, even by those who do not know the couple well or who cannot afford such purchases. Those who choose to have different kinds of heterosexual relationships (e.g. a nonmonogamous affair, a relationship that is sometimes platonic and sometimes sexual) or those who are gay, or deliberately or by default celibate, or who live alone or with friends, do not deserve such support. Their communities owe them nothing.

Given the punitive system of reward and punishment that wedlock entails, the thick veneer of sentimentality that is spread over the entire engagement process makes sense. Sentimentality is usually compensatory, obscuring cruelty by casting an emotional spell over people and encouraging emotion rather than thought. And for women who have still not gotten their piece of the economic pie, I can see why the idealized marriage narrative is almost impossible to resist. It entails total validation accompanied by the promise of financial security. It involves nurturance and approval, not just from a single man, but from an entire community. It means a justified existence.

I'm an unmarried woman who has spent the past six months sleeping on a single futon mattress on the floor of my studio apartment. My new boyfriend is six feet two inches tall; when he spends the night it's quite an adventure. We sleep on our right sides, squeezing together like spoons, and one of us inevitably rolls onto the floor in the middle of the night. I wouldn't trade my life for anyone's; I enjoy privacy, spectacular friends, loving relatives, brilliant professors, a tiny home lined with books in the most interesting city in the world, and a set of intellectual problems that continue to challenge me. But because I'm a graduate student with a limited income, and because in the eyes of my peers I'm "single," I lack domestic comfort. In fact, I have good taste. I love elegance: beautiful colors, fabrics, textures, patterns. I love to cook and entertain, despite the fact that my tiny kitchen doesn't accommodate very many guests. But were I to register for the housewares that I want, I would not receive a single one, because I have not and will not become anyone's wife. And at some level I feel that those around me—even those who care about me most—are unconsciously punishing me for my sexual autonomy. I will not enter into the institution that has secured gender inequity for four thousand years. Despite shifting cultural definitions, despite reforms and counterreforms, despite varying emphasis in different times and places, there is a fundamental marriage contract; women receive class privilege in exchange for sexual conformity. In rejecting the terms of this contract I (and those like me) remain unclaimed female sexual and reproductive agents, living apart from the sanctioning controls of the state as they are expressed in civic marriage. And despite the recent waves of sexual liberation in the American middle class, this stab at autonomy does not go unpunished.

In the environs of the Bloomingdale's registry, surrounded by fairy-tale icons of opulent romance, I was exasperated by the conventionality of what I saw but dazzled by its imagery. I felt more than ever before the allure of the wedding promise, the yearning to step inside the charmed circle of sanctioned domesticity. And I realized the potency of our culture's reverence for the couple. In offering financial support to the married, in feathering the nests of brides and grooms and leaving others to fend for themselves, we sanction a single paradigm for living, a single sexual ethic, a single form of social organization. And we deprive other styles of life that would create a productive, interesting, heterogeneous society. That people like myself are denied overt support in the form of gift giving is not merely unfair to specific individuals; it is culturally imprudent. The commonsense argument for financing the households of newlyweds is that communities owe support to those who will one day shoulder the expense of bringing up children and populating the world with another generation. Yet this implies that the only activity that creates meaning within a society is that of procreation. John Boswell has argued to the contrary, pointing out that,

> pair-bonding of various sorts, erotic and nonerotic, is manifestly advantageous to most human societies (providing as it does mechanisms for social organization, mutual assistance, care of offspring in the event of a parent's death, etc.), homosexual attachments and relations are no more peculiar biologically than friendships. If one took the

extreme view that only sexual or emotional activities directly conducive to reproduction would be favored in human evolution, one
would be constrained to reject the majority of human erotic behavior
as "unnatural."[31]

By naturalizing child-centered monogamy we tacitly denigrate
relationships that focus on other endeavors. By withholding gifts from
homosexuals, for instance, we convey the message that we do not value
or wish to nurture the remarkable contributions that gay men have
made, to, among other areas, the arts and humanities in this country.[32]
By denying household goods to the scholar we send the aggressively
anti-intellectual message that his or her work does not matter to us. By
withholding domestic necessities from the unmarried woman we invalidate female independence. And by ritually showering gifts on women
who marry, we enshrine both female dependence and the traditional
family, a unit that still divides labor largely by gender, that is characterized by possessiveness and the ideal of sexual ownership, that enshrines
male power through the still dominant masculine patronym, that
indicts children born outside of its boundaries as "illegitimate" and denigrates unmarried women.

Our reflexive generosity toward married couples is a retrograde
form of cultural monotheism. The Bloomingdale's registry and the consumers that it represents enshrine a single human activity—isolated
conjugal love. And the glossy magazine advertisements for registries that
I've recently spent time clipping are identical in their promotion of a
uniform society of isolated "couples," a culture that was most perfectly
realized in the middle-class suburban exodus of the 1950s and 1960s.
Department store registries like that of Barneys New York, which advertises, "Toasting All Brides; The Registry at Chelsea Passage: We Offer the
Best of Everything,"[33] prey on the female consumer's deepest fears that
life's optimum emotional and financial rewards will elude her if she does
not marry. Online registries like the the Service Merchandise Gift
Registry depict a photograph of a barefoot young couple dressed in
jeans and clasping coffee mugs, comfortably ensconced on a beige sofa
with a powerbook computer. The caption reads, "Get Together, Get
Comfortable . . . and Register for the Gifts You *Really* Want."[34] Here is the

marital consumerist ethic at its apex; the bride and groom burrow in their inner sanctum, secure in their mutual self-completion, safe from the diverting influences of the outside world. Electronic shoppers, they do not even have to leave home to obtain the camcorder, electric mixer, or ceramic tea set pictured in the photographs below. When we succumb to images like this one, when we bestow gifts upon the bride and groom and withhold them from the unmarried scholar, scientist, librarian, painter, solitary thinker, reader, sex worker, actor, mentor, aunt, lesbian, unwed mother, or friend, we do not innocently help a young couple in love to get a start. We negate the varieties of human experience and social organization that could only enrich us as a culture.

Whether they depict prewedding activities (shopping, packing, list making) or postwedding relaxation, advertisements in bridal and women's magazines project the myth of wedlock's happy inevitability. In a cluttered apartment, a young man and woman—both in shorts and T-shirts—pack framed photographs into a carton on which the hyphenated name "Miller-Heaton" is scrawled in black marker.[35] A bride and groom coast along a country road in a white convertible sports car bearing the sign "Just Married"; her veil trails behind her in the wind.[36] A young couple in bathing suits embrace on a beach above a caption that reads, "Alone, together. At last. Just the two of you, with nothing but love on your mind and the sun on your back."[37] These images blend notions of casual elegance and conjugal propriety, depicting people who have matured and in so doing entered into something inexorable, predestined.

Offsetting such photographs are articles that promote wedlock as the sole desire of the healthy adult. The January 1999 issue of the women's magazine *Mirabella* purports to answer the question, "Why marry?" with an article entitled "We Few, We Happy Few" in which marriage counselor Amy Bloom philosophizes, "Reasonably healthy people with food, work, and shelter long for something more, and we tell them that marriage will give it to them."[38] If by *we* Bloom means America at large, then this is certainly true. Marriage imagery saturates every culture, every region, every social class in this country. But like many representatives of the mental health industry Bloom falls back on hard-boiled folk wisdom rather than analysis. Her statement does not describe an objective state of affairs; it prescribes marriage as a universal panacea. And it assumes that the yearning to wed is a timeless ahistorical phenomenon, something almost physical and as impervious to analysis as the desire to eat or sleep. If wedlock is inevitable, if it requires no explanation, if it is as "natural" as breathing, than to question it is to question nature itself.[39] So that the series of exhausted, combative, depressed couples whom Bloom describes in her piece are not buckling under the pressures of an unrealistic institution; they just lack that special something, the right chemistry. Bloom concludes vaguely, "Nothing 'makes' a great marriage. Like jazz, like art, like orgasm, if you have to ask, that ain't it."[40]

Again, a quick glance backward at the material component of marriage tells us that this institution is anything but natural; it is overlaid with cultural artifice and legal doctrine. There is no western society that has not institutionalized wedlock in financial terms. Weddings have always involved transfers of funds between households underscored by elaborate contractual arrangements; often the wife herself has been not only the recipient or provider of these monies but has been part of the financial package. The oldest western law codes, the Mesopotamian Code of Hammurabi (circa 1750 BCE) and the later Middle of Assyrian Law Codes dictate the sealing of an engagement through gifts and money; bridal and betrothal gifts were paid to the bride's father from the groom's father, at which point the bride became her groom's sexual property. After the marriage's consummation, the bride's father provided dowry or settlement to be managed by the husband.[41]

Greek women were likewise bartered into marriage by their fathers, lacking the power of refusal or consent. Their dowries were the married household's chief source of support.[42] Although medieval Jewish doctrine granted women the right of refusal, Hebrew law codified in the Talmud throughout the first five centuries of the common era prescribed a three-part engagement process that began with *kesef* (money); a woman was acquired through the exchange of an object of value worth at least a *perutah* (an antique penny) and the exchange took place in the presence of two male witnesses.[43] Roman men of the empire's ruling class often married to obtain substantial dowries that would fortify their estates and transmit to their legitimate male heirs. The historian Paul Veyne writes that in Rome, "The nobleman's wife was not so much his life's companion as the object of a major decision. She was so much an object, in fact, that two noblemen could amicably pass her back and forth."[44] In contrast to the Roman husband who was paid to take a woman off of her father's hands, the German medieval groom, who lived in a culture in which there seems to have been a shortage of women, paid a bride-price for his wife. Arranged by male relatives, barbarian betrothal was followed by a communal meal at which the payment of the bride-price to the groom's family took place. Once purchased, a wife became her husband's rather than her father's legal subordinate.[45] As late as the fourteenth and fifteenth centuries, by which time the Church had come to dominate marriage in Europe, arranged unions based on the dowry system were still the norm, and the marriage contract entailed the transfer of a young woman from the guardianship of one male to another.[46]

By the eighteenth century, when mutual attraction had largely replaced the arranged dowry as the key objective of marriage, female dependence on male husbands/providers had reached its apex. The historian Lawrence Stone writes that in England this period witnessed the birth of the idealized middle-class wife: "She was a well-informed and motivated woman with the educational training and the internalized desire to devote her life partly to pleasing her husband and providing him with friendship and intelligent companionship, partly to the efficient supervision of servants and domestic arrangements, and partly to educating her children in ways appropriate for their future."[47] Caucasian European women first entered the American colonies as purchase brides, shipped to Virginia and sold, by their own consent, for the price of transport.[48] Eighteenth-century American women, almost all of whom married, lived, like their English contemporaries, under the aegis of William Blackstone's legal definition of husband and wife as a single, male-dominated economic entity. Under this definition, women had no right to matrimonial property. Yet wedlock was the fulcrum of female identity in colonial New England, where women went by the generic appellation *Goody*, which meant *good wife*.[49]

Because we have inherited the late nineteenth-century's marriage reforms, it is easy for us to believe that our romantic decisions are pure, that we marry solely out of "choice," that our unions are equal partnerships untainted by the sexism of prior ages. Marriage documents from the past, such as Victorian bidding advertisements, which commonly solicited donations for engaged couples in rural England, look strangely impersonal.[50] But they are no more utilitarian than contemporary online web sites through which betrothed couples register for gifts and money. The site, surprise.com, for instance, solicits donations for upscale dinners out, internet shopping sprees, and cash delivered in a suitcase. The site, stockgift.com, allows friends and relatives to invest in stocks and mutual funds for the bride- and groom-to-be.[51] Eighteenth- and nineteenth-century practices anticipate our own marriage customs quite directly.

In every era, economics have largely determined sexual behavior, and communal support has influenced romantic selection. Although it is difficult for us to see it, our own century presents no exception to this rule. Because they lack historical awareness, advice givers in the relationship industry focus erroneously on the issue of personal choice, urging women to marry if they feel the "need" to. Their rhetoric assumes that such impulses are autonomous, separate from the social forces that direct our deepest urges. Such experts do not acknowledge that, in our marriage-obsessed culture, a woman cannot feel the need to marry or remain "single" as she might feel the need to get a new haircut, or take a night course, or buy a house pet. Her feelings about marriage must be analyzed, understood, accounted for, since they emerge within a social context that equates happiness, self-completion, and fiscal security with wedlock.

In order to arrive at a more satisfying explanation of matrimony's enduring appeal we must therefore examine the claim of Amy Bloom and "experts" like her who assume that matrimony is the natural aspiration of reasonable people. We must return to Bloom's claim that marriage offers ultimate meaning for those whose survival needs have been met. Middle-class Americans learn that wedlock will fill the void in their lives in a very specific way. They receive enormous financial rewards when they marry. Engaged couples are showered with accolades and congratulations, dazzled with attention, and given something much more substantial as well: thousands of dollars in cash, expensive gifts, and housewares. In the early twenty-first century, when the cost of living in the United States is at an unprecedented high, this is a powerful incentive to sexual conformity. It is equally potent to withhold those rewards from homosexuals in amorous pairs, from celibates, from lesbians who live collectively, from women who have multiple sexual partners, from men who choose to live alone, from bisexual or heterosexual women who live with friends. Financial compensation is the tacit underlying promise of the middle class to its married young. It is ever present, in the registries at department stores like Bloomingdale's and on the covers of bridal magazines like *Wedding Bells*, the summer issue of which features a glowing bride with patrician features in a Christian Dior gown and Tiffany diamond earrings framed by lavender letters that announce, "It's All About You!" Our myths about wedlock—it is spontaneous, private, natural, personal, romantic—demand that its financial component remain unspoken. The advice columnist of *Wedding Bells*, for instance, admonishes a bride who asks if she can request cash gifts that, "It is never appropriate to solicit (or even mention) gifts of money...on a wedding invitation. Spread the word to your parents, future in-laws, and wedding-party members that, if anyone should ask, you would prefer a gift of money."[52]

But if we violate some of these rules of etiquette and begin to speak openly about the material dimension of the marriage contract—the contract between partners as well as the agreement between each couple and its community—then we can get a much clearer picture of the forces that fuel marriage hunger in twenty-first century American women. And we can better understand the desperation of the couples featured in Amy Bloom's article; men and women who are not necessarily mismatched but who have bought into a dazzling cultural lie; happiness, popularity and conformity rewarded by piles of money and baubles. But the question "why marry?" cannot be answered without examining the tacit, ubiquitous politics of marital entitlement.

In my midthirties I broke up with my male companion of six years. I left the apartment that we had shared together and found myself without a permanent address for six months as I tried to find decent New York City lodging. For three of those months I stayed in the Chelsea apartment of a friend, a female graduate student with whom I had recently become close, who was also dealing with a breakup. Two students living alone, reading and teaching, we soon fell into a rhythm that felt delicious—sinful. We slept late, woke up and ate a prolonged breakfast, speaking about our reading and thinking of the previous night. We separated for the middle part of the day for our respective teaching obligations, but we stayed up late into the night together sipping scotch and watching old movies on her VCR or lounging on her double bed and talking for hours, discussing what had brought us to academia and to New York.

We had and still have the kind of intense female friendship that was, according to Adrienne Rich, considered "regressive and neurotic" in America's post Freudian era.[53] With postwar suburbanization came the message that women should pour themselves unstintingly into a single marital relationship. Same-sex friendship was suspect because it diverted a woman's attention from her "family" and because it was said to obscure a latent sexual impulse; in Freudian epistemology, a dark libidinous secret lurks beneath each friendly surface. It is worthwhile noticing the extent to which our current habits of courtship, marriage, and communal support still rely on these retrograde assumptions. I loved living with my friend; I loved coming home to her, I loved waking up with her, and I loved the fluid boundaries of our relationship, which allowed other friends to pass through our life together. At some level I wished that our parents had reached out with financial support that would have enabled my friend and I to establish a home together. But I also believe that this very lack of financial incentive and societal intervention made the relationship possible. No one who knew Amy and me asked us if we were getting serious. No one asked if there was a future. No one asked if our friendship was exclusive. No one suggested that we open a joint checking account or consolidate our finances in any way. None of my relatives asked me if I was anxious about not having received a commitment from my friend. No one suggested that I take her name, and no material reward was held in front of us like a carrot to facilitate the formalizing of our relationship. It was never suggested that my love for my friend would stave off loneliness while providing fiscal security, social prestige, and emotional completion. To anyone who knew us, such a notion would have seemed incongruous, overreaching, bizarre.

Because it was private, the friendship was able to develop organically, on its own terms. It achieved a depth of intimacy and mystery that only the most powerful friendships have; the relationships that Cicero defined as "a complete identity of feeling about all things in heaven and earth: an identity that is strengthened by good will and affection."[54] (A typical ancient, Cicero considered such bonds to be far more powerful than blood relations.) While I was relieved to finally move into my own studio apartment in Brooklyn and set up a new life, I still recall the ease with which my friend and I slipped into a blissful existence in which rigorous debate coexisted with unconditional support, and mutual admiration for each other's seriousness was offset by a sense of the absurd. While I do dream of growing old with her in a house in New York filled with books and mutual friends (and if she has her way, a few children), there is no need to make promises.

Those who wonder what model would replace wedlock if the institution of marriage fell away fail to recognize that the model already exists. The paradigm is platonic friendship, unfettered by social institutions, unrewarded by financial gain, untainted by the legacy of gender inequity. The forces that guide successful friendship are privacy, uniqueness, the acceptance of other relationships, individuality, autonomy, open-endedness. If these qualities could guide amorous male-female relationships, replacing those that presently undergird the marriage bond—publicly declared love, state-mandated sex, joint property, conformity, teleology, exclusivity, and the exaltation of a single relationship above all others—then such depressurized unions would probably be much happier. As Cicero wrote, "Friendship does not develop out of advantage; the process works the other way around."[55] When I pick up the telephone to call my friend and describe my adventures as an undercover bride at Bloomingdale's, I am confident that it is she and not a romantic archetype that I am reaching for.

CHAPTER SIX

Prewedding Charades:
The Bridal Shower and the Bachelor Party

Law prefers to sanction only conjugal relationships. . . . No similar privileges are assigned to friendship. Yet, what law does not provide, people
legislate for themselves through gesture and symbol.

—John Gillis, *For Better, For Worse:*
British Marriages, 1600 to the Present

Marriage, for a woman at least, hampers the two things that made life
to me so glorious—friendship and learning.

—Jane Harrison, *Reminiscences of a Student's Life*

I. Milking the Community: The Bridal Shower

The stereotypical bridal shower conjures up images of a naughty sorority
in which women squeal with delight while unwrapping and displaying
erotic gifts such as silk teddies, satin camisoles, lace boustiers and edible
panties. As it is often represented in film and television, the shower is a
same-sex event sponsored by the bride's close female friends, some of
whom will serve as attendants at the wedding. The party's ostensible
purpose is twofold. First, it allows the bride-to-be a premarital female
bonding session, a last night to indulge in the pleasure of friendship
before retreating into marital isolation. Second, the shower sets the stage
for what has been billed as an evening of female sexual initiation and
rapturous physical bliss: the wedding night. At the classic shower the
engaged woman's mother, older sisters, aunts, and married friends pass

along sexual wisdom in preparation for the honeymoon—information that will ease her transition from "single" celibacy to the regular sexual activity of married life. Friends arm the bride-to-be with sensual gadgetry, garments, oils and sprays with which to tantalize her man. Scented candles, crotchless panties, bottles of massage oil, and even the occasional pair of handcuffs are unwrapped and exhibited with relish while guests nudge each other, giggle, sip champagne, and trade erotic secrets.

This cliched scenario assumes a high degree of gender segregation; the sorority-style shower is predicated on the notion that a woman's closest friends are other women, that only in the presence of girlfriends can a bride-to-be unwind, kick back, and share frank erotic talk. The old-fashioned shower also assumes sexual ignorance on the part of the unmarried woman, anticipating the wedding night as her first significant erotic adventure. Shower gifts such as black negligees, crimson garter belts, and sheer silk stockings are props for the production of the big moment when, having taken her vows, the bride makes a dramatic entrance, disrobes, and, for the first time, submits to the act of sexual intercourse with her partner.

In the early twenty-first century both of these assumptions are outdated. While total equality in the workplace has not been fully achieved, American women do coexist with men in the educational and professional ranks, sitting with male colleagues in classrooms, working side by side with them in laboratories, competing with them in corporate offices and board rooms, and serving with them on military bases. To a great extent coeducational friendship has therefore been normalized, as sex itself has been demystified for the population at large through the media, whose pundits and talk show hosts function as ad hoc sex education teachers and psychotherapists. A contemporary American teenage girl with no sexual experience can turn on the television in the late afternoon and hear extremely frank discussions of sexuality. She can watch married couples participate in counseling sessions where they reveal graphically intimate details of their relationships. She can hear pro and con arguments for same-sex marriage and listen as miserable spouses bewail their partners' infidelities and sex therapists dispense tips on how couples can perk up their sex lives. She can learn about subjects ranging from contraception to estrogen therapy, from trans-sexualism to s & m. Despite isolated prochastity movements throughout the country,[1] the 1950s mandate that women "save it" until the wedding night has lost its power; premarital sex and cohabitation have achieved widespread acceptance within the middle class, particularly if such activities foreshadow matrimony. With gender desegregation and the loosening of restrictions upon sexuality, the old-style bridal shower, in which young women model lingerie for each other while giggling uncontrollably, now seems faintly absurd. The image of credulous young females receiving candid sexual advice from their older married counterparts likewise seems nothing more than a cultural artifact of the past, when nice American girls were instruucted to at least *affect* ignorance about sex.[2]

The bridal shower remains a staple of wedding protocol, but it has been transformed, in the decades following the sexual revolution, into a coeducational event. Today's shower is often no more than a prewedding party for male and female friends at which the featured couple receives yet more recognition and more gifts. "A shower where the engaged couple are the center of attention is a growing trend that involves male and female relatives and friends," explains wedding expert Jaclyn C. Barrett-Hirschhaut,[3] and her coauthors in the wedding industry hail this development as if it represents a major marriage reform. Arlene Hamilton Stewart, for instance, praises the shower's marvelous versatility and its accommodation of social change: "With an ability to adapt that even a chameleon would admire, the bridal shower has reinvented itself in any number of socially and politically correct ways. For the feminist, there is the coed bridal shower, attended, of course, by both men and women.... There is a world of choice in specialty showers: the linen shower for the nest builder, the wine shower for *les amis du vin*, the tool shower for the home-improvement team...."[4] Janet Anastasio, author of *The Wedding Shower Book*, concurs, but she attributes the updated shower to newly relaxed standards of masculinity: "Today, as more grooms take an active interest in their homes, 'co-ed' showers are on the rise. As a result, there is more and more emphasis today on style and presentation in the shower. Is there a theme to the shower? What does the shower say specifically about the future bride and groom?"[5] The editors of *Signature Bride* magazine endorse the the mixed-sex shower enthusiastically, daring the African American bride to alter convention:

"Perhaps you want to put a new spin on the whole idea of 'Tradition.' Coed Jack and Jill showers are fast gaining popularity and can be a contemporary answer to the 'Traditional' tea party/stag party single-sex celebration.... He may be the cook in the house anyway."[6] Similarly, in *The Everything Jewish Wedding Book*, Helen Latner urges the Jewish bride to shatter old-fashioned, prewedding gender barriers: "Becoming more and more popular... is the egalitarian event known as the 'Mr. and Mrs.' or 'Jack and Jill' shower, to which men are invited.... A backyard barbecue is especially appropriate for a coed party, and for a change, let the men cook the meal!"[7]

For marriage advisors the mixed-sex shower is a positive trend, a sign of our enlightened times. Uncharacteristically, the authors of wedding primers discuss the coed shower in overtly political language, using such nouns as *feminist* and such adjectives as *egalitarian*, framing the word *tradition* in quotation marks to distance themselves from the idea of antiquated marital custom, and urging women to shift the burden of domestic work to their male partners, if only for one evening. The wedding industry's publicists perceive the coed shower as an event which reflects progress for both sexes, because it seems to point to increased female independence and heightened male sensitivity while fostering that paramount value of contemporary marriage: conjugal togetherness. The shower once provided the space for an engaged woman to separate from her fiancé and commune with friends, but the modern woman's fusion with her partner is now assumed to be total, so that such privacy is unnecessary.

The new bridal shower, therefore, perfectly exemplifies what John Gillis refers to as the "residue of puritanism" that has often infected feminism's equalizing initiatives.[8] Attempting to egalitarianize the family, late twentieth-century reform movements have focused on eliminating the Victorian notion of separate spheres for the sexes. While demanding professional access and reproductive rights for women, such movements have also called on men to become more attentive husbands, more informed lovers, and more involved fathers. Rather than challenging the justice of conjugality, mainstream American feminism has worked toward creating a new version of conjugal perfection and has perhaps unwittingly furthered the Puritan ideal of holy matrimony in which each couple is an autonomous, self-sustaining, and self-reliant unit.[9] Rather than questioning the ideology of the nuclear family, the contemporary woman's movement has promised to integrate and fortify the family through re-education, producing educated, professionally satisfied wives and sensitive, respectful, domestically involved husbands. ("This is the book that shows that a woman can be her own self and achieve her own goals without sacrificing either marriage or motherhood," declares the cover copy of a 1974 reprint of Betty Friedan's seminal women's rights manifesto, *The Feminine Mystique*.[10] The sentiment is echoed in the summer 1998 issue of *For the Bride* magazine, the cover of which reads, "Marriage & Career... Having it All!"[11]) Bolstered by the marriage-obsessed self-help movement, the women's liberation movement has fostered a new marital ideal, a more intensely romantic view of wedlock than has probably ever existed before. In this radically intimate vision of domestic life husbands and wives share work and friends, socializing as a team, laboring side by side in the kitchen and the laundry room, discussing their "issues" in the therapist's office or the couple's workshop, and "breathing" together in the Lamaze class and the hospital delivery room where the children are born.

To the extent that this transformative social project has succeeded, the privacy a woman once enjoyed with her female friends, sisters, cousins, servants, tutors, and midwives has now been relinquished in favor of total romantic symbiosis; marital fusion in which nothing is withheld from one's spouse. "In the present climate, there is a danger that love is being idealized as the only path to salvation,"[12] warns British psychiatrist Anthony Storr. A lone voice in an industry that naturalizes coupledom, Storr argues persuasively for a more diffuse valuation of human relationships: "Whether or not they are enjoying intimate relationships, human beings need a sense of being part of a larger community.... The modern assumption that intimate relationships are essential to personal fulfillment tends to make us neglect the significance of relationships that are not so intimate."[13] It is this modern bias toward amorous togetherness that underscores contemporary marriage custom, fueling such events as the mixed-sex shower, in which the *couple* rather than the bride is honored. But this new conjugality is not progressive in any simple way, and those who adhere to it should not feel too comfortably smug about their own correctness. While the West's recent mobilization of its female population is just cause for celebration, a brand of romanticism that privileges amorous love over friendship and community is not. The newfangled bridal shower, which eschews the closeness of homosocial friendship for a coed paean to coupledom, does not represent the victory of truly egalitarian values, and it should not be seen as a sign of our progress over the social mores of the past. The shower is now one more celebration of married love, one more opportunity for the engaged couple to revel in its own heterosexual glory, one more tribute to the myth of happily ever after in a society in which such tributes are not lacking.

For contemporary marriage experts the mixed-sex bridal shower is not only a politically liberating event, it is, like so much wedding festivity, an opportunity to bolster each couple materially. Handbooks agree that the new shower is open to interpretation. It can entail a formal sit-down dinner or a Sunday brunch, a wine tasting or a touch football game accompanied by pizza and beer. The coed shower has one requirement, though; gifts are prerequisite, regardless of the style of the party. The shower invitation, in fact, is the one document on which etiquette guidebooks permit couples to advertise their registry information.[14] Although the bride- and groom-to-be will soon celebrate themselves in an extravagant gala accompanied by an influx of cash and expensive presents, convention entitles each heterosexual pair to even more. It is as if sexual conformity cannot receive enough accolades, as if no amount of praise is adequate for the man and woman cemented to each other with the promise of monogamy. The duo is advised to further milk its community, extracting small practical items along with the more expensive booty. Because the shower gift anticipates a larger, more costly expenditure, wedding custom dictates an inexpensive purchase—a paperback cookbook, a bottle of wine, or a handy household tool. And while the gift may be small, for the wedding guest it is yet another economic burden, another required expenditure, another mandate to support institutionalized heterosexuality. "Modern etiquette dictates that if people are not invited to the wedding, they should not be invited to the shower, simply because its primary purpose is gift giving," explains an anonymous columnist in *For the Bride* magazine.[15] Janet Anastasio actually suggests a

"Money Tree" shower in which guests pin envelopes stuffed with cash and checks for the couple to a small potted plant.[16]

Among friends of the bride and groom, such mandatory purchases engender resentment. Overt expressions of hostility to the shower have appeared in the recent columns of bridal magazines and guidebooks. "One of my best friends is getting married, and I've been inundated with invitations to her engagement parties, showers, and then the wedding itself. Do I have to bring a present to each event...?" a distressed correspondent asks columnist Louise Lague in *In Style* magazine's millennial "weddings" issue. "Showers...exist only as magnets for gifts," replies Lague candidly, "usually modest ones of the household gadget or glamorous lingerie variety."[17] "One of my coworkers approached me with the information that she and her fiancé were having a 'Stag and Doe' prior to their marriage and inquired as to whether I would like to purchase a ticket for a certain sum to attend," a correspondent reports to etiquette expert Judith Martin. "I've always freely contributed to gifts purchased in our large office, but I admit that I was startled and embarrassed by this request."[18] Martin disapproves of such blatant matrimonial fund raising. "We have rapidly gone from a bridal couple's appreciating the generosity of their friends and relatives to their expecting it to their demanding it."[19] In Martin's *Miss Manners on Weddings* another anonymous author complains of an imminent bridal shower in which competitive games will be played, prizes awarded, and all prizes then returned to the bride at the end of the day. "Since every guest brings a gift for the bride, it seems that guests ought to be able to take home whatever little game gifts they have won."[20] Martin's reply is contemptuous: "Miss Manners can hardly think of a worse preparation for marriage than to allow the bride to believe that she should always win, regardless of whether or not this is fair."[21]

But this etiquette expert misses the point. When a woman is extolled by relatives, gushed over by friends, rewarded by society at large with ecstatic approval and treated to a series of Academy Awards-style parties accompanied by a cascade of cash and gifts, she is told in no uncertain terms that she is one of life's winners. Because the source of these accolades is a romance—a hit or miss relationship based on a set of random intangibles—the inequity of marriage custom is truly grotesque. Some do find long-term compatibility with a lover, and others find it for a short time, other don't find it at all, for reasons that range from the arbitrariness of personal taste to sheer happenstance. ("Love," mused Mary Wollstonecraft in her 1792 treatise *Vindication of the Rights of Woman*, "the common passion, in which chance and sensation take place of choice and reason...")[22] But our culture treats men and women in long-term romances as if their sexual relationships were indicators of virtue—as if they have *earned* a set of material benefits. While this practice provides a strong incentive to sexual conformity, it also fosters resentment among those who have not won the marital bonanza. Economic beneficiaries of the marriage system, on the other hand, rarely object to its incongruities. In *The Couple's Wedding Survival Manual* Michael R. Perry jubilantly observes, "One of the big material differences between getting married and 'just living together' is the sheer volume of cash and prizes that are rained down on married couples, almost as if they've won the lottery."[23] "When you get married people buy you the best, the best!" exclaimed the hostess of a Jewish sabbath dinner that I attended on Manhattan's Upper West Side several years ago. I was helping her to clear the table between courses; and she was nodding in the direction of a Cuisinart food processor sitting on her kitchen counter next to a set of elegant Nambe serving bowls.

"You'll see," she assured me.

"What if I don't get married?"

"But, why wouldn't you? You're a terrific woman.... Please, don't worry. Someone will find you very, very soon!"

"Oh, no," I explained, "that's not what I'm asking. I'm not worried that someone won't want to marry me. I mean, what if *I* make the choice not to marry? What happens then, in terms of getting, you know, 'the best?'"

"Well, then..." Her voice trailed off, and she looked away.

"Are those wedding gifts?" I asked, as we scraped plates into a trash can under the sink.

"Oh, no," she replied, "these are all shower gifts. The wedding stuff was much more elaborate."

Like so much wedding ritual, the contemporary shower mandates two simultaneous responses to romantic coupledom: material support and cheerful exaltation. And once again, the event's material nature is obscured by kooky thematics, creative programming that distracts the guest from his or her compulsory purchase. A party planner (usually the maid of honor) executes the shower's theme, coordinating decorations, activities, and refreshments. A favorite topic of wedding authors, shower motifs range from the utilitarian to the personal to the cloyingly cute. In accordance with an industry obsessed with personalization, showers must somehow reflect the couple's joint identity. For the outdoorsy pair, the editors of *Bride's* magazine suggest an "Into the Garden" shower in which invitations are clipped to assorted seed packets, salads are served, and gifts include gardening clogs, tools, a watering can, rosebush, sun dial, or lawn furniture.[24] For the professional duo, the magazine promotes a "Home Office" shower in which invitations come printed on computer paper, guests dine on coffee and sandwiches, and gifts include a desk lamp, stationery, and computer accessories.[25] Jaclyn C. Barrett-Hirschhaut advises the hostess to thematize according to room, planning a "linens shower where guests select sheets, blankets, and comforters plus towels for the master suite."[26] For the travel-oriented couple *Bridal Guide* magazine proposes an "Around the World" shower, in which international cuisine is served and gifts come from "faraway places" (e.g. a Japanese tea set, an Irish blanket, a silk sarong from India).[27] In her *Complete Book of Wedding Showers,* Diane Warner suggests a "Country and Western Barbecue"[28] decorated with lariats, cowboy hats, saddles, and bales of hay and a "Hawaiian Luau" complete with tiki torches, ukuleles, and women in grass skirts.[29] And for the sophisticated bride and groom, the couple with a "lifestyle," Janet Anastasio recommends an elegant "Champagne and Wine Shower" to which formally dressed guests bring bottles of fine wine.[30]

The coeducational shower is often billed as an athletic event in which men and women play team sports. *Bride's* magazine suggests a "Fitness" shower with tennis balls or headbands used for invitations and guests gathering at a health club to work out and sip vegetable juice (gift suggestions include a nonstick skillet for low-fat cooking, hand-held weights, or a gift certificate for ten sessions with a personal trainer) or a softball game at which outstanding players receive trophies.[31] The summer 1999 issue of *Bridal Guide* magazine recommends an athletic war of the sexes in which men and women compete against each other at volleyball.[32] These motifs incorporate the athletic imagery that Daniel Harris claims is integral to the new aesthetic of romance:

> In advertisements, the act of courtship has become nothing less than a contact sport in which scantily clad men and women tossing footballs and throwing frisbees are shown howling with laughter as they run piggyback through the surf, plunge into snow drifts, smash each other over the head with pillows, and douse each other with garden hoses. Romantic images no longer feature staid bachelors in swallow-tail coats politely tipping their top hats to ladies with parasols but half-naked savages in Bermuda shorts and bathing suits, who, hyperventilating with uncontrolled hilarity, hurl each other to the ground like professional wrestlers. Riotous scenes of rough-housing in romantic advertisements celebrate the death of the Little Lady and the expansion of women's outdoor activities, which are no longer limited to leisurely strolls in the garden, relaxing sets of badminton, and genteel games of croquet but include bruisingly athletic tournaments of Rugby and soccer.[33]

Even as she gathers for her trousseau such confining garments as underwire demi bras and satin merrywidows, to which lace stockings are attached with garter belts, the contemporary bride enjoys portraying herself as an Olympian competitor, a musclebound athlete of strength and agility. Even as she selects a bridal ensemble that advertises her delicacy—close-fitting dress, high heeled shoes, white gloves, veil, bouquet—today's bride projects the image of a tough quarterback, a sweaty sparring partner, a crackerjack pinch hitter who holds her own against male opponents. Even as she enters an institution that has restricted women's mobility, ensuring female dependence while ostensibly protecting feminine chastity, the modern bride asserts her own masculine raunchiness. The millennial weddings issue of *Us* magazine contains a photograph of rapper Sandra Denton ("Pepa" of the all-female group Salt-n-Pepa) on her wedding day. Dressed in a classic, sleeveless white gown, Denton eats a piece of wedding cake fed to her by her groom, fellow rapper, Treach (Anthony Criss), who describes the July 1999 nuptial as a day of "bonding" with his "soul mate."[34] Prior to the bonding session Denton hosted a coed prewedding party in a Kansas City tattoo parlor, where she and her groom had illustrations of barbed wire imprinted across their knuckles.[35] In accordance with a romantic ethos "in transition, portraying women as both jocks and dolls, defensive linebackers and porcelain figurines,"[36] today's bride embraces conflicting images of femininity. A Janus-faced creature, she is both a graceful ballerina and a staunch combatant, a virginal coquette in white and a brawling, whisky guzzling, tattooed sailor.

While the utilitarian coed shower is now a staple of the wedding industry, it has not eclipsed the girls-only night. Even as the mixed-sex shower gains popularity, the exclusively female bridal shower continues to hold its own. The female gigglefest, in which naughty party favors are bestowed on the guest of honor now coexists with the mixed-sex barbecue, softball game, cocktail party, or wine tasting, and many brides indulge in both celebrations, enjoying an evening of female camaraderie as well as a mixed-sex gathering and doubling their intake of gifts. (For her August 28, 1998, wedding to musician Robb Vallier actress Traci Bingham for instance planned "a perfect Cinderella fairy tale" in which she would "feel like Princess Grace and have a train like Princess Diana,"[37] and after the Ames, Iowa, based ceremony she gushed, "I felt like a queen."[38] Displaying the narcissistic self-importance of a monarch, Bingham enjoyed three separate showers, one of which was a women-only pool party at Las Vegas' Planet Hollywood Hotel.[39]) As is often the case with marital custom, egalitarianism has bred nostalgia. As gender difference threatens to fade, the myths that sustain it gain new luster. While hailing the coeducational shower as a feminist inroad, the authors of wedding guidebooks also write glowingly of the all-girls shower, describing it as a sentimental milestone in each woman's life and suggesting that even the most staunchly egalitarian bride to be indulge in a night with her women friends. While insisting upon the salutary effects of mixed-sex fraternity, marriage propagandists also encourage women to retreat into private female enclaves and engage in stereotypically feminine activities as if reliving, for one magical evening, the segregation, domestic isolation, professional exclusion, and sexual repressiveness of the past.

Janet Anastasio suggests reviving the 1950's shower tradition of the wishing well, a structure resembling a bird house that was placed near the bride's seat and stuffed with small kitchen items. "Today, with women rarely able to devote themselves to homemaking full-time, shower themes have changed considerably," remarks Anastasio, "but you could still pay homage to the past by having a traditional, time honored shower that features a wishing well."[40] This author does not explain why one would wish to honor a period that idealized female domestic servitude; like many marriage advisors, she simply enshrines the past, as if previous eras possess inherent value. "One of the interesting aspects of prewedding festivities is how they used to divide along gender lines," observes Arlene Hamilton Stewart, addressing the contemporary bride-to-be directly. "More and more of these divisions are blurring, but don't be surprised if you have at least one shower that is 'for women only.'"[41] *Modern Bride* magazine mandates the shower as a special duty of the bridal party and admonishes the bride to relinquish control of the event to her female attendants: "The shower and bachelorette party are a bridesmaid's two big duties—and the two obligations that give control-freak brides nightmares, because they have *absolutely nothing* to do with them."[42] But *Modern Bride* advises its reader to go with the flow, giving input without determining the process and enjoying her all female shower, whether it takes the form of a formal tea party or a lingerie-oriented sexcapade.

In wedding literature the focus of the single-sex shower has shifted slightly, from sex to folk wisdom about matrimony. The bride's older friends now attend the shower, not as expositors of sexual data but as sage married women, august elders who offer prescriptions for marital harmony. According to the editors of *Bride's* magazine, "At some prewedding showers today, friends circulate a beautifully bound blank book so married women can write their 'recipe' for a happy marriage."[43] Crammed with ideas for planning and implementing a bridal shower, Janet Anastasio's *The Wedding Shower Book* concludes with a fourteen-page lined section entitled "Advice," which, according to the author, will "allow family members and special friends the opportunity to share with the bride-to-be any words of wisdom or secret tips they might have on married life."[44] "Ask the bride's relatives to bring their wedding gowns and wedding photos to the party," suggests Diane Warner in *The Complete Book of Wedding Showers.* "Or, better yet, see if you can talk the bride's mother, aunts, or grandmothers into modeling their own gowns in a fashion show."[45] Warner also recommends that the bride's female relatives bring family heirlooms, and that they describe each item's acquisition and use.[46]

Such activities envision the couple as part of a tapestry of family history, naturalizing marriage as the sole means of establishing generational continuity. A colleague recently regaled me with a lengthy description of her prewedding event, at which each married woman brought her wedding album, passed it around for admiration, and then shared the story of her first marital spat and its resolution along with a maxim for easing tension within marriage. The brandishment of objects representing marital longevity, uplifting tales of matrimonial triumph, bromides for domestic harmony, and aphorisms on the conjugal good life characterize today's female shower. The event has become a virtual group therapy session—a women's retreat at which guests are mandated to care and share. As opposed to the raunchy bachelor party, the female shower is mawkishly sentimental and marriage oriented. It entails such activities as viewing a videotape of Sidney Pollack's 1973 tearjerker *The Way We Were* while sipping champagne and eating popcorn, or hiring a fortune teller to predict the weather for the imminent wedding day.[47] Like much dating and marriage-oriented activity, the shower has a salient, new age component. Through the employment of psychics, astrologers, fortune tellers, and tarot card readers and via adolescent games of prediction, the shower enables "single" women to cast an eye to the future, foretelling the arrival of their own respective prince charmings. Becky Long's wedding primer, *Something Old, Something New*, for instance, blatantly espouses the ideal of marital enchantment. Long's dedication to her parents thanks them for the "fairy-tale wedding" they threw her and acknowledges the groom who made her realize "that fairy tales really do come true."[48] Among Long's suggestions: reviving an old fashioned shower game in which ribbons from the gifts are tied together. "The bride's engagement ring is tied to the last ribbon. The long strand of ribbons is then wound into a ball. Unmarried girls in attendance stand in a circle, and the bride moves around the circle, unrolling the ribbon ball as she goes. When she gets to the end of the ribbon, the girl she's standing in front of will be the next to marry."[49]

Correspondingly, the sorority shower often prefigures female domestic activity within marriage. Toward this end it entails either home decoration or self-beautification. Courtney Cook's *The Best Wedding Shower Book* suggests a "Sewing Bee/Trousseau Party" in which guests contribute fabric and trim and work on the bride's wedding gown and trousseau items, a "Spice Shower" in which each guest brings a spice and recipe using that spice, and a "Powder Room Shower" in which guests bring bath oils, soaps, and towels.[50] *In Style* magazine reports that prior to marrying actor John Stamos in September 1998,[51] model Rebecca Romijn Stamos took her bridal party to a Korean "tough-love spa,"[52] for a day of physical therapy and beautification. For the woman on a more limited budget the cosmetics company Philosophy offers a beauty kit for the home-spa shower. Called "Here Comes the Bride," the kit consists of an aluminum tin containing "pampering treatments" such as facial cleanser and exfoliating foot cream.[53]

One of the most unabashedly Victorian of today's wedding propagandists, Don Altman suggests a "Baking Shower," in which the bride receives, "Rolling pins, measuring cups and spoons, paring knives, spatulas, cookie cutters, gingerbread molds, pie shells, . . . frosting decoration tools, and even some flour and ingredients" in preparation for a day of culinary fun.[54] Altman also recommends a "Recipe Shower," in which each guest brings a favorite recipe and the kitchen tools necessary to prepare the dish "and the bride goes home with recipes and cookware for preparing all kinds of goodies,"[55] a "Tea and Coffee Shower" in which the bride receives gourmet coffee, cappuccino mugs, exotic teas, tea pots and strainers, and ice tea makers,[56] and a "Wedding Quilt Shower" in which women create a quilt for the couple's marriage bed.[57] For those lacking in domestic industry Altman suggests an "Angel Shower" in which the bride-to-be is regaled with angel-decorated mirrors, candles, paper weights, and mugs ("Any bride who loves angels will long remember this gathering of her own personal angels."),[58] a "Jewelry Shower" in which she receives costume jewelry as well as a jewelry box,[59] or, finally, a "Perfume Shower," which includes gifts of "potpourri, incense, aroma therapy oils, room fresheners, and scented candles."[60]

In 1930 Virginia Woolf famously described her internal battle with the previous century's ideal of femininity, the Victorian wife and mother who was celebrated for her selfless devotion to home and hearth. A voice whispering in the author's ear, this soothing maternal "angel in the house" distracted Woolf from the work of book reviewing, urging the author to treat her subject gently: "be sympathetic; be tender; flatter; deceive; use all the arts and wiles of our sex."[61] This icon of maternal altruism tortured and seduced. "She was intensely sympathetic. She was immensely charming, writes Woolf. "She was utterly unselfish. She excelled in the difficult arts of family life.... Above all—I need not say it—she was pure. Her purity was supposed to be her chief beauty—her blushes, her great grace. In those days—the last of Queen Victoria—every house had its angel."[62] It was this spectre of female virtue that Woolf claimed to have strangled in order to relinquish the sentimentality that impedes intellectual rigor ("My excuse, if I were to be had up in a court of law, would be that I acted in self-defence. Had I not killed her she would have killed me.")[63] If organized feminism's succeeding generations have committed themselves to eliminating the Victorian angel and her ideals of female purity and altruism, the modern wedding industry seems determined to revitalize her. Authors like Altman draw directly on Victorian imagery, envisioning groups of women in domestic settings. At the optimal bridal shower, women outfit their kitchens, bake up fragrant pies, brew tea, sew quilts, administer home pedicures and facials, spritz perfume, adorn themselves with jewelry, and decorate their homes with Victorian angel motifs.

These tendencies should perhaps not surprise us, since the same-sex shower emerged in full force during the nineteenth century, although its origins probably extend further back into history. Folk legend traces the bridal shower to seventeenth-century Holland, where an anonymous miller who regularly gave his flour away to the poor, lacked the requisite funds to marry. Barred from the woman he loved because of his poverty, the miller received help from his neighbors, who descended on his beloved en masse and "showered" her with objects necessary to start a home, so that her father finally consented to the match.[64]

Like much wedding parable, this tale has the ring of an apocryphal sentimental fable; it presents a heterosexual pair beleaguered, impoverished, and oppressed by tyrannical parental authority in order to justify the custom of community support for married couples. By the nineteenth century, however, the bridal shower had a different iconography. In keeping with the general tendency of bourgeois Victorian wedlock, the shower's focus had shifted from the bride and groom to the bride herself. Standing poised at the threshold of meaning, about to achieve social significance, she was ushered to the center of a room and "showered" with gifts that had been tucked into a Japanese paper parasol or a crepe paper wishing well.[65] This deluge suggested the social, emotional, and material plenitude of married life. Nineteenth-century rural America did indeed inaugurate the quilting bee shower at which women spent the day stitching a wedding ring-patterned quilt for the engaged couple.[66] An object of talismanic power in frontier courtship, the quilt was a cautionary symbol of spinsterhood and female chastity and a metaphor for married life. Folklore imported from England proclaimed that a girl who finished a patchwork quilt alone would never marry, a girl beginning a quilt would not marry until the last stitch was drawn,[67] and the couple that warmed its bridal quilt through sexual activity prior to the wedding day would have bad luck.[68]

Wedding advisors frequently deploy the nostalgic image of the quilt, recommending quilts as bridal shower gifts or prescribing showers at which women quilt together or to which guests bring individual panels of handmade fabric that the bride can craft into a final product. These suggestions evoke the eighteenth and nineteenth centuries as periods of bucolic simplicity. Like the shower at which modern women can preserve or embroider samplers, the quilting shower enables each bride and her entourage to return to an imaginary, salubrious, uncomplicated past and bask in its wholesome glow. Such events elide the painful realities of colonial marriage; the biased laws that fostered female dependence and sanctioned controlled domestic violence. Bound by the English system of common law, eighteenth-century American wives could not own property, sign legal documents, or bequeath their goods without spousal permission. According to the old English law of a colony like Virginia, wife beating was acceptable within bounds; any stick smaller than a husband's little finger was suitable for disciplinary use.[69] Folksy wedding primers omit to mention the quotidian difficulties of nineteenth-century marriage; hardships recorded in the journals of pioneer women who give harrowing accounts of abandonment, unwanted pregnancies, the fear of death from childbirth, sudden widowhood as the result of illness or frontier violence, backbreaking domestic labor, and overriding powerlessness, particularly in the case of mail order and child brides.[70]

A New Hampshire denizen lured west by her husband, Abigail Bailey wrote in 1767 of her despair over his infidelities and his sexual advances toward their third child: "My heart was torn with grief and my eyes flowed with tears, while I learned...the *inconstancy* of a husband!"[71] Harriet Ann Ames recorded the loneliness of marriage in mid nineteenth-century Texas: "In the first sad years of my married life one of the hardest things for me to bear was my husband's indifference to his children. He did not seem to care anything at all about us.... Night after night the lonely hours sped by; usually he did not come home until three o'clock in the morning."[72] Oregon resident Bethenia Owens-Adair complained of the man she had married in 1854, "He simply idled away his time, doing a day's work here and there, but never continuing at anything. Then too, he had a passion for trading and speculating, always himself coming out a loser...."[73] (After four years of marriage Owens-Adair decided she had had enough and sought divorce. Despite the burden of supporting a son, this remarkable lady ultimately attended medical school, receiving her degree in 1880, when she was forty years old.)[74] Two hundred and ten women in San Joaquin County, California, petitioned for divorce between 1852 and 1877; their claims ranged from fraud, neglect, and cruelty, to adultery and desertion.[75] These painful accounts do not represent the totality of pioneer marriage, but neither are they rare. And for the contemporary wedding author they simply do not exist. The American past is a folksy tableau. Colonial New England is a Currier and Ives print. The nineteenth-century frontier is populated by hearty rustic couples dwelling cheerfully in log cabins. With a shower focused on quilting, sewing curtains, pickling vegetables, or stewing preserves, the modern bride can return to this prelapsarian America in which bustling pioneer women produced quaintly primitive handicrafts.

Similarly, when they enshrine the all-girls shower as an event that honors female friendship, the authors of wedding primers do not seriously consider the real and very complex issues of women's relationships within a conjugally organized, male-dominated society. A discussion of this sort might touch on the difficulty of maintaining such relationships in a culture that denigrates friendship in favor of conjugal romance. It might also analyze competitiveness between women in a matrimonially oriented and youth obsessed country whose media fuels fears of female failure on the marriage market. Or it might present emulative models of female friendship—historical alliances that have catalyzed feminist activism. Marriage specialists do not pursue any of these lines of inquiry. They simply flatter their female readers with trite aphorisms while romanticizing the past's most oppressive forms of sexual segregation. Waxing sentimental, they praise the same-sex shower as a venue for women to share their allegedly special brand of intuition, what ideologues often refer to as "women's ways of knowing": "While the bride-to-be unwraps cooking utensils, tableware, and linens, hilarious jokes and stories fly," gushes Arlene Hamilton Stewart. "Women share valuable insights and secrets about the art of being married, and all bask in the warmth of sisterhood."[76] "Celebrating sisterhood" is how Anita Diamant describes the Jewish bridal shower in her primer, *The New Jewish Wedding*.[77] Diamant praises the Middle Eastern Jewish shower, at which women eat, sing, and paint the bride's hands and feet with red henna, as a day of joyous ethnicity. She urges women to imbue their showers with ethnic flavor and suggests that American Jewish women adapt the Sephardic custom of a group visit to the *mikveh* (the ritual bath in which traditional Jewish women must immerse themselves after menstruation and childbirth to regain their ritually pure status) as a "special women's party."[78] This suggestion again typifies the misguided nostalgia of the ethnic marriage propagandist. Determined to provide a new and improved alternative to tradition-bound Jewish nuptials, Diamant appropriates a degrading obligation as if it was ideologically neutral. The ancient commandment of female immersion originates in the biblical book of Leviticus, which addresses a male readership, and forbids intercourse with a woman during her period[79] and states that any object that touches a woman during her menstrual cycle is "unclean."[80] Later rabbinic writings interpret this mandate with a muddled view of female biology,[81] insisting that women wait seven days after the end of each period to immerse themselves in order to avoid contaminating their husbands. Diamant overlooks the ignorance and antipathy to the female body in which the ritual of the *mikveh* is steeped and instead re-envisions the ritual bath as the ideal site for a female lovefest, a girl's only rap session, a big group hug for members of the contemporary Jewish bridal party. Once again, wedlock is imbued with magical qualities that can, it seems, transform an instance of shameful misogyny into a ritual of female empowerment.

In one of its renditions then, the bridal shower as a social institution still insists upon gender difference, envisioning women as nurturant, domestic, and intuitive about matters of the heart. Its publicists hearken back to two periods of intense gender subordination: the nineteenth century and the midtwentieth century. Marriage primers recall an imaginatively quaint Victorian age in which gracious ladies sipped tea, ate finger sandwiches and crumpets, and regaled each other with dainty gifts. Or they conjure up images of a pioneer era when unspoiled wives produced handicrafts in an atmosphere of bucolic cooperation, quilting, pickling, darning, and churning butter. The shower also recalls a postwar America that never was, in which beaming suburban women fulfilled themselves through the nascent art of home economy, collecting recipes and stocking their pantries as their husbands toiled in urban offices.[82] While promoting the coeducational shower, today's marriage primer simultaneously recommends the same-sex event, betraying nostalgia for this enchanted period of postwar female domesticity; an imaginary era of happy gender segregation, when beatific housewives gathered for bakeathons and Tupperware parties or assembled in each other's homes to sample perfume and model jewelry.

Like virtually all of the current wedding's festivities the shower is an event in transition. It accommodates the modern woman who wishes to project a dual image of herself as both a virgin and a sexual connoisseur, a porcelain figurine and a tough athlete, a retiring coquette and a worldly professional, a homespun rustic and an urban sophisticate. As long as she maintains her primary commitment to the traditional family, the wedding industry embraces all these female archetypes, encouraging the bride to milk her community for gifts and providing two versions of the shower to meet her schizophrenic needs. One shower takes place in the twenty-first century when gender lines have blurred, the two sexes mingle socially and professionally, unmarried women are erotically experienced, and discussions of sexuality permeate the public domain. The second version of the shower occurs in an imaginary time warp in which males and females operate in separate spheres and women require privacy to pursue their exclusively domestic interests and discuss matters of the heart. Marital advice literature itself reflects the two-faced nature of today's bridal shower, celebrating both events as if their underlying assumptions were not contradictory

II. Graduating from Friendship: The Bachelor Party

Whether it is coed or single sex, the contemporary bridal shower entails a community of friends honoring a woman who is about to get married. Wedding authors therefore describe the shower as an event that celebrates friendship, reinforcing the bonds between a woman and those nonrelatives who are central to her. But this is not simply the case. The shower does not extol friendship so much as it ritually marks the end of friendship necessitated by the onset of married life. Today's marital system is based on couple worship, and the etiquette of wedlock demands that each new bride reorder her priorities, according central status to her husband and relegating friends, colleagues, mentors, teachers, students, and neighbors to the periphery. Many of the single-sex shower's activities function to demarcate the boundary between "youthful" friendship and "mature" conjugality. In a chapter of their handbook, *Going to the Chapel*, entitled "Goodbye to the Single Life: Pre-Wedding Parties,"[83] the editors of *Signature Bride* magazine, for example, suggest that friends of the bride-to-be hold a slumber-party shower in order to relive junior high school days: "Have the girls park their overnight cases and head over to the hostess's house for pizza and beer. Dance to old records, get out the old year book, play Truth or Dare, and pin-the-tail-on-the-hunk. Gifts might include sentimental items from school or dating days."[84] In this spirit, Playboy model Jenny McCarthy combined cosmetic and new-age motifs in her prewedding, all-girls sleepover. Prior to her 1999 wedding to director John Asher,[85] McCarthy hired a manicurist and a psychic for her shower, a party that culminated with a 3:00 A.M. viewing of the low budget horror film, *The Blair Witch Project.*[86]

In suggesting that grown women playact the roles of pubescent girls by staying up too late, dancing to oldies, salivating over teen heartthrobs, indulging in games of Truth or Dare, doing their nails, and clutching each other's hands and shrieking as they watch scary movies, marriage primers draw a dividing line between "single" and married life. These contrivedly nostalgic activities permit women to recapture the the glow of early friendship before leaving friendship behind. The "Bride's Basics" column of the February/March 2000 issue of *Bride's* magazine deals explicity with the transition from "single" to married life. Editor-in-chief Millie Martini Bratten describes the modern "single" girl's metamorphosis into a bride:

> At work your status undergoes a subtle shift from that of the single gal who'd jump at a month's assignment in the Far East to someone who weighs personal obligations with devotion to her career. And among friends, you morph from that great soul mate who's always up for Thursday-night daiquiris to a woman who keeps one eye on the clock, lest she return home after her honey has hit the sack.
>
> In short, you've become an adult. Even if you already own a condo, spend vacations in the great museums of Europe, and run the family business, in most societies that diamond on your left hand is a signal that you've really grown up.[87]

Martini Bratten veers off in the direction of politically correct sexual politics, urging women to develop careers and nurture friendships after the wedding day. But her magazine, which features images of beaming brides in white sobbing as they embrace tuxedo-clad grooms and scantily clad honeymooners running barefoot on the beach or necking in the woods, attests to a purely conjugal social vision. The back cover of this issue of *Bride's* depicts an advertisement for Noritake china; in a color photograph several young women dressed in soft pastel tones are caught in a sudden downpour of rain; they giggle while carrying teapots, tureens, and platters of food from the backyard where they have been dining to the home's interior. "Noritake and bridal showers," the caption reads.[88] The image is one of bittersweet sorority in which a group of women laugh together for the last time, basking in the company of their guest of honor prior to her departure to the realm of the married where she will commence life in the plural, making less time for her friends, socializing as part of a couple (generally with other couples), and relinquishing the pleasure of moments like these. No longer the "great soul mate" of other women, the bride will maintain primary emotional allegiance to her husband. In the wedding industry's iconography, the bridal shower provides a space in which women can utter a symbolic bon voyage to their soon-to-be-married friends.

If the bridal shower marks the transition from communal to conjugal life, then the bachelor party performs this task even more rigorously. Wedding experts admit that the two events are diametrically opposed and that their differences illustrate men and women's disparate perspectives on marriage. Whether it entails a group of women bestowing kitchenware on the bride or a cadre of coed friends painting the couple's new apartment, the bridal shower is a paean to domesticity and a tribute to the stability of married life. By contrast, the American bachelor party is, optimally at least, a night of drunken revelry that glorifies premarital sexual excess. Emphasizing domesticity and feminine elegance, the bridal shower takes place in the staid environment of a suburban backyard, the living room of a friend's apartment, or the dining room of an elegant restaurant such as the Four Seasons in Los Angeles, where, according to *Bride's* magazine, "showbiz bride" Melissa Rivers celebrated with girlfriends prior to her December 1998 wedding to horse breeder John Endicott.[89] Contrastingly, the bachelor party celebrates unfettered male sexuality and therefore occurs in a vaguely illicit venue: first the back of a rented limousine, then a bar, strip joint, or hotel room. The female bridal shower joyfully anticipates the beginning of a monogamous relationship, providing erotic props to initiate the physical activity between husband and wife. The bachelor party appears to celebrate sexual licentiousness, lamenting the loss of male freedom that wedlock entails.

Stereotypically, the American bachelor party is a Dionysian celebration in which men cheer as buxom blondes emerge from oversized wedding cakes that are wheeled into hotel rooms on dollies, or puff Cuban cigars while hooting at x-rated videos, or guzzle scotch in upscale clubs, occasionally stuffing hundred dollar bills into the g-strings of lap-dancing strippers. In *The Best Man's Handbook*, James Grace adumbrates a plan for just such a festival of debauchery. It involves furtive machinations that can only take place in the bride's absence ("Remember, this is a covert operation.")[90] and must include arrangements for the groom to sleep away from his intended ("Remember, women at strip bars wear enough perfume to fell a rhino at thirty paces. Any bride will smell it a mile away.").[91] Grace suggests beginning at a restaurant, casino or pub, and proceeding, at the end of the evening, to an adult entertainment venue after jettisoning such troublesome guests as the bride's father ("Would you want to watch your future son-in-law with a handful of one-dollar bills, getting accosted by naked women?").[92]

Similarly, Michael R. Perry frames the bachelor party as an act of male rebellion against the wedding's "female dominated rituals."[93] To foment the insurrection, Perry provides a list of preposterously named bachelor party drinks that combine various kinds of hard alcohol: the zombie (five types of rum and orange juice), the kamikaze (vodka and triple sec), the stealth bomber (vodka, gin, tequila, and pineapple juice), the screaming orgasm (vodka, Bailey's Irish Cream, and Kahlua), and the suffering bastard (triple sec, champagne, light and dark rum). The names of these drinks convey the idealized mayhem of the bachelor party, an event that combines self-destructive violence with sexual release to produce the archetypical shell shocked, hung over groom; an exhausted party animal who is carried home by his buddies at dawn. His clothing rumpled, his eyes swollen and red, his body fluids and wallet depleted, this Lothario is a standard bearer for contemporary masculinity. A few primers recoil from his image, reinterpreting the orgiastic bachelor party as a milder event aimed at male companionship—a get together that might entail a baseball game or an evening of bowling. But these recommendations are a minor departure from the mainstream tradition of the bachelor party as a Bacchanalian frenzy. Despite wedding advisors' occasional cautionary admonitions to rein in the licentiousness, the event remains, in the wedding industry's mirror image of the popular imagination, an evening of decadent excess which Michael R. Perry's *The Groom's Survival Manual* describes as, "a bad-ass blowout with the boys."[94]

The contrived tawdriness of such events necessitates premarital discord, and in the modern nuptial scenario it is practically de rigueur for an engaged couple to have at least one spat about the bachelor party. The woman is scripted in the role of the proprietary wife-to-be who must impose middle-class standards of decency and taste upon her husband as a prelude to her domestic function within marriage. Bourgeois decorum mandates her objections to the groom's "last taste of 'freedom' (read:

twenty-dollar lap dances, tequila shots, and drunken antics)."[95] According to Carley Roney, author of *The Knot's Complete Guide to Weddings in the Real World*, "the historical bachelor party—and the underlying ball-and-chain message—has been the source of friction in many a to-be-wed relationship."[96] But in this case the event becomes a self-fulfilling prophecy; angry at her groom's participation in an event that treats marriage as a punishment, the modern bride punishes him, acting the part of the stern disciplinarian. The advice sections of bridal magazines often contain queries from brides distressed by the iminent bachelor extravaganza. In a recent issue of *Bride's* magazine, an anxious wife-to-be confides her anxieties to pop psychologist, entrepreneur, and advice columnist John Gray. Her lament about her partner's impending bachelor party combines sexual possessiveness, distaste for the pornographic milieu, and the disgruntled wife's standard complaint that she's being ignored:

> My fiancé Don and I have one problem: his bachelor party. Don's best man is pushing hard for a trip to Atlantic City and a tour of the strip clubs. I've heard stories that men actually have sex with the strippers! This scares me....
>
> The thought of him having sex with anyone else —particularly a stripper—makes me totally nauseous.... I just don't understand why men have to get drunk and watch naked women prance around right before the wedding. How do I say this to him so he hears me? Aren't my feelings important to him?[97]

"Of course your feelings matter to him," replies the reigning guru of gender difference, attempting to mollify his distressed correspondent. Like a cultural anthropologist addressing a mentally impaired child, Gray explains the event's "significance"; "In our society, the bachelor party is a traditional rite of passage. Particularly for younger men, these parties are very important: Metaphorically, they are closing the door on their uncommitted lives before committing exclusively to one woman.[98] Gray urges this bride to permit the party, securing from her groom the promise that he will not have sex.

Another distraught bride lodges a complaint with columnist Lisa Milbrand in a recent issue of *Modern Bride*: "My husband-to-be said his bachelor party was going to be tame: just a little poker, beer, and cigars with the guys. A few weeks after the party, my best friend told me that there were strippers, and apparently they were all over my fiancé. (Her husband spilled the beans.) I feel so betrayed."[99] "Your fiancé really may not have been lying to you in the beginning—maybe the guys told your fiancé it would be a tame night, then surprised him with naked women," Milbrand speculates. "Hopefully, once you've reached mutual guidelines for your behavior in the relationship—and your hubby proves his trustworthiness by adhering to them—you'll be able to forgive him his lapse in judgment and move on."[100]

Feminist social critics have long noted the conservative role that women play in the family, as wives and mothers who manage households, contain their husbands' predatory sexual impulses, and socialize their daughters for marriage, perpetuating the very conjugal system that is disadvantageous to them. In the late eighteenth century Mary Wollstonecraft observed that girls are commonly taught by their mothers that "*outward* obedience, and a scrupulous attention to a puerile kind of propriety, will obtain for them the protection of a man...."[101] Writing approximately one hundred and sixty years later, Simone de Beauvoir observed the wife's stabilizing function within marriage: "Thanks to her, the existence that man disperses through the outside world in work and activity is concentrated again within her immanence: when he comes home at night, he is once more at anchor on the earth; through his wife the continuity of his day is assured...."[102] But as she nurtures and fortifies her husband, the middle-class wife also controls him, curtailing his excesses; "above all, a whole tradition enjoins upon wives the art of 'managing' a man; one must discover his weaknesses and must cleverly apply in due measure flattery and scorn, docility and resistance, vigilance and leniency.... A husband must be granted neither too much nor too little freedom."[103]

In her 1970 *The Female Eunuch*, Germaine Greer took a similar view of the married mother's lot as one of possessive management: "The home is her province.... She wants her family to spend time with her for her only significance is in relation to that almost fictitious group. She struggles to hold her children to her, imposing restrictions, waiting up for them, prying into their affairs."[104] The conventional wifely behaviors of clinginess, containment, and the insistence upon propriety begin early, with the advent of premarital festivities. In the weeks before the wedding, the modern bride enacts a mandatory ritual of sexual ownership, establishing herself as the moral center of the conjugal household. Fearing the bachelor party as a divisive event that will lead her groom away from her, down the path of sexual excess, the bride-to-be attempts to control the situation, imposing time constraints on the party and setting limits on the groom's sexual activities. Her confidantes soothe her, minimizing the evening's overall importance and assuring her that the grand prize she worked so arduously to secure—male commitment—remains intact. In her wedding primer, *Jumping the Broom*, Harriette Cole, for instance, addresses the anxieties of African-American brides. Cole placates her readers with the assurance that grooms experience only visual titillation: "There are times when the boys will hire a female dancer or have some exotic element included. Rest assured, sisters, they tell me that even under those conditions, he's looking from a distance."[105]

But engaged women who fear the bachelor party as a debauch and clinicians and wedding advisors who tolerate it as a sexual catharsis are equally confused about the event's true meaning. The stag party does not really take place in order to give each groom-to-be a final extramarital thrill, allowing him to gape at a stripper, grope a call girl, or receive a full-body massage from a pretty masseuse. Such encounters may take place at prewedding shindigs, but they are insignificant. The bachelor party's raison d'etat is something more powerful than anonymous sex and more potentially disruptive to wedlock than pornography ever could be: male friendship. The contemporary bachelor party celebrates same-sex friendship as it marks the groom-to-be's passage from fraternal to conjugal life. Because marital isolation is far more intense for men than women, the male prewedding event is charged with greater emotion. The bachelor party takes an overtly hostile derogatory stance toward marriage by celebrating hyperactive masculine sexuality, because recognizing the degree to which wedlock impedes male friendship would be too painful.

Victor J. Seidler has written that in our Protestant, marriage-oriented culture men are not socialized to cultivate extramarital relationships, so that heterosexual males tend to lose their friends as they grow older, solidify romantic ties, and advance professionally.

Describing the male experience of unconsciously eschewing friends, Seidler writes:

> We unceasingly take them for granted, as they are part of the private realm, part of the background that we assume, and from which we move into the public realm where "important" things happen to us in relation to our identities. We never learn to pride ourselves in being good at friendship because, within the split between public and private that it so integral to modernity, we never learn to value or give meaning to these aspects of our experience, even if we pay lip service to them.[106]

The celebrated public roles of husband and careerist are ritually legislated through marriage proposals and weddings, graduation ceremonies, professional examinations, and parties to celebrate job promotions. Husbandly devotion is also reinforced by the mental health industry, whose high profile representatives, like John Gray, describe single male existence as "uncommitted," as if friendship did not entail responsibility. These sanctions encourage middle-class men to invest in family and career while casting off friendship, a vague bond that receives no formal acknowledgement. As well, the increasingly rigid demands of the capitalist workplace and the social expectations of family life radically limit the time that American men can devote to cultivating friends.[107] And as many psychologists and sociologists have noted, competitiveness, homophobia, and modernity's construction of masculinity as a state of stoic invulnerability combine to prohibit intimacy between men.[108] The passionate expressive vocabulary that characterized platonic male relationships in antiquity and the Renaissance is absent from modern discourse, the language of which consists of firm handshakes, unflinching gazes, and monosyllabic replies. Richard Miller's 1983 study, *Men and Friendship*, reports a common exchange in which a man, when confronted by the author with the question, "Do you have friends?" replied, "A few." When asked if these people were important to him the individual typically responded, "Sure."[109]

The American male's stony taciturn mask is anything but natural; it is the product of socioeconomics. American culture assigns to men the role of provider and earner. The successful entrepreneur represents the apex of masculine achievement in our culture, and he operates as a corporate shark who swims with other sharks, protecting his offspring and warily fending off potential attackers. Built into this corporate winner's psyche is the notion of other men as predators to whom one must not let down one's guard. Equally important to his enterprise are the American ideals of autonomy and self-direction. For an American man to confess love or admit need to another man is tantamount to stating that he lacks the two qualities that capitalism most enshrines, so, at a certain point, his inevitable recourse is to the all-purpose matrimonial relationship that he has strenuously resisted. In a society whose male population derives meaning from work and romance, men, according to Victor J. Seidler, regard the need for friendship as a sign of weakness and learn to live without networks of friends.[110] And when an American male in his thirties, forties, or fifties does take stock of his social life and realizes that his high school and college friends have slipped away, he experiences a sensation that is "unutterable."[111]

American women mythologize their romances in unhealthy ways, and they certainly assign their friendships lesser status after marriage. But even the most maritally self-satisfied wives maintain ties to other women, preserving some degree of extramarital intimacy. For men, however, wedlock means emotional seclusion—a steady process of withdrawal from life with other men. Theodore F. Cohen describes this as moving from a peer group to a "coupled identity"[112] and claims that the process begins prior to marriage, when a sexual relationship intensifies and its male partner redistributes his time accordingly. Among the focus group of married men that Cohen recently surveyed, "Time formerly shared within a small network of friends became the property of the now central male-female relationship, and this allocation of temporal resources was seen as both legitimate and appropriate."[113] Viewed in light of the American male's exit from friendship as he enters wedlock, the bachelor party is a pivotal event, not because it involves high stakes poker, cocaine, or sweaty sessions with female mud wrestlers, but because it marks the groom's final embrace of a joint marital identity. Although they do not explicitly state that the bachelor party signals forfeited friendship, those who plan and implement the festivities appear subliminally aware of the event's strong emotional undercurrents. Male respondents to a survey conducted by James Grace use ambiguous language to describe the bachelor party's function. "A ceremony to honor friendship and to acknowledge how it changes as we go through life,"[114] is how one subject characterized the event. According to another anonymous male the bachelor party is "a send off in many ways. Like a guy going off to war."[115] "Men experience 'the change of life' and it begins after the bachelor party,"[116] a third respondent stated.

Men can only allude cryptically to a social transformation that is somehow related to marriage and is somehow sinister. Because our culture restricts the expression of homosocial male sentiment, it would be impossible for a group of middle-class men to gather and quietly say a real goodbye to their engaged friend, recognizing that as part of a couple, this individual will be forever changed in relation to them. It is generally impossible for unmarried men to describe publicly the abandonment they feel as marriage takes over and their circles of male acquaintance contract. So American males stage an event comprised of childish acts of aggression and adolescent displays of sexuality: a party at which they can smash into each other in games of football, wipe each other clean in rounds of poker, ply each other with drugs and alcohol, and bond by sharing women. (James Grace's *The Best Man's Handbook* actually claims that "single" men at bachelor parties punish the groom for his shifting social allegiance by mixing strong, unappealing drinks.)[117] The hoopla and contrived tawdriness of the bachelor party obscure the reality of male isolation within wedlock, and misdirect the American man's justifiable anger at marriage, channeling his rage toward the woman who hampers his sexuality rather than the conjugal system that separates him from his companions. In order to ritually mark each groom's departure from same-sex community, today's bachelor party must distract both the groom and the revelers from a painful social reality. It does so with an arsenal of pathetic devices and stratagems: x-rated videocassettes, masseuses, strippers, call girls, and naked women blurting out singing telegrams. The louder, raunchier, and more ostentatiously vulgar the party, the more effectively it blots out the reality of truncated friendship.

The best film I have seen on the political tensions underlying marriage is a small, independent, 1989 production ironically titled *True Love*. Directed by Nancy Savoca and cowritten by the director with screenwriter, Richard Guay, the film is set in the 1970s in an Italian enclave of the Bronx that has maintained the social atmosphere of the 1950s. It depicts the weeks before the wedding of young Italian-American Michael (Ron Eldard), a counter man at a local delicatessen, to his girlfriend, Donna (Annabella Sciorra). Michael and Donna both live with their parents, and their three-year relationship has consisted of trysts in vaguely public areas or late-night make out sessions when he creeps into her apartment after Mom and Dad have turned in. Now these two are ready to assume the mantle of adult life by getting married, a process that entails such landmark activities as renting an apartment and ordering a bedroom set with a Mediterranean floral motif. There are also arguments about the wedding's color scheme during a visit to the local catering hall; Michael wants to wear a black tux, but Donna envisions the whole bridal party in pastels. The caterer himself promises a "classy" affair with such details as a menu with mashed potatoes dyed sky blue to match the bridesmaids' gowns. There is an evening during which the two take a magazine quiz to see if they're compatible as a couple. (The quiz reveals that Michael's dream home is a two-family house in the Bronx.) For Donna there are daunting anecdotes and advice from her aunts, caustic hard-bitten ladies whose faces do not tell a tale of domestic bliss. In one scene Donna, her sister, mother, and aunts sit in a crowded Bronx kitchen eating cheesecake. One aunt complains that since purchasing a videocassette machine her husband has taken to renting pornography, most recently Bernardo Bertolucci's *Last Tango in Paris*. "Filthy; saw the bush," she exclaims with disgust. "Then, last night, he brings home this *Deep Throat*. Yeah, I told him not to get any ideas. I mean, they pee through that thing." These women assuage Donna's prewedding anxieties, instructing her to solve all future marital conflicts by telling Michael to "take gas" (i.e. to asphyxiate himself by sticking his head in the oven).

Herself a native of the Bronx, Savoca has an amazing feeling for her subjects, and the movie captures its blue collar, prewedding milieu perfectly. Critic Janet Maslin has accurately described *True Love* as *Moonstruck* "made by, for, and about real people,"[118] and Savoca and Guay's screenplay reveals the underlying social pressures that a commercial film like *Moonstruck*, with its seamless plotting and slaphappy, ethnic characters, can only elide. Michael and Donna are Italian, but they are never ethnic cartoons. They are good looking, but they are not air-brushed. Provincial kids living in a provincial community, they have become engaged in response to cultural mandates, not because either one has a burning desire to be married. Happy as boyfriend and girl-friend, they have nevertheless heeded the call of a society that believes a heterosexual romance must "go" somewhere. They are neither unusual nor inquisitive enough to question this assumption. (The fact that nei-ther one has a last name suggests that they are archetypes rather than formally realistic characters: what's special about Michael and Donna is their averageness. They might be any young ethnic couple living in one of Manhattan's outer boroughs.)

One might expect a film that does not romanticize wedlock to vil-lianize or trivialize its protagonists for buckling to social convention, but *True Love* does neither. Rather, it scrutinizes its characters in a manner both sympathetic and rigorous. It has profound empathy for two people who don't possess the language to express their emotions, individuals who don't understand that their desires and phobias have a political con-text. And in its presentation of wedding banalities (e.g. an evening spent haggling over the price of rings with the local jeweler, Donna's bridal gown, with its weird puffy sleeves) *True Love* has a sharp satiric edge. Eldard and Sciorra underplay the roles of two inarticulate people who genuinely care for each other. The actors allow us to see just how the rela-tionship's new status has placed a strain on their characters; what was once private, covert, and excitingly sexual has become public and cere-monial. Very young and very scared by the social pressures threatening to destroy their bond, Michael and Donna have no recourse to action. Terrified performers in a heterosexual drama, they are filled with stage fright and unsure of their lines, and there is no director to guide them. So, they numbly follow the momentum of the production, allowing the wedding's big chugging structure to carry them along. In between acts they privately confess their anxieties to friends. Donna admits to her bridesmaid J.C. (Star Jasper) that she feels it's simply too late to call things off; doing so would isolate her from the community she loves, all of whose members intertwine in various ways. "I can't live here if I don't marry him," she says quietly and desperately. And Michael confesses to a bartender friend, "I just don't wanna end up hating my life."

The crux of the problem is propriety. Being engaged has made Donna possessive in a new way, or, rather, it's made her feel empowered about expressing her possessiveness. As a soon-to-be-married woman she is less willing to share Michael with his friends, the three men with whom he appears to have hung around since childhood. Her magazine-fed notion of married life entails institutionalized togetherness—bride and groom attached at the hip like conjoined twins. She now keeps tabs on Michael, tracing his whereabouts as he proceeds from work to gatherings with the guys at a local bar to view the 1950's television sitcom, *The Honeymooners*, a series to which he is slavishly devoted. As much as he enjoys Donna, Michael enjoys his male friends more, and Donna's semi-conscious knowledge of this fact fuels her jealousy. Michael's love for his friends is not covertly homosexual, as a mistaken Freudian interpretation might claim. It is homosocial; despite his physical chemistry with Donna, in her presence Michael is constricted, fraudulent, not quite himself. With his friends he is spontaneous and relaxed. They have the same frame of reference and the same impulses, they enjoy the same activities, and the same moments strike them as humorous. But custom dictates that he establish a household with the person to whom he is erotically connected. No laws or rituals exist by which Michael could marry his friends; he has to marry Donna.

The psychologist Lois M. Tamir, who has studied patterns of male friendship, reports that among educated men self-esteem is largely contingent upon a single marital relationship, whereas among less educated males it derives from "the sense of social connectedness" to a larger network, a set of relationships that may or may not include a spouse.[119] While it details a wedding, the subtext of *True Love* is the powerful unspoken attachment between working-class men, a bond that marriage can only weaken. The tension between conjugal and homosocial alliance culminates early in the film, and it focuses, appropriately, on Michael's bachelor party. Playing the part of the nagging fiancée, Donna demands that Michael spend the night with her after the party, presumably to ensure that he does not end up with another woman. She is willing to allow him a final evening of male fraternity as long as he checks in with her afterwards. Intimidated, Michael capitulates. The bachelor party takes place in a seedy Bronx bar at which Michael's best friend and male relatives gather to watch pornography on a two reel movie projector. The room is dark, lit only by the projector, and Savoca's camera pans across the older men's delighted faces as they view the film. "A lot of miles on that," one man remarks. "That's the girl I should have married! A girl like that," exclaims an elderly viewer. "You couldn't handle a girl like that," a friend chides. Although we don't see what the men see, we can pretty well imagine the source of their glee. But when the camera reaches Michael's face, his expression registers only boredom and discomfort. He has a sexual relationship; the seedy vicarious eroticism of this all-male ritual is not what he wants from his last night of social freedom, and he makes an excuse to leave with his friend, taking the keys to his uncle's Lincoln Continental. They hit another bar for some *Honeymooners* inspired dancing, hook up with the other two members of their group, stop at an A.T.M., and drive to Atlantic City for an ill-fated night of gambling. The boardwalk, as it turns out, is deserted and the casinos closed, so they end up sitting on the ground and eating fast food while Michael complains about the oversized furniture that Donna has ordered. He has completely forgotten his promise to visit her.

She, in the meantime, has become increasingly furious. Retaliating against Michael for what she's sure is an evening of sexual ribaldry, Donna has taken her bridal party to a local Chippendales-style bar to view male exotic dancers. This sequence exemplifies a popular new trend in premarital festivities: the bachelorette party. No longer content with the staid brunch in her aunt's living room at which she smiles demurely while unwrapping packages of lingerie and potpourri, today's woman must also enter a public sexual arena, proving herself to be every man's raunchy equal. Accompanied by a posse of women friends, the feisty modern bride now visits a male strip joint prior to her wedding, and guidebook authors again present this custom as a sign of equity and sexual progress. "Just remember, guys, if you can do it, she can too.... What's fair is fair,"[120] explains John Mitchell to those lusty carousing grooms who may not expect the same from their brides. "It may serve you both well to talk about the bachelor and bachelorette parties far in advance and discuss your plans to make sure that you are both comfortable with them."[121]

Carley Roney's discussion of the bachelorette gala is a virtual call to arms to engaged women everywhere:

If your honey and his crew just *gotta* go out for one last look at some T and A, we say, two can play at this game—and should. If it's really that important for the groom to have that one last free-falling sleazefest, the bride should get one too—but hers will be a "night out with the girls." Bridesmaids and/or girlfriends should plan the bachelorette party for the exact same night. Let the ladies don their skimpiest skirts and tightest tops (or coolest clubbing ensembles) and head for the all-nude male revue.[122]

Even the more conservative wedding primers now promote the bachelorette party, albeit in more staid language. The tastefully discreet *Bride's Book of Etiquette* acknowledges each bride's right to a final night of single "fun" at an event that has "a raucous feel."[123] "A bachelorette party is the female equivalent of the bachelor party. This too can be a somewhat indelicate event if you want it to be," write Donna A. Bankhead and Lynnette Blas in *Last Minute Weddings*.[124]

Yet, as *True Love* demonstrates, the bachelorette party is a gesture of retaliation rather than a real sensual adventure. When Donna briefly climbs onstage and dances with one of the male strippers she looks stiff and uncomfortable rather than excited. The bachelorette escapade sounds wonderful to her mother, whom Donna slips away to call from a pay phone in the hopes that Michael has turned up. But it sounds better than it is. Actually, there are few sights less genuinely erotic than that of a male bodybuilder with capped teeth, Farrah Fawcett hair, and an oiled chest, gyrating in a leopard-skin thong to the rhythms of 1970s disco. Yet today's bachelorette must cheer, clap, hoot, and ply the male stripper with bills as he swivels his hips. She must feign arousal in order to establish herself as a sexual conqueror, thereby evening the score with her fiancé. This disingenuous display of sexuality is absurd, because it is so clearly performative and because it answers an imagined insult, responding to the bachelor party's text (lewd sexuality) rather than its subtext (lamenting lost friendship). But, as always, the American bride must perform rather than analyze. Here she must respond to one charade with another even more ludicrous exhibition in which she plays the role of an incorrigible, sexually indiscriminate party animal. Angela Lansbury's *Wedding Speeches and Toasts* suggests the following opener for a bachelorette party toast: "Dear Friends: I appreciate your message of goodwill, and your charming gifts. Don't you dare tell Steven that you found this pair of red socks under my bed!"[125] But Lansbury's carefree wanton bride immediately white-washes her own image, conjuring up visions of home and hearth. The text of Lansbury's toast continues, "You'll all be at my wedding in six weeks/six months time, and frequent guests in my house, and in my garden. I shall throw my bouquet to one of you at the wedding and who knows, there might be another wedding in the not too distant future. My mother says there's one for everyone."[126] Marriage etiquette allows the modern woman to pose as a sexual renegade as long as she does so temporarily, and always as a retaliatory gesture. The industry has no place for the female who is truly sexually adventurous—whose libidinous energies cannot be contained.

Despite the bachelor party conflict and despite Donna's father's assurances that she does not have to go through with the nuptial, the wedding at the center of *True Love* does take place and comprises the film's final sequence. The cavernous catering hall, the Catholic cere-mony, the plates of prime rib accompanied by sky blue mashed pota-toes, are all genuine and believable details, as are the comments of guests caught on video camera. "A lot of people would like to be in your shoes," exclaims a young female wedding guest with sharp features and a penetrating Bronx accent. "This is the most beautiful wedding I ever saw." "Many children!" an elderly Italian woman shouts heartily. "Boys, boys—no girls, please!"

But the bachelor party conflict is replayed at the wedding in an especially painful scene. Toward the end of the party, Michael asks Donna if he can drink with his buddies for an hour or so and hook up with her afterwards; he is not, apparently, aware of the wedding night's mythological implications. Devastated by his lack of romantic finesse, she retreats so the ladies' room, shuts herself in a stall, and collapses on the floor in her frilly white gown, sobbing. He finds her in the bathroom and speaks to her through the stall door, which, of course, tangibly sym-bolizes their inability to communicate.

"You know, I had the right idea tonight, Donna," states Michael angrily. "I had the right idea. I wanted to go out and be with my *friends*;

my very good *friends*. My real *friends*. I had the right idea." She pounds
on the stall door and cries.

"Goddamn you Michael! It's our wedding night! You can't go out
with your friends on our wedding night!" She continues to sob and mut-
ters, "Stupid," as Michael slides onto the floor and sits with his back
against the wall, looking shell-shocked, shaking his head in disbelief.
Finally, she exits the stall appearing calmer.

"Michael, Mikey," she says gently, "this isn't going to work."

"Don't say that," he replies.

"It's not what I want," she says disparately. "It's not normal, you
know.... I don't want to live like this." He stands up, pleading with her.

"Donna, what do you mean? Donna, please..." He hugs her and
continues to plead, "Don't say that, Donna, please, please..."

The power of this scene comes from its lack of resolution.
Annabella Sciorra's Donna appears limp and traumatized; Ron
Eldard's Michael seems genuinely fearful of losing her, but neither
character retreats from his or her respective position. For Michael, an
hour with friends is not something to beg for, not something to apologize for, not something to ever sacrifice, wedding night or no wedding
night. For Donna, the thought of leaving her wedding alone, as her
husband departs with his friends, is intolerably humiliating, and the
mere request indicates callous disregard. There is no middle ground
for these two—no way that either can understand the depth of the
other's feelings. "We should probably go back outside," Michael finally
says, and they exit the bathroom, returning to the wedding, which is
still in full swing.

In the next scene Michael and Donna are being photographed
outside the catering hall. It's evening, and they stand together stiffly,
looking miserable. We see only these two, although we hear the voices
of the photographer and several of the guests who stand in close proximity as the pictures are taken. In a single, beautifully sustained shot
the camera moves in on Michael and Donna's faces as the photographer's voice shouts instructions: "Okay, beautiful. You got the bridge in
the background. You got the water. Just wait 'til you see this picture.
You're gonna love it." In an unintentionally ironic reference to their
dispute he remarks, "now think about tonight, and smile." They

attempt forced smiles, but both look away at the last minute as the camera clicks. The photograph is ruined. "You guys fucked up!" an anonymous guest calls out. And of course, Michael and Donna have done just that.

True Love demonstrates how achieving public social distinction can entail a private betrayal of self. And it shows the imprudence of any culture upholding a single model of love. With its demands of intimacy, exclusiveness, and fusion, the companionate marriage ideal is simply wrong for someone like Michael. He belongs in a relationship that exists in harmony rather than opposition to his friendships, a relationship that does not culminate in a series of romantic performances that he cannot execute. He would be better off setting up a household with his friends. But there are no rituals to inaugurate such a home and no manuals on how to establish a nonbiologically based family, and Michael's community would provide no economic support for such a venture. Companionate wedlock is equally wrong for Donna, who would benefit from basic education and self-discovery. But Donna's relatives and friends have always viewed her life in terms of wedlock's narrative, and she has internalized this perspective and has no other way of viewing herself. Her future consists of being Michael, or someone else's wife, and the biological mother of his (hopefully male) children. Instead of gaining access to the world outside the twenty block radius that has defined her existence, Donna will be further sequestered in wedlock, isolated with a man who frustrates her and to whom she does not have much to say. To alter her fate she would have to relinquish many apparent securities: the centrality of the marital contract, familial approval, community support, the reassuring sense that she is, in her own words, "normal," and the emotional safety that comes with having a warm body in one's bed at night.

These are the securities that keep actual modern women primed for marriage. They are difficult to resist. When we become able to resist them, when we become willing to relinquish the privileged role of bride and assume the more dignified role of friend, the bachelor party's overt displays of contempt for women will become unnecessary, as will the foolish retaliatory gesture of the bachelorette event. When we stop demanding the paramount position of spouse and feel honored to be another one of our partner's good friends, the prewedding's absurd gender charades will become obsolete. But agreeing to the status of friend means relinquishing the fanfare of wedlock: the bouquet, the floral arrangements, the music, the elegant place settings, the confetti, the photographs, and, especially, the gown, that quasi-mystical garment to which we will now turn.

CHAPTER SEVEN

An Angel in White: The Wedding Dress

> She is the Proper Lady, guardian and nemesis of the female self.
> —Mary Poovey, *The Proper Lady and the Woman Writer*

"**EVEN SULTRY, SEXY,** five-time grammy winner Toni Braxton has learned firsthand that the path from solo act to half of a loving duet can be a bumpy one,"[1] a recent issue of *In Style* magazine proclaims. Beaming from the adjacent page in a full-skirted, ivory satin bridal gown, the thirty-three-year-old singer clasps a bouquet of red roses. The article profiles Braxton and the man who recently became her fiancé, musician Keri Lewis, who proposed in his Minnesota home, dropping to one knee and presenting his beloved with an oval-cut diamond with two heart-shaped diamonds on each side. "Keri says I'm corny for thinking this," gushes Braxton,"but when I look at this ring, I see the world with two hearts together."[2]

Braxton is one of a handful of high-profile brides-to-be featured in *In Style*'s regular bridal segment, in which celebrities model various gowns, apparently in preparation for their own nuptials. Actresses and singers go through the motions of shopping for a designer dress and appearing indecisive about which one they will select to make their jaunt up the aisle. *In Style*'s photo spread shows Braxton in a variety of ensembles that range from traditional to modern. "She may pick one of the dresses on these pages; therefore she swears her fiancé will be forbidden to see the pictures beforehand,"[3] the copy explains. Her hair dotted with tiny flowers, she samples a white halter beaded gown designed by Pamela Dennis. She also appears standing beside a swimming pool in an Elie

Saab white-and-silver floral lace gown offset by an enormous veil that trails to the ground behind her. Seated on a beautifully appointed double bed, she clasps her left hand to her heart and tilts her head backward ecstatically, modeling a beaded Chantilly lace short-sleeved gown enhanced by a diamond tiara. Braxton emphasizes her preference for traditional wedding attire over the more revealing contemporary designs. "The sexy way I dress is just my image, but who am I in reality? I like fantasy. To know me is to know I'm into old movies and old fashions."[4] "The diva known for baring her midriff, and more, plans to play storybook princess,"[5] *In Style* declares approvingly. Although she models a skimpy, silk-chiffon Richard Tyler gown with a plunging neckline, Braxton plans to wear a regal cumbersome ensemble inspired by the ultimate fictional bride, Cinderella.

An enduring symbol of female redemption in wedlock and a means by which women announce their adherence to traditional marriage ideals, the white dress is the most salient visual object of the modern wedding. Since the early twentieth century it has been the piece de résistance of the nuptial celebration and the focal point of feminine hopes and dreams. John Gillis explains that,

> By the 1930s . . . virtually all women who could afford it were marrying in lustrous white, by then the universal symbol of female purity and virtuous womanhood. Grooms were renting morning suits, but their dark tones in no way competed for attention. His sober attire highlighted her ceremonial presence. The attention was not on the couple, but on the bride. He could be himself; she could not, for this was the day when she ceased to be herself and become his wife [sic].[6]

Seventy years later, wedding primers still present the white dress as the focal point of the event and understand the bride's fashion choices as those that determine the other principals' outfits. Because the wedding signals the transformation that she has dreamed of since childhood, the bride's dress is a garment of talismanic power, a gown created to provoke an intense emotional response in her audience. The groom's dark tuxedo or suit, which is identical to those of his groomsmen, and the bridesmaids' bland, matching, monochromatic ensembles, are designed to make no visual impression. These outfits are intended to take no attention away from the star of the wedding, the standard bearer for heterosexuality whose amorous dreams are culminating in a single jaunt up the aisle. "When the bride's dress has a long train and a headdress holding the bridal veil, the bridegroom wears formal dress and all that goes with it to complement her. The bridal ensemble determines what everyone else wears,"[7] instructs Yetta Gruen in *Weddiquette*. The *Bride's Book of Etiquette* concurs and addresses the modern women directly and fervently, stressing the wedding gown's sacrosanct importance. "Ever since a Victorian bride wore the first white wedding dress, women have devoted weeks, months, even entire childhoods to the contemplation of this utterly romantic garment. Your wedding gown is the dress of a lifetime— and will set the style for the entire wedding."[8]

Because the gown retains its mystique, the process of buying it is unlike any other single purchase. Despite the fact that it is an impractical garment that is only worn once, the wedding gown is the most expensive sartorial acquisition of the average American woman's life. A five-hundred-dollar dress is considered cheap; midrange gowns cost between eight hundred and twelve hundred dollars, and top-of-the line dresses go for between three thousand and seven thousand dollars. The quest for the perfect gown, the fantasy dress, the garment that flatters the bride's appearance while conveying her romantic hopes is laboriously described by wedding primers and bridal magazines alike. Advisors admonish brides to begin shopping for their gowns at least nine months before the wedding and to cinch the deal with a formal contract attesting to the dress' manufacture, style, size, color, and embellishments as well as its price and delivery date.[9] Another recent issue of *In Style* magazine offers a sampling of dresses to flatter every figure. The magazine's experts assert that all women are instantly glamorized by the very fact of being a bride. "All brides—we repeat, *all* brides— are beautiful. For what better beauty treatment is there than happiness? Long as you're ready to say, 'I do,' you're going to glow like moonbeams."[10] Nevertheless, these advisors provide a range of designs for the plus size woman (an overlay dress) as well as the bride with a thick waist (a gown with heavy draping), wide hips (an off-the-shoulder bodice), or a big bust (a two-tone number with a straight, Bateau neckline), or the client who is too thin (a bias cut gown) or unusually small (a simple organza silhouette).[11] Experts instruct women to make the wedding dress the focal point of their prewedding physical regimens, paying attention to the body parts that the gown displays during their workouts, and planning their hair and makeup to accommodate the dress.[12] Brides-to-be themselves are often overheated and impassioned by the entire subject of the dress. A correspondent wrote recently to the editors of *Modern Bride* in a state of despair about her experience shopping for a wedding dress that the magazine had featured: "when I went to try it on at a store, which I drove hundreds of miles to ... I was crushed. The sample was ruined: the zipper was ripped and puckered, the train was black with dirt and the bodice was crooked. I looked in the mirror and wept. I had admired the dress in the magazine every day for weeks, and this is what it was diminished to."[13] (Alerted to the distressed woman's quandary, the designer of the gown, Randy Fenoli, created a sample and sent it to a store near her, making it possible for her to happily order "her dream dress" in the end.)[14]

Designers who specialize in bridal couture maintain strict protocols. Mill Valley, California, couturiere Nancy Taylor, who specializes in Victorian dresses, describes the process by which she designs bridal gowns as entailing an initial telephone screening by a member of her staff and an in-shop meeting during which a salesperson learns the specifics of the wedding and the client reveals what she hates most about her body; usually her bustline ("some think it's too big, but most think it is too small; we probably sew pads into half the dresses we make")[15] and is presented with a sampling of gowns. The bride-to-be's initial choice is followed by the creation of a muslin pattern ("to make sure we're all talking the same language"),[16] the cutting of the actual fabric, the shaping of the headpiece and veil, and four separate fittings. "The last meeting is a complete run through with accessories."[17] Wedding consultants and bridal designers alike understand that the nuptial celebration is not about private love; it is a public event that offers its principals a unique performative opportunity to project images of themselves as happy healthy heterosexuals. The wedding industry's representatives therefore speak of the day in theatrical terms, preparing their clients with practice run-throughs, walk-throughs, and dress rehearsals, for their moment in the spotlight.

Women who cannot afford such personalized service have to take a more aggressive stance, often visiting the sample bridal sales held throughout the country, where designer gowns are available at drastically reduced prices. One such event takes place at Filene's Basement in Boston, where, four times a year, gowns ranging from one to three thousand dollars are sold for two hundred forty-nine dollars apiece. Because the scene at this sale gets ugly—impatient brides have broken down the store's door at least five times over the years and fistfights frequently break out over choice dresses—Alan and Denise Fields, coauthors of the 1999 *Bridal Gown Guide*, offer some ground rules for braving the crowd. They advise the bride on a budget to arrive a few hours before the store opens. At 5:30 A.M. gown-hungry women begin lining the streets. They also suggest bringing an entourage to help hold the dresses, wearing a leotard, as women strip in the aisles of the crowded store, trying on dress after dress, and grabbing every interesting gown off the racks: "All the gowns are gone in thirty-two to forty-six seconds." (This has been timed by more than a few amazed reporters says Filenes.)[18] Once she has seized enough booty, the bride-to-be can negotiate with other customers, trading her wares for theirs. "If you're a size eight and you've grabbed a size fourteen, never put it back on the rack," advise the Fields'. "Instead, trade it with another bride for a dress that you like. You might have to barter several times before finding 'the dress.'"[19]

While the custom designer offers personalized service to an upscale clientele and sample sale offers bins of shopworn white dresses to hoards of desperate women whose financial resources are stretched thin, both retailers provide the same ultimate service. Both fan the flames of marraige mania, offering an outfit that is synonymous with social victory for women. The atmospherics are different, but the underlying message is not. Bridal gown providers congratulate women on having found a man, achieved social distinction, and succeeded in a competitive marriage market on which so many women fail. The professional woman who visits a Northern California bridal consultant or an exclusive Madison Avenue shop is really no different than the Boston secretary who storms the doors of Filene's with her posse, ready to club anyone who threatens to take "the dress" away from her. Both participate in the same retrograde fantasy; both enshrine the same destructive myth; on balance, both devote enormous time, money, and energy to selecting the perfect heterosexual costume. Both perceive the wedding garment as one that transforms the lowly "single" girl into our culture's version of valorized femininity: the wife.

For New York brides, Kleinfeld's in Brooklyn is a popular destination point. An enormous bridal emporium located deep in an Italian section of the borough, it attracts women from the entire tristate area. Over the years, many of the brides I've known have made the pligrimmage to Bay Ridge by subway, accompanied by their entourages: mothers, aunts, and bridesmaids. All have giggled about the process afterward, finding the place hopelessly declasse yet somehow unavoidable: Kleinfeld's houses one of the largest collections of bridal and bridesmaids' dresses in the country, so the selection it offers is unparalleled. An older coworker of mine who found herself a mother of the bride summed it up: "At first we went to chic shops in Manhattan and looked at sample dresses in Soho... you know, vintage forties gowns and very modern designs... and then we ended up where all Jewish mothers and daughters from New York eventually end up before a wedding: Kleinfeld's."

Because this bridal warehouse is an important stop along the way to heterosexual legitimacy, at least for northeastern brides, I decided to check it out. Resuming my identity as an undercover bride, I phoned ahead to find out the store hours. A customer service representative named Veronica took my call.

"This is Veronica. What is the date of your wedding?"

"Uh... September... second... And my name is Jackie, by the way."

"Okay, Jackie, we've got plenty of time then. It's only February."

"Yeah, so, can I come out and look around? What are your hours?"

"Jackie, all our work is done by appointment. You'll meet with a bridal consultant for an hour and a half. You'll view a selection of dresses and then we'll take your measurements and order the gown. We do suggest that you bring some photographs of dresses that you like, to show us what styles you're interested in."

"So, I can't come out and just browse?"

"No. We only offer individualized service."

"Well, it just seems to me that there would be a lot of pressure to buy under these circumstances."

"There is no pressure to buy if you don't see a dress you like. But most people do buy, because our selection is so extraordinary."

"Well, okay. How about tomorrow?"

"Tomorrow, Monday, I can squeeze you in at 4:30. I'll need a credit card number over the phone right now to hold your appointment. And we have a forty-eight-hour cancellation fee. If you don't notify us within that time-frame you'll be charged fifty dollars, and since there isn't forty-eight hours between today and tomorrow, we'll have to consider this appointment final."

In my research on the wedding industry I have read about the ways that bridal shops make additional money, adding extra charges for unnecessary fittings, marking up individual gowns and headpieces, and even falsely advertising generic dresses as designer gowns. I wasn't sure whether to believe such stories. Suddenly, face to face with the wedding industry's economic opportunism—the financial incentive that lies beneath so much of the lavish romantic imagery—the accounts seemed believable.

"Veronica, excuse me for saying so, but there seem to be more rules in just looking for a dress than there are in scheduling a surgery at a city hospital."

"Well, these are our policies. As I've said, we have an enormous selection. Our customers find just what they're looking for, and we do all the fittings on the premises. Our dresses range from eighteen hundred dollars and up."

"Excuse me, did you say your cheapest dress is..."

"Eighteen hundred dollars."

"For a dress that's worn once?"

"For a dress that's worn on the most important day of your life, dear."

"You know what, Veronica? Let me get back to you."

Even if I was planning to marry, I would not dream of burdening my parents with the expense of an eighteen hundred dollar dress. So, the next day, I find myself riding the subway out to Bay Ridge in the late afternoon to visit another bridal emporium, David's, which offers middle-range gowns. Climbing off the R train and following the crowd out of the station, I'm deep into Brooklyn. What was once a heavily Italian neighborhood has become more eclectic; there are Middle Eastern, Chinese, and

Indian restaurants, and I hear a lot of Russian and Hebrew being spoken on the street. I walk for two blocks along Eighty-sixth Street, the main commercial drag in this part of Brooklyn, and arrive at David's, a moderately sized, brightly lit shop with two blank-faced mannequins wearing —of course—white gowns, in the window. I pause briefly outside the store to view these monstrously oversized dresses, with their billowing skirts. "Will I be able to go through with this?" I wonder. Registering for china was one thing... but trying on bridal gowns. . . .

A few feet away from me, two young men stand together, smoking cigarettes and talking. They are, apparently, a groom-to-be and his compatriot. Eavesdropping on their conversation, I overhear the groom's standard lament and his stalwart married friend's advice.

"Listen, it's a woman's day. You rent a tux, put in on, and show up."

"I know, but she's dragging me all around town. She's in there matching her bridesmaids' shoes to the exact color of their dresses. She wants me to see this. With the hours I work, I have to be involved with this nonsense?"

"Just do it. Make her happy. It's gonna all be over soon, and life goes back to normal. Trust me; I've been through it."

With renewed resolve, I enter David's. The store is sparsely populated. I see a bevvy of saleswomen but only two other female shoppers. There are racks of colored dresses: salmon- and lavender-colored satin gowns with wraps and sleeveless blue cocktail frocks. I realize that the top floor of the shop offers bridesmaids' dresses. I quickly head downstairs to the more spacious section of the store, where row after row is lined with enormous white gowns, each wrapped in its own plastic garment bag. I'm met by a friendly West Indian woman in her midfifties named Carole. Wearing a charcoal grey suit and clasping a clipboard, this warm efficient saleswoman seems like an older version of the woman I had spoken with at the Bloomindale's registry.

"Hello, Jackie, I'll just have to quickly take some information down, and then we'll look at dresses. Is this your first stop?"

"Uh, yes, actually, and, just looking at the dresses I see, they're really formal. I was thinking of something a little more casual . . . a little smaller."

"Well, many women feel that way at first. But you should try on some traditional gowns and see how they feel on you. And our dresses can be tailored and made smaller; you can make a skirt shorter or alter a train."

"Okay."

I tell Carole my fictitious wedding date, home and email address, and telephone number. She then asks me about the style and size of my wedding. It will be small—sixty guests—and informal, I decide on the spot. Will there be a color scheme? I don't know, I concede.

"Well, that's okay. A white dress goes with everything. That's what's so wonderful about it."

Once again, I'm uncomfortable lying to this pleasant stranger, a working woman who is treating me nicely, to whom every commission probably means a great deal. But, once again, I don't see any other way. In order to understand the psychology of wedlock I need to experience certain things firsthand. The process of shopping for a wedding dress is fundamental to the marriage narrative. I can't just read about it in guidebooks; I have to go through the motions myself.

Carole puts down her clipboard and asks if she can take my coat. As I hand her the coat, she quickly looks me over. A seasoned salesperson, she knows that one doesn't ask a woman's size. She hangs the coat and leads me to the back corner of the the store.

"Let's start here," she says, "What do you think of these?"

She holds up two white dresses. One is short sleeved, with a boatneck, a lace top, and a broad white ribbon encircling the waist. The other has long sheer sleeves and an elaborate, lacy Queen Anne neckline. With their wide, multilayered, bulky skirts, both garments, to me, appear absurd. I cannot imagine marching up an aisle in these heavy prissy costumes, which seem to have been designed for Walt Disney characters rather than modern working women. Carole reads my mind.

"Not for you. Too formal. Let's keep looking."

She keeps going, aggressively rifling through the rows of hanging dresses. She produces two gowns that are more understated: a sleeveless matte satin a-line gown with no ribbons, lace, or decoration, and another similar design with a boatneck, cap sleeves, and a beaded bodice. The first, she informs me, is a Gloria Vanderbilt, the second an Oleg Cassini. Both designers produce bridal gowns exclusively for David's.

"Those are pretty nice," I admit. "How much?"

"Very reasonable. Each of these is four hundred ninety-nine dollars."

I take the dresses from Carole and head for a dressing room. Once inside, I remove my sweater and jeans and begin the process of attempting to put the first dress on over the sleeveless white bodysuit I'm wearing. At first the endeavor seems futile. The Gloria Vanderbilt gown is not just large and stiff; it's skirt is lined with what appears to be mosquito netting, and I can't get my hands through the netting to even find the waistline. Finally, I feel the opening, but the netting and skirt bunch up as I try to get the dress over my head.

"Sweetie, are you allright in there?" calls Carole.

"Yeah, but I think the dress is trying to strangle me."

"Do you need help?"

"No, I think I'm okay."

I get the gown down over my neck. The bottom seems much too large, while the top section is too tight. I can't get the back zipper up.

"Carole, this isn't right," I call out.

She knocks gently on the dressing room door and then enters.

"Let's see. Oh, I see. You're not wearing a bra. You have to wear a pushup to try these dresses on. I'll get you one. . . . We have spares. You see, when your bust is pushed up, your back is smaller, and we can get the zipper up."

"I think I'll just try the other one," I tell her.

"Okay."

She vanishes, and I'm soon into the Oleg Cassini gown, which has the same heavy netting, wide skirt, and tight bodice. I can get it on though. I pull the back zipper up and walk, barefoot, out of the dressing room to the mirrors located in the middle of the store. Carole follows me.

"Oh, beautiful, beautiful!" she exclaims. "I thought this dress was too plain. It doesn't really look like much on the rack. But it comes to life on you. It's gorgeous, and it's going to be a favorite of mine from now on."

I pinch at the sides of the dress.

"Is the top supposed to be tight like this?"

"Yeah, that's the traditional style. You'll wear white pumps with that dress—closed shoes—and you'll look even better," she rhapsodizes.

I pull at the skirt and catch my own reflection in the mirror. For a moment I don't recognize myself. I'm a New Yorker with short, spiky brown hair who consistently wears black—but only because there's no darker color. A graduate student and college instructor, I wear pants and sweaters, pantsuits, the occasional skirt if I'm giving a conference paper. No white, no satin, no beading, no long dresses. In this a-line gown, with its long smooth skirt, I look like a different person, the heiress to the throne of a small country, a duchess, or the protagonist of a Harlequin romance novel.

I actually think to myself, "I look amazing. I look like a queen. It would be worth getting married just to be seen in this dress for a few hours. I will never take this dress off."

Carole interrupts, intruding upon my private rapture.

"The boatneck is very flattering. It suits your face. And your neck is bare now. Remember, you'll wear pearls or something, which will really flatter the dress and bring out your blue eyes."

I feel that I have been summoned back to reality by the sound of her voice. I scurry back to the dressing room, close the door behind me, and collapse in the corner. Sitting, barefoot, on the cold dressing room floor, with the wedding gown's a-line skirt pulled up around my waist, I begin to laugh. At first it's a quiet muffled laugh, a giggle. But I can't contain it, and it starts getting louder. Soon it's out of my control. . . . I'm rocking from side to side, shuddering with laughter. Carole is suddenly hovering outside the door.

"Jackie . . . are you allright in there?"

"Yes. I'm having a laughing fit, and I can't stop." I choke the words out.

"Oh, okay, I thought you were crying, you know, which some girls do. It's an emotional time."

By now I'm laughing so hard that I'm twitching. My whole body is convulsing, and the harder I try to muffle my own guffaws, the louder and more hideous they become. To those outside the dressing room it must sound as though I'm choking or strangling a small animal. Tears are streaming down my face. I'm wiping them quickly with my fingers, so that my black mascara doesn't run down my neck and stain the boat-necked, cap-sleeved beaded gown that Mr. Oleg Cassini designed exclusively for David's Bridal and that, temporarily, had me in its spell.

"You take your time, and come out when you're ready, dear," enjoins Carole.

During the subway ride home, I review some of the David's Bridal promotional literature that Carole gave me as I shook her hand and staggered out of the store. I learn that David's has revolutionized the bridal industry by selling directly to its customers, thereby bringing the costs of designer gowns way down. It is now the largest bridal retailer in America, with over one hundred twenty-five stores nationwide. I discover that David's specializes in quick, special order deliveries. I find out that the bride ordering through David's receives substantial discounts—15 percent off the price of dresses for her entire bridal party. David's offers matching ensembles, enabling the client to carry a color scheme—like rum pink accents—through from her gown to the dresses of her bridesmaids and flower girls. On page after page of the David's catalog, I see the same familiar image: a beaming young woman in a white gown, standing motionless, her hands clasped demurely at her waist. This archetype of female fulfillment is the wedding industry's most powerful image. She appears in advertisement after advertisement, magazine after magazine. She haunts the imaginations of American women. For a moment, she captured mine.

Because of its peculiar potency, the bridal gown is the single object most often used in bridal advertisements and most frequently employed in film and television to evoke a mystical state of romantic bliss. Even more than a woman marveling at her engagement ring, the figure of a bride in white proceeding up the aisle on her father's arm, followed by costumed attendants, is employed to suggest rapture and finality. In popular culture the bridal gown is a metonym for female aspirations, hopes, and dreams. Advertisements for gowns differ from the fashion industry's other commercials. The models featured are, for one thing, anonymous. In the era of the supermodel, when the women who strut down designer runways earn unprecedented incomes,[20] act in films, run their own multimillion dollar clothing and makeup empires, chair charitable foundations, and philosophize on late-night talk shows, bridal gown models remain generic to the point of invisibility. Prior to Cover Girl's 1961 international campaign to locate seven top models whose distinct faces would advertise the company's products, models looked blandly indistinguishable from each other. Since the 1960s, the fashion industry has featured the faces of exceptionally beautiful women with distinct features, and this shift has created a star system among models.

The model is no longer merely a vehicle for clothing; she is a persona, a celebrity in her own right.

But in the age of Cindy, Christy, Claudia, and Naomi, when models have such high-profile personalities that they are recognizable to the public by their first names, wedding gown models are anonymous. The women who model gowns for companies like Alfred Angelo, David's Bridal, Eden, L'Amour Bridals, Lazaro, Monique Bridal, Mon Cheri, and Sweetheart Gowns, appear stuck in a 1950s time warp. The layouts in bridal magazines do not highlight each model's particular look but demonstrate their sameness. The bridal gown—not the model—is the focus of each image. Magazines like *Bridal Guide, Bride's, For the Bride, Modern Bride,* and *Martha Stewart Weddings,* and catalogs like the one offered by David's Bridal, feature page after page of advertisements for wedding attire. In photograph after photograph, the same genteel, brown-haired Caucasian woman in her twenties appears against a dark backdrop in traditional wedding costume—white dress, white gloves, pearl choker—clasping a bouquet or standing with her hands placed delicately on her hips, staring into space. In wedding iconography, models are not superstars. They are what they were in the 1950s: young women with well-proportioned bodies on which clothes are hung—hired help.

Perhaps this is because the dress itself is meant to be the pièce de résistance of each ad. The model serves as a universal emblem for marriage rather than a fashion icon with a unique look. But it is also because the wedding dress is itself a throwback garment. In a period of dark neutral clothing—black, brown, and various shades of grey—the bride wears pristine white. In a time of sleekly functional clothes created for female professionals by designers like Donna Karan and Calvin Klein, both of whom specialize in utilitarian bodysuits, minimalist pant suits, turtlenecks, and streamlined jackets and overcoats, the bride wears a stiff dress with a close-fitting bodice and an elaborate skirt that is often accompanied by a veil and a headpiece and always offset by a bouquet of flowers. In an era whose clothing is made of such simple, functional, multiseasonal fabrics as cotton and merino wool, the bride wears a gown comprised of heavy satin, shantung, moire, tulle, crinoline, chantilly lace, or taffeta. Often these fabrics are combined, woven into intricate multilayered patterns, embroidered, decorated with beads, or affixed with bows. In the heyday of the satchel, backpack, and the briefcase, in which the working woman carries her calendar, cellular phone, notebooks, and professional papers and journals, the bride needs only a tiny bejeweled purse containing a makeup compact, a lipstick, and few tissues with which to blot her tears. She leaves even this purse behind as she begins her journey up the aisle to meet her romantic destiny.

The bridal gown hearkens back to an era in which female dependence was a given and women's mobility was severely hampered by layers of heavy uncomfortable clothing. With its tight, corsetlike top piece and broad cascading skirt, the traditional gown takes us back to the nineteenth century, when women's breathing was restricted by tightly laced bodices and their movements impaired by enormous cumbersome hoop skirts. In this era female clothing was so elaborate that monied women often required the help of servants to make even the simplest excursions. Victorian fashion extended the philosophy that female mobility was unimportant, as a women's real work was at home. The ideal lady might venture out for tea at neighbor's house, carrying only a tiny purse or a parasol, but she would not stay long away from the loving bosom of her family, where she was most needed and appreciated. With its heavy fabric, elaborate detail, and stiff shape, the formal wedding dress transports us visually back to the gilded age of the late nineteenth century.

The first white wedding dress on record was actually worn in 1499, by Anne of Brittany, in her wedding to Louis XII of France. Prior to this, European women had been married in their finest dresses, which were often brightly colored. In the seventeenth and eighteenth centuries brides often wore brocades of gold and silver; with their disdain for finery, Puritan women wore grey.[21] The white wedding dress became a staple after the February 1840 nuptial of England's Queen Victoria, whose pristine gown was accompanied by an eighteen-foot train and white gloves and slippers and enhanced by a crown of orange blossoms studded with diamonds. The sight of the most powerful woman in the western world—a stout, plain, matronly girl of twenty—conjoined to her tall elegant cousin, Prince Albert of Saxe-Coburg-Gotha, struck a sentimental chord with the English and American publics. Wedding propagandists gush about Victoria's nuptial to this day, celebrating the ugly duckling queen's transformation, through matrimony's magical elixir.

Arlene Hamilton Stewart writes, "The fact that this young queen had found the great love of her life—and showed it, touched the hearts of women, ordinary and aristocratic. . . . So evident was Victoria's happiness that reporters for women's publications were moved to call this 'the hour of her beauty.'"[22] Following the event, many middle-class and aristocratic women imitated the queen, and by the turn of the twentieth century the white wedding dress had acquired its current symbolism, compressing images of virginity, purity, wealth, and privilege.

The white dress remains a potent symbol of Victoriana. The garment's impracticality bespeaks its origins in an era in which women relinquished control of their bodies, their offspring, and their money when they married. (From the moment a Victorian woman even verbally accepted a marriage proposal, her property belonged to her fiancé.)[23] It is not just that the bridal gown seems designed to confine, to contain, to impede movement and facilitate dependence. The white dress intended to announce each bride's virginity has never lost its prissiness; it emerges from a period in which popular culture had decarnalized women to the point of ethereality, and a powerful ideology claimed that ordinary women possessed no sexual feelings at all.[24] The nineteenth-century bride clad in white was chaste, both inside and out, and her twentieth-century successor maintains this pristine asexuality.

The wedding gown's origins account for the distinct tone of its advertisements. Commercialized images of bridal gowns are like no other current fashion statements. They are oddly anachronistic, like throwbacks to a presexual era of cloistered femininity that etherealized women. According to Victorian cultural ideals, married women devoted exclusively to childrearing were more divine than human, more angelic than mortal. With its presentation of brides as sylphs, modern periodicals capture this prototype perfectly. The bride does not walk; she floats. Even if the fabric of her gown is heavy, she is expected to defy the laws of gravity, soaring up the aisle like a sprite or a fairy. The summer issue of *Bridal Guide* magazine includes a spread of gowns purported to make their wearers resemble "blithe spirits," like Pronovias' ivory silk crepe a-line gown featuring "white yards of chiffon float willowlike around the skirt and sleeves";[25] the sleeves are enormous bat wings that extend several feet beyond the model's wrists, giving her the appearance of a bird about to take flight. A model wearing Alfred Angelo's "ivory silk crepe a-line sheath with a flowing silk chiffon chapel train" lets her chiffon throw blow behind her in the wind, as if she too is about to take flight. "You flow, girl," announces the copy. "Translucent fabrics seemed designed to catch the breeze."[26] Yumi Katsura's satin gown has been crafted to enable its giddy enthralled wearer to walk on air. "Attached to one shoulder is a transparent organza shawl that promises to float down the aisle. A low-waisted silk organza overlay with Alcenon lace appliques enhances the gown's celestial spirit."[27] "Imagine wearing a breeze,"[28] exclaims model Kimora Lee of the Jean Paul Gaultier tulle-and-satin bridal gown she wears in the February 1999 issue of *In Style* magazine. "Modern yet so romantic, it could help you float through a daytime or outdoor wedding like a dream."[29] Enraptured by love, enthralled by her newfound social validation, the modern bride walks on air.

In actual advertisements, however, the bride often appears strangely wooden, especially in comparison with other fashion models. Today's model is usually photographed moving exuberantly, and she is shown in glamorous locations. Even in haute couture, the high fashion model of *Vogue* and *Elle* rides on horseback along the sands of a Caribbean beach, bicycles through New York's Central Park, sips espresso in a Parisian cafe, or rows a gondola in Venice. Often she is photographed walking briskly, caught in midstride, throwing a haughty glance at the camera or glaring contemptuously at a group of male admirers. The wedding gown model, by contrast, is photographed in color in what appears to be a 1950s photographer's studio, standing against a heavy, monochromatic curtain, her body motionless, her head tilted to one side, her hands clasping a small bouquet of white roses. Her formal garment, her seclusion, and her odd stilted posture announce her to be the representative of yet another period of female subordination and decarnalization: the postwar era. It was in the 1950s that photography supplanted illustrations in advertisements for clothing, and the photographs used in early advertising show the influence of generations of previous illustrators. Models' upward-tilting chins, demurely lowered eyes, or flirtatiously slanted heads and their dainty hand placement seemed like the representations of drawings rather than photographs.[30] It is these oddly controlled, stylized presentations of brides that dominate contemporary wedding advertisements.

In an advertisement for the company Mon Cheri, for instance, a brunette stands in front of a cream-colored curtain. The photographer has shot her from the back; she wears a white gown with short sleeves, a scooped back, and a large bow affixed just above her rear end. The gown's enormous train, decorated with a floral pattern, has been spread out behind her and covers almost entirely a large, cream-colored chaise lounge. The model's hair is swept up in a bun on top of her head and held in place by pearl-encrusted hair pins. In her left hand she holds a white bouquet of flowers to her chest; her right hand delicately clasps one of the folds of her dress.[31] In an adjacent image, a blonde model for the company Bianchi wears a sleeveless gown, stole, and crystal tiara. She smiles faintly, her head tilted downward as she clasps the arm of the model posing as her bridesmaid in a purple floor-length gown. The copy reads, "Twinkle like a star in this stunning ivory satin strapless a-line gown with a delicately embroidered band at the top of the bodice that sparkles with tiny pearls and crystals. Inverted pleats open up just under the waist, creating a sweeping, full skirt from a very narrow bodice. Wrap yourself in the matching organza stole, which has a crystal-and-pearl-encrusted satin border that matches the dress. Gown, about two thousand five hundred dollars, and stole, about five hundred dollars."[32] These women combine the baroque extremes of Victorian excess—beading, lace, yards of heavy fabric—with the rigid stylization of 1950s portraiture and fashion advertising, expressing nostalgia for these two periods of sexual conformity. Both are presented, not as individuals, but as all-purpose prototypes for wedlock.

The repertoire of some of the more deliberately hip, contemporary bridal designers contains sleek streamlined versions of the wedding dress, and these designers' updated renditions of the gown are captured in photography that is more in tune with the aesthetic of contemporary fashion. Vera Wang, the reigning designer of urban chic wedding ensembles, promotes her wares with photographs of icy stoic adolescents. These are the models one generally sees featured in high-end fashion magazines: androgynous males with chiseled features who appear either apathetic or faintly menacing and women with elongated bodies who stare directly from the page with an air of cold nonchalance. In one of Wang's advertisements a young man wears a sleek, single-breasted black suit. In a seated position, he is clad in this deliberately minimalist alternative to the frilly fussy tuxedo. He stares at the camera blankly, leaning forward. Because the black-and-white photograph is cropped, we cannot see the right half of his body. Next to him a female Asian model sits in a sleek, sleeveless white dress that hugs her body. She also slouches forward, looking bored and insolent, and her body is also blocked; standing in front of her is a dark-haired model in a strapless gown with a full skirt who is so thin that her formal dress seems to be slipping from her torso. Looking unconcerned, she turns her body toward the camera and gazes from the page with haughty composure.[33]

This photograph deliberately overturns the conventions of the standard bridal advertisement. Its mixed-sex models are not deferential—poised in poses of gratitude or psuedoreligious abnegation to the marriage ideal. Rather, they are the standard purveyors of cool depicted in current fashion iconography; emaciated, smooth-skinned icons who seem to be neither children nor adults but perpetually bored adolescents. The photograph's lack of symmetry, the casual arrangements of the models themselves, and their bad posture, slovenly body language, and conspicuous detachment from marital ritual all express mild contempt for the proceedings. While they may represent members of a wedding party, these individuals, the photographer tells us, are above caring about such old-fashioned ideals as happily ever after. Their languid poses and apathetic stares are carefully staged to show how little marriage matters to them—how far above conventional matrimony these young rebels are. In another black and white photograph for the Vera Wang Bridal Collection a young man with a mop of brown curls is again seated, this time with his legs thrust open. Between them, on the floor, sits a brown-haired model in a strapless white gown, her head resting on his thigh, her arm wrapped carelessly around his right knee. To his left stands another gaunt brunette in one of Wang's signature sleek pieces: a straight, white, body-hugging gown with spaghetti straps; no veil, no jewelry, no bouquet. She leans limply down toward the young man, draping her tubular arms around his shoulders.[34] The image is one of decadent boredom among the very young and very rich. The underlying idea is that these, limpid, pubescent young people dressed in wedding finery are too jaded to pose for choreographed photographs, too cool for wedding bric-a-brac, too sexually liberated for monogamy, and too sophisticated for wedlock's sentimental excesses. (They don't even mind soiling their wedding-day outfits by slouching carelessly on the floor.) By implication, the designer herself is presented as a sophisticate who produces ultramodern garments that are far superior to the suffocatingly frilly Victorian gown, with its hodgepodge of lacy ribbons and bows. Vera Wang's ad campaigns thus brilliantly flatter the modern bride-to-be. Wang's client can think of herself as glamorous in a very contemporary way; too independent, self-sufficient, and coolly knowing for the very institution she is embracing.[35]

In both conventional bridal photographs and sleek, revisionist wedding advertisements, the bride's face is a perfect alabaster mask. Without wrinkles, blemishes, or any signs of discoloration, the airbrushed countenance of this beauty stares tranquilly at the reader. In wedding magazines the bride is always young; her porcelain complexion and air of serenity indicate knowledge of having achieved that which wedding propagandists say is paramount: a public display of sanctioned monogamy. But in every photograph, behind the bride's mask of self-satisfaction lurks another face, the implied face of the "single" woman. The model for the company Cococ Voci, who wears a spaghetti strap gown with a billowing skirt that resembles a shower curtain embroidered with tulips and reclines on a chaise lounge, admiring her own features in a hand mirror, is shadowed by the image of another face.[36] Confronting her own flawless countenance and her social success, she is haunted by the specter of the hag who failed to find a man. Beneath the small precise face of the petite short-haired model for Riva Mivasagar, who wears a strapless gown with a full skirt that cascades to the ground in a tangle of strange pleats and tilts her head toward the camera, is the face of the crone who lives on the margins of marriage culture without companionship or sexual fulfillment, lacking a single individual for whom she comes first. The model whose "groom" "loves the way she looks" in a "satin a-line gown" with "satouche embroidery" and "scalloped edge"[37] beams in grateful recognition of the fact that she might have fallen between the cracks, growing old without the prestige of male partnership. The bride with small gold butterflies in her hair, wearing a "silk satin organza princess-line gown" featuring "three-dimensional pink embroidered buds with pearl centers" and a "detachable, semi-cathedral train"[38] clasps her white-gloved hands together and bites her lip, staring away from the camera in what appears to be happy reflection. Behind her perfectly symmetrical features, framed by a bob of dirty blonde hair, is the face of the aging "single" pariah—the woman who didn't read her husband-hunting manuals carefully enough and failed to capture a man. Behind the beaming countenance of the bride who ascends a stairwell, gathering the skirts of an Impression gown so full it resembles a large pup tent[39] is the aging unmarried woman who was too caught up in work and friends to focus on marriage, or who was undesirable, or who was unlucky.

The wedding industry thus functions through silent intimidation, compressing notions of youthful happiness, social prestige, and physical perfection into a single image: the happy bride. This ultrafeminine creation cannot really function without her counterpart, the dessicated spinster. The source of joy fueling the nuptial extravaganza is the bride's narrow escape from the desuetude of spinsterhood. When she wafts down the aisle in a "sexy sheath" of "bias cut silk chiffon"[40] or a "silk satin mermaid dress that dares to reveal a little leg,"[41] her sartorial splendor announces her triumph to the world. When she stares knowingly at the camera from beneath her veil, clasping the hand of a young flower girl clad in a white, puffy-sleeved dress, who gazes up at her in adulation, she presents herself, in contrast to her homely "single" counterpart, as a model of social perfection.

In an ad for David's Bridal, a luminous blonde bride is seated, wearing a heavily beaded, sleeveless tulle dress with a gigantic skirt. The cumbersome dress overwhelms her small frame; the outfit is like jungle gym covered in brocade. Beside her stands a young attendant who is perhaps five or six years old, wearing an Imitation sleeveless white dress. Her platinum hair is swept up in a headband of daisies, and she carries a basket of pink and red flowers. Mirror images of perfect femininity, the two stare at each other, mutually transfixed.[42] The bride sees what she once was: a child fantasizing about marriage. The girl sees what she hopes to become: a successful woman starring in her own romantic production. This typical image presents wedlock as a transfer of values, from one generation of women to the next, in which "single" existence has no place.

Whether she wears a ball gown (fitted waist with full skirt), an Empire gown (cropped bodice and high waist), a princess gown (vertical lines flowing from the shoulder to the hemline), a sheath (linear, body-hugging form), or an a-line dress (fitted bodice that steadily flares outward toward the hemline),[43] the contemporary bride always wears an expression of social victory. She wears a dress that she will not wear on any other day, a garment designed, purchased, and worn to mark the happiest occasion of her life. This is not, as marriage advisors mistakenly claim, the day a woman is joined in marriage. It is the day she escapes the stigma of being "single." It is the day her relatives breathe a sigh of relief as she enters sanctioned coupledom. Her carriage, self-presentation, and apparel are therefore the visual centerpiece of the contemporary wedding.

Ellen Willis' hilarious 1981 essay, "The Last Unmarried Person in America," is set in a futuristic dystopia—an America in which marriage has been accepted by all as a necessary and universal good. Congress has passed a National Security Act making divorce and premarital sex illegal, enabling local communities to prosecute "single" people as vagrants, and requiring all civil servants to take a monogamy oath. "Singles" are forced to identify themselves publicly by wearing a scarlet S. Prior to this bill, a debate has raged between purists and the pragmatists. The former consider homosexuality a sin; the latter believe that to deny same-sex lovers the sacrament of marriage would keep dangerous communities of gays alive and thriving. The final compromise: homosexuals who have sworn not to have sex are permitted to marry. (Those who decline to take advantage of the privilege are deported to Saudi Arabia.) The Swiftian persona who writes glowingly of such measures is not one person but two, a married couple whose members do not identify themselves but write in the first person plural. The couple glowingly chronicles a number of recently married teams who declare their happiness and protest that peer pressure and the threat of deportation had nothing to do with their decision to tie the knot. "It was so cute the way he proposed,"[44] one of their fictional subjects recounts. "He came over one afternoon while I was sewing scarlet S's on my clothes. . . . He kissed me and said, 'Why spend your time doing that when you could be sewing on my buttons instead?'"[45] A pair of radiant married lesbians announce that they can't wait to start a family and are delighted to be celibate. "We think sex is dirty just like you do."[46]

The essay culminates in its "authors'" meeting with Ruby Tuesday, the last unmarried person in America. A Jewish woman who sleeps in an empty New York City subway car and sports green hair and rhinestone-covered eyelashes, Ruby wears a satin jumpsuit made entirely of scarlet S's sewn together—the perfect visual antithesis to the white wedding dress. This unapologetically "single" girl sneers at the idea of sharing her space ("It's taken me fifteen years to get this car just the way I like it. . . . Why should I share it with some asshole?")[47] and when asked if she prefers to sleep with men or women replies, "Yes," with great enthusiasm.[48] She turns the tables on her married interviewers, accusing them of buckling to sexual intimidation. "'Not at all,' we said hotly, 'we got married because we wanted to! We needed intimacy and community and commitment!'" "'Bullshit,'"[49] Ruby replies, forcing the couple to admit that the fear of deportation actually spurred the jaunt up the aisle.

Willis' essay is the most effective piece of satire I have found that exposes the typical married duo's double talk, demonstrating the extent to which those in couples valorize their own mundane intimidation. When couples claim to have married for the most stellar of personal reasons—commitment, intimacy, friendship, connection—their voices ring peculiarly hollow. It is not just that there are many ways to nurture loving relationships without bringing the government into our bedrooms. It is not just that equating the highest form of commitment with a single matrimonial package is bigoted. The statements themselves elide the whole public consumerist aspect of marriage: the blockbuster party with its flowers, gifts, pageantry, costumes, food, libation, music, celebratory toasts, and dances. Apart from all other considerations, the wedding's splendor provides a strong incentive to sexual conformity. As powerful as wedlock's material rewards are, the thrill of celebration in the heterosexual spotlight is probably even more intoxicating. The contemporary nuptial offers women in particular the sole opportunity of being queen for a day. Relinquishing the chance to plan and execute an extravaganza in honor of one's own love life when such an event is the cultural norm, when relatives wait eagerly to bankroll the party, and when an entire industry exists to cater to each bride's fantasies, is difficult indeed.

But in conversation most couples treat the wedding itself as an afterthought—a superficial nicety. Avoiding the subject of the nuptial, with its excesses of narcissism and financial waste, allows them to present their own marriages in terms of strong self-admiration as a choice based on transcendent love rather than sexual conformity, depth rather than attention-seeking vanity. Six years ago I spent a weekend at a bed and breakfast in Connecticut with my then boyfriend and his three best friends and their wives. It was a celebration of his birthday. After a large Friday night dinner, everyone was tired and staggered off to their rooms to go to sleep. I sat up with the only other nocturnal member of the group, a Harvard graduate working in the field of public health. As generally happens when a married and a "single" woman speak, the subject turned to matrimony. As usually happens in such instances, the "single" woman suddenly finds herself the subject of cross-examination, asked to justify her unmarried state. Is her lover a cad? Why won't he commit? Why won't he make her an honest woman? Why doesn't she pressure him? Doesn't she care about monogamy?

I explained that I didn't. I offered my usual antimarriage polemics: the institution has an intolerably sexist history, the wedding is inconsistent with values of community as it extols one relationship above all others, and, finally, officialized coupledom devalues solitude, and solitude was the basis of the intellectual life I was hoping to build. She smiled at me and explained that she knew what I meant, having been there herself. She was a radical feminist in college and had decided on principal to never become a wife. Skeptical about the ideal of lifelong monogamy and cynical about the wedding's promise of fairy-tale happiness, she had even given herself an "autonomy ceremony" when she turned thirty, asking friends to bring household gifts to which she felt entitled despite her status as a "single" woman.

I was curious to know what had changed her mind, and she explained that it was simply a matter of outgrowing such ideas, getting on with the business of life, which, at some point, she realized, was marriage and children. "When I got into my late thirties, it was like someone had thrown a light switch and I suddenly felt this tremendous desire to start a family," she explained. Feminist critiques of marriage were, she continued, fine at a certain stage of life, but they were analyses that one moved past; I would see what she meant in a few years. She told me proudly that she had recently passed on a job that would have put her line to become the secretary of state of Pennsylvania, because it would entail too much time away from her husband and child.

"And the main thing," she said, "is the wedding day. You look at all those faces of friends and family... they're just so happy for you, so happy. Nothing comes close to it."

"Wouldn't it be great if our friends could be equally happy if we decided to live with friends that we loved, or alone, or even with multiple partners?" I asked.

"Oh that's never going to happen," she replied. "We live in a world of couples. It's very unfair—tragic—that gay men and lesbians don't have the same privileges, though."

Married men and women who consider themselves to be politically enlightened often suggest extending conjugal privileges to gay people. It seems to me that such noblesse oblige does not address fully enough the marital double standard that plagues our culture. The debate over gay marriage has come to a boil in recent years, with activists of all stripes entering the fray. From *New Republic* editor Andrew Sullivan to lesbian author E.J. Graff, openly gay intellectuals have demanded access to matrimony's many privileges, pursuing their goals in the courts and seeking validation from gay-friendly clergy. The Hawaii Supreme Court's 1993 ruling that stated bans on same-sex marriage violate the state constitution's equal privacy clause was a landmark victory for such activists—a triumph that led to backlash in the 1996 Defense of Marriage Act and generated a good deal of alarmist vitriol among conservative pundits.

The desire for marital inclusion is certainly understandable. Income tax advantages, inheritance rights, awards of child custody, post-divorce options relating to support and property division, the benefit of confidential marital communication, and the ability to bring a wrongful death action are all very real privileges—painfully real for those to whom they have been historically denied. "Because literally hundreds of important legal, economic, practical, and social benefits flow directly from marriage, the exclusion from this central institution wreaks real harm on real-life same-sex couples every day,"[50] proclaimed Evan Wolfson, Marriage Project director of the Lambda Legal Defense and Education

Fund. During the 1996 Hearings of the House Judiciary Committee on the Defense of Marriage Act, Massachusetts Congressman Barney Frank, one of two openly gay members of Congress, echoed this lament. "What we're saying is, if we pay taxes, if we work, we simply want to be able to get the same financial benefits and the same responses other people do."[51]

On the other side, heterosexual marriage propagandists put forth arguments that always boil down to the perception of homosexuality as deviant. The belief that gays and lesbians are, in some sense, morally aberrant perverts who do not deserve matrimony's sheltering benefits fuels antigay marriage polemics, no matter how sophisticated such arguments seem at first glance. Conservatives like author William Bennett, who likens same-sex marriage to incest, or Los Angeles KABC radio talk show host Dennis Prager, who presents the Hebrew Bible as an optimal guide to sexuality,[52] cloak their arguments in fancy language and stud their think pieces with literary allusions from antiquity, but their position is finally one of bigoted self-interest. They do not wish to grant homosexuals the right to marry because they think homosexuals inferior. Marriage, that most lofty of human institutions, is designed for the heterosexual elite.

It seems to me that gay people should not buy into their opponents' logic. The desire for same-sex marriage is not only about legal inclusions. It is fueled by intangible desires as well. For many gay men and lesbians, matrimony is a normalizing club that they desperately wish to join. When we're on the outside looking in, it's always tempting to assume insider status. But gay rights advocates, as well as their homophobic adversaries, share the same blind spot. Participants in both sides of the debate overlook the possibility that the couple—gay or straight—is not an intrinsically virtuous unit. I can think of no logical reason why a male-female couple or its same-sex counterpart deserves the special privileges that married heterosexuals now possess. Should conjugality, after all, be a precondition to health insurance? Should being part of a couple determine whether one can immigrate to the United States? Shouldn't each person have the right to determine who his or her primary partners in life are and then have the ability to grant life insurance to and share a lease with these special friends, one of whom might be a lover? It seems to me that all people deserve the basic protections marriage offers. Instead of imbuing gays and lesbians with the rights of the straight majority, I suggest resolving the debate by stripping the heterosexual couple of its privileges. This measure would eliminate not just one but two of our society's cruelest double standards.

In our present, conjugally organized world, though, women who choose to remain "single" are few and far between. Confronted by marriage ideologues, particularly those who possess the zeal of the recently converted, we often feel disoriented. We feel that they perceive us as Ellen Willis' Ruby Tuesday: outré sexual outlaws who are young, misguided, and pointlessly iconoclastic. In the confusion and emotion of such encounters, it is important to remember one thing: we are not the ones expressing a radical point of view. The real extremists are those who believe in marriage as an all-explaining totality and a way of life for everyone despite the institution's unworkability. The zealots are those who believe romantic matrimony can last a lifetime and sustain each individual emotionally. The fanatics are those who, like the couple in Ellen Willis' essay, believe that intimacy can and should exist only within wedlock and that amorous relationships take precedence over all others. With its profusion of flowers, candles, costumes, cameras, music, and fireworks, the contemporary wedding enacts these ideals. At the heart of each nuptial is the figure in the white dress who casts an image of herself as a woman uplifted and improved by love. She enacts this narrative in opposition to her own doppelganger, the female loner who is destined to be bereft, without support, without intimacy, without the only commitment marriage propagandists value: sexual fidelity from a single man.

The terror of spinsterhood implicit in bridal advertising and in the white wedding itself is the explicit subject of the popular television comedy *Ally McBeal*. When this program's protagonist, a "single" attorney living in Boston, fantasizes about her future, she does so solely in terms of the white dress, and her nightmares center on growing old without a husband. Created and largely written by David E. Kelley, the series features Calista Flockhart in the title role. *Ally McBeal* presents Flockhart as an updated version of the husband-hunting heroines of 1930s films. Ally is not a switchboard operator or a department store salesgirl, though; she's a high-paid lawyer with a degree form Harvard, a vibrant group of friends, an apartment out of the pages of *Architectural Digest* that's located in a prime section of Boston, and a closet full of designer clothes. But all she does is pine away for a man. More aggressively marriage-centered than any of the vixens from *Sex and the City*, Ally perceives her life in terms of the marital trajectory, yearning to don the white dress that will signal her participation in a couple. "My whole life, I had a plan," she explains to a colleague bitterly. "When I was twenty-eight I was gonna be taking my little maternity leave, but I would still be on the partnership track. I would be at home at night, cuddled up with my husband, reading *What to Expect When You're Nursing*. Big home life. Big professional life."

Ally has a big professional life, but because she has accepted the cultural lie that a home life must revolve around a husband, she doesn't perceive the significance of her loving domestic partnership with her roommate, the voluptuous, easygoing district attorney Renee Radick (Lisa Nicole Carson). The two share dinners and holidays and throw parties together. They confide in each other and step out regularly to dance at the local bar where much of the show takes place. They date a battery of professional men but always have each other to come home to. They give each other unwavering emotional support. But Ally is so destructively marriage-centered that she cannot appreciate the ways in which this partnership enriches her life. Perceiving her existence in terms of the timeline set by marriage propagandists and understanding her relationships in terms of marriage culture's devastatingly limited definition of family, she cannot enjoy the quotidian pleasures of her daily routine with Renee. Like *Sex and the City*'s Carrie Bradshaw, Ally is oddly unaware of the fact that she possesses a loving, open-ended, nonbiological family, so she dwells on her yearning to "start" a family. She openly admits to the belief that emotional gratification hinges on wedlock. A "single" woman, Ally defers happiness, in her own words, living as if her entire life as "one big Christmas Eve" and anticipating the bonanza of her wedding day, the ultimate Christmas morning, when she will greedily unlock matrimony's rewards.

Calista Flockhart herself is sympathetic to her character's quandary, explaining, "She's looking for somebody to share her life,"[53] as if Ally's close friendships are just a way of passing the time until an all-purpose emotional partner appears. Flockhart has described her signature character as being "beyond" feminism.[54] It's not clear to me what this means.

Ally McBeal is certainly a portrait of a 1990s woman made deeply uncomfortable by feminism; she perceives equal rights activists as humorless hyperaggressive shrews. In her imagination they sometimes appear out of nowhere and bark orders at her, demanding that she abandon the marriage search, toughen up and live like a role model to younger women. Flockhart's costar, Lisa Nicole Carson, appears equally estranged from the goals of organized women's liberation. "There's a lot of women out there like Ally McBeal,"[55] she observes, nonjudgmentally, admitting that she sometimes thinks women should be "in the kitchen with an apron on, barefoot, and pregnant."[56] Like the professionals they play, these two highly paid, successful actresses don't have to embrace feminism, having inherited its achievements. Spoiled by privilege and professional opportunity, such women maintain a private romantic focus, conveniently forgetting the political struggles of the past century that have made their own careers possible.

Ally McBeal doesn't hide the fact that she's on a single-minded quest for state-sanctioned coupledom. More than any other female protagonist on television, she is obsessively, unabashedly husband hungry. She admits that she doesn't really date men so much as she interviews prospective husbands. On her first date with a friendly district attorney, Ally thinks not about him but about the trajectory of their relationship. "This guy has 'future' written all over him," she speculates. When she flirts with the idea that her boss and close friend John Cage (Peter MacNicol) might be a suitable partner for her, she immediately envisions the two of them in wedding attire, posing for snapshots. She sees John in a tuxedo and herself in a ruffled, white bridal gown with a headpiece; they sip champagne and feed each other wedding cake, performing for an invisible imaginary crowd. When she begins dating an elegant British lawyer, she falls into a romantic trance. Traipsing giddily through Boston's early morning streets, she stops at a storefront to view a mannequin wearing a full-length bridal gown. Fantasizing, she substitutes her own face for the mannequin's blank featureless countenance. It's no accident that Ally's private theme song—the tune she hears in her head—is a 1950s hit, the Exciters' song, "Tell Him"; "Tell him, that you're never gonna leave him, tell him, that you're always gonna love him, tell him, tell him, tell him tell him right now," she sings to herself in her more upbeat moments as she bops along, hoping that Mr. Right will turn the next corner. In the show's opening credits singer Vonda Shepard croons, "I believe I am ready, for what love has to bring; got myself together, now I'm ready to sing..." as the opening montage shows the gaunt Flockhart looking intense as she walks hurriedly along a Boston street. This song summarizes Ally's frustration—a quandary that the millions of female viewers who tune in to *Ally McBeal* each week apparently know well. Ally has followed her culture's mandates, "getting herself together," with an education and a profession and starving herself to apparent physical perfection. Creating what she has been told is a desirable package, she's primed for what love has to bring: the white wedding dress, with its promise of conjugal permanence. But somehow, infuriatingly, this magical garment keeps eluding her.

To Ally the dress does not merely represent happiness; it is happiness. It is also popularity, success, prestige, finality, closure. Her yearning to prance up the aisle in the sacred gown, finally part of a couple on display for all to see, is so powerful that she cannot perceive men as individuals. She views them solely in terms of marriage imagery and alludes to each new suitor in the vocabulary of fairy-tale romance as "the one" or not "the one." The premise of the program is that she lost the one; the show began in medias res in 1997, with Ally taking a job at Cage & Fish, the law firm where her exboyfriend Billy Thomas (Gil Bellows) and his wife Georgia (Courtney Thorne-Smith) are employed. The bland innocuous Billy hardly seems an appropriate object for Ally's grand passions, but viewers learn that he had been Ally's other half throughout childhood and high school and had left her heartbroken with no explanation halfway through college. The gaping emotional hole in her life has never been filled, and she has spent the ensuing eight years missing him. The sight of Billy with his blonde nonentity of a wife proves too much for fragile Ally. The members of this lovey-dovey professional couple, after all, share a name, a home, and an office. They enjoy just the kind of enmeshment that she craves. (Because the office has a unisex bathroom, they can even visit the john together.) Billy and Georgia have the kind of social validation Ally aches for, and their married status is made more painful by the fact that Ally feels Billy to be, in some basic way, hers. In the program's first two seasons, before Billy meets an untimely end, Ally stumbles around the office and the streets, despairing over the impossibility of her love for him and crying herself to sleep at night with an inflatable plastic doll in her arms.

Perhaps out of awareness that Ally McBeal's marriage mania might be too much, even for viewers who believe in matrimony, David E. Kelley has adorned his creation with a set of odd mannerisms—quirks intended to show that Ally is really a lovable oddball, a square peg in a round hole. He has mitigated her sexual conventionality with personal eccentricity. The adjectives *quirky, bold, creative,* and *politically incorrect,*[57] which have been applied to the program as a whole, are often likewise used to describe its central character. Like the zany bride-to-be of 1980s and 1990s films, Ally is often described by friends as "strange" and "abnormal." "Do you know that you're odd?" Ally's boss John asks her, and her therapist Tracy (Tracy Ullmann) declares her to be "not a normal person." But like her cinematic predecessor, Ally's alleged uniqueness consists of a few trademark idiosyncrasies rather than an independent point of view. Ally has hallucinations. She sees unicorns (a sign of her romantic nature). She regularly sees a baby in a diaper, chucking spears at her (a reminder that her biological clock is ticking; she was supposed to have snagged the man who would father her child by now). Although stylishly dressed, she is an uncoordinated klutz who stumbles around her office, often falling flat on her face or careening down flights of stairs (a sign that she walks to the beat of her own drummer and lives in her own reality).

These qualities are superficial rather than substantive. Beneath her veneer of oddness Ally McBeal is as conventional a heterosexual romantic as one could hope to find. Kelley's attempt to create a free spirit whose rakish charm is meant to entice viewers doesn't succeed. His overtly nasty characters, such as the unfazable attorney and entrepreneur Ling Woo (Lucy Liu) and her sidekick, the icy lawyer Nelle Porter, (Portia de Rossi) are far more effective. These two coworkers seem to have arrived at the law offices of Cage & Fish to deflate Ally's romanticism. Ling believes that men are gluttonous animals driven by the appendage she refers to as the "dumb stick," and Nelle claims to have awakened from the belief in marital romance when she was nine years old; both women disdain sex due to its messiness. Ally, by comparison, just seems like a woman desperate to be married who needs a neurological workup followed by heavy doses of medication and immersion in a fulltime curriculum of feminist reading.

Ally's work life itself is an extension of her commitment to the marriage ideal. As an attorney, she represents a series of spouses whose complaints highlight the show's conventional marriage philosophy. Ally sues for fraud on behalf of a husband who has recently learned that his wife is not in love with him. She represents a woman whose husband claims sex addiction to excuse his constant infidelities; upon cross-examining the husband, she berates him and calls him an ass. In one episode she brings legal action against a hospital, trying to force its staff to sedate an elderly female patient with A.L.S., so that the unmarried patient can exist fulltime in her private dream world, where she lives with her imaginary husband, Henry. This woman is, in the show's view, the epitome of pathos: old, ugly, sick, and unmarried. Her plight embodies the "single" woman's worst fear—growing old alone without a caretaker. The only realm into which she can retreat is one of pure fantasy, in which she enjoys the companionship of a husband. In her dream sequences she is elegantly dressed, and she and her husband ballroom dance together. Of course, the coldhearted hospital administrators and physicians don't want to drug this patient; they want her to live cognizantly in the real world. But the softhearted female judge presiding over the case orders the hospital to grant the client's wish. By sanctioning an act in which an ailing unmarried woman is literally put out of her misery with sedatives in order to enable her escape the horror of "single" existence, *Ally McBeal* demonstrates the view that wedlock is not just happiness but salvation, a perspective that the program's heroine embodies.

Despite constant whining about her "single" girl status and fear of losing her looks before snagging a male partner, Ally is somewhat aware of the ludicrousness of her own self-abnegating romanticism. She's been drawn specifically as a character whom educated, high-powered urban women would relate to. Ally is intended to be the one who violates social decorum by expressing the retrograde fantasies that female professionals have but can't vocalize. When, in one episode, she and her roommate sip wine at home, Renee philosophizes about the mixed messages modern women receive, pointing out that society prescribes both traditional full-time motherhood and professional advancement, judging harshly the mother who does not care for her children fulltime. "We could change it, Renee," replies Ally. "Society is made up of more women than men, and if women really wanted to change society, they could do it. I plan to change it. I just want to get married first."

Perhaps *Ally McBeal* has struck a deep chord in our culture because so many women leave it to others to effect social change, postponing every meaningful activity until after the day that they have walked up the aisle in white. But a gender neutral, equitable society will never emerge as long as the big white wedding maintains its hold on the female psyche. And, for contemporary women, the bridal gown is the focal point of the marriage fantasy, the visual emblem of matrimonial grandeur. Wedding primers devote entire chapters to the gown and its accouterments, bridal magazines devote half of their space to articles and advertisements for wedding gowns. Magazine and newspaper accounts of celebrity and high society weddings focus inordinately on the dress as a conduit through which women achieve happiness and upward social mobility. The woman dressed in a white gown is almost always described as a "princess" or a "queen," expressing the belief that her married fate represents a startling turn of good fortune. The fantasy at the heart of wedlock's costumes and pageantry is still that of catching prince charming. The traditional wedding outfit does not consist of commoner's clothing; with its beading, train, veil, gloves, and tiara, the bridal ensemble is the clothing of a nineteenth-century female monarch. Regardless of her educational pedigree, profession, or economic situation, today's bride is viewed as a lucky Cinderella who captured the heart of a man who is her social superior and whose commitment elevates her.

The Cinderella narrative at the heart of the wedding day explains—and sustains—the ongoing popular fascination with royal weddings. Husband-hunting literature and wedding primers alike express a fetishistic concern with the love affairs and nuptials of monarchs, aristocrats, and wealthy, high profile families who function as pseudo-aristocrats. "Snag Your Prince!"[58] admonishes the December 2000 issue of *Mademoiselle* magazine. Its "no shame guide to the world's most eligible royals" includes portraits of eighteen-year-old heir to the British throne, William Windsor (described as "eye candy"), who can most easily be found at Ayers Rock in Australia, where he winters. ("You'll need to set up shop there for a while—as an unforgettable waitress or chambermaid.")[59] *Mademoiselle* also suggests pursuing the twenty-eight-year-old Italian Emanuele Maria de Savoia ("granted, his great-grandfather was an asshole for collaborating with Mussolini, but just look at Prince Emanuele's cheekbones")[60] and offers tips on how to land the thirty-two-year-old Spaniard Felipe Santos de Borbon y Grecia ("Memorize the entire works of Bach. Felipe adores Bach almost as much as he adores American women....."),[61] and how to snare the twenty-year-old Jordanian Hamzah bin Al Hussein, who has spa treatments at the Sanctuary Zara Spa on the Dead Sea ("Get your massage credentials in the U.S....and land yourself a job there.")[62] The "single" girl who wishes to climb the social ladder through marriage to the thirty-two-year-old Dane, Prince Frederik Henrik Christian, is advised to move to his native Copenhagen and take up marathon running, a hobby of the prince's.

This article is only partially tongue in cheek. It plays to a common fantasy of snagging the social superior and expresses the sense that marriage always effects upward social mobility for women. We have seen how, despite her immense efforts to secure marriage, at the moment of the proposal scene, the bride-to-be must appear shocked, caught off guard, totally disoriented. The decorum of heterosexual romance dictates that each woman, despite angling to gain access to her suitor, must appear to have met him by happenstance. This is the convention of fated, fairy-tale love. Cinderella differed from her stepsisters in that she didn't prepare laboriously for the ball and set out to catch the eye of the prince; she caught it accidentally. Snow White was asleep—totally unconscious of her prince's gaze—when he happened upon her. To win a monarch, or a husband's heart, the bride must seem like the girl who just happened to be in the right place at the right time rather than the woman who obtained commitment through strenuous machinations and Machiavellian efforts. This contrived nonchalance is also required in the wedding scene, when she must elide her hard work and preparation by appearing in ethereal costume and floating up the aisle, more divine than human. Somehow, the wedding scenario tells us, magically, and without trying, this simple girl found herself a princess/bride.

Wedding propagandists convey this fantasy through their obsessively pious descriptions of the nuptials of monarchs and aristocrats. Bridal reporters are especially impressed with the pomp and circumstance of royal weddings. Certain blockbuster celebrations continue to appear in women's magazines and coffee table books, spawning photographs, articles, memoirs, and hymns of praise. The April 18, 1956, wedding of actress Grace Kelly to Prince Rainier of Monaco has received so much press coverage that it has taken on a life of its own. Wedding nostalgists continue to memorialize this cinematic bride whose fashion sense still inspires bridal trends among the wealthy. A Philadelphia girl from an Irish Catholic background, Kelly had failed to get into college before embarking upon a career as a model and ascending to Hollywood stardom in the 1940s and 1950s. She then moved even farther up the social ladder in her marriage to Rainier, an event that took place in the throne room of the royal palace in Monte Carlo. Her cinematic wedding had seven hundred guests and a dress created by Hollywood designer Helen Rose. In her homage to upscale matrimony, *Legendary Brides*, Latitia Baldridge memorializes Kelly, focusing on her gown:

> The exquisite wedding dress she wore accentuated her translucent skin, classic features, and cover girl figure. It had been fashioned from twenty-five yards of silk taffeta, another twenty-five yards of silk *gros de longer*... and three hundred yards of silk tulle. Not surprisingly, the bridal ensemble was awkward and heavy to wear, but Grace walked into the salon with the elegance and regal bearing of a born princess.[63]

In this account and in others like it, Kelly's ability to manage the difficult bridal attire—her composure, dignity, and good posture—demonstrates her true mettle and her rightful place at her husband's side. She is a bride, because she endures the difficult physical ordeal of the dress, even appearing graceful as she proceeds up the aisle, and, afterwards, waving and laughing from a castle window at her adoring fans. Newspaper coverage at the time applauded Kelly, presenting her story as a hopeful tale of upward social mobility for women.[64] Forget professional ambition and educational achievement, the story promised. Marriage was the path to distinction. Even an anonymous girl from

Philadelphia could win the love of a monarch, become a princess, host a formal wedding for seven hundred and depart for her honeymoon on a yacht accompanied by a flotilla of small boats.[65] Kelly's premature death in a car accident in 1982 seemed only to add luster to her marital legend, enabling the sentimentalization of her story as "the last fairy tale."[66]

Perhaps the most overreported celebrity wedding of the twentieth century, however, is the September 12, 1953, union of John F. Kennedy and Jacqueline Bouvier, then, respectively, an ambitious senator and a glamorous debutante and newspaper reporter. As with Kelly's wedding, storytellers rely on a narrative framework. While Kelly's wedding dress represents upward social mobility within marriage, the Kennedy dress serves as a symbol for the clash of two cultures and the antagonism between family ambition and private love. And, as in Princess Grace's narrative, the bride is given hurdles to overcome and praised for her dignity and restraint. Latitia Baldridge explains that Bouvier's mother, Janet Auchincloss, wanted a private affair, but the groom's mother, Rose Kennedy, wanted a large, Catholic wedding to further her son's political career. Rose's ambition prevailed. The ceremony was performed by Boston's Archbishop Cushing, a Kennedy family friend, and, as Kelly's had, the celebration attracted roughly seven hundred guests. It took place in St. Mary's Church in Newport, Rhode Island, and strained the bride's family budget to the point where certain concessions had to be made. Bouvier could not purchase the top-of-the-line designer dress she yearned for, but, in popular accounts, her natural taste triumphed. "The gown, although not lavish, was beautifully worked—its taffeta skirt was embellished with large circles of interwoven bands of tucking and tiny wax orange blossoms, and its creamy ivory color matched her grandmother's rosepoint veil."[67] The October 1999 issue of *Ladies Home Journal* features a portrait of the young bride in full heterosexual regalia, her gown billowing below her, her veil cascading down her back to the floor, her face tilted demurely downward, her hands clasping her bouquet of pink and white spray orchids, stephanotis, and miniature gardenias. "Nearly fifty years after that September afternoon in Newport, Rhode Island, the images still captivate us," the copy reads.[68] Beneath the photograph is a before-and-after shot of Jackie Kennedy's engagement ring, a 2.84 carat emerald matched with a 2.88 carat diamond, which she had redesigned during her tenure as first lady. On the day of her wedding, the article explains approvingly, Jackie Kennedy wore two magnificent gifts: "a diamond bracelet from her husband and a diamond pin from her father-in-law."[69]

The cult of Jackie Kennedy—the obsession with her clothing and jewelry and the affirmation of her taste—is symptomatic of a culture generally obsessed with women as brides. Of the many biographies that have documented the life and times of this career wife, the most recent refers to her as "America's queen."[70] There is something tellingly vulgar about authors' references to Jackie Kennedy as a princess, a monarch, a ruler, a queen. There is something almost pornographic about her constantly reproduced image and its use to conjure up feelings of awe at the sight of wealthy women marrying even wealthier men. Jackie Kennedy was not, after all, a national leader or a titled aristocrat. She was not a career politician who led America, shaping domestic or foreign policy or making military decisions. She was a good-looking, high-profile married woman who enhanced her husband's political career and cared for their children, and for this reason she continues to spawn hagiographies and inspire worshipful gossip. In magazine layouts she is shown as a beaming young bride, standing at the top of a stairwell, poised to throw her bouquet. Or, in collections like Mark Shaw's *The John F. Kennedys*,[71] she is depicted as an affectionate mother, nuzzling her toddler son, cuddling her young daughter, or frolicking on the beach with both her children. A woman of undeniable physical beauty, she is like a walking advertisement for graceful selfless matrimony.

Viewing photographs of the ultimate celebrity wife nearly fifty years after her wedding, I'm fascinated, not by her, but by the allure she manages to generate even posthumously. In her I see a disappointing picture of female achievement and wasted talent. I see an intelligent woman who accepted the socialization process that taught her how to attract men by modulating her voice to a soft whisper and projecting a defenseless, little-girl persona.[72] I see a person of privilege who received an outstanding education, yet chose to mortgage her future on wedlock, marrying a succession of rich powerful men. Selecting a career as a wife rather than an actual career was not unusual in postwar America, but the decisions of high-profile women validated this choice in powerful ways.

When I look at Kennedy in her flowing veil, appearing to bask in her own self-completion as she contemplates her bouquet, I also see an abbreviated wish list of femininity that many mothers must have had for their daughters in the 1950s and 1960s. Like many women born in the 1960s, I was named for Jackie Kennedy, because, as I was told, she embodied dignity and grace. Her name was mentioned around our house in tones of hushed reverence. She seemed to possess all that a good bride and a successful woman should: beauty, quiet warmth, reserve, delicacy, that sense of being an extraordinary version of someone ordinary, and the quality that bridal handbooks refer to as a "glow."

More than anything she possessed popularity. Her bridal costume announced publicly that she was the object of male desire who had attained the ultimate female prize: a husband. On top of that she possessed awareness of the wedding day as the day that would seal her fate. She knew that, despite behind-the-scenes turmoil, the momentous nature of the wedding procession demanded composure; the show had to go on. The drama written into Jackie Kennedy's wedding photos is the absence of her drunken father, who, having gone on a bender as his daughter was getting ready for her big close-up, was not available to escort her up the aisle. But this crisis did not ruffle the bride's surface calm. One of her bridesmaids admiringly recalls "the splendid way in which she comported herself, her ability to rise above the problems of the day, namely the enforced absence of her father."[73] Latitia Baldridge praises the young bride's perseverance: "It is a measure of Jackie's courage and sense of duty that she was able to overcome her personal disappointment and present a smiling, confident face to the world on her wedding day...without any sign of nerves, she walked up the aisle...."[74] Biographer Sarah Bradford is equally glowing in her praise: "What should have been the happiest day of Jackie's life so far, her wedding day, turned out to be one of the bitterest and in concealing the pain the episode caused her, she showed courage and self-discipline."[75]

Women like Jackie Kennedy are not just famous for being famous; they are famous for being brides. They naturalize femininity through their performance as brides, carrying off the wedding gown with flair, maintaining requisite solemnity during the nuptial proceedings, demonstrating courage in the face of personal adversity, understanding their central role to be that of spouse, handmaiden, helpmate, and projecting this role as a universal female ideal. After Jackie Kennedy, perhaps the second most photographed woman of the twentieth century is another underachieving celebrity wife, Diana Spencer. The sanctification of this unremarkable woman—a celebrated representative of the people who actually came from a wealthy family with court connections,[76] a celebrated feminist icon who could not muster enough ambition to attend college and married rich at the age of nineteen, a celebrated royal spokesperson who could barely utter a sentence without stuttering, a celebrated beauty who had the looks of a toothy British flight attendant—is only explicable in terms of the marriage mystique. Diana's hold on the popular imagination is undeniable, and the outpouring of grief in the aftermath of her sudden accidental death in August 1997 demonstrates a worldwide obsession with her that some scholars have likened to a form of folk religion. In their study, *Diana: The Making of a Media Saint*, Jeffrey Richards, Scott Wilson, and Linda Woodhead describe the week of unprecedented national mourning in England that followed the Princess of Wales' death on August 31, 1997, culminating in her funeral. They also recall grief over her passing as a global event; thirty countries issued Diana commemorative stamps within a month of her demise. "We have seen Italian Christmas cribs with a painted figurine of Diana lining up with the shepherds and the wise men, and private shrines to Diana. We have heard Diana's brother ask that Diana should not be turned into a saint, only for him to construct an island shrine in her memory. And we have read the conservative Catholic Paul Johnson confess in *The Spectator* to praying to Diana."[77]

Whatever the actual facts of her life, the narrative imposed upon Diana was that of a fairy tale romance in which a shy children's nanny captured the heart of the heir to the throne of England and the two prepared to live happily ever after, their dreams ultimately thwarted by the prince's infidelities and the machinations of a cold, snobbish royal family often presented as a gang of haughty blue bloods who ostracized the young princess. Hagiographers do not mention the fact that Diana Spencer had been an unmotivated student who, at the age of fifteen, failed her O-level exams twice, a circumstance that left her unqualified to proceed through the English university system and rendered her virtually unemployable. (She responded to the crisis by busying herself with preparations for her sister Jane's 1978 wedding to Robert Fellowes, the Queen's private secretary.)[78] They do not focus on her marriage-obsessed imagination, which described wedlock in terms of the fairy-tale plots penned by her stepgrandmother, prolific romance writer Barbara Cartland. Admiring biographers of the "people's princess" omit her early ambitions to achieve distinction through marriage to a promi-nent man.[79] They do not include her reliance on spiritual advisors: astrologers, clairvoyants, hypnotherapists, soothsayers, and tarot-card readers, in whose predictions she expressed the utmost confidence.[80]

Spelled out explicitly, these are the behaviors of a directionless woman who dreams of rescue through marriage to a social superior and waits for the strokes of good fortune predicted by spiritualists rather than forging her own career path. They suggest an almost pathological brand of passivity. But because the purest, most undiluted version of the wedding fantasy *is* a tale of female passivity and redemption, the unglamorous details of Diana Spencer's life must be omitted and her inertia woven into the tale of superlative romance that is the basis of her popularity. It is not just that her dreamy-eyed, faraway expression and shyness express a kind of female vulnerability that many find attractive. Her story contains elements irresistible to the public: fate, charmed courtship, engagement at a young age, and a sudden, radical transforma-tion effected through matrimony. The female ability to attract a power-ful male admirer—not with any particular plan but with a quiet static charm—is the quintessence of the Diana narrative and the focal point of photographic accounts of her wedding. Photo spreads of the July 29, 1981, nuptial depict Diana as dazzled and dazzling—a lucky Cinderella and the ultimate princess in the tradition of Princess Grace of Monaco. (Jeffrey Richards reports that immediately following her death, com-poser Stephen Stahl announced his plans for a musical based on the Princess of Wales' life entitled *Queen of Hearts*, which would feature Princess Grace as Diana's guardian angel. Princess Grace and the Princess of Wales are likewise named as two of *In Style* magazine's "iconic brides)[81] Like her predecessor, Diana has an enormous, cumber-some, costly dress. Latitia Baldridge describes how, "Looking every bit the fairy-tale princess, Diana stood at the steps of St. Paul's Cathedral.

Her gown of ivory silk taffeta and old creamy lace, with its delicate embroidery and frilled neckline, captured the imagination of the world—and signaled the return of romantic bridal fashions."[82] The dress is an object of fetishistic concern for other memoirists as well:

> The sumptuous silk taffeta dress, with its lace-trimmed puffed sleeves and frilled neckline, was encrusted with tiny pearls and sequins and had a twenty-five-foot-long train—the longest in royal wedding history. The train was marked by an equally long ivory tulle veil. For luck, a tiny diamond-studded gold horseshoe and a "something blue" bow had been sewn into the waistband.[83]

Diana's butler, Paul Burrell, recalls that her designers, David and Elizabeth Emanuel, actually had two backup dresses on hand in case of a mishap. He remembers that "the bridal bouquet, made that morning by Longman's of Fenchurch Street, the royal florists, included orchids, freesias, Mountbatten roses, a sprig of myrtle grown from Queen Victoria's original wedding bouquet and, as is customary for royal brides, stephanotis for good luck."[84]

As the focal point of the royal wedding, the dress as much as the bride herself requires special maintenance, attention, and surrogates on hand in case of emergency. The bridal ensemble's direct connection to the popularizer of the white wedding, Queen Victoria, is significant. Victoria is envisioned as the progenitor of the royal wedding; as she was transformed, temporarily, into a beauty through marriage, Diana was said to be transformed from a wallflower into a glamorous powerful monarch. The dress, which in photographs appears so huge that it seems ready to attack the petite princess, is the agent of her metamorphosis. Its layers of cumbersome white fabric, its jumble of lace, bows, and jewels, and its incongruously long train announce Diana's celebrity to the world while serving as the ideal metonym for her life. Photographs of the royal wedding show a person whose power rested on her commonness—her lack of direction, distinctiveness, and ability. They show a woman, who, despite an absence of identifiable qualities, generated a marital spectacle, encoding to girls everywhere the silent message that even the most ordinary, unaccomplished young lady can snag a prince if she wishes for marriage hard enough and sits still long enough. Beneath the layers of taffeta, the puffy sleeves gathered at the elbows, and the incongruously long veil, is a young girl who appears lost and underdeveloped. Diana's interior life was, by recent accounts, rather empty, but her exterior life, like her bridal gown, was an enormous, dramatic, overproduced affair that riveted the world. Her dress was the ultimate talismanic object of marriage, the prototypical garment that transforms each "single" girl into a bride, each commoner into a princess. The princess' seamstress, Nina Missestzis, recalls, "How Diana had gazed at herself in the mirror as she stood transformed from a kindergarten teacher into a fairy-tale princess. With tears in her eyes, she kissed the seamstress, 'Oh thank you, Nina, thank you!'"[85] The dress also served as the prop with which the new bride, often described as fragile and childlike, demonstrated her glee at being safely married. After the wedding, Paul Burrell reports, "She went against royal protocol, gathered the train in her arms, shed her satin slippers, and ran barefoot down the length of the principal corridor."[86] In a century in which women have done pioneering research in the sciences, served on the United States Supreme Court, and walked in space,[87] this pampered, giddy child bride remains our most popular and cherished icon.

CHAPTER EIGHT

"I Do"
The Contemporary Wedding Ceremony

All the world's a stage,
And all the men and women merely players...
—William Shakespeare, *As You Like It*

I. Revisiting the Past: Traditional Wedding Ceremonies

When the bride and groom stand in front of a minister or a priest, before a judge, or under a *huppah* (the traditional Jewish wedding canopy), they occupy center stage in a way that they will at no other time in their lives. They are the leads in the drama of heterosexual couplehood, actors in an extravaganza that is both generic and personal. All eyes are cast admiringly upon them. We have seen how, despite its claims about intimacy, modern marriage is profoundly materialistic. It is equally true that in spite of its assertions to be about private feelings, to express the most personal kind of love between two people, the contemporary nuptial is actually a public exhibition, an often garish display of sentimentality. While traditional western marriages took place in the presence of spectators in order to legally solidify the matrimonial bond and establish a new family alliance, such ceremonies involved no real paperwork.[1] The witnesses themselves legitimated the union. Current wedding ceremonies invert this process; they culminate a plethora of bureaucratic procedures such as registration, blood tests, and the procurement of licenses but serve a performative function. Wedding guests act not as witnesses in the legal sense but as members of a rapt admiring audience assembled to ooh and aah over the couple, gasping at the appearance of the bride in white and choking back sobs as the groom slides the wedding band onto her ring finger. The modern bride and groom have the unique opportunity to command group attention, casting an image of themselves as cinematic leads in a stylized romantic production. Toward this end, the contemporary wedding ceremony, with its departures from tradition, its ad hoc additions and subtractions, its quirky combinations of incomputable religious materials, and its by now de rigueur personal flourishes, embodies the values of our age. It affirms the conjugal couple as the ordering principal of society and extols romantic love above all other forms of attachment while advertising its principals' uniqueness as individuals. It also champions such psychological ideals as self-awareness, mutual support, commitment, communication, and respect for each other's "space," and, in a bizarre and fascinating turn, it uses what were once religious mandates aimed at regulating sexual behavior to enforce the modern value of connubial intimacy.

Although the noun *wedding* conjures up images of rapturous romantic feeling, the word's etymology is utilitarian in ways that allude directly to matrimony's sexist origins. According to legal scholar Homer H. Clark, the Anglo-Saxon form of marriage is the original prototype of American wedlock.[2] The Anglo-Saxon word *wedd* referred to a man's pledge to marry a particular woman but also to the purchase money or equivalent in livestock that he paid the bride's father. A wedding was, literally, the purchase of a woman for the purposes of breeding: its original root means to gamble or to wager, perhaps referring to the element of risk involved in the common early medieval practice of taking a bride whom one had not seen and whose face was revealed for the first time when the betrothal was formalized.[3]

Like other forms of medieval wedlock, Anglo-Saxon marriage concluded a process of negotiations between men resulting in a settlement: the groom was required to pay a bride-price, early on to his future father-in-law but in the later Anglo-Saxon period to the bride herself. In the immediate aftermath of the marriage he also presented her with a *morgengifu*, a gift—usually of land—which acknowledged the surrender of her virginity and his acquisition of sexual rights to her. There is minimal extant information on the Anglo-Saxon wedding ritual, although a tenth-century document indicates that betrothal involved the promise from a groom to a bride's kinsmen to "maintain her according to God's law as a man should maintain his wife," and that marriage was optimally formalized by a priest.[4]

Medieval Christian marriage coalesced into a ritual that directly prefigures the modern wedding in the Anglo-Norman world of the eleventh and twelfth centuries: a ceremony that involved the giving away of a bride, an exchange of promises, blessings, and the placement of a ring upon the bride's third finger (followed by a mass) is recorded in this period in the church records of Normandy and England.[5] By the thirteenth century marriage had been further formalized by the required reading of banns by a priest three times prior to the ceremony, with a few days between each announcement. On the wedding day the bridal parties assembled at the church, the dowry was announced, and the couple stood before the church door and recited vows that remain a staple of nuptial celebrations: "I take thee to my wedded wife, to have and to hold, from this day forward, for better or for worse, for richer, for poorer, in sickness and in health, till death us depart." (The verb *depart* connoted separation: in later centuries it was altered to *do part*.) Rings were exchanged with the vow, "With this ring I thee wed, and with my body I thee honor." The wedding then might move inside for a formal mass, but many couples apparently opted to omit this part of the ritual, which entailed additional cost.[6]

By the sixteenth and seventeenth centuries the ceremony had moved from the church door to the building's interior. The ritual began with the fetching of a bride from her parents' home and her accompaniment to the church by her siblings and peers, who were key players in the ceremony. In a period in which conjugality had not yet totally eclipsed the ideal of friendship, in which the word *friend* could mean either a blood relative or a companion, and in which "homosocial relationships ... had an intensity and volatility that is rarely encountered today,"[7] a young couple's friends set the tone for the day. Given away by her brothers and/or friends, the bride undertook the standard vows, although in this period the central part of the ceremony was the blessing of her ring and the confirmation of the groom's dowry, symbolized by the placement of coins on the priest's service book.[8] The ceremony concluded with the priest's symbolic kissing of the bride and and was followed by a free-for-all in which all present scrambled to steal her garter. Before she surrendered the garter, the bride addressed the entire company, asking if there was any blemish upon her groom's character. Assured of his honor, she lifted her gown, relinquished the garter, and was saluted with a round of song that often expressed hopes for the optimal outcome of marriage, the speedy arrival of male progeny: "And bless the bride wheeas leg this graat. An' bless the bridegroom too!/May their love be trusty/The'r bairns be lusty/We wish ye bairs, an'graith and gear/ Long life, good health an'joy/An from this night's embraces spring/In good time a bouncy boy."[9]

By the eighteenth century, when English marriage was conducted with the *Book of Common Prayer*, these customs had eroded. With the idealization of the nuclear family cut off from larger community ties, the role of friends in the marriage service had diminished, and that of parents had increased. The ritual placement of coins fell into disuse, and the custom of the clergyman kissing the bride was abandoned. The peer-dominated wedding gave way to a rite that focused on the dramatic appearance of the bride in white and accorded her father a central role. Despite or perhaps because of its retrograde political message about the propriety of transferring female identity from one male to the next, the somber ritual of a father escorting his daughter up the aisle and depositing her with a waiting groom remains a signature moment of the marital scenario that elicits tears at many contemporary nuptial celebrations.[10] By the late eighteenth and nineteenth centuries the revelry that followed a typical wedding ceremony had been replaced by an elegant party; the pristine choreographed event was sponsored and controlled by the bride's parents, as is often still the case with today's nuptials.[11]

While the modern wedding was (and is) said to represent the culmination of a process by which two people have spontaneously "fallen" into romantic love, with the traditional economic exchanges undermined by a personal quest for happiness in the form of a romantic partner, it was clearly an economic enterprise essential to mobilizing social power and channeling wealth. Among the eighteenth- and nineteenth-century aristocracy, gentry, and increasingly prominent middle class, marriage-oriented courtship was monitored to prevent erroneous alliances, regulated by parents and staged at seasonal balls and assemblies held for young people to meet and mingle, events that are famously depicted in novels of the period.[12] The appropriate generational transfer of family resources to male heirs, a process symbolically enacted through the wedding ceremony, depended, of course, on a woman's chastity. The white dress signaled this virginal state: to ensure her sexual purity, domestic law limited her agency. When an eighteenth-century husband and wife exchanged vows, the wife immediately lost all power over any property she possessed as well as the ability to sue or make a contract on her own. Even the drawing up of a will required her husband's consent, and if he wished to forcibly confine her he was within his legal rights. With all its pageantry and splendor, its effusions of sentiment and purported beneficence, the early modern white wedding was an elaborate event in which a woman celebrated her own subordination.[13]

Whether it is religious or secular, Christian or Jewish, Catholic or Protestant, the contemporary wedding ceremony relies on traditional material, resonating with images from matrimony's troubled past. Because it de facto represents a tradition, no wedding, conventional or innovative, occurs autonomously. Despite the frequent desire of contemporary brides and grooms to create their ceremonies anew, shedding the misogynistic trappings of previous eras by authoring their own personal wedding vows or modifying religious and legal elements of the ritual to create something vaguely humanistic, such transformations are finally not possible. The celebration of exclusivist conjugality, the privileging of romance over friendship, and the idealization of wifely propriety are the D.N.A. of matrimony, and these ideas are embedded in the foundational structures of the wedding ceremony itself. Contemporary marriage propagandists frequently celebrate the new wedding as an innovative personal ceremony that bears little if any resemblance to the staid rites of the past. Gerard J. Monoghan, president of the Association of Bridal Consultants, claims, for instance, "There are two big trends in weddings in the last decade. The first is personalization of the wedding—celebrating heritage. The other is the weekend or destination wedding. Couples are saying, 'This is our special day. We want it to express us.' There are no rules anymore. There are only guidelines."[14] This rhetoric romanticizes the most conventional act that a male or female adult can undertake as something daringly individualistic. Monoghan presents the ethnic flourishes and personal statements and keepsakes that adorn the current wedding as triumphant innovations over the bland formulas of the past, and, like many brides and grooms, he erroneously perceives the personally expressive wedding as a new ritual that shatters the paradigms of previous ages. But in vocalizing their emotions via the wedding industry, today's couples follow a particular and oppressive set of rules that privileges male-female partnership, celebrating wedlock as the ultimate earthly good. Rather than disrupting the hierarchies of the past, today's pseudosensitive wedding represents a basic continuity with conventional marriage and traditional gender norms.

Whatever its religious or ethnic denomination, the contemporary wedding inevitably begins with a cinematic procession up the aisle marked by the bride's appearance in white. Whether it consists of Hebrew blessings or a Catholic mass, the wedding commences with the powerful visual statement of wedlock as the pivotal moment in a woman's life. Whether she is accompanied by an organist's rendition of the wedding march, a gospel choir singing Baptist hymns, or an audiotaped version of John Lennon's "Imagine," today's bride marches toward her amorous destiny clad in the only ritual garment she will ever wear. Whether her ceremony consists of traditional biblical texts or personally authored vows, whether it combines readings from the Song of Songs with Wallace Stevens poems and letters from her grandparents or blends Jewish wedding prayers with a Korean tea ceremony, the bride's first task is to cast a glamorous aura over her audience. Clasping her bouquet and proceeding demurely up the aisle, she basks in the gaze of her onlookers. Both a paragon of female delicacy and a larger than life diva, she is matrimony incarnate. Her arrival at the ceremonial site inaugurates the ritual.

The wedding officiant's opening words, which typically signal the beginning of the ceremony, are equally reactionary. Whether they are religious or secular, sober or humorous, philosophical or anecdotal, they reinforce the message of the bridal procession by announcing that the occasion of uniting a man and woman in sexual/economic union is momentous in a way that the bond between two platonic friends or a community of caring individuals never could be. The readings that follow, the bride and groom's statement of their intent to marry, and the taking of formal vows, all reinforce the notion of gender dichotomization and the ability to find perfection only in heterosexual partnership. Whatever its version, the wedding ceremony presents male and female opposites uniting to create a complementary and self-sustaining unit purported to magically improve both its partners, regulating their desires and thereby promoting a larger kind of social stability. And the exchange of wedding rings hearkens back to a tradition that considered wives as property. Probably worn by Roman women originally, the wedding band gave public notice that a woman was obligated exclusively to her her husband, who didn't wear a ring.[15]

It is important to remember the wedding ceremony's central iconographic source. The western tradition's seminal presentation of male-female partnership occurs in the Bibles's book of Genesis, a text that has never lost its popularity at weddings and is still quoted frequently in the vows of contemporary brides and grooms. The most important heterosexual pair in the western imagination remains Adam and Eve. Revisiting their narrative sheds considerable light on the modern religious wedding as well as its recent newfangled interpretations. Genesis, which offers an account of the creation of the world, also presents a matrix of primordial gender relations. Its initial chapters tells a story of physical reversal so familiar that it has ceased to to startle us. "In the beginning, God created the heaven and the earth." Creation does not, as in much ancient mythology, result from a mingling of male and female deities. In Genesis 1, without female participation, a single male agent creates the universe, separating day from night and water from dry land and creating plant and animal life.[16] The female ability to give life is oddly effaced, and a masculine agent is imbued with procreative powers. This initial vision of male omnipotence recurs in the book's second creation story, in which God, having created the first man from dust, shapes a partner for him after declaring, "It is not good for the man to be alone...."[17] In a reversal of the actual process, a woman emerges from the male body and is fashioned from the man's rib; he subsequently names her as he has named the animals: "This one at last/is bone from my bones, flesh from my flesh!/She shall be called woman, for from man she was taken."[18] The text strikingly inverts the only relationship that fits this description, the bond between a mother and her biological child. After investing the male with procreative power and the exclusively female ability to commingle with, share, and create another body, the biblical narrator finally envisions matrimony: "That is why a man leaves his father and mother and attaches himself to his wife, and the two become one."[19]

Here is the classical language of wedlock: interdependence, enforced lifelong partnership, and for women, domination. After she occasions the fall by eating from the tree of knowledge of good and evil, a division of labor ensues in which the woman is cast in the perpetual service position of childbearer and subordinate to her husband.[20] Gerda Lerner notes that

> the consequences of Adam and Eve's transgression fall with uneven weight upon the woman. The consequence of sexual knowledge is to sever female sexuality from procreation. God puts enmity between the snake and the woman (Gen. 3:15). In the historical context of the times of the writing of Genesis, the snake was clearly associated with the fertility goddess and symbolically represented her. Thus, by God's command, the free and open sexuality of the fertility-goddess was to be forbidden to fallen women. The way her sexuality was to find expression was in motherhood.[21]

The first book of the Hebrew Bible is, obviously, an attempt to provide mythical answers to basic ontological and social questions. Who or what generated temporal existence? Where do the earth and the sky come from? Why do people have dominion over animals? Why must human beings work for their survival? Why are women treated as social inferiors? Why do women suffer while giving birth? Why do people marry? It is important to note that the Jewish (and later the Christian) traditions answer these questions as a seamless totality, presenting a vision of creation in which unequal male/female partnership is legitimate and natural, as inevitable as the beginning of time, the separation of the earth from the sky or the division of water from dry land. The most influential of all western myths entails a metaphoric transfer of procreative power from women to men, the condemnation of solitude, the disenfranchisement of female sexuality, the denigrating punishment of the female body, and a gendered division of labor as prerequisite to marriage. Genesis' ensuing chapters further enshrine the ideal of the couple as a basic social unit with the flood story in chapters 6:9-8:22, in which one male-female dyad of each animal species is preserved to populate the earth after God's purge.[22] But in the Bible the conjugal unit is never removed from its original patriarchal context. When God establishes a covenant with the first Hebrew patriarch, Abraham, he blesses the latter's descendants, in some translations Abraham's "seed," as if, once again, procreation was a purely male act and semen a self-generating fluid that could ensure the survival of future generations.[23] The deity's chief demand is that of circumcision, a physical mark on the bodies of Hebrew males, with no corresponding requirement for females.[24] And the subsequent lists of generations marked by patrilineal descent confirm the Bible's supernaturalization of the penis and its corresponding demotion of married women to the status of subordinates: daughters, wives, mothers, fetal containers.

It would of course be ridiculous to apply contemporary standards to a narrative written between the tenth and the second centuries B.C.E. and compiled from oral legends that had circulated throughout the ancient near east for centuries, legitimating social hierarchies and providing a small embattled tribe with its own national mythology. In the ancient world it was indeed "not good" for a man to be alone. It was not even possible. Human survival was based on an elaborate set of contractual relationships between individual men and women, discrete households, and tribes. In the Babylonia, Assyria, and Canaan of the Bronze and Iron Ages the threat of expansionist empires, rogue bands of nomads, and the violent caprices of nature itself made it essential for each individual to ally him or herself with a protective network, the most basic unit of which was the individual household within which a woman performed domestic service in exchange for physical and economic security for herself and her children. Texts like the Hebrew Bible record this ancient society, demonstrating the ritualized manner with which personal alliances were formed. But they also mythologize conjugal relationships of dependence and subordination.

Jewish and Christian constructions of wedlock still recur to the Genesis story, celebrating Adam and Eve as emulative models. According to the Midrash—a body of imaginative Jewish literature that interprets and fleshes out scripture—Genesis included a wedding at which God functioned as matchmaker, wedding coordinator, and officiant: "The wedding of the first couple was celebrated with pomp never repeated in the whole course of history. God Himself, before presenting Eve to Adam, attired and adorned her as a bride.... The angels surrounded the marriage canopy, and God pronounced the blessings upon the bridal couple, as the *hazzan* does under the *huppah*. The angels then danced and played musical instruments for Adam and Eve...."[25] Judaism's most important mystical text, the thirteenth-century Zohar states that God creates the world continually "by causing weddings to take place."[26] The *Catechism of the Catholic Church* advocates for Catholic marriage because, "Sacred Scripture begins with the creation of man and woman in the image and likeness of God,"[27] claiming that, "Holy Scripture affirms that man and woman were created for one another: 'It is not good that the man should be alone.' The woman, 'flesh of his flesh,' his counterpart, his equal, his nearest in all things, is given to him by God as a 'helpmate'; she thus represents God from whom comes our help."[28]

The ethos of Genesis permeates the contemporary wedding ceremony. Virtually all variations of the religious ceremony now allow participants to select biblical passages: God's proclamation in Genesis 2:18 that it is not good for men to be alone and the subsequent verse in Genesis 2:24 that depicts a man leaving his parents' household and merging with his spouse are perennial favorites among couples and wedding advisors alike. David Glusker and Peter Misner's *Words for Your Wedding: The Wedding Service Book* for example suggests Genesis 2:18-25 as an appropriate reading for the modern wedding. In their 1998 *Sacred Threshold: Rituals and Readings for a Wedding with Spirit* Gertud Meuller Nelson and Christopher Witt likewise offer Genesis 2:18 as a suitably spiritual reading for the contemporary wedding, rendering their own verse translation of the chapter that begins, "Yahweh God said/'It is not right that man should be alone./I shall make him a helper...."[29] Collections of wedding vows for the semireligious couple that do not quote Genesis verbatim tend to use its symbolic language. "John, do you pledge to be trustworthy and true, to cleave to Naomi and to none other, and to make her the center of your life and your thoughts?" is an example of one of the nondenominational vows offered by Michael MacFarlane in *Wedding Vows: Finding the Perfect Words*.[30] The notion of marriage as a man and woman adhering to each other exclusively, yoked together as part of a larger cosmology, is integral to the wedding ideal.

The ideas of Genesis are embedded in formal parts of the nuptial ceremony as well. "Grant great joy to these loving companions as You once gladdened Your creations in the Garden of Eden. Blessed are You, Adonai, who gladden the bridegroom and the bride (*mesameah hatan v'kallah*)."[31] is the sixth of the seven wedding benedictions read at Jewish weddings after the groom has symbolically acquired his bride under the wedding canopy (by taking and returning an object such as a handkerchief and placing a ring on her finger) and two (traditionally male) witnesses have signed the wedding contract. In *The New Jewish Wedding* Anita Diamant explains that the final act of the Jewish ceremony—the groom smashing a glass with his foot—signals an "explosion" that terminates the "silence and hush of mythic time under the *huppah*—when the bride and groom stood as Adam and Eve, when redemption was almost tangible...."[32] In *Your Catholic Wedding* Chris Aridas praises Genesis 2:18-24 as an ideal Old Testament reading for the modern Catholic couple. Aridas explains that the passage is a blueprint for universal gender relations in which a female is created to comfort and aid a primary male agent: "In this beautiful passage from Scripture, we hear God's plan for us unfold. Adam, the man, was in need of a helpmate. The Lord, therefore, proceeds to beasts and birds for him to have; none is a suitable partner. And so God takes Adam's rib and forms from it the woman, Eve, who is indeed a suitable helpmate."[33]

Taken from the Episcopal *Book of Common Prayer,* the basic Protestant ceremony alludes to Christ's quotation of Genesis 2 in the Gospels:

Our Saviour has declared that man shall leave his father and mother and cleave unto his wife. By His apostles He has instructed those who enter this relations to cherish a mutual esteem and love; to bear with each other's infirmities and weaknesses; to comfort each other in sickness, trouble or sorrow; in honesty and industry to provide for each other, and for their household, in temporal things; to pray for, and encourage each other in the things which pertain to God; and to live together as heirs of the grace of life.[34]

The biblical notion of primordial institutionalized togetherness for men and women is here augmented by a harmonious view of companionate marriage—the Protestant marital ideal that has been steadily popularized throughout the West for three centuries and is now the norm. In this model, two complementary heterosexual partners bolster each other, providing more than practical methods of survival, financial alliance, adherence to codes of honor, and biological offspring in accordance with the mandates of a potent and threatening deity who has ordered them to be fruitful and multiply. Here the benefits of wedlock are psychological and consist of such intangibles as "esteem," "love," and "honesty." But when the officiating minister asks, "Who giveth this Woman to be married to this Man?" and takes her hand from that of her father, giving it to her groom, he evokes a long tradition of passing women from one male household to the another. The ceremony signifies her evolution from a literal daughter to another kind of symbolic daughter—a wife. When he pronounces the couple husband and wife and states, "Whom therefore God has joined together, let no man put asunder,"[35] the officiant revives the biblical notion of man and woman as enmeshed inseparable opposites: two who are one. The Protestant ceremony contains two preexisting paradoxes, double messages that reverberate throughout earlier wedding rituals and continue in almost all variations of the present ceremony. The partners are two individuals, but they are also one entity; the woman is an agent but she is also an object of transfer. The Protestant wedding, however, adds to these traditional components of marriage a third layer of meaning: the wedding is not only the marker of a legal alliance but the recognition of a relationship that will be joyful—the wellspring of happiness and self-worth—for both partners. The ceremony's emphasis on the interpersonal psychological aspects of marriage is relatively new and has led to the current situation in which wedding vows are almost always personally expressive.

While it reflects the still potent influence of biblical imagery, non-Protestant, religiously oriented wedding propaganda clearly indicates the predominance of Protestant wedlock as a cultural ideal. "God Said, It Is Not Good For Man To Be Alone," is the title of chapter eight of David C. and Esther R. Gross' recent rhapsodic ode to Jewish marriage, *Under the Wedding Canopy: Love and Marriage in Judaism.*[36] The Grosses echo

the biblical marriage ethos, as centuries of Jewish matrimonial proponents have, alluding to the Bible as a timeless source of wisdom on sexual
relationships:

> In the closing years of the twentieth century, when life for virtually
> everyone is lived at a super-frenetic pace, a person who does not have a
> lifetime companion—a husband or wife—is missing out on one of life's
> most natural, gratifying dimensions. A spouse is someone with whom
> to enjoy the everyday pleasures or problems and heartaches; a spouse
> can bolster the other partner in the marriage in times of need or crisis,
> and in so doing, over the course of time, a bond between them grows
> ever-stronger, and life as a whole does not loom quite so daunting.[37]

In primers like this one, Protestantism's infiltration of Jewish marriage is striking. The biblical and Talmudic mandate of arranged marriage as a means of controlled procreation has been replaced by a
reassuringly sensitive view of the institution. Here the comforts of conjugality are emphasized, and its stresses and difficulties elided. Marriage
is presented as a panacea to the rampant anxiety produced by the late
twentieth century's fast-paced lifestyle. It is sentimentalized as a source
of psychic comfort and relief for both men and women rather than the
traditional obligation—which did not necessarily entail pleasure—
imposed exclusively on Jewish men. The Gross' underlying message is
that those without a single domestic partner suffer from a deficit of emotional support, lacking a key individual with whom to share daily pleasures or turn to in times of crisis, and that this is as it should be. Primers
like these naturalize marriage as the sole source of companionship in an
isolated modern world, failing to acknowledge that it is the modern
institutionalization of marriage at the expense of other equally valid
emotional ties that heightens twenty-first-century isolation.

Catholic sources now tend to concur. Pope Pius XI, writing in 1930,
described marriage in traditional Catholic terms as a divine institution,
"entirely independent of the free will of man, so that if one has once con-
tracted matrimony he is thereby subject to its divinely made laws,"[38]
which entail, "the ready subjection of the wife and her willing obedience,
which the Apostle commands in these words: 'Let women be subject to

their husbands as to the Lord, because the husband is the head of the wife, as Christ is the head of the Church.'"[39] Yet he added that conjugality "blooms more freely, more beautifully, and more nobly, when it is rooted in that more excellent soil, the love of husband and wife which pervades all the duties of married life and holds pride of place in Christian marriage."[40] Religious obligation is not replaced but enhanced by romantic fondness. In his recent Catholic wedding primer, Chris Aridas echoes the sentiments of myriad psychologists and relationship experts by stressing the importance of keeping the modern marriage "spicy." While he insists upon the Catholic precepts of sacramental, permanently binding marriage in which no contraception is used, he urges his readers to keep conjugal romance alive:

> While I was interviewing an engaged couple, the husband-to-be jokingly said to me, "I only ask that she use salt in the macaroni water. I can't stand my pasta unless it's boiled in salted water." Being a priest of Catholic background, it seemed like a reasonable request. But more than that, it brought to my attention just how important salt is for the flavoring of food.
>
> What will be the "salt" of your marriage? What will you need to flavor the routine of daily living? Perhaps it will be a weekly movie, a candlelight dinner, or a time structured into your day when you can share your dreams. Every marriage has its own flavor pods which add the necessary dimension to married life.[41]

That most austere figure of clerical authority, the celibate Catholic priest, now assumes the role of a sensitive marriage counselor concerned, not with the salvation of his parishioners' souls but with the amorous activities of husbands and wives. Rather than instructing his readers in matters of religious doctrine Aridas urges them to literally spice up their relationships, mandating movies, candlelight dinners, and interpersonal communication sessions as means of sustaining conjugal happiness.

The Protestant elevation of wedlock in religious and psychological terms has penetrated traditional wedding ceremonies directly. "Do you, Len, promise to be patient with Rebecca, to laugh at her jokes and to comfort her tears, to live together as lovers?" is a format for wedding vows suggested by Anita Diamant in *The New Jewish Wedding*.[42] Although the Jewish ceremony traditionally has no vows, no "I dos," proclaimed by the couple itself, the modern American convention of self-expression as part of the wedding rite has become so powerful that it has been absorbed into the Jewish ceremony, which now often entails declarations of personal intent in which brides and grooms prove their mental fitness for marriage, listing the numerous ways in which they will bolster each other emotionally. "Do you Dina [sic], promise to be patient with Roger, to learn alongside him what it means to be human, what it means to love another person for a whole lifetime?" is another possible formula offered by Diamant.[43] The verbal exchange between married partners is such a powerful moment in American culture that minority groups have coopted it into their own wedding rituals as a way of demonstrating not just their conformity to the conjugal ideal but their sensitivity, depth, and self-awareness. Harriete Cole's *Jumping the Broom: The African American Wedding Planner* suggests traditional African rites, attire, and cuisine for the modern black couple. But when it comes to the exchange of vows Cole reverts to pseudosensitive convention: "With this ring I wed you and pledge my faithful love. I take you as my wife and pledge to share my life openly with you, to speak the truth to you in love. I promise to honor and tenderly care for you, to cherish and encourage your fulfillment as an individual through all the changes of our lives."[44]

The stated goal of helping each other to maximize individual potential is now part of many wedding ceremonies and is particularly salient in the vows exchanged by brides and grooms. Once a verbal contract intended to harness a woman's sexuality to one man and ensure his lifelong protection of her, the wedding vow is now deployed as an advertisement of a couple's personal growth. This exhibition of sensitivity evidences one of the unstated but central purposes of the contemporary wedding: to demonstrate the modern couple's high degree of emotional advancement. It is no longer necessary, in many states, to have witnesses at a marriage, yet the blockbuster wedding, with its lengthy guest lists, continues. The larger the audience, the more people there to indulge the bride and groom's vanity, watching as they cast a fantasy image of themselves as loving, spiritual, committed adults completing themselves and each other through the sanctifying gesture of matrimony.

II. Sentimentalizing Patriarchy:
The Politics of the Contemporary Wedding Ceremony

Despite its claims to the contrary, the modern wedding ceremony rein-forces the Bible's antiquated notion of male-female enmeshment, female dependence, and sexual ownership. Like all of the accouterments of mar-riage, the contemporary wedding ritual encompasses several conflicting tendencies. It is fraught with the tension between conformity and indi-vidualism that we have seen to characterize virtually all current wedding iconography. The wedding ceremony, however, is the arena in which even the most secular couples can affect religious sentiment, playing at spiritu-ality by combining biblical readings from the Psalms or the Song of Songs with passages from Kahlil Gibran's *The Prophet,* interspersing passages from the Koran or St. Paul's Letters to the Corinthians with Beatles lyrics. A substantial number of psuedoreligious wedding planners that instruct couples in the art of politically correct, religious self-expression have appeared in recent years. While they purport to elevate the wedding cere-mony to new spiritual heights, correcting the sexist excesses of the past, such new age guidebooks actually confirm patriarchal marriage's basic tenets while obscuring those tenets with sentimental doggerel.

The odd hybrid of religious incantation, confessional, and psy-chobabble that comprises today's wedding ceremony is present from the initial words spoken by its officiant. In the traditional Catholic wedding the priest inaugurates the ceremony with the following sentence: "Father, you have made the bond of holy marriage a holy mystery, a sym-bol of Christ's love for his church."[45] The Protestant ceremony begins, "Dearly Beloved: We have come together in the presence of God to wit-ness and bless the joining of this man and this woman in Holy Matrimony."[46] Today, whether the officiant is a priest, minister, rabbi, judge, or, friend,[47] he or she tends to wear many hats, functioning as preacher, psychologist, poet, and sage, and these different roles are apparent in the opening address. Sentimentality rather than religious sanctity dominates the modern wedding's convocation. Daphne Rose Kingma's collection of free-form wedding ceremonies, *Weddings from the Heart,* is a rich source of opening addresses so maudlin they appear parodic. Rose Kingma suggests the words, "We are all gathered here today because love gathers us, and especially, because love had found _____ and _____ and woven them together into the great web of life,"[48] as an ideal introduction to the modern nuptial. This address envisions each marriage as a metonym for a larger great chain of heterosexual being in which all couples are magically connected. The text continues, "We are gathered to remember and rejoice, to recount with one another that it is love, always love, that leads us to our true destination and to celebrate that _____ and _____ have finally arrived."[49]

As in the gooiest Hollywood melodramas, marriage represents the final destination, the consummate happy ending. In another convocation that orders guests to relinquish their analytical capacities, Rose Kingma presents the bride and groom as regal monarchs: "Come on now, pull up your chairs, open your hearts, turn off your minds. We've come here together to celebrate and have fun, to see what magic and moonlight have done, to see how love can make a king and queen out of a man and a woman."[50] For a marriage of "love and commitment" Rose Kingma suggests a psychoanalytic address:

> it is important to remember that, more than you can possibly imagine, you are unconsciously drawn to that person who possesses the attributes you need to be affected by in order to change. These are the very qualities which, because of their capacity to irritate and inspire you, will encourage in you the very dimensions you lack, the qualities which, as you acquire them will represent an enlargement of your soul.[51]

Interestingly, this speech draws on Freudian assumptions while overturning them in fascinating ways. As in psychoanalytic doctrine, men and women are purported to operate in a trancelike state of unconsciousness, the hapless victims of furtive impulses that they cannot perceive or control. Buried in the psyche, however, is not rage, aggression, or sexual desire, those staples of Freudian epistemology, but rather positive romantic pursuit. The subterranean desire that fuels each one of us is, according to Rose Kingma, the yearning for a romantic "other" who will correct our personality defects. Sweetening Freud with the magical thinking of heterosexual romanticism, Rose Kingma naturalizes wedlock by constructing a universal human psyche in which self-improving marital pursuit is the primary urge.

When the contemporary wedding officiant is not condescending to the couple with sentimentalized distortions of psychoanalysis, he or she is posturing in the role of the politically correct ideologue. Gloria Steinem for instance officiated at the August 1998, Los Angeles wedding of actress Kathy Najimy and actor/dancer Dan Finnerty. This wedding was staged, not so much as a nuptial but as a demonstration that its principals were not submitting to sexual convention; it was a self-conscious display of their nutty iconoclasm and politically enlightened views. *In Style* magazine describes the affair as a celebration of Najimy and Finnerty's commitment "to each other and the causes they they believe in."[52] Held at a posh, private men's club in which the portraits of Republicans Ronald and Nancy Reagan and George Bush had been covered with swathes of velvet,[53] the wedding began when the couple's corgi-mix dog trotted up the aisle bearing their wedding rings, Najimy followed, accompanied by the Pogues song "Fairy Tale of New York," and Finnerty followed her, wearing black Converse high-top sneakers. Steinem addressed the celebrity studded audience, noting that while the "couple was thrilled to celebrate their own marriage, they felt sadness for gay friends who don't share the legal right to wed."[54] "I'd hesitated to to have a wedding because my gay and lesbian friends don't have that right," Najimy later explained,[55] and her wedding, which was preceded by drag queen RuPaul blessing the room with sage and included a version of "Ave Maria" by lesbian singer Melissa Etheridge, seems to have been conceived as a festival of gay camp. The event's every kooky detail highlighted both the couple's freewheeling zaniness and their friendliness toward homosexuals. Steinem's remarks seem staged, in fact, as a kind of disclaimer—a statement that while Finnerty and Najimy appeared to be getting married, they were not actually doing so in the way that others might understand that act. But the wedding photographs featured in *In Style* magazine's 1999 special weddings issue show a glowing bride in white, beaming at onlookers in one image, clasping her groom in a passionate embrace in the next. While Najimy might lament American marriage's denial of domestic privileges to gay men and lesbians, her Loree Rodkin engagement ring, Mon Atelier white silk dress complete with beading and a plunging neckline, and three-tiered white wedding cake, all demonstrate her ultimate seduction by the most traditionally homophobic of cultural institutions, a choice as dully conventional as that made by any other bride.

Integral to the political correctness of the new wedding officiant's opening speech is the assertion that the bride and groom will not—or must not—relinquish their individuality within wedlock. "Friends, _____ and _____ have invited us here today to share in the celebration of their marriage—their wedding," begins a suggested convocation in Roger Fritts' primer, *For as Long as We Both Shall Live.*[56] The address continues, "For the giving of yourself in love is difficult. Therefore, you must learn to give of your love without total submission of yourself. Therefore, in your giving, give your joy, your sadness, your interest, your understanding, your knowledge. But in this giving remember to preserve yourself—your integrity, your individuality. This is the challenge of love within marriage."[57] The kind of compensatory rhetoric often found in today's wedding invitations again crops up in modern marriage vows. Philosophical adages assert that even as the bride and groom merge legally, socially and financially, asking that the society in which they live view them as a unified team, they will not lose their independent identities. Married couples of the past, many of whom enjoyed far more solitude and independence within wedlock than do current husbands and wives, would not have thought it necessary to protest the nature of their actions, publicly assuring friends and relatives that they would remain unfettered individuals, even as they joined with another to form a dyad. But the American spirit of individualism demands that today's brides and grooms preserve a fantasy image of themselves as simultaneously fused with another and utterly autonomous, and wedding consultants therefore attempt to allow their clients to have it both ways. Modern ceremonies enable men and women to publicly claim both the freedom that an independent identity offers and the conventional securities of wedlock.

This tension between two dominant American ideologies—heterosexual romanticism and individualism—persists in the next segment of the wedding, the readings. Because this part of the ceremony is pieced together by the bride and groom, it is here that each couple's self-presentation is most dramatic, and it is in this portion of the nuptial that we can perceive the degree to which the modern heterosexual identity is at war with itself. Read by the officiant or by members of the bridal party, the readings are typically literary selections chosen by the couple, ostensibly to express a philosophy of relationships, but actually to project an image as husband and wife. In the contemporary wedding the readings tend to combine incompatible values, celebrating both the ruggedly self-reliant individualism championed by American capitalism, the commitment to institutionalized romance sanctioned by psychologists, and the contemplative tranquility of eastern religions. Today's wedding reading insists that its bride and groom are rugged free agents, romantically committed consorts, and individuals who possess the superior wisdom of Buddhist monks or Hindu yogis.

A standard in the new wedding is the following reading from Kahlil Gibran's *The Prophet*: "Give your hearts/but not into each other's keeping./For only the hand of Life can contain your hearts./And stand together yet not too near together:/For the pillars of the temple stand apart,/And the oak tree and the cypress grow not in each other's/ shadow."[58] This syrupy passage was selected by photographer Ling Li and beauty editor Holly Turchetta, a couple praised by Sally Kilbridge and Mallory Samson in *Real Weddings* as having "exceptional vision."[59] Married barefoot on the beach in Bridgehampton by a Unitarian minister, Turchetta describes her September 9, 1998, wedding as "Flaky, casual, and wonderful."[60] Kilbridge and Samson extol the crashing waves, the sand, the aisle of seashells down which Turchetta's father escorted her, and the casually dressed assembly as components of a wedding "in harmony with the sea."[61] Each natural element seems intended to emphasize the bride and groom's free spiritedness; the fact that they are nature children high on love who cannot be constrained by the legal strictures of matrimony. The feel-good Kahlil Gibran excerpt amplifies this wedding's overall theme. Its metaphor of two separate cypress trees announces that this couple is at one with nature and that the elements of the physical landscape itself sanction their partnership. Integral to this vision is the bride and groom's view of themselves as deeply autonomous—as unique as cypress trees—as they merge into a single socioeconomic unit.

The cultural fear expressed through such readings from *The Prophet* or from the high-blown prose of Rainer Maria Rilke ("Loving does not at first mean merging, surrendering, and uniting with another person—it is an inducement for the individual to ripen, to become something in himself, to become world, to become world in himself for the sake of another person. . . .")[62] is that of enmeshment. Today's bride and groom seem to feel accused of intertwining with each other to the point of mutual strangulation, and their defensiveness underlies the entire matrimonial process. Current wedding readings indicate a pervasive anxiety that husbands and wives will become fused in a pathological symbiosis, unable to subsist without each other for long periods of time. To assuage their own fears and reassure their friends and relatives, brides, and grooms therefore enact ceremonies that assert their independence as married individuals, claiming that they possess the best of all psychological combinations: the allegedly mature ability to "commit" as well as the capacity for solitary self-reliance.

Social enmeshment within marriage and its concurrent devaluation of both solitude and fraternity with friends is certainly a pitfall of marriage and one that could be deterred by eschewing the ceremony altogether. Another equally serious problem, which is not articulated in the current wedding or considered in marriage manuals, is losing oneself, not to the other partner, but to the marital narrative. Once she has obtained the promise of commitment from a man, the modern woman's concern with the jewelry, costumes, announcements, save-the-date cards, bridesmaids, invitations, registration, showers, floral arrangements, music, cuisine, and photographs, constitutes a different kind of romantic vortex in which she can easily lose herself. This fetishistic obsessiveness, ironically, effaces her lover and exists independently of him. A seemingly anomalous materialistic binge, the American bride's immersion in nuptial preparation is comprehensible when we recall that it is through marriage that women still prove their validity and assert their successful femininity to the world at large. A serious attempt at shattering conventional notions of femininity will entail putting the marriage narrative to rest and allowing relationships between men and women to evolve organically. This would mean forgoing symbols of heterosexual joining—the jaunt up the aisle, the name change, the joint tax return. But for most, wedlock's tangible rewards, which include the singular experience of performing as a couple in a public ceremony celebrating one's independence, eroticism, and sensitivity, is too tantalizing.

Despite the wedding's widespread emphasis on individualism, many of today's ceremonial readings are still unabashedly romantic, trumpeting the couple's rhapsodic transformative love that is said to test or even create religious faith. A common reading through which brides and grooms advertise their bliss is Elizabeth Barrett Browning's poem, "How Do I Love Thee?" which actress Kate Mulgrew read at her April 1999 Sanibel Island, Florida, wedding to foundation consultant Tim Hagan. Immediately following the reading Hagan regaled the wedding guests with the story of their first meeting and subsequent separation. "I looked into his face," gushes Mulgrew, recalling the ceremony, "and thought, I'll have to work on his agnosticism, because there certainly is a God!"[63] In his primer *As Long as We Both Shall Live*, Roger Fritts offsets the sobriety of Barrett Browning's verse with the cutesy eroticism of e.e. cummings:

> i like my body when it is with your
> body. It is so quite new a thing.
> Muscles better and nerves more.
> i like your body. i like what it does,
> i like its hows. i like to feel the spine
> of your body and its bones, and the trembling
> -firm-smooth ness and which i will
> again and again and again
> kiss...[64]

Actress Molly Ringwald incorporated cummings into her July 28, 1999, wedding to novelist Valery Lamegniere, which took place in Bordeaux, France. Family members read selected cummings poems along with excerpts from the children's book *The Little Prince* and Vincent Van Gogh's letters to his brother, Theo,[65] in a wedding whose readings seem intended to declare that its bride and groom are both innocently playful, overgrown kids and cultivated aesthetes.

Roger Fritts suggests including readings of letters written by parents to the bride and groom. A benevolent, endearingly inarticulate father of the groom, for instance, might write, "Dear Son, I don't have all the answers. I feel things more than I know things. I married your mother because I loved her, and I felt strongly that it was the right thing to do. That feeling has stayed with me for more than twenty years," and continue, "Today this marriage of yours feels right to me. It it more than the fact that you and Sharon have fun together, or that you share many interests and values. These things are important, but your relationship feels right to me at a much deeper level. It is a feeling that I cannot explain in words."[66] Here the contemporary ceremony integrates self-help techniques like journal and letter writing, allowing relatives to openly express their feelings about marriage, working those emotions out as part of a cathartic "process." But in such readings there is room only for sentiments, never for ideas. Analysis and critique have no place in the modern nuptial. When Fritts' hypothetical father claims that he feels rather than knowing things, he obeys the wedding's unspoken mandate that its principals relinquish the clarity of thought for the visceral satisfaction of romance-derived emotion. Without questioning the assumptions underlying his or his son's choice to marry, this archetypal parent can thereby confidently offer himself as a role model for sexual normalcy, a committed steadfast husband.

To bring participants to this trancelike state of intellectual oblivion, the contemporary wedding author often uses nonwestern prayers and incantations. Daphne Rose Kingma suggests that couples read Hindu marriage poems ("We are word and meaning, united./You are thought and I am sound.") and hymns from the Great Plains Indians ("May our trails lie straight and level before/us. Let us live to behold. We are all your/children and ask these things with good hearts.").[67] When the contemporary nuptial reading is not indulging in such prolonged exercises in sensitivity it is enforcing reactionary notions of gender difference, as in a suggested quotation by Benjamin Franklin in Michael MacFarlane's 1999 collection, *Wedding Vows: Finding the Perfect Words.* "It is the man and woman united that makes the complete human being. Separate, she lacks his force of body and strength of reason; he her softness, sensibility, and acute discernment. Together they are most likely to succeed."[68]

Wedding protocol dictates that readings are followed by vows, promises that the bride and groom make to each other. Setting the stage for these declarations, the officiant typically asks the bride and groom of their intentions. Religious ceremonies reflect the emphasis that each sect places on marriage. The traditional Catholic line of questioning asks if the couple has come to the alter freely, if bride and groom will love each other as "man" and "wife," and if they will eschew contraception and "accept children lovingly from God, and bring them up according to the laws of Christ and his Church?"[69] The Protestant minister asks, "Will you have this man to be your husband; to live together in the covenant of marriage? Will you love him, comfort him, honor and keep him, in sickness and in health; forsaking all others, be faithful to him as long as you both shall live?"[70] He or she then poses the same question to the groom.

In the new ceremony, the focus is no longer on legal doctrine. The theme of the ritual is now emotional support: "_____, do you come before this gathering of friends and family to proclaim your love and devotion for_____? Do you promise to affirm her, respect her, and care for her during times of joy and hardship? Do you commit yourself to share your feelings of happiness and sadness? Do you pledge to remain faithful to her?"[71] Current wedding vows continue this tone of feel-good sloganeering. Today's bride often utilizes the moment of taking her vows as an opportunity to demonstrate empowerment and heightened self-esteem. Actress Diane Ladd, for instance, in her February 1999 wedding to businessman Robert Charles Hunter, authored her own vows. In a ceremony presided over by actress Della Reese, a minister of the Understanding Principles for Better Living Church, Ladd vowed to be loved, at which point, "All the women screamed, 'Yes!' Because you have to vow to accept love as well as give it."[72] When the bride is not engaging in consciousness-raising exercises by affirming her own amorous entitlement she is coyly displaying the quirks of her romance through her wedding vows. In her July 2000 Malibu wedding to actor Brad Pitt, actress Jennifer Aniston, for instance, promised to always make his favorite banana milkshake, while he pledged to "split the difference on the thermostat."[73]

Michael MacFarlane offers numerous sets of vows for the religious, religiously mixed, or nondenominational couple: his self-proclaimed intention is to "instruct, inspire, comfort, warn, and validate."[74] Writing as a psychotherapeutic marriage coach and a seemingly delirious champion of conjugality, he offers vows that are mawkish (Bride: "My wonderful, beautiful lover. The hero of my childhood and the subject of my girlish dreams. You have carried my books and stolen my heart."),[75] conventional (Bride: "David, my friend, how I have come to love you...I knew I needed to be part of your life, and you a part of mine. I knew of no other way than for me to marry the wonderful man of my dreams, but feared you would never ask.[76])," and patently insane (Groom: ... "The crown of creation, however, is a wise, handsome woman, as ripe as the summer fruit. Grown strong in mind and body, and ready to meet a noble and appreciative companion. My lady, I vow to be that companion....").[77] Some have the cadence of children's nursery rhymes:

> Bride: I love you and you love me and soon we two shall marry
> I hold your hand and know your heart, and give myself
> This day,
> For I love you and you love me,
> And love will show the way.

> Groom: I love you and you love me and soon we two shall marry
> I take your hand and leave my heart, what more can I
> Give [sic].
> For I love you and you love me,
> As long as we both shall live.

The Hallmark card quality of these declarations demonstrates that today's wedding is for some an opportunity to mythologize their romantic attachments through excessive imagery, cloyingly sweet metaphors, and embarrassingly sentimental ballads. For many, personal success is tantamount to romantic fulfillment, and the new wedding offers an opportunity for brides and grooms to flaunt their amorous achievements in readings that cannot be too ardent, passionate, or hyperbolic.

While they consciously deviate from the vaguely ominous, doctrinaire vows of the past, contemporary wedding vows display little evidence of independent thought. The vows promoted by wedding advisors and mouthed by brides and grooms almost uniformly promote fused romantic attachment and envision a hierarchy of relationships in which one's spouse is paramount. In *With These Words I Thee Wed*, for instance,

Barbara Eklof suggests an exchange in which the groom intones, "You and I, coming together as one," and then each partner states, "I . . . promise to honor and cherish you above all others from this day forward. I bring to you this flow, the flower of my heart, as my wedding gift,"[78] and another vow in which the groom proclaims, "This love means more to us than anything else in life."[79] Yet, in today's marital marketplace, even a wedding propagandist unabashedly committed to the nuptial relationship at the expense of all others, must nod deferentially to the ideal of individualism within matrimony. Eklof also suggests vows in which partners list the ways that romantic attachment has strengthened them, enhancing their individual identities: "I have been told that love carried with it dependency and weakness, but I found a new and stronger expression of my place in this world,"[80] or, "We have learned to respect our individual outlooks, to share our thoughts and experiences with one another . . . we come together willingly today as distinct, growing individuals, each true to our love, each sound in spirit, each free to explore the dimensions of life in the spirit of unity, cooperation, trust."[81] "I commit my life to our partnership in marriage. . . . I promise to express my thoughts and emotions to you and to listen to you in times of joy and in times of sorrow," is a vow suggested by Roger Fritts.[82]

Alternate formats for the exchange of vows now exist for the same apparent purpose of tweaking tradition, but such formats inevitably reify our culture's pervasive idealization of the romantic couple. Daphne Rose Kingma proposes that after taking their own vows, the bride and groom ask those present for a "vow of support": the promise to encourage and sustain them as a couple, as if the requisite party and expensive gifts were not quite enough.[83] In Style magazine suggests that the modern bride and groom "share their vows," not by opening up the conjugal circle and making declarations of commitment to their friends, but by asking their officiant to "invite all married guests to renew their vows" as part of the celebration.[84] Rather than serving as the kind of communal celebration that marriage is often erroneously claimed to be, this wedding becomes a heterosexist house of mirrors in which each couple gazes at its own amplified image in that of the bride and groom, sets of married lovebirds affix to each other in self-congratualtory devotion, and "single" participants are made to feel profoundly inadequate.

Immediately following the exchange of wedding vows is an exchange of rings. The American wedding ring has decidedly homespun origins. In the colonial period an engaged woman customarily received a thimble—a perfect symbol for preindustrial female domesticity—from her fiancé. After the wedding, the cup of the thimble was cut off and its plain top became her wedding band.[85] Like most components of matrimony, the modern wedding ring has been shaped by the forces of commercialism: it is now a costly and elegant trinket. Wedding bands now consist of elaborate designs combining yellow and white gold and strands of braided silver. Today's rings have intricate engravings and are embedded with precious stones, or they are shaped to express ethnicity, like those from Charriol's Wedding Collection, "A passionate celebration of Celtic art... available in exquisite styles incorporating eighteen karat white gold, yellow gold, and stainless steel cable with diamonds."[86] Women's rings are not the only elaborate ornaments: contemporary male wedding bands are forged of gold and brushed platinum and studded with diamonds or decorated with the grooms' birthstones. Marriage consultants treat the rings as objects with talismanic power. Addressing the modern bride directly, the editors of *Wedding Bells* magazine claim that, "An engraved inscription gracing the inside of your wedding band can be a powerful declaration of hope and love."[87] They suggest epigrams that emphasize marital permanence and fidelity, such as "*Semper fidelis*" (Always faithful), "You and I will lovers die," "Forever in love," and "Always."[88] Today's wedding band does not advertise its wearers' sentiments through language alone. It uses ethnic and even mathematical symbols and incorporates designs that function as amatory hieroglyphics, such as the mathematical indicator of infinity or the figure of a gold dragon swallowing its own tail as a symbol for eternity.[89] *For the Bride* magazine suggests "banding together" with the fourteen- or eighteen-karat-gold wedding rings from the Bradford collection. This line of customized rings offers both "forever" and "eternity" designs and allows brides and grooms to encode "cryptic messages" such as "hugs and kisses," "blinded by love," "lucky in love," or "star crossed lovers" into their designs.[90] Sometimes, however, wedding band inscriptions are jokey. Actor David Arquette and his wife Courtney Cox Arquette wear bands inscribed with the slogan, "A deal's a deal," an expression that comes from a friend's father whose marriage Cox Arquette admires.[91]

The exchange of rings is one of the key moments of the ceremony, the point at which the bride and groom don symbols of marriage that are ostensibly permanent, as opposed to the temporary white dress and black tuxedo. Directly following the exchange, the officiant declares the couple married. In Jewish tradition, because a man acquires a woman in marriage, only he decorates her with a ring, stating, "By this ring you are consecrated to me (as my wife) in accordance with the traditions of Moses and Israel." However, many modern Jews have egalitarianized the ceremony, rendering it a ritual of mutual acquisition, as if extending the right of possession to both parties eliminates the problematic nature of sexual ownership of another individual. Anita Diamant suggests that today's Jewish bride intone the biblical phrase from Song of Songs, "I am my beloved's and my beloved is mine," when slipping a wedding band on his finger.[92] The Roman Catholic ceremony entails the priestly statement, "May the Lord bless these rings that you give to each other as the sign of your love and fidelity. Amen," and the Protestant wedding contains the affirmation, "Bless, O Lord, this ring, to be a sign of the vows by which this man and this woman have bound themselves to each other, through Jesus Christ our Lord. Amen."[93]

The contemporary blessing has been, of course, psychologized and transformed into personal anecdote: "We looked for the perfect ring for a long time. As I wear this ring, it will remind me that you and I will be together for a long time. I will remember that when I am struggling, you will struggle with me. When I rejoice, you will rejoice with me. When you struggle, I will struggle with you. When you rejoice, I will rejoice with you."[94] And of course, in keeping with the current wedding's overall goals of sanitizing the power dynamics embedded in traditional marriage ritual and differentiating its principals from brides and grooms of the past, the wedding officiant must now protest that the rings are not besmirched by the sexual mores of antiquity: "Some say the ring is a sign of ownership. I prefer to believe it is a symbol of a union that has no beginning and no end. I believe the gold is symbolic of beauty and value, and of something so precious, it may not be removed or replaced."[95]

Master purveyors of interpersonal hype, contemporary wedding advisors provide formulas through which the most sexist customs of the past are rendered benign, alchemized into feminist affirmations. Similarly, they transform the most legalistic of religious rituals into moments of pure self-expression. The traditional declaration of marital status, the Catholic, "What God has joined, men must not divide," the Protestant, "I pronounce that they are husband and in the Name of the Father, and of the Son, and of the Holy Spirit," and the generic American, "I now pronounce you husband and wife," are announcements that have remained largely intact. Most guidebooks refrain from suggesting personal versions of these statements, but the occasional wedding consultant offers an individualized rendition. Roger Fritts provides a new version of the declaration in which the bride and groom themselves make the announcement in a moment designed to highlight their self-awareness, adventurousness, and assertiveness: "Because we have grown in knowledge and love for one another; because we agree in our desire to go forward into life seeking a richer and ever deepening relationship and because we have pledged ourselves to meet sorrow and joy as one family, we affirm that we are now husband and wife."[96] Daphne Rose Kingma suggests that the wedding officiant express his or her her own pleasure at making the declaration, praising the effusiveness of the bride and groom: "Because, _____ and _____, you have showered our hearts with expressions of your love, and promised each other the joy of all your days, it gives me great pleasure to now pronounce you husband and wife." [97]

Today's wedding ceremony can end in many ways. The ritual's closing demands a celebratory note, so primers suggest such upbeat antics as the joint shattering of a glass underfoot, a choir beating tambourines and bursting into joyous song, the release of doves into the air, or a display of fireworks that emblazen the bride and groom's name across the sky. In formulas for concluding wedding ceremonies, the religiously oriented, new age wedding advisor tends again to hearken back to traditional religious sources and amend those sources in inadequate ways. His or her standard move is to reinterpret or alter an ancient ritual or text, sanitizing it according to the precepts of popular psychology. One such effort is Debra Orenstein's essay, "*Yihud* and the Holiness of Matrimony," published in her volume, *Lifecycles: Jewish Women on Life*

Passages and Personal Milestones. A compilation of anecdote, poetry, and reminiscence by Jewish women, *Lifecycles* is one of many recent attempts to expand the traditionally male-dominated realm of Jewish ritual to include women. It contains newly written prayers for such events as menstruation, miscarriage, having a child by caesarean, and coming out as a Jewish lesbian as well as simplistic recipes for creating one's own religious rituals that resemble the "How to Write Your Own Vows" sections of current wedding handbooks. Many of the newly created prayers in Orenstein's anthology are intended to console Jewish women in moments of trauma (e.g. incidents of sexual abuse), to "affirm" their emotions during weighty decisions (e.g. divorce, the choice to have an abortion), or to aid them through difficult periods (e.g. the struggle to conceive a child, menopause).

With its emphasis on healing and psychological validation, the book exemplifies an unfortunate trend reflected in the new wedding itself: the transformation of feminism from an organized initiative with an agenda of political demands to a kind of life-affirming self-help movement with such intangible aims as empowerment, emotional recuperation, and increased self-esteem. Orenstein's assumption appears to be that well into contemporary American feminism's third wave, Jewish women remain in a state of emotional convalescence from which they must be gently coaxed with rituals that serve as emotional salves. With its chronicling of the kind of epiphanic "click moments"—sudden, life-changing emotional breakthroughs—frequently experienced by female guests of the *Oprah Winfrey Show,* this soporific anthology also demonstrates new age philosophy's infusion of traditional religions like Judaism, a phenomenon that has impacted directly on the Jewish wedding. But as Orenstein's own marriage ritual demonstrates, the sensitive flourishes of the new Jewish wedding are superficial additions that infuse the proceedings with a warm glow without altering the ceremony's unacceptable tenets.

An ordained conservative rabbi, Orenstein concedes that, "in its classical form, the Jewish wedding seals and celebrates acquisition of a woman by a man," and she admits to the forces of socialization that encourage women, from childhood, to anticipate wedlock as the pivotal event of their lives, acknowledging, "Most girls are still raised to dream of their wedding day."[98] Her solution to this dilemma is the egalitarianizing of ancient ritual, as if double ring ceremonies and the smashing of a glass by both a Jewish bride and groom could correct the imbalances of wedlock or puncture the marriage mystique. "Times have changed!" she exclaims jubilantly.[99] She rewrites the traditional Jewish *Yihud*, a custom now gaining popularity at non-Jewish weddings, in which the bride and groom separate from the celebration and spend a few moments alone.[100] She presents her revised *Yihud* as part of what she sees as a widespread and laudatory trend toward matrimonial reform, but the biblical epigraph to her essay is all too familiar: "Therefore a man leaves his father and mother and cleaves to his wife, and they become one flesh."[101] In selecting this quotation Orenstein validates the familiar paradigm of enmeshed conjugality in which the family regenerates itself through heterosexual partnership.

Despite her self-advertisement as an expert on gender studies, she appears unaware of the retrograde gender assumptions embedded in her essay, which is a kind of ode to the modern Jewish version of insular coupledom depicted in Genesis. The *Yihud*, she explains, "implicitly asserts that one feature of marital status is being separated from others—from one's family of origin, from other potential partners—and joined, first and foremost, with one's spouse."[102] Orenstein laments the abandonment of this tradition to the Anglo/American receiving line as a sign of ethnic assimilation, "A sad turn of events. The communal aspects of weddings are pressing and important, but it is wonderful, I think, to preserve a moment of privacy in the midst of a day devoted to being 'on display.'"[103] Her ritual is as follows:

CELEBRATING THE MOMENT
AND PUTTING EACH OTHER FIRST

Once in seclusion the couple reads: Now, with friends and family outside celebrating, we take our private time: Time to drink each other in, to be alone together, to acknowledge that we are married! *Yihud* comes from a root that means both aloneness and togetherness. No matter how much we are partners in this new marriage, we will always be our individual selves. No matter how alone each of us may feel, we will always have each other.

These first few minutes of our marriage, we take for us—for *our* joy, *our* privacy, *our* chance to laugh or cry. There are many times and occasions when we serve the community, but sometimes, we as a couple come first. Sometimes, we close the door and say, "They will wait. I need you."

After this miniorgy of heterosexual self-affirmation, the partners give each other mouthfuls of food, reciting, "I will feed you forever./I will feed you with righteousness./I will feed you with justice./I will feed you with love./I will feed you with compassion./I will feed you with faithfulness."[104] The therapeutic *Yihud* continues with a quotation from Genesis that marks the biblical patriarch, Isaac, acquiring his wife Rebecca: "*Groom*: And Isaac took Rebecca and made her his wife. And he loved her and found comfort."[105] It concludes with Judaism's traditional prayer for momentous occasions, the *Sheheheyanu*.

While Orenstein contrasts the public acts of self-display that occur throughout a wedding with the private union of *Yihud*, she omits to mention that this ancient custom once entailed a different kind of display: the ritual was originally intended to allow the groom his first sexual access to the bride and to enable the couple to exhibit the bloody undergarments that evidenced her virginity prior to the marriage.[106] Any reenactment of the *Yihud* occurs on a historical continuum in which female sexual and reproductive capacities were reified by men and chastity imposed upon women, often with draconian consequences for those who pursued independent sexual destinies. But even if it attempts to sever itself from the sexual double standard of the past, a ceremony like this one is hardly private. Retreating into romantic isolation in the midst of a gala event celebrating oneself is, in fact, an act of utter exhibitionism. Like the bride and groom's dramatic departure for their honeymoon, in which they wave, blow kisses to those whom they imagine to be their adoring fans, and retreat conspicuously into erotic isolation, this kind of retirement demonstrates the emotional attentiveness to one's partner championed by mental health professionals. While allowing the modern Jewish bride and groom to exhibit their capacity for "intimacy" through this performative moment of alone time (during which they, of course, proclaim their uncompromised individuality), the new *Yihud* as well allegorizes the couple as a unit discrete from biological family and friends. As it uses the standard compensatory rhetoric of the new age wedding, praising personal autonomy, Orenstein's ritual enacts the modern marriage system's hierarchy, demanding that bride and groom intone the belief that they as a couple "come first"; that the romantic bond precedes—and therefore diminishes—all others. Echoing the sentiment of her chosen epigraph, the ritual asks the members of each pair to drink each other in and feed each other. In this vision the heterosexual relationship is autonomously self sustaining: the couple is a nucleus that supplies its own protein, living off of love and fidelity. And the hackneyed romanticism is offset by a biblical quotation in which a patriarch "takes" a woman, finding comfort in her domestic partnership/subordination. Despite its ostentatious sentimentality and its claims to the contrary, this ceremony, like so many others that characterize the new wedding, does not alter wedlock's basic paradigms. "We have great attachments to and nostalgia for the Jewish wedding ceremony as a whole,"[107] Orenstein writes, and nostalgia rather than analysis informs her approach to marriage ritual. Her *Yihud* compresses and sweetens images of romantic fusion, marital primacy, and masculinist domination, naturalizing the inequitable but allegedly happy ending in marriage that our culture promises each bride and groom.

Orenstein typifies the new age wedding propagandist's dual anxiety. On the one hand such authors express concern that the bride and groom will relinquish their independence. On the other hand they appear worried that the partners will succumb to distraction, failing to put each other first. Such authors seem oddly unaware that abandoning oneself to an erotic relationship and sacrificing other aspects of one's life *is* the formula for modern American marriage. When married men and women make this error, they do so, not as psychological deviants, but as individuals responding to the mandates of a social institution. In a romance-saturated culture such as our own, it is rare that men and women who have declared themselves to be "in love" and committed to the social arrangement of the couple will fail to elevate their partners to the appropriately lofty status. The second concern—neglect of work, relatives, and most often, friends—addresses a more serious pitfall. But a way to eliminate both problems is to eschew marriage. Without a person to whom we are legally yoked, the prospect of losing our autonomy becomes less probable and less threatening. When we abandon the fantasy of a ceremony that announces to the world that this man or woman is the most important person in our lives, we as well become less likely to neglect our other relationships. Our lover can be more easily woven into the everyday fabric of our lives. He or she becomes one of many valued emotional allies, not the primary individual on whom our happiness rests.

But nostalgic yearning for the marriage ceremony makes it difficult for modern women—and men—to relinquish the conjugal ideal. A deep attachment to marriage ritual persists, even during periods of social upheaval and transformation. A counterculture favorite, the film *Alice's Restaurant* contains an archetypal, large-scale, alternative wedding ceremony. Directed by Arthur Penn from a screenplay by Penn and Venable Herndon, this 1969 film appeared at the end of the decade that gave birth to the free-form wedding. It is based on Arlo Guthrie's satirical antiwar ballad, "The Alice's Restaurant Massacree" and features Guthrie (as himself) in the lead role. The movie chronicles his truncated college experience and his subsequent attempts to launch a musical career by playing on the folk circuit. Guthrie shuttles between an apartment in New York City and his second home in Stockbridge, Massachusetts, where in a deconsecrated church Ray and Alice Brock (James Broderick and Pat Quinn) run a restaurant while serving as surrogate parents to a group of adolescent drifters. When in New York he frequently occupies a chair alongside the hospital bed in which his father, legendary singer Woody Guthrie (Joseph Boley), is dying of a degenerative nerve disease. And he makes occasional stops at the draft board office on Whitehall Street in lower Manhattan. The Vietnam war is raging; his number may be up.

In the draft board scenes, which involve waiting on lines, submitting to invasive physical exams, spilling urine samples, and attempting to fill out baffling forms, we see that this affable young man is as powerless over large impersonal institutions like the United States Army as he is over his father's deterioration from the congenital disease that may one day take his own life as well. This amusing film is very much about accepting one's own powerlessness with a sense of humor. It's also about those who galvanize to challenge social and political authority, including Pete Seeger (played by himself), who, in a great scene, sings "The

Pastures of Plenty," a haunting ballad about the abuse of migrant laborers; the incapacitated Guthrie; and Alice and Ray Brock, who challenge the ideal of the closed nuclear family by building their own open-ended, nonbiological community. But the film ends on a cliched romantic note with an enormous, tumultuous flower ceremony. The Brocks stage a wedding at their church in which they affirm their original vows, attempting to rekindle lost passion and repair a faltering relationship. (The actual Brocks divorced.)[108]

With its wild costumes and orgiastic consumption of drugs, alcohol, and food, this event seems to epitomize what, in the 1960s, was called a "love in." Arlo Guthrie participates, wearing a shiny turquoise costume that resembles a medieval jester's robe purchased at K-Mart. The groom, Ray, wears a top hat and tails, and Alice wears a white dress, carries a garland of flowers, and has daisies strewn in her hair. She smiles demurely as Ray escorts her up the aisle of the balloon-festooned church. The "minister," clad in a tuxedo and a crimson ascot, shouts the words of the ceremony like a carnival barker:

And Adam said, "wherefore a man shall leave father and mother and shall cleave to his wife, and they shall be two in one flesh." Alice, do you take this man for your lawful, loving man, for bad or for better, for drunk or for sober, for high or for lower, for husband and lover, today and tomorrow, til death do you part?

"I do," replies Alice. The officiant continues:

Ray, do you take this woman to be your ever wedded woman, for bitchy and for giving, for love and for living, in peace and in dissension, in health and affliction, today and tomorrow, til death do you part?

"I do," answers Ray, beaming, and the large crowd whoops with approval and shouts, "We now pronounce you man and wife!" Alice and Ray kiss, and he slips a wedding band on her ring finger. In the following shots guests dance, shower each other with confetti, hug, jam on electric guitars, smoke marijuana, guzzle red wine, and gorge themselves on the turkey buffet as if they were attendants at a Roman orgy. Dessert is a purple three-tiered wedding cake decorated with a red flower. But finally the party ends. Despite Ray's protestations and his drunken ramblings, the guests drift away one by one, as if returning to the sobriety of their real lives. Ray and Alice's social experiment, like the psychedelic 1960s themselves, is over. In the film's eerie final shot Alice stands alone outside the church in her white dress looking lonely, frightened, and lost, as the words of Arlo Guthrie's "The Alice's Restaurant Massacree" are heard in the background.

Despite its obvious attempts to thwart convention through wild visuals, zany costumes, and drug and alcohol consumption, this ceremony contains all the familiar elements of the standard wedding. The bizarre costumes, hallucinatory decorations, and hyped up Bible reading may distract viewers from the underlying message of the wedding, assuring us that we are viewing an unprecedented extravaganza rather than a standard nuptial, but these additions do not alter the goals of the ritual: to yoke a man and a woman in enforced partnership according to biblical precedent. As in many actual weddings, the unusual components appear to have been put in place in order to compensate the principals, reassuring men and women who wish to perceive themselves as dangerously antiestablishment that they are not buckling to middle-class social pressure by getting and staying married. But Alice's white dress, the officiant's reading that depicts women as helpmates, the sanction on heterosexual fusion, and the ecstatic approval of a roaring crowd of onlookers all render this a ceremony as ordinary as any taking place in the late 1960s in a white clapboard church. Only Penn's eerie last shot of Alice, who has been exhausted by her husband's neediness, irresponsibility, and manic excesses, deflates the proceedings with a note of skepticism. We see that, bereft of her community, this woman, like so many before her, has entered a social contract that will isolate and disadvantage her. No amount of Technicolor distraction can obscure this reality. Even a ceremony that consists of protestations to the contrary cannot ultimately conceal the fact that, for women, marriage is an act of conventionality rather than personal expressiveness. Traditionally, it has been a gesture of self-abnegation rather than self-assertion.

Thirty years later, in a computerized era deficient in pageantry and spectacle, contemporary weddings allow men and women to project their own self-images through extravagant statements of romantic intent. Personally authored wedding vows tend toward the saccharine and the hyperbolic and are almost always peppered with moments of spiritual and ethnic self-expression. In an age that is increasingly secular, the modern nuptial allows brides and grooms to broadcast their religious sentiments. Individuals who are not especially religious can play at piety for a day, and, in a period of widespread assimilationism, couples can briefly and publicly return to their roots, demonstrating pride in their ethnic traditions. They can accessorize their weddings. Mix and match ceremonies that combine the Mexican lasso ritual, in which the bride and groom are intertwined with a rope, with the African American jumping over the broom, to symbolize jumping over the to a new family, are now common. Weddings in which a Scottish Catholic groom in a kilt intones Hebrew blessings under a *huppah* or a Baptist minister reads excerpts from the Book of Genesis combined with musings from the poet Rumi are not unusual. Marriage ceremonies can freely combine incompatible material, as long as they hit the appropriately heady note of romantic excess.

Today's weddings are, of course, not the first nuptial celebrations to gratify their principals' vanity or to express paradoxically opposing sets of beliefs. Western marriage has never been a uniform or neat institution: its goals and definitions have always been contested, and its rituals have always expressed multiple purposes among the various parties involved. Medieval marriage, for instance, which spanned one thousand years and blended customs derived from various cultures and theologies, was utterly chaotic and self-contradictory. As the historian Christopher N.L. Brooke points out, "One tradition ancient in European society claimed carnal union as the essence of marriage; another, canonized by ancient Roman law, made a stated consent the heart of the institute; another made mock of this consent by the assumption that a girl was always in her father's gift; the fourth, increasingly powerful...made marriage the key to the passage of estates and kingdoms."[109] Weddings have inevitably encompassed glaring ideological contradictions: the current tensions between individualism and effusive romanticism, between sexual conformity and individuation, represent the latest set of conjugal paradoxes to beset the institution.

But there is one social circumstance surrounding modern marriage that is absolutely new. For the first time in western history women have the option not to marry. Although they are oppressive and psychologically powerful, the pressures to become part of a heterosexual couple are now intangible. The twentieth and twenty first-century American woman has often been cross-examined by her parents about her personal life: if she lacks a husband and biological children she has frequently been diminished, insulted, or pitied. But she has not, like her female ancestors of antiquity, the Middle Ages, and the Renaissance, been bartered into an arranged marriage by her father.[110] Today's women may be instructed by magazine columnists and the authors of pop-psychology primers to consider sexual partnership as the one true source of personal fulfillment and self-worth, but she is not forced into a nonconsensual union in order to solidify family alliances. She may feel seduced by the wedding scenes that seem to always conclude the plots of film and television romances, but no one drags her up the aisle or forces a ring onto her finger. She may be awed by the photographs of celebrity brides who fill the pages of glossy magazines. But, unlike her eighteenth-century female predecessors, she is not forced into marriage through a socioeconomic system that denies her professional and educational opportunity, leaving dependence on a man as her sole option.

This remarkable and relatively new freedom is so precious that it entails awesome responsibility. Out of respect for our anonymous female ancestors who had no choice, we must summon the courage to choose differently. We should no longer envision our lives in terms of the marital trajectory, perceiving ourselves as fragmentary "single" beings living in quiet anticipation of the pivotal moment of our lives, the wedding ceremony at which we will receive public sanction, fusing with a man in order to complete our social identities and become whole. Gerda Lerner has exuberantly described the mobility that modern western women have achieved, and the potentials created by this new freedom:

> More then thirteen hundred years of individual struggles, disappointments, and persistence have brought women to the historic moment when we can reclaim the freedom of our minds as we reclaim our past. The millennia of women's prehistory are at an end. We stand at the

beginning of a new epoch in the history of humankind's thought, as we recognize that sex is irrelevant to thought, that gender is a social construct, and that woman, like man, makes and defines history.[111]

In order to shape a meaningful history different from the history of those who came before us, women must relinquish the sentimental excess of the current wedding ceremony and let go of marriage, the institution that has sheltered our female ancestors, sometimes granting them safeties and protections but always furthering their subordination. An epoch of equality will only come to fruition when this ceremony, which enforces gender difference, is abandoned. By denying ourselves the short-term rewards of the nuptial rite, resisting its temptations and relinquishing the opportunities it provides for narcissistic self-presentation, we can begin to construct a vision of female selfhood untouched by the marital agenda.

CHAPTER NINE

Aesthetics and Politics
of the Wedding Day

According to the modern civilised scheme of life, the good name of the household to which she belongs should be the special care of the woman; and the system of honorific expenditure and conspicuous leisure by which this good name is chiefly sustained is therefore the woman's sphere. In the ideal scheme, as it tends to realise itself in the life of the higher pecuniary classes, this attention to conspicuous waste of substance and effort should normally be the sole economic function of woman.... So much that the women have been required not only to afford evidence of a life of leisure, but even to disable themselves for useful activity.

—Thorstein Veblen, *The Theory of the Leisure Class*

I. The Design Scheme

A recent advertisement for the hair-relaxing product Optimum Care contains the following description: "Before sensitivity was cool, there was a confident, attractive, financially secure Harlem princess, whose love life had the potential of getting stuck in a quagmire of noncommitment."[1] The photograph shows a youthful black woman sitting cross-legged on a sofa in a sumptuous white bridal gown that falls around her ankles. Her hair, which appears to have been straightened, is piled on top of her head in a dramatic upward sweep. Her half smile is beatific, her gaze confident and knowing. A glamorous professional who takes her man in tow, this is the kind of savvy lady who appears in the current beauty industry's ad campaigns, promotions that present the modern woman's ability to domesticate her man as a laudable sign of drive and self-esteem. The advertisement tells the rest of the Harlem princess' story:

> Just when it seemed like she'd be alone on another "Saturday boys' night out," an angel appeared on her remote and reminded her that nobody controls her happiness and her destiny but her. Filled with inspiration, the princess took control of her love, she took control of her Reggie. And once she took control of her Reggie, she took control of her wedding dress, her bridesmaids, her invitations, her seating arrangements, and her honeymoon.[2]

Of modern wedlock's many paradoxes, perhaps the most salient is the woman who is both a fairy-tale princess passively awaiting the male redeemer whose arrival will secure her happiness and a motivated self-starter who makes marriage occur through sheer force of will. Marriage ideology demands that women occupy both roles simultaneously. The American bride must maintain her femininity, preserving the image of a charmed woman who just happened to be standing in the right spot at the right time when the man who was her destiny appeared and whisked her away. She must also demonstrate the all-American values of hard work, earnestness, and perseverance, the qualities with which she secured male commitment. Professionally successful and financially autonomous, she needs no man to rescue her and in fact dominates her male partner, "taking control" of him by limiting his access to his friends. The modern bride must project an image of herself as the steward of her domestic affairs, and it is as both ethereal icon and micromanager that she appears on her wedding day, her costume announcing her own frail beauty, her floral arrangements, seating plan, menu, and entourage, demonstrating massive, behind-the-scenes effort. While she wafts down the aisle in a white gown that bespeaks femininity, chastity, and delicacy, she must also appear to be "in control" of the romantic production. The interior design scheme, the pageantry, and the vows are all intended to reflect her personality. Every aesthetic detail is meant to highlight her appearance, to offset the glow that wedding propagandists tell us can only come from romantic love. "On the most important day of her life, Ms. Together Forever chose Optimum Care to make her hair elegant, stunning, and beautiful."[3]

To highlight the modern woman's transformation from insignificant "single" girl to culturally empowered wife, the space in which the wedding takes place must be transformed. The modern blockbuster wedding rests on alchemizing a once plain sanctuary, room, backyard, field, or beach front, into a magical landscape. This usually involves a cadre of professionals; in upscale weddings, the team is headed by a single coordinator who makes it all happen, implementing the bride's vision. Groom-oriented wedding literature urges men to refrain from to the entire process of aesthetic planning, alluding to the flowers, table settings, and cake as mysterious, incomprehensible, and trivial female affairs. ("Does is really matter to you if you have pansies instead of daisies? Will you simply die without baby's breath?"[4] asks John Mitchell, the disingenuously caustic author of *What the Hell Is a Groom and What's He Supposed to Do?*) The notion that each wedding's look should represent a purely female initiative stems from an underlying belief that this is an event for the bride rather than the groom. It is her day to shine, her ultimate moment, the ritual that marks her improvement. The design motif exists to enhance her appearance and set the mood for her metamorphosis. She must therefore dominate the aesthetic production, laboring over flower arrangements, table settings, and centerpieces. The official host and hostess of the event, her parents, must foot the bill for these costly props. Wedding planners unanimously proclaim the bride's mother and father to be responsible for all the details of the wedding day, with the exception of the marriage license, clergyperson's fee, engagement ring, and, perhaps, the liquor. The bride's parents are responsible for the real expenses of the affair: the invitations, dress, flowers, hall and furniture rental, photographer and/or videographer, catering, and wedding cake. In the supposedly enlightened era of the two-income household, wedding protocol still treats each woman as an economic liability to be taken off her grateful parents' hands, and women who star in the big white wedding accept and perpetuate this idea. In one of our culture's most shameless gestures of sexist sentimentality, a man and woman customarily demonstrate their happy relief at their daughter's assimilation into another man's household, and her newfound sexual respectability within wedlock, by footing the bill for a lavish party.

Because the party is one at which they too cast an image of themselves, debuting as effective parents who have socialized a successfully feminine daughter, the bride's mother and father must purchase a range of accouterments, props, and costumes that set the tone for the day. Wedding coordinators orchestrate the event, arranging the details into a harmonious whole that showcases the bride and her family. Such consultants speak with both brides and grooms, but their real ongoing work is always with the star of the wedding, the bride. Wedding planners tend to present themselves in quasi-mystical terms, as conduits for each bride's creative energy. St. Helena, California, based consultant Mary Ellen Murphy explains that the first time she sits with a client, she tries to get a feel for what the bride is after, asking, "When you close your eyes and see your wedding day, what do you see?"[5] Even a bride without a clearly defined aesthetic vision usually spits out a key word, which becomes the starting point of the wedding's thematic plan. Premiere wedding coordinator Colin Cowie, founder of the New York and Los Angeles-based special events company, Colin Cowie Lifestyle, utilizes a similar pyscholanalytic process. He surveys each bride before arriving at a wedding design scheme, asking each client to delve into the recesses of her unconscious and recall her favorite restaurant, food, cocktail, and vacation spot. He asks which books or stories inspire fond memories and which scenes from film speak to the bride. What is her favorite time of day? Does she have a special collection—vintage linen, crystal decanters—that could be incorporated into the wedding? Does she have a particular image of being a bride that she has cherished from childhood? With nothing to do, how might she spend an afternoon? These exercises are intended to unlock secret recesses of aestheticism that Cowie then transforms into a "look," planning weddings that exude the rustic safari atmosphere of Ralph Lauren advertisements or mimic the art nouveau elegance of 1930s black and white films. Cowie, like most wedding coordinators, perceives the nuptial as a glorious moment of personal expression rather than a generic religious ceremony. His philosophy expresses the misconception common among those employed by the wedding industry that the act of marriage is a highly personal unique event rather than a humdrum act of sexual conformity. His recent, meteoric rise to prominence as a wedding consultant to the rich and famous demonstrates the extent to which brides and grooms of means require this kind of flattery—how badly they wish to be told that they are artists with unique sensibilities that require special expression in wedding thematics rather than men and women following a cultural script. "A visually beautiful wedding is one where the decor elements have been planned to work together in a harmonious manner," Cowie explains. "When guests enter your wedding site, whether it is a backyard or a ballroom, they should immediately sense that this celebration has a unique look that expresses the personality of the bride and groom."[6]

Like many consultants, Cowie is zealous on the subject of flowers, urging brides to unleash their creative spirits and shatter the convention of white flowers and baby's breath with bold floral patterns. Wedding flowers, which decorate the church or synagogue as well as the reception area, the bride, her attendants, and the wedding cake, are a paramount detail and the focal point of attention for the bride and her entourage. Symbols of romance, fertility, and pastoral utopianism, that are the necessary commodities that transmute a mere day into a wedding day, a mere woman into a wife. Flowers have traditionally been used at weddings as fertility symbols; the first flower girls on record were the young girls who carried sheaves of freshly cut wheat at Greek weddings,[7] a custom that continued into the Middle Ages.[8] Elizabethans adorned their weddings with rose petals and fresh herbs, a practice recommended by modern wedding consultants; the tossing of the bridal bouquet, in which "single" women desperately scramble to seize the object said to bring matrimonial luck, also originates in the English Renaissance, as part of the melee that characterized the early modern wedding. Victorians held the bouquet as a sentimental keepsake; unwilling to part with this personal treasure, the bride often tossed a second bouquet to her anxious "single" guests.[9]

In today's nuptials the flowers are decorative and are used to create a nature scene, transforming a pedestrian space into something magically bucolic that expresses the bride's sensibility. Cowie's recommendations include a Mediterranean-style fountain filled with rose petals, church aisles lined with ivy and lemon leaves, a gazebo with trellising covered with rosemary, vines, and bunches of grapes, trees adorned with lemons, limes, and kumquats, a bridal bouquet of tulips or bear grass,

Virginia roses, and freesia tied with a cuff of rose leaves, and, for a Jewish ceremony, a *huppah* fashioned by gluing galax leaves to cover four poles with white spandex stretched overhead. While they are important for the ceremony, flowers, Cowie emphasizes, can make or break the reception. He likens the wedding reception to a theatrical event, reminding brides that, as with a play on opening night, the first five minutes set the tone for the evening.[10] Guests who enter Cowie's wedding sites are meant to be struck dumb by the lavish floral arrangements: doorways draped with blossom-studded garlands, towering candelabra adorned with ivy, centerpieces of ornamental kale, rosemary, kumquats, apples, and bunches of gilded grapes, tall topiaries studded with ivory and pink roses. Cowie fondly recalls a fall wedding held on a tennis court in which he swagged the ceiling with mint-colored chiffon, hung chandeliers to provide an evocative glow, and decorated the space with roses and amaranthus combined with grapes and pomegranates.[11]

Whether they are bold baroque arrangements in which tables are crowded with magenta flowers, country settings in which glass milk bottles are filled with daisies, or modern affairs with calla lilies and long-stemmed tulips, the arrangements signify marital bliss. Wedding flowers have an opulence that no other single event would justify. Their symbolism is twofold. They are meant to suggest the "natural" quality of each couple's relationship, diverting guests' attention from the institutional aspects of the wedding by suggesting that each pair exists in a pastoral utopia, that each bride and groom's love has been as spontaneous, organic, and perfect as the earth's seasonal bounty. They also demonstrate the financial ability of the bride's parents; flowers, are expensive, impractical, and temporary, typically lasting about a week before perishing. They are therefore the ultimate symbols of conspicuous consumption in an extravaganza of brazen ostentatious spending. The arrangements of peonies, hydrangeas, Casablanca lilies, and French tulips that embellish the contemporary wedding site demonstrate the bride's personal style, foreshadowing her role as a married consumer, as they simultaneously announce her parents pecuniary strength.

Wedding planners, however, emphasize flowers as accouterments for creating atmosphere. Martha Stewart, America's reigning guru of horticulture, suggests adding luster to a wedding's interior space with strands of white silk flowers illuminated by holiday string lights[12] or giving reception tables a warm glow by creating a centerpiece of votive candles on a bed of pink and orange rose petals[13] or fashioning a centerpiece by nestling green and white posies on a tiered wire stand.[14] While Cowie's overproduced arrangements are theatrical, Stewart's are intended to appear spontaneous and unplanned. Her countrified wedding aesthetic suggests a natural abundance in which the lives and loves of men and women are harmoniously attuned to the seasons. At the archetypal Stewart affair, baskets of herbs and fruit and bowls brimming with fresh flowers appear to have been haphazardly left on tables and chairs, and folksy handmade wreaths of daisies adorn church doors. Hydrangeas, sweet peas, viburnum, and blackberries burst from such utilitarian containers as fish bowls, beat up wooden milk cartons, or antique aquariums. Lilies of the valley fill simple juice glasses, and rose petals are strewn along a wedding aisle with calculated haphazardness. A blue plastic butterfly is inserted into a white bridal bouquet, as if it had landed there accidentally. "A butterfly, like the bride and groom, already lived in one form but has begun a new life as something completely different and beautiful,"[15] Stewart explains. Most importantly, bowls of flowers are everywhere. "Place a bowl filled with florets of hyacinth, narcissus, or another fragrant flower on a table, along with a card, beautifully calligraphied, inviting guests to take one as they enter the ceremony or reception,"[16] she suggests.

In the blockbuster weddings of celebrities, costs skyrocket to the millions, with the flowers themselves often totaling hundreds of thousands of dollars. Each year, celebrity-oriented glossies provide worshipful accounts of weddings of the rich and famous, chronicling how the heterosexual elite celebrates itself. Such accounts focus on wedding consumption, praising the spectacular sums of money that fuel each celebration. Flowers, for instance, absorbed one million of the seven million dollars spent on telecommunications executive Chris Edgecomb's September 19, 1999, Santa Barbara wedding to entertainment executive Maryann Antell. "The couple worked nine months with a staff of six planning the event,"[17] reports *People* magazine, explaining that Edgecomb flew his eight hundred guests in on private jets, built two stages to accommodate the musicians and comedians hired to perform, ordered seven hundred twenty bottles of Dom Perignon champagne and two kinds of caviar, and had oysters flown in from Nova Scotia. The ceremony concluded with one hundred fifty thousand dollars worth of fireworks and was followed by a reception featuring palm readers, hand-rolled cigars, and a sushi bar.

Documenting a more modest affair, *In Style* magazine praises the actor Christopher Lambert's 1998 Los Angeles wedding to film producer Jaiymse Haft as "a glorious ode to love."[18] Flowers dominated this event. Working from a palette of red, burgundy, persimmon, and coral ("to reflect the bride and groom's sensual side")[19] floral designer to the stars, Walter Hubert, trimmed the Beverly Hills Hotel's Rodeo Ballroom with Italian cypresses and antique urns filled with blossoming peach branches. "Each table at the banquet was draped with layered cloths in vibrant shades and set with centerpieces of hot-hued roses, lavender, and rosemary mixed with purple grapes and red pears. In the bar area, Hubert created an arrangement of oak twigs, Spanish moss, and orchids to evoke the forests of Bali, where the two had recently vacationed."[20] The article hails Haft's sudden appearance, amidst the dense foliage, "dressed like a Renaissance princess in a Vera Wang gown."[21] At some celebrity weddings the flowers are not just set pieces; they're props. John Stamos' September 1998 Beverly Hills wedding to model Rebecca Romijn involved guests in the floral arrangements. To make friends feel like part of the ceremony, wedding consultant Sharon Sacks asked each one to bring a flower and insert it into an archway of greenery at the head of the aisle. As the blissful bride and groom passed under the arch, guests were instructed to shower them with rose petals. The floral motif was reflected in the cuisine, which culminated with an angel food cake covered with sugar flowers that had taken one hundred hours to make. In *In Style's* photo layout the confection, which appears to be a pile of white flowers rather than a cake, sits at the center of a table surrounded by bouquets of red roses and bathed in angelic light.[22]

Because they compress the two elements Americans value most—amorous love and money—celebrity marriages elicit worshipful descriptions. Reporters often describe famous brides as cultural royalty, alluding to them as princesses and queens and marveling at their enchanted marriages marked by cinematic wedding festivities. Actress

Traci Bingham, whose role models were Princess Grace and Princess Diana, and who celebrated her August 29, 1999, wedding to musician Robb Vallier with a series of lavish prewedding events, hosted three hundred fifty guests at an Ames, Iowa, based nuptial that was "pure Hollywood."[23] Crystal vases of roses and Asiatic lilies adorned the tables, and the bride carried a bouquet of white Casablana lilies, denodrobium, orchid sprays, and Ecuadorian roses to enhance her opulent gown. Bingham's white duchesse satin Escada dress featured a ten-foot train, a tulle embroidered skirt with seven overlayers hand sewn with sixty silk roses, and a bodice overlaid with hand-sewn sea pearls and beads. The gown, which weighed thirty-seven pounds, was enhanced by a five-hundred-thousand-dollar diamond tiara borrowed from Los Angeles jeweler Fred Leighton. The oval five-tier cake was topped by a scale model of the swing in the groom's parents' backyard on which the groom proposed.[24] Actress Peri Gilpin's July 1999 wedding to artist Christian Vincent also took its cue from Grace Kelly. The event was held at the Malibu home of the bride's friend and television costar, actor Kelsey Grammar. Gilpin wore a sleeveless, "fairy princess" Badgley Mischka gown and carried a bouquet of ivory gardenias and stephanotis; her eight bridesmaids wore sleeveless blue gowns designed to resemble the frock that Kelly wore in the 1954 Hitchcock thriller, *Rear Window*. According to *In Style* magazine, the sight of Gilpin in her costume prompted hysterics from her groom, who burst into tears when she began her march up the aisle.[25] This wedding, *In Style* explains approvingly, exuded the feel of old Hollywood in its every detail. Wedding planner Janine Micucci of the company Along Came Mary was commissioned to transform Grammar's tennis court into a chapel (with vine-covered pews and a stone path as an aisle) and his horse ring into a forties supper club (with an aged mahogany floor, art deco lamps, tables topped with burnt orange calla lilies in silver cups, and a big band to play 1920s standards). While the atmosphere was elegantly cinematic, the white cake featured a garden of eden motif, with piles of artificial, sugar paste flowers and figurines representing Christian and Gilpin as Adam and Eve. To announce their married love to California's population at large, the bride and groom hired a skywriter to draw two hearts in the sky.[26]

Actor Michael Douglas' November 18, 2000, nuptial to actress Catherine Zeta-Jones, which took place at New York's Plaza Hotel, was, of course, a consumerist extravaganza. *Us* magazine celebrates this lavish affair in which a woman from humble origins—the thirtyish daughter of a Welsh candy salesman—married into Hollywood royalty, joining herself to a wealthy successful man in his midfifties. The young ingenue who enchants an established older man, breathing new life into him as she seals her own financial future, is a favorite narrative among wedding celebrants. *Us* praised the setting of the 2 million dollar "fairy-tale wedding"[27] as "sublime,"[28] extolling the interior design scheme in which the Plaza's Grand Ballroom was "draped in deep-peach silk taffeta and brimming with peach and red roses and stargazer lilies."[29] Zeta-Jones, who admits that, prior to the big day she had been "hopping around all week shouting, 'I'm getting married,'"[30] wore an ivory duchesse-satin Christian Lacroix gown and a diamond tiara. She exchanged vows beneath a canopy of white roses and tulips in a ceremony that represents the apex of marital exhibitionism, sentimentality, and free enterprise. The bride and groom sold their story, along with photo rights to the event, to England's *OK!* magazine for an estimated 1.5 million dollars.[31]

The story of the confirmed bachelor struck by love is another favorite of wedding reporters. This narrative underscores *In Style* magazine's coverage of hip-hop artist D'Mon "Mack 10" Rolison's August 19, 2000, Palos Verdes, California, wedding to singer Tionne Watkins. "When I first met D'Mon he was all, 'I'll never get married.'... it's great to see him eat his words,"[32] exclaimed musician Ice Cube, a friend of the groom. Apparently, the love of one good woman redeemed Rolison, who proposed on New Year's Eve, 1999, with a ten-karat diamond solitaire ring imported from Belgium. The ceremony took place at an oceanside bluff under a swagged chiffon canopy bedecked with ivory, champagne, and white roses and cascading amaranthus. Friends gathered to witness Robinson's conversion from degenerate bachelor to upstanding heterohusband, but they also served as decorative props for the bride and groom; wedding guests were asked to wear only shades of cream or beige to accentuate the natural scenery. In Olympian fashion, four rhythmic gymnasts waving ivory ribbons heralded the arrival of the bridesmaids; the bride, clad in a forty-seven-thousand-dollar Monique Lhuillier

Empire-waist gown with a sixteen-foot train, emerged from a white Rolls Royce. She proceeded up the aisle on the arms of her father and a close family friend; after taking her vows and sliding a ten-karat diamond wedding band onto her groom's finger, a flock of white doves was released into the air.[33]

An equally popular wedding myth is that of the older bride and groom who find each other late in life, when both have abandoned their dreams of love. The conventions of this narrative shape accounts of actor James Brolin and actress/singer Barbra Striesand's July 1, 1998, nuptial, which was held at their Malibu home. The February 1999 issue of *In Style* magazine details the entire production, explaining how the perfectionistic bride placed flowers throughout the house, working them into the flower girls' baskets and head wreaths and decorating nine dinner tables with floral arrangements in red, lavender, and burgundy to echo the colors of the china service. Small bouquets were also clustered around hurricane lamps and grouped with gardenias and roses. Streisand herself came to the day armed with two bouquets to accommodate a possible change of clothing; she carried a cluster of gardenias enhanced by her birth flower, lily of the valley, and had as a backup a monochromatic bouquet that was the color of antique lace, which she didn't end up displaying at the wedding but took on her honeymoon.

The great drama of the Brolin/Streisand nuptial, however, was the dress. Custom-made for the event by designer Donna Karan, the hand-beaded crystal tulle fabric from India was draped and fitted in a rush to accommodate the last-minute nuptial. When Karan initially flew from New York to Los Angeles to drape the fabric on her friend and client, according to Streisand, "it looked like hell."[34] In a panic, the stressed-out bride-to-be assigned her groom the task of shopping for gowns on the internet, but when Karan returned the second time with the reworked garment displayed on a mannequin, "It was extraordinary."[35] *In Style* provides Karan's initial sketches of the dress adjacent to a photograph of Streisand wearing the final product, beaming like a regal drag queen as she stands at the foot of a staircase, her hands clasped behind her, the skirts of her close-fitting, off-the-shoulder white gown spread in a dramatic, circular swirl around her feet. In another photograph set in the same stairwell, she and a tuxedo-clad Brolin clutch each other and stare passionately into one another's eyes. Here Striesand's gown is offset by a tulle veil dusted with sparkles and affixed to a crown of antique wax flowers; the veil covers her body entirely, trailing onto the floor behind her. The copy quotes Brolin's postceremony address: "I can't tell you how lucky I am that this should have happened to me so late in life.... Every day, every night, every morning is a new adventure.... I love you, Barbra."[36]

Whether they represent starry-eyed young lovers, May-December romances, conversions from "single" debauchery to married virtue, or the unions of aging lovebirds, magazine accounts of celebrity weddings present the myth of happily ever after as being especially sweet when the bride and groom are famous and wealthy. Overt displays of prosperity and effusive proclamations of love render the celebrity wedding an event of garish exhibitionism that sets the current tone for nuptials among the anonymous mass of middle-class Americans. As the actors and actresses transported into our homes each day via the television screen influence our fashion choices, body language, and styles of speech, they also set wedding trends. Perhaps the most ballyhooed blockbuster wedding of the millennium was the July 29 Malibu ceremony of television actress Jennifer Aniston and film star Brad Pitt. *People* magazine tells the familiar tale of a famous young couple hounded by paparazzi and determined to keep their love secret and pure. By September of 1999, however, the two had come out as a duo, and Aniston was "flashing a diamond-and-platinum engagement ring" from Italian jewelry designer Silvia Damiani, with whom Pitt had worked on the ring design over a period of seven months.[37] Reporters for *People* estimate that the Aniston-Pitt wedding cost one million dollars but add that such an expenditure is "Not a problem for Pitt, who raked in 40 million dollars last year, nor for his bride, who'll take home seven hundred fifty thousand dollars an episode for the next season of *Friends*."[38] The army of employees who erected tents, hung lanterns, laid a linen canopy for the bridal walkway, set tables with roses and wisteria, floated lotus flowers in a specially built slate fountain, and lined the site with brown sugar candles imported from Thailand, worked toward creating the Zen effect that Pitt demanded. When he and his bride, who had recently gotten matching blonde highlights at a Beverly Hills hair salon, took center stage, the two hundred guests were appropriately awed. "It was so beautiful," gushed Aniston's hairstylist, Chris McMilan. "It just made me want to get married."[39]

Clearly, wealthy Americans devote a great deal of money to non-marital activities; entrepreneurs and famous performers flaunt their wealth, spending outrageously on clothing, cars, travel, interior design, food, and fitness regimens. But reporters are not on hand to chronicle every expenditure with the kind of astonishment reserved for the special weddings and Valentine's Day issues of popular magazines and the Weddings of the Year specials broadcast by television networks. Lavish weddings receive a special kind of fanfare in the press; wealthy couples garner a unique kind of celebrity. They are not merely successful; they are romantically successful. They are not merely wealthy; they are wealthy as a couple and are therefore entitled to special pampering and self-indulgence. The flowers, lighting, costumes, champagne, and cake signify their ascent into heterosexual legitimacy; the wedding itself is a synergistic fusion of public eroticism and absurd levels of luxury spending. Big white weddings present each duo as a fated pair of upscale consumers who can and should reward themselves with a series of enormous parties, demanding gifts from friends and indulging in those crazy prewedding impulse purchases: gold cufflinks, diamond broaches, silk boxer shorts and negligees, sable coats.

Often today's blockbuster wedding is a lavish display, not just of the bride's taste and spending power but of the couple's ethnicity. Sally Kilbridge and Mallory Samson's *Real Weddings* pays homage to recently married Erica Lennard, an American photographer based in Paris. The authors stress the fact that this "highly individualistic" woman "never imagined herself as a traditional bride—or any bride, for that matter."[40] But when she met and fell in love with architect Dennis Colomb, "one of the better dressed men in France,"[41] the matrimonial narrative took over, and before they knew it, the two were planning a full-scale international extravaganza to celebrate their feelings for each other, publicize their heterosexuality, and demonstrate their offbeat sense of style. Set on Bastille Day, 1998, in the groom's Provençal home, the marriage of this Jewish woman to a French Catholic was officiated by a priest who purported to be more interested in spirituality than religious dogma. The reception, which featured a sitar player and a traditional Indian dancer, seemed, however, to have a Hindu theme. Preparations for the costly affair included relandscaping a series of terraced gardens, chopping down trees, and resetting a stone stairway. Argentinean decorator Roberto Bergero was brought in to embellish the pool area with dozens of colorful throw pillows in a mix of French and Indian fabrics and to erect a black-and-white Moroccan tent. The couple's sartorial choices were in keeping with the wedding's strenuous ethnic diversity. Determined not to don the standard white gown, the bride wore a mauve jacket with kimono-style sleeves lined in Indian fabric and an eighteenth-century tail. Her friend, designer Isaac Mizrahi, contributed a white taffeta "fairy princess skirt," which Lennard claims she never would have selected. Topping off the ensemble was a gold-threaded Indian silk shawl, which the ecumenical priest held over the couple during the ceremony to form a *huppah*-like canopy. Colomb sported a black Helmut Lang tuxedo that he had purchased on a whim, unsure if he would ever need it.

Like many nationally and ethnically themed weddings, the Lennard-Colomb event seems staged as a protest against conventional boilerplate matrimony. It features an independent woman who flouts marriage but somehow ends up at her own wedding, a bride who disdains the traditional wedding raiment but ends up proceeding up the aisle in frilly white taffeta, and a western couple asserting that they are really eastern. It also features a Catholic ceremony that claims to be not Catholic but spiritual in a nonthreatening new age way combined with a Jewish wedding canopy that is not really a *huppah* at all. In classic, modern married doublespeak, the bride and groom seem to be saying that in bending all the rules, traversing all the boundaries, and melting traditions together into a chaotic cultural stew, they are defying wedlock's mandates. The wedding's religious and ethnic hodgepodge extended to the reception, which included the bride in an orange and red sari, beaming attendants in Indian garb, trellises of olive branches and rosemary, Japanese paper lanterns, metal chairs painted green and orange, tables covered with tangerine-colored cloths, eighteenth-century reproduction vessels filled with five hundred white roses, a Provençal repast of fruit and vegetables, and, for dessert, a large edible man made of melons, plums, grapes, and lemons, which the bride described as, "Way, *way* over the top."[42] With their cadre of international professionals, this upscale bride and groom seem to have planned an event that would fly in the face of wedding protocol. With its visuals intended to jar guests, its baffling mixture of national and religious customs, and its older sophisticated bride and groom, who, in Kilbridge and Samson's photographs appear faintly bored, the Lennard-Colomb affair wants badly to jar, shock, and titillate with its many breeches of bridal protocol. But, finally, this ethnic pastiche was an expensive wedding like any other—a celebration of one woman being yoked to one man, forsaking all others and, by implication, relinquishing all others to a secondary tier in their lives.

Like most jet-setting married couples, Colomb and Lennard admit that price was not an issue in planning their big day. This is not the case for the vast majority or brides and their parents. But because they represent the pinnacle of heterosexual self-presentation, large-scale weddings are the single events for which otherwise sensible middle-class people are willing to drain their bank accounts and even go into debt, emulating, on a smaller scale, popular icons from the entertainment industry. ("Because love and marriage are two things we share with our celebrity heroes, we can't get enough of their weddings,"[43] explains *Modern Bride* magazine.) Contemporary American weddings represent a 70 billion dollar a year business—up 230 percent from 1982.[44] The lion's share is spent on receptions: dresses, flowers, food, photographs, videotapes, and tent and furniture rentals are costly and indispensable elements of the big day and are often modeled on the accouterments of celebrity extravaganzas. (Jennifer Aniston's floor-length, silk and satin, low-backed white gown designed by Lawrence Steele is already inspiring cheaper knockoffs for noncelebrity brides.[45]) The *New York Times* reported recently that sixteen thousand dollars is the average national cost for a wedding, pointing out that, in most parts of the country, this represents the downpayment on a house. This same article notes that in New York City, where prices are inflated, caterers consider one-hundred-thousand-dollar weddings to be midrange; twenty-five thousand is the cost of a lower-end celebration.[46] In part because of escalating wedding costs and the increased pressure to celebrate lavishly and publicly, a new matrimonial trend has recently burgeoned; the corporate-sponsored wedding, in which companies loan bridal dresses, jewelry, and flowers in exchange for publicity. Brides like Cincinatti-based financial broker Natasha Allen, who married in 1999, receive complementary or reduced items, listing corporate sponsors on their wedding invitations or featuring company brochures prominently at the reception.[47] While traditional wedding experts like the knot.com founder Carly Roney find such measures unspeakably crass, the practice of eliciting sponsors is a minor exaggeration of the entitlement and economically self-interested romanticism advanced by mainstream bridal publications. That a woman's biological parents should serve as her sponsors, paying extraordinary sums of money for a romantic extravaganza, is a custom taken for granted by most Americans. That her friends should chip in for gifts and costly prewedding parties is another given. Asking for additional forms of sponsorship is a logical extension of this practice.

Why do parents strain their budgets to cover the cost of blockbuster weddings? I think it is partly because they themselves find the emotional rewards of the day irresistible. The "high" of pulling off one's daughter's nuptial is powerful. For parents as well as brides the modern wedding elicits praise, acclaim, and popularity; it offers the opportunity to deck oneself out in sartorial splendor and pose for photographs like a movie star. But this kind of narcissistic gratification offers only a partial explanation for the average American's reckless matrimonial spending. The party's real justification comes from the unstated notion that marrying one's daughter off secures her financial future. In traditional societies in which divorce was unavailable, when a woman was taken off her father's hands and ensconced in the home of another man, she was supposed to be provided for. Her possible unhappiness and the limitations placed on her freedom were accompanied by what was at least a promise of certain lifelong material securities. The belief that this is still the case underscores the modern nuptial, justifying its extravagance. The contemporary American father may not state or even think it consciously, but his actions indicate that he believes his daughter to be another man's financial responsibility after the big day. One big blowout in which I shoulder all the expenses, and then she's set for life, and I will no longer have to worry, the logic goes.

But this logic degrades fairly quickly once we hold it up to the light. Like most myths of male benevolence, the fiction underlying the modern wedding is that each groom will be loyal, responsible, hardworking, professionally successful, and healthy. We have all heard the tangible relief in the voices of mothers of newly engaged women—the joy they take in alluding to their daughters as members of a couple. "How is Mimi?" we ask a neighbor or a coworker. "Oh, Ted and Mimi are fine," the relieved mother-of-the-bride replies smugly. Encoded in her reply is the belief that Mimi, being part of a couple, is set for life economically and emotionally.

But Ted's penis does not guarantee his competence. He may well turn out to be a philanderer or a professional failure. He may be unlucky, or he may become disabled, or he may get sick. He may want a divorce at some point, and divorce is now readily available. His immediate intentions are good, and his romantic feelings seem genuine enough, but they are no guarantee of Mimi's future. Before they spend one hundred thousand dollars on a party rather than putting it in trust for her, Mimi's parents ought to consider this, as they peruse some of the recent studies on divorce. In an era with a 50 percent divorce rate, the idea of marriage as protection for women is truly untenable. There is a high probability that every newly married couple will separate and that the wife's economic position will decline severely after the marriage has ended. Research indicates that the standard of living of newly divorced women drops dramatically, partially because women are still lower wage earners, partially because female divorcees tend to become "single" parents, while divorced men tend to become newly "single" again,[48] and partially because child support regulations are notoriously difficult to enforce.[49] Historian Rochelle Gatlin reported that, in the mid-1980s in California, where half of all marriages end in divorce, a divorced man's standard of living increased by 49 percent on the average, while his exwife's fell by 74 percent.[50] More recent national studies report the postdivorce drop in standard of living for women at 30 percent.[51] Currently, half of all homes headed by females are below the poverty level.[52] Journalist Rhona Mahony explains that this body of research shows

> that divorce means something completely different for women and men. That should not be surprising, since marriage means something completely different for women and men. The sexual division of labor in the home means that women almost always do much more unpaid work than men.... If they do less paid work—no matter how much

they love their families and enjoy their daily accomplishments—they live in a state of permanent economic peril.[53]

The wife who operates as a full- or even a part-time homemaker, relying on her husband for support, makes herself very vulnerable. "If she separates from her husband, she separates from most of her income."[54] For women, marriage is simply not the security that people think it is. And once that promise of lifelong financial protection is removed, the blockbuster wedding loses its already dubious justification.

Despite the staggering sums of money poured into wedding celebrations each year, the consumeristic aspect of marriage generally goes unquestioned. Even the most vocal feminists tend to take a hands-off approach to a day that most still consider to be a sentimental milestone.[55] American feminism has traditionally villainized two industries: the beauty business, which is often said to engender in women unrealistic standards of physical perfection, and the pornography industry, which is accused of degrading women by turning them into sex objects while causing violence in men.[56]

These critiques have always appeared misguided to me. Since good makeup and skin care products can dramatically improve an individual's appearance, women who purchase beauty products with the desire of looking their best seem to me to be behaving quite reasonably rather than acting the part of self-hating brainwashed victims. I have likewise always believed that pornography exists to offer an enjoyable sexual outlet to men and women who like it. However, even if these two areas of commerce *were* somehow damaging to women, I do not understand why they have elicited so much criticism while the wedding industry has remained virtually untouched. With very few exceptions, feminists have failed to recognize the bridal business' stranglehold on the female imagination and have not acknowledged the ludicrous amounts of money with which the average middle-class woman celebrates the institution that has disenfranchised her sex. Speaking anecdotally, in the past year, I have spent one hundred fifty dollars on skin and hair care products, including makeup, and no money on pornography. Had I gotten married and had my wedding bankrolled by relatives, I would have spent twenty-five thousand dollars.[57]

Feminist analysis aside, it is peculiar that Americans continue to invest so much financially in an institution with a 50 percent failure rate,[58] which, despite the clamor of nostalgists, has not proven to offer the optimal environment for childrearing. Since the 1970s researchers in California have studied deliberately unconventional families, unmarried parents and parents who live communally or enjoy sexually open relationships. The results: "The children are as bright, as healthy, and as well-adjusted as children who live in more conventional families."[59] As well, no important differences have emerged between children raised by heterosexual and homosexual parents. Yet the myth of parents who come off a biblical assembly line, stepping from Noah's ark in neat heterosexual pairs, endures, fueling the marriage mystique. The ideal of a nuclear family comprised of a doting husband and wife and two children living in a private home and carrying out their activities free from the prying eyes of neighbors and friends, is intractable. And while this new institution has not proven superior or particularly viable, it is still presumed worthy of a kind of launch or send-off in the form of a costly party.

When viewed as the historical wellspring of female subordination, a social contract that no longer binds, a romantic commitment that will likely be rescinded, and an arrangement with no identifiable social benefits, marriage seems less a workable institution than an engrained superstition, and today's wedding expenditures become truly incomprehensible. But, as the anthropologist Lionel Tiger has observed, wedlock is reflexive rather than analytical and those whose marriage's end tend to personalize the experience rather than questioning the feasibility of the paradigm itself. Most divorced men and women do remarry. "The more divorces there are, the more experienced marriers exist, ready to remarry—and many do. The divorce rate has jumped 250 percent in the past twenty-one years; about 80 percent of the formerly married remarry."[60] Those whom experience should have made skeptical about state-sanctioned commitment are ever ready to take the plunge once again, planning the elaborate party and binge-buying on invitations, flowers, costumes, gourmet food, photographs, trinkets, and the always costly postwedding honeymoon. If a small business failed 50 percent of the time, it would not attract venture capitalists as investors. If a stock underperformed 50 percent of the time, brokers would not promote it and individual investors would not buy it. Yet the big white wedding—the single largest financial investment middle-class men and women make apart from their homes and college tuitions—remains impervious to economic analysis. The event commands such veneration that its principals, lost in sentimental euphoria, remain unwilling to recognize the wedding as an unsound expenditure. "This is astonishing,"[61] Tiger exclaims.

> It is also astonishing that, under the circumstances, marriage is still legally allowed. If nearly half of anything else ended so disastrously, the government would surely ban it immediately. If half the tacos served in restaurants caused dysentery, if half the people learning karate broke their palms, if only 6 percent of people who went on roller-coasters damaged their middle ears, the public would be clamoring for action. Yet the most intimate of disasters . . . happens over and over again.[62]

I am not sure that illegalizing marriage would provide the appropriate remedy to wedding excess, although few things would please me more than seeing bridal consultants, dressmakers, florists, caterers, and pastry chefs forced underground, compelled to use code names and meet with their clients in seedy clandestine locations where they would pass fabric samples and menus under tables in brown paper bags. However, with marriage as the backbone of our country's system of family law, its illegalization will not take place any time soon. A more realistic remedy to marriage mania and the fiscal extravagance it engenders would be the creation of a serious economic alternative for women. If the relatives of each American woman, instead of coming together to invest in her romantic future with a costly party, would instead put their thousands of dollars into a woman's health and education fund, the female members of our society would have a future as a group rather than the illusion of a romantic future for lucky individuals. No national fund now exists to finance young women's college tuitions, provide them with birth control, and enable those in need to travel to parts of the country where doctors perform abortions in order to terminate pregnancies. The institutionalization of such a fund would revolutionize female existence in this country. Making intellectual and preprofessional training and safe contraception available to all women rather than an elite few would build the foundation of an egalitarian society. But this practice would entail a very basic shift in consciousness on the part of biological parents. People of means would have to retrain themselves to hope for their daughters' mobility rather than their dependence within marriage. Fathers and mothers would have to learn to dream of their daughters' commitment to learning rather than their commitment to men. Women themselves would have to begin to fantasize about professional achievement rather than the romantic triumph signaled by the blockbuster wedding. And parents would have to relinquish the wedding's private satisfactions in favor of a broader kind of emotional gratification. This would mean coming to think of all young girls as their daughters and committing themselves to the aspirations of an entire generation of women rather then financing the amorous dreams of their own female progeny.

II. The Reception

Couple fascism is evident throughout the matrimonial narrative, but it is nowhere so powerful as in the wedding reception. Advertised in wedding planners as an elegant postceremony party at which friends and relatives of the premiered couple meet, mingle, and fete the newlyweds, the reception is actually an event that trumpets the conjugal ideal by publicly rewarding marital longevity and thrusting "single" people together in a minimarriage market.

Traditionally, wedding meals were casual events that required no formal invitations, seating plans, or party favors. In England, until the eighteenth century, a wedding ceremony was typically followed by a feast that an entire village would attend. Admission was charged to subvent the cost of the party; guests would bring a penny or a dish to add to the meal; and a bush placed outside the site was a sign that all were welcome, even strangers. Gaming, singing, dancing, and athletics would accompany the event, with many guests so full from food and libation that they would sleep over for the duration of the event.[63]

With its emphasis on community, the premodern wedding reception marked an attitude toward marriage markedly different from our own. "Although husbands and wives were supposed to show consideration and respect, conjugal love was a means to marriage, not its end. Too much conjugal affection was perceived as unnatural and a threat to the broader social obligations that came with the establishment of a household."[64] The tradition of two or three days of exuberant feasting accompanied by rough music faded during the 1700s, when the companionate marriage ideal emerged in full force while the middle class grew, became more prosperous, and consciously emulated the aristocracy in its planning and implementation of social events. The open-ended feast became a one-day celebration that usually started in the morning. Etiquette-conscious Victorians in both England and the United States hosted wedding breakfast teas in their homes. The diminishing number of full-time domestic servants after World War I, however, made the at-home wedding meal difficult, and the increasing desire to display wealth through an elaborate meal in a public venue gave rise to the current reception: a catered meal in a hotel, restaurant, or banquet hall.[65]

Today's wedding primers stress the reception as something personal and open to interpretation. "Your reception should be as special—as memorable—as your ceremony," states the *Bride's Book of Etiquette*. "It can include a sumptuous seated dinner and dessert buffet with a ten-piece band or just you two, your parents, and a few close friends around a big table at your favorite inn or restaurant."[66] While 1950s handbooks offered hard-and-fast rules for reception seating, with a parents' table, for the mothers and fathers of the couple and the wedding officiant, a head table from which the bride and groom and their attendants faced the guests, and fixed seating plans for each table, current planners are more casual and emphasize flexibility and spontaneity. Wedding advisors urge the modern bride not to become overly obsessive about arranging the perfect reception seating chart; the point of the event, they claim, is to celebrate in a relaxed atmosphere.

However, the arrangement of guests is still a notorious source of anxiety and prewedding conflict between brides and grooms. Who should sit next to whom, which guests should be kept apart, and which "singles" will likely hit it off, are topics of intense concern. This is because, while the rules for seating wedding guests (e.g. the bride's parents across from each other, the father of the bridegroom to the right of the hostess, the officiant to her left, the bridegroom's mother to the right of the host, etc.) may have relaxed, the reception is not like any other mere party. Its ritualistic components and its subtext distinguish it as an event. Decorative touches, ceremonial dancing, toasts to the bride and groom, party favors, and the placement of guests render this a meal whose every detail emphasizes the ideology of the couple. The newly-weds seek to reinforce their choice to marry by surrounding themselves with couples and arranging mating opportunities for those who are not yoked together in partnership. Today's wedding reception is, in effect, one big group date.

The wedding invitation that requests the pleasure of our presence at a ceremony followed by dinner, and asks us to bring our "significant other," does not allow us to select the person who is most important in our life as a chaperone to the event; it makes the choice for us. It does not beckon us with our closest friend or mentor or niece or nephew. It invites us to bring our spouse or our lover, assuming that the lover has made the appropriate overtures and appears "serious" as a candidate for marriage. On the occasions when I have responded to such invitations by asking if I could bring, as my date, a close woman friend, I've been told that the wedding budget could not accommodate additional guests. This is clearly a legitimate concern; wedding receptions now run from fifty to one hundred dollars per person for a sit-down dinner, so it is understandable that the hosts might not wish to cater to a lengthy, unmanageable guest list. However, brides and grooms seem willing to find the additional money for romantic dates, because lovers, in marriage ideology, are more important than friends. Nothing else explains the standard refusal to invite a woman with her girlfriend of twenty years or her gay male friend and mentor of sixteen years, when the same bride and groom are happy to include her boyfriend of six months, a man whom they have heard about but never met. Celebrating their elevation of each other above all others, the bride and groom typically impose the same dubious priorities on their guests. The wedding reception thus makes explicit the belief that the entire marital process has implied; lovers are primary and friends are secondary: lovers are essential and friends are dispensable.

Because the reception is so couple oriented, and because it often brings young people together to drink, dine, and dance in a festive setting, relationship advisors consider it an ideal venue for husband hunting. Dating coaches urge their female clients to aggressively prowl each wedding reception for potential spouses, even advising women to leave commitment-phobic lovers behind and go stag in the hopes of finding more substantial prospects. *In Style* columnist Louise Lague, for instance, reminds an anonymous correspondent who wants to bring her boyfriend to a wedding, that receptions are "terrific places to meet men who have marriage on their minds." Lague instructs the woman bluntly and directly to "make this special request only if you and your honey are already joined at the hip and you can't imagine spending a day apart."[67] The guiding assumption seems to be that music, flowers, champagne, and elegant cuisine put everyone in a relaxed mood, so sentimental liquored-up males who are normally resistant to marriage will temporarily reconsider the arrangement, and, before long, find themselves happily conjoined.

But how-to-snag-a-man experts also remind women that reeling in a husband takes work; attitude is everything at such wedding receptions. "Work that Wedding!"[68] commands the December 1999 issue of *Glamour*. The husband hunter is instructed to attend each reception in smashing attire, armed with such original opening lines as, "How do you know the groom?" and "How would you rate the singer?" She should also request a ladies' choice dance from the band, so she can snag an available usher, and she should not feel shy about asking the bride and groom for personal introductions throughout the party. The article includes what is meant to be an inspirational tale of matrimony regenerating itself. A Dallas schoolteacher identified simply as "Jenny" hooked up with her husband at her sister's nuptials, where he served as best man. Tipsy from champagne, the two strolled through a nearby garden and began kissing; soon they were an item. To complete what this bride refers to as a "karmic cycle,"[69] two of her close friends met at her wedding and married shortly thereafter.

The May 1999 issue of *Cosmopolitan* contains a "Have-More-Fun-Than-the-Bride-Guide," which addresses the reader directly: "Be even ballsier than your usual flirtatious self. Go ahead, plant yourself in front of him during the Macarena so he can see every seductive swivel, or ask him to dance when the band plays a slow jam."[70] Dateless women can bask in the company of eligible men in the hopes of hosting their own nuptial celebration—and inspiring envy and adulation—in the not-too-distant future. Those accompanied by their serious beaus, however, should not use the environment to hint for a marriage proposal. *Cosmo* admonishes women that their dates will "freak" if they catch the bouquet and quotes wedding expert Carly Roney, who advises, "Never use this day to put pressure on your guy.... He's probably freaked out enough without your dropping hints about how *his* cousin would make an adorable flower girl or how *you're* going to have a cathedral-length train on *your* big day."[71] "Single" women, who have less to lose, should prowl confidently at weddings, but those whose prey is within their reach—who are zeroing in on the kill—require subtlety, finesse. Snaring a man, after all, is a hunt, and a hunt involves timing and patience. Roney advises women with dates to conveniently find themselves in the rest-room during the bouquet toss.

One of the reasons that weddings are considered to be such excellent man-meeting venues is the opportunity they provide for dancing. The husbandless girl who meets a man at a wedding reception can find herself gliding around the dance floor in his arms within moments. Traditionally, nuptial dancing is a group affair, and contemporary ethnic weddings maintain vestiges of old-world festivity, featuring raucous dances such as the Jewish horah, in which celebrants link arms, the Polish dollar dance, in which men dance with the bride and fill her pockets with gifts of money or pin dollars to her veil, and the Greek handkerchief dance, in which the bride and groom are linked by a handkerchief and others hold shoulders and weave around them. But even ethnic weddings now tend to include the more staid American couples dancing; every wedding band, whether it plays swing music, Klezmer, salsa, disco, or generic standards, is cued to the dictates of wedding protocol. Wedding singers, such as the now popular Dakota Horvath (a.k.a. "Little Blue Eyes"), a pint-sized, thirteen-year-old crooner with greased black hair who belts out Sinatra songs,[72] or thirty-four-year-old Cookie Gonzalez, lead singer for the New York wedding band, Sound of Infinity, whose repertoire includes such Celine Dion tearjerkers as "My Heart Will Go On" and "Because You Loved Me,"[73] know the routine. The stars of the show, the bride and groom, first circle the floor to their favorite song as onlookers ooh and aah. The bride's father soon cuts in, at which point the groom dances with his new mother-in-law. The bride then dances with the father of the groom and the best man, while the groom cuts the rug with the maid of honor. Finally, the bandleader invites all present to join in.[74]

The reception's atmosphere of oppressive romanticism reaches its apex during the wedding dances. First-dance standards like Louis Armstrong's "A Kiss to Build a Dream On," Bryan Adams' "(Everything I Do) I Do it for You," and Harry Connick, Jr.'s "It Had to Be You,"[75] reinforce the ideals of marital salvation and inevitability. When the bride and groom glide along the dance floor, they make the same self-satisfied claim that they have issued throughout the marriage narrative, and they request the same outpouring of approval. "We've decided to have sex with each other exclusively for life and put each other on a romantic pedestal, so please give us lots of applause," they proclaim. In honoring her father with the next dance, the bride displays her loyalty to the two most important men in her life. She reiterates, symbolically, the message that she had affirmed throughout the whole process, that she has found a new father in her husband. Daddy-daughter dances to the strains of Al Martino's "Daddy's Little Girl," George Gershwin's "Someone to Watch Over Me," or, that perennial Jewish wedding tune, "Sunrise, Sunset," from the Bock and Harnick musical, *Fiddler on the Roof,* reverberate with the wedding's promise of protection of women within the conventional family, first by fathers and then by husbands. By honoring their parents as couples, and by then pairing and repairing to form temporary units, the wedding dancers again convey the naturalness and rightness of heterosexual partnership. Wedding planners constantly invent new ways to further enshrine marriage through the activities of the reception: they recommend tables arrayed with family wedding photographs that span back generations, the lighting of unity candles by august pairs of grandparents, and the performance of special songs, such as the one that the bride's father sang to her mother on the night that he proposed marriage. New York planner Elizabeth K. Allen suggests that her clients follow the example of a bride and groom who, at their wedding, asked every *couple* present to come to the dance floor. "Little by little, they narrowed the couples down by saying, 'If you have been married for three years, if you've been married five years, please leave the dance floor.' In the end, only the couple wed the longest remained; the bride gave them her bouquet in the hopes that she and her husband might be married as many years."[76]

Groom's manuals offer tips on dancing, because the wedding, which is usually the first time a man has danced in public, is a source of anxiety for many men. The focal point of male wedding stress, however, is the toast, another reception feature. Customarily, wedding toasts are made by the male principals. Anytime after champagne has been served, the best man makes the first reception toast in honor of the bride and groom. The groom, who, since the proposal, has functioned as a supporting player in the marital drama, again takes center stage and thanks the best man, toasting both sets of parents.

The wedding toast is an interesting moment in the festivities, because it punctures the cloyingly romantic atmosphere and evidences the same hostility and confused homosocial anger that characterized the bachelor party. The toast is a masculine affair; the best man and groom assume their roles as public speakers while the ladies look on quietly and demurely. Occasionally a bridesmaid or mother of the bride may make a toast, although handbooks provide no instructions for such speeches. (Most primers suggest that, when the bride's family wishes to speak, and her father is deceased or absent, the man who gave her away—an uncle or male friend—should take the microphone.) Bridesmaids rarely toast, and those who do are considered unusually aggressive. In *The Best Man's Handbook,* James Grace in fact provides instructions for how to keep an inappropriately loquacious bridesmaid in her place. "If she does have the chutzpah, the least you can do is give her a nice introduction. This will cement the crowd's understanding that you're an MC, this is your little show, and she's only a bit player."[77] The narrative of female passivity in wedlock, with men assuming public leadership roles, continues through the reception.

During the toast, the best man is supposed to thank the hosts of the event for a wonderful party, recount some amusing anecdotes about his friendship with the groom, describe how the couple met, and wish the pair well. However, since marriage is a particularly intractable obstacle to male friendship, and since, as we have seen, men find the subject of their isolation from each other impossible to broach, the toast often becomes an embarrassing display of misplaced hostility—a roast, at which the speaker channels his aggressions toward the bride and groom as a couple. Groom's manuals are aware of the pitfalls of the best man's toast and provide lengthy lists of cautionary instructions. Best men are not to drink too much prior to the speech. ("Alcohol is a depressant—it works first to depress your common sense, then it compromises your ability to speak."[78]) They are not to indulge in backhanded compliments while describing how they met the guest of honor. They are not to deliberately embarrass the groom, mention his sexual history or past relationships, or insult the bride, despite the temptation to do so. ("If you don't agree with the groom's choice in a bride, it can show during the best man speech [sic]. Try out the speech on a friend who understands your feelings and see if he or she can see through your mask of civility," recommends James Grace.[79]) They must, when reminiscing about past episodes with the groom, omit incidents of drug and alcohol abuse or brushes with the law. "You want to make fun of the groom in a way that only you can because you're his relative or best friend. This isn't the bachelor party, so when in doubt, leave it out."[80]

Why the lengthy what-not-to-say lists in groom's manuals? Because violations of decorum are so common at this point in the reception. The subtext of the best man's speech is resentment and frustration. Mixed with alcohol and the stress of public speaking, the simmering emotions that men experience when their companions retreat into conjugal isolation reach a boiling point in the toast. The convention of the American wedding toast is to embarrass the groom slightly, with affection and to express love without becoming maudlin. It is easy to cross the line in both cases. Speakers who recount drunken weekends during college and spring break parties, emphasize the groom's poor taste in women by dwelling on his depraved exwife, mention his messiness and poor work habits, comment negatively on his physical appearance, make smutty allusions to the couple's relationship, *or* ramble on inaudibly and sentimentally produce intense discomfort in the audience. But the emotions of the toast are just the tip of an enormous iceberg of ambivalence about wedlock. A wedding is no longer the celebration of both a new husband and a set of communal relationships. It is the lionization of a heterosexual couple embracing each other at the expense of all other relationships. Perversely, wedding protocol now demands the the person who will feel the loss of the groom most acutely—his best friend—put on a happy face and fete the duo. And the results are, predictably, uncomfortable, or at times even disastrous. *The Best Man's Handbook* includes cautionary examples of toasts in which best men condemn the marriage ("I give them six months.")[81] or share their own sexual knowledge of the bride ("I had your wife and she was the best.").[82]

To provide a verbal outlet for the hostility and divert *faux pas,* some contemporary primers offer lists of insulting, humorously antimarriage toasts that allow the best man to contain his hostility within an elegant epigram. Angela Lansbury, in *Wedding Speeches and Toasts,* suggest utilizing a Samuel Butler quotation: "A man's friendships are, like his will, invalidated by marriage—but they are also no less invalidated by the marriage of his friends."[83] Usually, however, groom's handbook's provide aphorisms that do not address the issue of lost friendship directly but, rather, enable the best man to skewer his friend, depicting the groom as a patsy, a henpecked husband whose masculinity has been compromised. Guests can chuckle uncomfortably while the best man, without losing his composure, describes his newly married friend as the dupe of feminine wiles. Barbara Jefferey, in her 1998 *Wedding Speeches and Toasts,* provides material for just such an occasion. She suggests pithy literary quotations to satirize the marital ideal, adding that the speaker should distance himself from the cynicism of his epigrams. Her suggested material includes sayings such as, "Marriage is a wonderful institution, but who wants to live in an institution" (Groucho Marx), "Marriage has many pains, but celibacy has no pleasures," (Samuel Johnson), "What delight we married people have to see these poor fools decoyed into our condition" (Samuel Pepys), "All husbands are alike, but they have different faces so you can tell them apart" (Ogden Nash), "A husband's last words are always, 'O.K., buy it!'" (N.P. Willis), "Who follows his wife in everything is an ignoramus," (the Talmud), "Marriage is based on the theory that when man discovers a particular brand of beer exactly to his taste, he should at once throw up his job and go to work in the brewery" (George Jean Nathan), and "The man who says his wife can't take a joke, forgets that she took him" (Oscar Wilde).[84]

These brief but direct assaults on matrimony, in which a male speaker quotes male antimarriage satirists in order to insult his closest male friend, hint at the dark undercurrent of the contemporary wedding reception. It betrays the loss of homosocial friendship to wedlock—a loss so profound that it cannot be addressed. When the groom takes the microphone from his friend and delivers his own toast, it is his role to obscure this schism between friends and promote happy matrimony once again, first thanking his mother-in-law for her work in planning the reception and then addressing his bride directly. "Gush,"[85] advises Michael R. Perry in *The Groom's Survival Manual.* "In most other situations in your life, you're expected to speak modestly, in careful, hedged terms. But this is your new wife, so you'll appear sweet, sensitive, and loving if you fill your toasts with superlatives." John Mitchell's *What the Hell Is a Groom and What's He Supposed to Do?* is equally direct in its advice on toasts: "Thank your parents. Thank her parents. Thank all the guests. Most of all, thank your new wife."[86]

The groom's role as toastmaster is far less rhetorically complex than that of his predecessor. While the best man must keep his emotions in delicate equipoise, balancing his private loss with his public role as happy celebrant of the marriage, using humor to mask his ambivalence, the groom's role is that of the unabashed romantic. His job is to pay tribute to his wife, displaying his excessive love for her, suggesting the endless romance that their marriage will be, and validating his own choice to become part of a couple. He must express what the medieval writer and abbess Heloise called the "blessed delusion between man and wife,"[87] the belief that one's spouse is the worthiest, loveliest, most perfectly realized man or woman on earth. (Heloise pointed out that, while this mental error safeguarded the marriage tie, it was never true. How could it be in every case?) But the groom must present himself as the luckiest man alive, the winner of amorous sweepstakes in which numerous men competed for a modern-day Helen of Troy—a woman in whom beauty, poise, intelligence, and virtue are smoothly amalgamated. Wedding author Angela Lansbury suggests the following opening: "As you all know Annabelle has been a much sought after girl/woman. I'm pleased to announce the winner of the competition, me. There are no runners up or associated prizes."[88] Other advisors suggest lavish poetic addresses, such as Ben Jonson's "Drink to me only with thine eyes,/And I will pledge with mine;/Or leave a kiss within the cup,/And I'll not look for wine," or Yeats' "Wine comes in at the mouth/And love comes in at the eye;/That's all we shall know of truth/Before we grow old and die./I lift the glass to my mouth,/I look at you,/and I sigh."[89] Or they recommend appearing humble and struck dumb by love; a man whose verbal abilities are inadequate to the task of praising his bride: "What has really made this the happiest day of my life is the lovely girl sitting next to me. Public speaking is not my scene, nor can I easily find the words to say how wonderful Paula is. In fact, if it wasn't for getting married, I wouldn't even be here! I really am a man of few words, and never more so than now."[90]

The groom's main task, when he takes the microphone and toasts his bride, is that of marriage propagandist. It is a job that will continue into the honeymoon, and through the period of composing thank-you notes. It will extend into married life itself, because matrimony, for the first time in western history, is now purported to be an endless honeymoon in which erotic and romantic delights continue to unfold. When he toasts his new wife, gushing over the beauty and accomplishments, the groom does so performatively, showing his finesse as a lover, his attentiveness as a husband. His job at the wedding reception is to wax sentimentally, obscuring the incongruities and paradoxes implicit in the institution of marriage: its invalidation of friendship, its imbalances of social and economic power, its requirements of romantic fusion and social isolationism. The groom's toast must naturalize matrimony to the point where that most artificial of states appears organic, and the wedding reception's flowers, food, and music seem to be spontaneous outcroppings of a deep and intrinsic bond between two star-crossed lovers. The groom's job is to leave every married wedding guest feeling good about his or her social standing and every "single" member of the company pining to become part of a couple.

Martha Stewart suggests sending guests off from the wedding reception with handcrafted party favors: candies wrapped in vintage white paper or almonds stuffed into cups fashioned out of doilies.[91] For less ambitious hosts, a conventional gift is a wrapped slice of cake. According to one piece of folklore, a piece of wedding cake taken from the reception and placed under a "single" person's pillow will lead to dreams of an actual future spouse.[92]

III. The Cake

"On this one day looks are everything,"[93] cautions an advertisement in a recent issue of *Martha Stewart Weddings*. "For this reason, the most exquisite cakes you will ever serve should be presented with style." This advertisement, for Van Horn-Hayward, a company that manufactures acrylic cake stands and candleholders, shows four white lattice-work cakes topped with white roses, surrounded by white candles flickering from what appear to be tall lucite pillars. The cakes, which sit on clear lucite stands of varying heights, appear suspended in midair. Their presentation is meant to suggest the opulence associated with wedding food. Apparently floating, these pastries are not merely desserts; they are visual sculpture intended to impress wedding guests and demonstrate the bride's finesse. With their shiny glazed surfaces, the confections do not look especially appetizing. They seem crafted to be admired—oohed and aahed over and photographed—rather than eaten. The advertisement then confronts the modern bride directly, proclaiming: "Everyone is watching, noticing each single detail you have carefully chosen."[94] It is not just the flowers, the dress, and the menu that distinguishes today's bride. The cake, icing, cake toppers, cake stands, and candleholders are among the nuances that display her taste to the world on the most public day of her life, a day when no detail is unimportant, no decision too small to be overlooked.

Like the white gown, the tiered white wedding cake is a crucial visual emblem of the blockbuster nuptial. Bridal magazines and coffee table books on famous marriages include enlarged photographs of every couple's cake, images that emphasize each concoction's glazed surface and ornamental details: its piping, sugar paste flower buds, buttercream ribbons, filigrees, sprinkles, and chocolate shavings. The ritual in which bride and groom together cut the cake and feed each other slices is a favorite of photographers and guests alike—a moment of public intimacy intended to symbolize the sustenance that each partner has found in marriage. Guides like *Modern Bride* offer specific instructions for freezing the first slice of wedding cake so that it can be saved as a cherished memento.[95] The frozen slice, which is defrosted and eaten only on a special anniversary, is intended to represent a figural slice of the literal heaven that is each couple's wedding day.

The majority of modern cakes are still white, although their surfaces may vary, including thick wavy frostings sprinkled with coconut or vanilla icing sculpted to form a latticework surface. While they are commonly decorated with artificial flowers made of a sugar and oil combination and shaded with food coloring, today's white cakes are also decorated with actual foliage—draped with strands of ivy, sprinkled with rose petals, or studded with purple grapes. Whether real or synthetic, such decorations are said to express the wedding's themes and continue its decor: cakes for orchard weddings are frequently topped with real or marzipan grapes, cakes at beach nuptials are studded with chocolate seashells, etc. For her July 19, 1998, East Hampton wedding to Brown University Chancellor Stephen Robert, public relations executive Pilar Crespi, for example, selected a lemony cake by pastry chef Gail Watson, who is known for her sugar tableaux. Covered with white frosting, the cake was topped with a tiny, copper beech tree inspired by the symbolism of the actual tree Crespi had given her groom as a wedding gift. According to the bride, "Trees, like marriage, need a lot of care."[96]

Cakes have long been an integral part of weddings. Roman nuptials featured the preparation of a special wheat or barley cake, which was broken over the bride's head; wheat crumbs were also thrown by the guests.[97] Medieval feasts among the highest reaches of European society used decorative food, and it is in medieval England that the plum cake, cooked with dried fruit, sugar, and spices, and served after a meal, originates.[98] By the early seventeenth century recipes for "bride cakes" cooked with butter, cream, milk, cloves, mace, and cinnamon, existed; at this point the wedding cake was less of a pastry and more of a celebratory bread.[99] Both plum and bride cakes were served at weddings. The direct antecedents of the modern wedding cake, however, are the elaborate creations served in England during the reign of King Charles II (1160–1185), when French chefs imported from the continent turned this traditional English spice cake into an visual spectacle, icing it with white sugar. It became the custom for English newlyweds to pile small cakes on top of each other and then try to kiss across the vertical structure without knocking it down. Superstition decreed that those couples who succeeded would enjoy a lifetime of prosperity. (To ensure each couple's success, discreet bakers would weld the tiers firmly together with icing.)[100]

In 1769 the English cook Mrs. Raffald published a collection of recipes that reproduced the wedding cake of a Spanish confectioner, including instructions on how to ice the cake with a layer of almond paste and then a layer of white frosting. The recipe became standard, crossing the Atlantic in 1830 and inspiring imitators who toyed with ingredients and amounts to create a richer product.[101] The nineteenth-century discovery of baking powder, baking soda, and finely milled flowers enabled bakers to create light fluffy cakes as opposed to the heavy fruit puddings of previous generations. Francatelli, a French-trained chef employed by Queen Victoria, provided the innovation of marzipan, which became a popular substitute for icing in the second half of the nineteenth century. Substances "more or less plastic"[102] could be rolled out and attached to the cake with egg white, sieved apricot jam, or puree. A popular late Victorian practice imported from France was piping, in which sugary icing was pressed through a funnel to shape ornamental designs on the cake.

Throughout the nineteenth century food became more and more elaborate, taking on a powerful vertical dimension, partly due to the influence of the French chef Marie-Antoine Carême, who had studied classical architecture and who, as a pastry chef, created formal culinary sculptures called *pieces montees*.[103] Towering, tiered wedding cakes became standard at the nuptials of high society couples, and these cakes, while white, were decorated with swags, cupids, bows, and filigrees, and, to celebrate the nuptials of figures of state, enhanced with allegorical figures. In typical high style, the 1840 wedding of Queen Victoria was marked with an elaborately topped, round plum cake. Covered with white icing, the cake was topped with symbols of the bride and bridegroom dressed in ancient Roman costume. At the feet of the groom was the figure of a dog (to denote fidelity). At the feet of the queen was a pair of turtle doves. The figurines were also surrounded by a host of gambling Cupids and bouquets of white flowers tied with true-lovers' knots.[104] Eighteen years later the queen attended her daughter's wedding and witnessed a far more elaborate concoction; a tiered white cake between six and seven feet high, topped by a dome supported by eight columns. The dome enclosed an altar on which stood two Cupids with the profiles of the Princess Royal and her groom, Prince Frederick William of Prussia. The columns supported busts of the Queen and her consort as well as the Prince and Princess of Prussia and statues representing innocence and wisdom. The side of the cake displayed the arms of Great Britain and Prussia, shown alternately on panels of white satin. Between each coat of arms was a medallion of the Princess Royal and her consort encircled by orange blossoms.[105]

With the commercialization of baking, tiered wedding cakes have become available to all strata of society in the twentieth century, and the stacked white cake makes its appearance at even the humblest wedding parties. Its image fills the pages of special "wedding cakes" sections of bridal magazines, and the ritual cutting of the wedding cake is often included in magazine accounts of weddings of the rich and famous. As is generally the case with wedding custom, this apparently neutral gesture has paternalistic connotations. Jaclyn C. Barrett-Hirschhaut explains that, while cutting into the wedding cake, "The groom traditionally places his hand over the bride's as a symbol of his desire to take care of her."[106] "We didn't do special toasts or any of that stuff,"[107] says actress Kim Weeks of her December 22, 1998, Los Angeles reception celebrating her wedding to actor Charles Bronson. But *People* magazine displays an adoring photograph of the thirty-seven-year-old bride and her seventy-seven-year-old groom cutting into the bottom level of a four-tiered white cake decorated with tiny pink, purple, and green florets and topped with what appears to be a bouquet of dried white flowers. "I *finally* found somebody who appreciates me,"[108] gushes actress Rue McClanahan in *People*'s June 1998 special weddings issue. A photograph of McClanahan at her December 25, 1997, New York wedding to actor Morrow Wilson shows the bride, for whom this is a sixth marriage, decked out in white and flanked by her smiling groom. The couple cuts into a tiered white cake topped with a plastic bride and groom framed by a wire oval covered in delicate white lace. This ubiquitous image—a glowing bride and nervous groom jointly cutting into a towering pile of white icing and sugar paste—is not just a key sentimental moment in the wedding's narrative. It is an act fraught with cultural significance. Simon R. Charsley points out that, within the history of marriage, this ritual is an indicator of social change. In antiquity and the Middle Ages, and perhaps well into early modernity, the folk custom of breaking a dry cake over a bride's head had sexual symbolism related to the imminent loss of her virginity on the wedding night. It demonstrated the common view that marriage was "something done by a man to a woman, and essentially about change for her."[109] Breaking cake over a bride was a physical act performed upon a woman by others; the modern joint action in which the bride and groom cut the cake together suggests equity within a reciprocal identity. The once passive bride is now presented as half of an equal couple.

Wedding cakes in the latter part of the twentieth century have become more visually eclectic, incorporating new styles of icing and intricate designs, adding tiers and applying colors to the standard white palate.[110] Although Victorian cakes were elaborate, ideally, they were completely white, relying for effect on piped decoration. Whiteness has been the rule for American cakes throughout most of the twentieth century, but today's confections draw on a range of bold color schemes and futuristic patterns. Bakers and their clients often describe these new style cakes as acts of bold iconoclasm:

> By the 1970s, in Los Angeles at least, cakes were to be seen in an array of fantasy styles, sometimes with ethnic titles or motifs. One firm was offering "Pure Bridal White, Daring German Chocolate, Classic Italian Marble, and Secret Danish Gold." They claimed that they had "innovated chocolate wedding cakes in L.A., to keep up with the new freedom of expression," and went on to comment that "it really upset people. It's wild what we're doing, but who says it has to be the same old four-tiered white cake year after year?"[111]

The impulse to do something "wild" is still dominant among upscale contemporary bakers. Their motivation toward visual outrageousness has resulted in a popular wedding cake that achieves two ends: it astonishes the viewer with its scale and color scheme, and it does not look like a cake.

A square four-tiered cake featured in a recent issue of *Martha Stewart Weddings,* for instance, is covered with tiny round dots that give it the look of "a vintage chenille bedspread, yet the effect is surprisingly modern."[112] The tiers of another white cake in this same issue are covered with what appear to be scalloped fabric embroidered with dainty Victorian patterns. "The lacy fondant decorations on the dazzling wedding cake resemble cutwork table linens,"[113] the copy explains. New York based baker Ron Ben-Israel specializes in art deco cakes that have industrial patterns, featuring linear and geometric combinations of grey and white. His cakes appear to have been graphically designed rather than frosted; they are topped with sculpted, edible white deco vases filled with actual white roses. The July/August issue of *Bridal Guide* magazine features a "Hooray for Hollywood" cake inspired by the gowns worn by actresses to Academy Awards ceremonies. The five-tier white confection is decorated with gold ornamentation and red and pink hearts and stuck throughout with pearl studded, curly cue-shaped wires. *Bridal Guide* uses the image of the wedding cake to remind the modern bride of her awesome social ascent through marriage. It showcases a four-tier white cake topped with a lavender sugar castle from whose towers and turrets fly tiny purple flags. "For your reign as princess (with your own Prince Charming) feast on a double-iced cake (buttercream topped by English fondant) in a sophisticated, subdued palette of lavenders, blues, and grays, dusted with real silver for shimmer. A floral trail—cattyla, orchids, lilacs, roses, morning glories, hydrangeas, and silvery trailing ivy, all made of sugar—leads up, up, up, to a removable keepsake castle. Being royal rules!"[114]

Often wedding cakes incorporate nature themes, like the classic snowflake cake, a white tiered confection covered with tiny meringue "snowflakes" that is "as magical as the season's first flurry."[115] Or they hearken to a particular period of artistic flowering. Polly Schoonmaker's five-tiered wedding cake is covered in fondant and decorated in a pattern "reminiscent of the Italian Renaissance interiors, beaded with gold dragees and strewn with fresh roses."[116] An iconoclastic, Portland, Oregon, based baker whose work is often featured in bridal magazines, Schoonmaker is a master of off-kilter cakes with wacky visuals. Her philosophy is anti-Victorian. "When I got into this business, I wanted to take the idea of a wedding cake and strip it of all the Victorian froufrou, making something that is fairly tailored and contemporary. Basically, I clean up all the Baroque stuff and make the cake classical yet modern."[117]

Schoonmaker's repertoire includes a Halloween wedding cake with a tiny haunted house, complete with crooked windows and shutters, perched on the top tier and a summer confection covered with three layers of fondant cherries, peaches, and bows, which simulates a patchwork quilt. Her "topsy turvy cake," featured in the spring 2000 weddings issue of *In Style* magazine, contains three tiers decorated with geometric designs in purple, lavender, and orange, embellished with what look like swags of green fabric and studded with what appear to be tiny pearls. The cake's tiers are uneven; each one appears to be leaning dangerously to one side, so the entire structure looks like it's about to fall sideways in both directions. New York baker Collette Peters offers a similar "quake cake," in which four shiny tiers, which look like they have been hand wrapped in gold fabric, lurch precariously to the right. Katrina Roselle, a baker in Alamo, California, prepares a "Golden Arches" cake, in which two of the three tiers are suspended on stiff gold columns, fashioned out of powdered sugar and egg whites. This confection is designed to evoke the look of a church courtyard. Brooklyn-based Cheryl Kleinman's signature creation is a cake reminiscent of the Greek themes of bas-relief china, in which two blue tiers are piped with white garlands and images of dancing meanads, and a final tier is suspended on nine Ionic columns. New Yorker Margaret Braun, who created the desert for actress Sarah Jessica Parker's wedding, offers a "bejeweled" cake intended to evoke Faberge eggs. Five tiers of pink cake are embellished with elaborate gold piping; topping the confection is a pink, gold, and white goblet.[118]

Roland Barthes has observed that heavily glazed and ornamented food is often used as a means of displaying wealth and gentility.[119] Such cookery, according to Barthes, operates in two contradictory directions, with its artificial ingredients and methods, it recoils from nature. It simultaneously reconstitutes the natural world through artifice, with rococo features like buttercream roses, sugar paste beech trees, fondant ivy, and plastic cake toppers that represent the biblical Garden of Eden. The visual gimmicks of today's wedding cakes are certainly nouveau riche displays, but they are also more. As opposed to the generic wedding cakes of the past, today's designs are personal, whimsical, and purely secular. Like the creative wedding invitation, they are undertaken to demonstrate the bride and groom's unique sense of style and joie de vivre. In the eighteenth and nineteenth centuries *pieces montees* were allegorical in nature, depicting timeless religious truths or national heroes. The contemporary wedding cake is, by contrast, a showcase of its principals. It is intended to highlight the bride and groom's madcap spirit and therefore represents yet another conspicuous act of public rebellion against matrimonial convention. Wedding advisors encourage this kind of desperate individuation in the planning and execution of one's cake. Don Altman, author of *201 Unique Ways to Make Your Wedding Special* lists creative possibilities: "A fashion designer might want a cake to resemble a quilt or other fabric. For avid publishers, writers, or readers, the cake could resemble a favorite volume of books. A cake can even represent a fairy-tale castle or a favorite locale, such as the Leaning Tower of Pisa and the Great Pyramids."[120]

Modern brides follow such advice, genuinely appearing to believe that their multicolored desserts comprise a dangerous threat to the marital order. "I wanted to stand out in a way that was very like me. I didn't want to be a typical bride," explains jewelry designer Tarina Tarantino of her October 30, 1999, Silver Lake, California, wedding to her business partner, Alfonso Campos. Tarantino wore a white Christina Perrin gown dusted with more than seven thousand five hundred Swarovski crystals and dyed her hair bright fuschia for the occasion, a choice documented and reported with shock and delight. "And the bride wore...fuschia hair? You bet,"[121] exclaims *In Style* magazine's Monica Corcoran, apparently overwhelmed by her subject's bold iconoclasm. To complement her hair and her fuschia bouquet studded with crystals, this bride selected a six-foot-tall cake prepared by the Los Angeles company, Different Cakes. Like others of its ilk, this dessert appears to be anything but a cake. *In Style* shows a photograph of what looks like a pile of bright pink hatboxes decorated with small crystal jewels, hung with strands of beads, and stuck randomly with hat pins. Its tiers appear to be suspended on a long steel rod, and, like its cousins, the topsy turvy cake and the quake cake, it is deliberately lopsided. This confection announces that its bride, who strolled up the aisle in virginal white and married in a traditional Catholic ceremony, is also a little bit lopsided, a little bit zany. It addresses the free-floating cultural anxiety that permeates the contemporary nuptial, assuring both guests and readers that this crazy, lovably off-center *artiste* will keep her spirit alive within wedlock. The cake reassures guests that marriage will not alter this adorable kook—that she will retain her raffish individuality, despite having embraced the most conventionalizing of social contracts.

The zany cake is more than just another of the wedding industry's controlled forms of rebellion, however. With its extreme degree of artifice, it is the nuptial's purest expression of camp. Wedding literature often laments the fact that despite its high cost, wedding cake doesn't taste very good and often goes uneaten. But it is not meant to be eaten or to inspire any degree of hunger in onlookers. The dessert's spuriousness as a food item distinguishes it from all other fare on the wedding menu. Contemporary wedding caterers tend to stress the freshness and naturalness of their dishes, describing their menus in terms of color, texture, taste, and regional origins. Today's bride and groom typically dine on grilled fish from the Mediterranean marinated in virgin olive oil and fresh herbs or Pacific rim prawns accompanied by organic green salad and rustic bread and followed by assorted Oregon berries with yogurt dipping sauce. Caterers offer such appetizers as melon with Parma ham or crispy vegetable dumplings accompanied by Napa Valley Chardonnay. They proffer such main courses as fillets of mullet with herbes de Provence or Chilean sea bass in port wine sauce with fresh mushrooms or Sonoma lamb skewered on rosemary branches or free range chicken breast dusted with pecans and seared. The modern wedding table features such side dishes as fresh corn cakes with Alaskan smoked salmon or couscous with golden raisins and crunchy pine nuts or creamy goat cheese and olive salad or summer vegetable platters of green and yellow beans, sugar snap peas, and zucchini, with fennel. The current aesthetic of deliciousness demands that today's caterer describe his or her offerings in Technicolor, characterizing food according to texture, hue, place of origin, and degree of freshness, no matter how processed and saturated with preservatives it may be.[122]

The wedding cake, by contrast, advertises its own artifice. By the time it has been baked, molded, colored, and frosted to resemble the Empire State Building or the holy grail, the cake has come to utterly disguise its own beginnings in flour, eggs, and butter. Suspended on lucite pillars, draped with ivy, or stuck with rhinestone covered hat pins, the wedding cake has no regional point of origin and no mouthwatering texture or scent. It is a visual spectacle rather than a dish prepared to stimulate the taste buds, and whether traditional or modern, the cake is therefore an emblem of marital camp. Susan Sontag defines the camp sensibility as one that loves artifice for its own sake. She identifies two types: pure undiluted love of the artificial that she terms naive camp, and the jaded and more self-conscious aestheticism that comprises self-conscious camp.[123] The conventional white wedding cake that originated in the Victorian era and is still served at nuptial celebrations, is pure camp. It combines exaggeration, fantasy, passion, and naivete. Consisting of three round tiers, decorated with inedible sugar paste roses, and topped with a porcelain bride and groom, it says, in effect, "I am here to celebrate the undying love of this man and this woman. It is pristine. It is beautiful. It is forever." The nineteenth-century cake topped with figurines of royal monarchs and decorated with their families' coats of arms, was similarly sincere. It said, in effect, "Victoria is our ruler, our monarch, and our mother. We love her. We pledge undying loyalty and deference to her. We salute her union with Albert, the man of her dreams." Because this confection, like this sentiment of naive patriotism, becomes absurd over time, the cake itself becomes an item of kitschy humor—a figure of camp. The contrast between the heartfelt emotions it represents and the absurd baroqueness of its decoration create, finally, an absurd effect that inspires affectionate laughter rather than tears.

This discomfort with marital sincerity has given rise to the off-kilter cake. The dessert designed to appear deliberately kooky, tilting to one side or emulating an object as mundane as a bedspread or a soup can or stunning the viewer with its profusion of glittery bows and strands of sugar paste pearls, mocks its predecessor. It pokes fun at the ideals celebrated in moments like the wedding toast: matrimonial permanence, fidelity, domestic happiness, and undying love between spouses. "Camp," writes Sontag, "sees everything in quotation marks. It's not a lamp but a 'lamp'; not a woman but a 'woman.'... It is the farthest extension, in sensibility, of the metaphor of life as theater."[124] The wedding cake that resembles a vintage bedspread or a patchwork quilt or a first snowfall or a medieval tapestry or an art deco vase or a Faberge egg or a pile of flowers or a bunch of silk roses or a skyscraper encodes profound self-consciousness about the possibility of happiness within marriage. It puts the very idea of companionate marriage in quotation marks, drawing attention to the excessive labor that precedes the wedding day, announcing that marriage is not a natural state but a humanly shaped institution. It is not a cake but a "cake." Like the campy, art deco lighting fixtures that take the form of flowering plants or the T-shirt that masquerades as a formal tuxedo, the new wedding cake is "off" in a special way. It channels modern marriage anxiety into an aesthetic that represents things as what they are not. It says, "I am not here to celebrate the lifelong union of one man and one woman. We all know that such commitments don't last. Instead, I am here to mock the convention. I am here to tweak the tradition. I am here to amaze you with my own artifice. I am here to represent a staggering sum of money spent on what amounts to flour, sugar, cream, and food coloring that is flavorless and will be hard and stale by tomorrow morning."

Addressing the actual inequities of marriage and relinquishing the big white wedding and all that it stands for would, of course, eliminate the need for such indirect forms of antagonism. For women, this would mean channeling our hopes (and our parents' money) into different, diverse projects and events. Modern cake cutting may, at some level, represent female progress within marriage, symbolizing egalitarian participation in a pivotal moment. But it still promotes the tyranny of the couple, celebrating woman as half of a heterosexual whole. It would be interesting to conceive of a less elaborate and costly cake prepared, customarily, in celebration of all women coming of age, with or without male companions. At the signature moment of such an event the guest of honor would cut the cake alone, to celebrate her independence and her potential as an individual rather than inaugurating her new status as Mrs. Attached-to-Somebody-Else.

CHAPTER TEN

Institutionalized Eroticism: The Honeymoon

They flaunt their conjugal felicity in one's face, as if it were the most fascinating of sins. —Oscar Wilde, *The Picture of Dorian Gray*

A man is always a teller of tales, he lives surrounded by his stories and the stories of others, he sees everything that happens through them; and he tries to live his life as if he were recounting it.

— Jean Paul Sartre, *Nausea*

I. Romantic Isolationism

"Maybe it's because you toasted your union with coconut milk.... Maybe it's because tonight you'll wear your tiara flower to the right side.... Maybe it's because you always knew who you wanted to be alone with on a deserted island.... Whatever it is, it's working.... Tahiti. Where Love Lives."[1] "It's as if Fiji were created with romance in mind. Think of long walks on deserted white-sand beaches, moonlit swims in warm, clear waters and intimate moments in secluded coves—Fiji is a honeymooner's paradise. Where else could you stay in a private, thatched-roof bungalow (*bure*) just steps away from the crystalline waters of the South Pacific?"[2] "You cannot confine the emotions of new love within four walls. With this in mind Allegro has a simple philosophy: honeymooners are treated like guests of honor. From your intimate living quarters and candle lit tables in the corner to the calm Caribbean waves lapping at your ankles, here, romance has no boundaries."[3] "You said yes to the greatest guy in the world. Now say yes to the most romantic resorts on earth!

337

Beaches Negril in Jamaica and Beaches Turquoise Resort & Spa in Turks & Caicos are the new wave in ultra all-inclusives."[4] "Maui's warm evening breeze whispers. This is no ordinary honeymoon. Every moment at Kea Lani is special. Every flavor, every aroma, every sunset. Our magnificent suites entice you to linger, but the warm sun and turquoise sea beckon you each morning. You deserve more than a little indulgence on your honeymoon. You deserve Kea Lani."[5] "You've found the perfect person. Now discover the Westin resort, St. John. . . . Our special touches include fresh flowers and chilled champagne waiting in your deluxe gardenview room, a couple's massage, breakfast in bed, romantic island adventures, and a sunset cruise."[6] "You'll call it heaven. We call it Breezes. Alone, together. At last. Just the two of you, with nothing but love on your mind and the sun on your backs. On your Breezes honeymoon, you need only think of each other, because we've thought of everything else."[7] "Romance, Passion, Indulgence, Privacy. . . and Fun! All the elements of a perfect honeymoon and the ideal way to begin your life's journey together. Caeser's Pocono Resorts, four secluded honeymoon resorts nestled in the rolling hills of the beautiful and peaceful Pocono Mountains, offer the ideal romantic atmosphere for you to be alone together."[8]

Modern bridal magazines conclude with page after page of advertisements aimed at would-be honeymooners. Placed by chains of hotels, commercial airlines, travel agencies, or chambers of commerce, these spreads feature photographs of lovers in tropical locales. Muscular sun-bronzed brides and grooms embrace passionately against the backdrop of coastal sunsets, frolic half-naked on vast empty beaches, snorkel in aquamarine ocean waters, sip fruity drinks while reclining on the decks of ocean liners, kiss beneath cascading waterfalls, soak in jacuzzis, uncork bottles of champagne in lavish hotel suites, or dance ecstatically to calypso music in the nightclubs of upscale island resorts. Draped in wet clingy swimsuits or decked out in festive island attire—colorful Hawaiian shirts, flower necklaces, splashy sun dresses, enormous sombreros—the lovers embrace on flower-filled sun decks or nap together on hammocks beneath immense palm trees. Photographed alone, in empty, unpopulated spaces, these iconic figures represent the bliss of marital exile, which, according to one advertisement, occurs in a nonspecific locale "somewhere between Vacation and Isolation."[9]

Commercials for honeymoon destinations constitute a discrete part of the wedding industry: erotic tourism for the newly married. Wedding merchants merge with the travel industry to promote sun spots that promise emotional, sexual, and spiritual renewal, beckoning brides and grooms to travel to edenic island retreats where they can enjoy an array of sensual delights, basking in "the scent of night blooming jasmine, accompanied by the sound of waves lapping gently on the beach," or visiting "Mineral springs bubbling in hidden grottoes, where legend has it their powers revitalize the soul with romantic energy."[10]

Such landscapes are presumed to function aphrodisiacally. Modern advertisers depict young couples in one of two states: either the bride and groom are preparing for sexual intercourse—gazing at each other across a candlelight dinner or disrobing together as they step into a hot tub—or they are languishing in a postcoital haze, lying intertwined on a heart-shaped bed draped in red satin sheets or playfully drawing hearts in the sands of secluded coves. The honeymoon destination spot is a place where they can copulate day and night without fear of interruption. One ad depicts two pairs of feet peeking from beneath rumpled sheets: "For honeymoon couples just starting out. Room service, twenty-four hours a day. No charge,"[11] the slogan reads. Romantic advertisements tend to employ natural phenomena as metaphors for marital permanence, assuaging their clients' anxiety by suggesting that in an era of escalating divorce, their unions will remain as permanent and pristine as the beaches of Bali, as rock solid as the mountain ranges of Bora Bora. Honeymoon advertisers go further; they deploy images of nature to symbolize marital eroticism, running photographs of Hawaiian volcanoes alongside copy that announces, "Honeymoons Sizzle on the Big Island";[12] Such advertisers present immense natural phenomena—vast oceans, endless beaches, gaping canyons, and starlit panoramic skies—as the appropriate backdrops for unleashing marital passion. The images imply that the hurricane of each couple's sexual fervor would destroy the flimsy constructs of mere man-made dwellings. Newlyweds require the appropriate landscapes in which to set free the forces of their cataclysmic libidos. The appropriate venues for their sexual rampages are island coves, moonlit fields, or the thunderous waters of that perennial American honeymooner's spot, Niagara Falls. With their erotic focus, honeymoon advertisers also instruct couples to explore each other's bodies in new ways: "Kiss Every New Freckle on Her Shoulder,"[13] an ad for a Bermuda resort entreats. The accompanying photograph shows a man and woman wrapped in terry cloth bathrobes, reclining on a hammock, and gazing into each other's eyes.

Honeymoon advertisers reinforce the sense of marital entitlement that characterizes the entire wedding narrative. They pander to the couple's sense of itself as exceptional and deserving of privilege; sometimes promoters go so far as to exclude troublesome "single" travelers with advertisements that read "for couples only." With their endless lists of newlywed extras—complimentary massages, bottles of champagne, fruit baskets, breakfasts in bed, island tours, and moonlight cruises—the erotic tourist industry perpetuates the notion of each newly married couple as heterosexual royalty deserving special treatment. Honeymoon advertising in fact takes a sympathetic view of the newly married couple, purporting to understand the extreme anxiety generated by the process of planning one's own tribute. Commercials present the honeymoon as an antidote to the tension of wedding production, a rejuvenating tonic for stressed out newlyweds. A feature for the Sheraton Hotel and Resorts in Hawaii depicts a woman in a blue bathing suit sitting on a rock formation from which water drips, gazing adoringly at her male partner, who waves at her from the ocean beneath. "Ten months of wedding planning instantly forgotten,"[14] the copy reads. This young couple is promised the tranquility of "White beaches that go on for miles," "Sunsets that last and last," and "An ocean with more shades of blue than the world has names for."[15]

The iconography of the contemporary honeymoon makes conjugal solitude the precondition for sexual happiness. Each commercial image promises that which newly married couples are presumed to want most: a natural landscape in which bride and groom can sequester themselves in order to enjoy a lengthy sexual marathon. "Feel like you are the only two people in the world," an ad for a chain of Mexican hotels admonishes: "The Sol Melia hotels and resorts of Mexico make your decision on your honeymoon getaway very simple. You choose the location and we take care of the rest. Let Sol Melia take care of your escape while you enjoy the stuff that dreams are made of."[16] The honeymoon advertiser takes a hostile tone to the newlyweds' friends and relatives, treating them as antagonists to young love. In an odd turn, the bridal party, wedding guests, and staff that has populated the big event, gathering to pay homage to the couple and do its bidding, have suddenly been transformed into the lovers' oppressors—a band of prying busybodies and overbearing relations whose presence can only inhibit. The photograph of the remote island untouched by civilization's corrupting forces conveys this idea forcefully. The dominant notion of newlyweds as amorous refugees who have taken flight from society explains why the image of honeymooners strolling alone on a tropical beach recurs in advertisement after advertisement. Photograph after photograph depict a young bride and groom, alone in an island setting, looking happy, relieved, and mutually entranced. The message is that, having found the desert island on which they can frolic unabashedly, traipsing along the sand half naked or in native costume, the lovers can breath a sigh of relief and let go of their inhibitions.

In this misanthropic aesthetic husband and wife doff the phony masks society has imposed on them only when they are with each other. Friends, relatives (who have often made the honeymoon financially possible), coworkers, teachers, mentors, and others all form a sinister horde that imposes artificial obligations on the duo. The honeymoon thus represents the signature moment at which they can break free of all nonconjugal obligations, putting the wedding's social occasions and bureaucratic procedures behind them and basking in a state of romantic primitivism. "The formalities are over. Let the honeymoon begin,"[17] enjoins an ad that shows a half dressed couple relaxing on a sun deck overlooking the beach.

While sun spots most commonly represent the contemporary honeymoon's ideal of romantic isolation, those advertisements promoting winter travel resonate with the same misanthropy. They show young couples burrowing cozily beneath down comforters, sipping hot cider alongside crackling fires in the great rooms of rustic lodges, leading horses along remote country trails, huddling together to contemplate the glory of snow-peaked mountain precipices, piloting snowmobiles through enormous snowdrifts, or carousing on motor bikes through piles of brightly colored autumn leaves. Promotions for continental honeymoons weave the couple into a European tapestry of historical romance, urging the bride and groom to leave behind the world of boorish Americana and journey to the seat of courtly love:

How do you say "I love you" in France? The French say "I love you" in many ways, since all of life is a celebration of love. Whether it's a picnic with Champagne in the shadow of a medieval chateau, ballooning in Burgundy, strolling in the Luxembourg Gardens, immersing yourself in great art at the Louvre, or dining on the finest cuisine—sharing the joys of France is the best way to say "I love you." Come to the country where romance is a way of life. A honeymoon in France is where "happily ever after" begins.[18]

The contemporary honeymoon concludes the marital narrative that began in courtship. It provides the bride and groom, who have received a series of celebratory parties and a plethora of expensive gifts, with one final reward: a sybaritic vacation in which they are mandated to unwind in erotic seclusion. The honeymoon reinforces our culture's widespread belief in heterosexual privilege, marital virtue, and conjugal primacy. Purported to represent the beginning of a married couple's life together, it provides a transitional period in which the bride and groom construct a marital identity in opposition to their community at large, completing the process of social withdrawal that began with prewedding festivities. During this symbolically charged interval of enforced leisure, the newlyweds become, in some new sense, a couple. Whether it takes place in a lakeside cabin, a Caribbean island resort, a Tahitian bungalow, a New England bed-and-breakfast, a luxury ocean liner, or a French chateau, the modern honeymoon demands not just isolation but isolationism; the idea that husband and wife are enmeshed lovers who are united, in some sense, against the rest of the world. To forge this corporate identity the modern honeymoon has two prerequisites: physical retreat and nonstop sex.

This was not always the case. Until the twentieth century, honeymoons were more about community obligations than conjugal intimacy. As is the case with most wedding rituals, the farther back we look in our search for origins, the more sexist the customs become. In their earliest manifestations honeymoons were probably periods in which male kidnappers sequestered their female captives. Some historians suggest that prehistoric couplings commonly took place by abduction. A man who had "taken" a wife would bring her into hiding for a full month, until the tempers of her kinsmen had cooled. A characteristic moment in the modern wedding's romantic narrative, the custom of carrying the bride over the threshold of her honeymoon suite is probably a residual practice of the abduction mode of patriarchal marriage.[19]

The term *honeymoon* first appears in English in the sixteenth century, although it refers to the early stage of married life rather than the custom of wedding travel. Sociologists Kris Bulcroft, Linda Smeins, and Richard Bulcroft explain.

> Common usage of the term today has come to mean a specified period of time in which the newlyweds exclude themselves from their social networks, engage in passionate and sexual behaviors, and establish themselves as an autonomous unit. It is generally believed that the origin of the term refers to the element of time, but the earliest recorded use of the term takes us back to 1546 when it was thought to refer to the couple's emotional state rather than a length of time in relationship to lunar cycles.[20]

Thomas Blount's 1656 *Glossographia* defines the honeymoon as "married persons that love well at first, and decline in affection after wards: it is honey now, but will change as the moon."[21] The contemporary American honeymoon has its origins in the English Renaissance custom of the bridal night, an event staged as an explicit sexual milestone. In the sixteenth and seventeenth centuries friends and relatives would accompany the newly married couple into the bridal suite, indulging in crude jokes and bawdy singing, and departing after the bride and groom, who might be meeting for the first time, had been tucked into their four poster bed and the bed's curtains tied in preparation for what was supposed to be an initial sexual encounter.[22] This custom persisted well into the eighteenth century, when brides entered their marriage beds with gloves on and emerged gloveless to indicate that they were no longer virgins. It ebbed by the end of the century, when upper class Englishmen and women began to shun public sexual rituals and dispense with the ribald singing, joking, firing of guns, and other revelry that were integral to the weddings of earlier periods.[23]

The convention of the honeymoon as a period of travel existed by the late eighteenth century, but the trip did not require privacy or isolation. Upper-class couples who honeymooned in Europe's urban centers brought chaperones, often the sisters of the bride. "The need for supportive female assistance in this time of psychological and physiological crisis shows how strong was the social attraction of each sex for its own company, even in those days of companionate marriage,"[24] explains historian Lawrence Stone. By the nineteenth century, status-conscious Victorians had developed the custom of the postwedding bridal tour, a lengthy trip in which the bride and groom, accompanied by relatives and servants, visited those who had not been able to attend their wedding. The tour was often elaborate and costly; it could last an entire summer and include the entire bridal party.[25] Although it featured the newly married couple, it was not intended as a period of amorous seclusion or sexual experimentation. Its purpose was to cement each couple's bonds to extended family and friends, fortifying the bride and groom's relationship to a broader social network.[26]

The private honeymoon emerged in the late nineteenth century, when a chorus of marriage advisors, many of whom were physicians, wrote about the sexual component of the wedding night in cautionary terms. "Experts" were particularly worried about the initial meeting between predatory oversexed grooms and chaste brides presumed to be virgins disinterested in sex who were probably further exhausted by wedding planning and travel. While both are stylized cultural constructions, the delicate frail brides of late Victorian marriage manuals are a far cry from the magnificent sexual animals featured in contemporary honeymoon literature. Sylvanus Stall, author of the 1897 marriage primer *What a Young Man Ought to Know*, described brides with "pallid cheeks and colorless lips"[27] traumatized by the physical demands of the wedding planning and organization, and in 1890 the physician George Napheys objected to the strain that postwedding travel placed on women, writing that "to be hurried hither and thither, stowed in berths and sleeping-cars, bothered with baggage, and annoyed with the importunities of cabmen, waiters, and hangers-on of every description, is enough... to test the temper of a saint."[28] Although late Victorian culture assumed new brides to be timid and sexually apathetic, its advice literature was already beginning to assume an antagonism between the newly married couple and those around it. Already the experts were demanding romantic isolationism of honeymooners.

By the early twentieth century the honeymoon had become, in the popular consciousness, a sexual escapade. According to historian Jonathan Katz, this period witnessed a shift in attitudes toward the erotic; sex was increasingly located as the core of human personality, and the sexual dimension of marriage was accordingly viewed as central— more important than wedlock's economic or reproductive functions and more significant than any of its psychological purposes.[29] Angus McLaren explains that, "In the twentieth century marriage was supposed to be sexually satisfying and experts daringly took it upon themselves to proceed to describe what happened—or should happen—after the bedroom door was closed. New story-tellers emerged: sexual enthusiasts and therapists... marriage experts and marital counsellors."[30] The honeymoon was the focal point of debate among these new pundits of the helping professions. As predominantly sexual partners, married couples were expected to take erotic postwedding trips. Manuals appeared that offered explicit advice about sexual techniques, and brides and grooms, who were still presumed to be profoundly ignorant about each other's bodies, were advised to undertake premarital medical interviews. The gynecologist Robert Dickinson was one of many medical experts who instituted the practice of separate interviews with brides and grooms, "which included a lecture on the ideal of mutual sexual pleasure as well as information about birth control and other practical wedding-night tips."[31] Women's magazines reinforced the notion that physicians were the optimal prehoneymoon advisors and sanctioned the frank, premarital sexual discussion in a doctor's office as a healthy measure.

Early twentieth-century experts presented themselves as radical innovators; Victorian doctors had, after all, found it impossibly embarrassing to broach the technicalities of sex, even married sex. But the early treatises relied on essential notions of gender difference and conjugal normality, and their aim of defending and strengthening the nuclear family was basically conservative. Both doctors and magazine writers assumed an imbalance of desire among the sexes; men were still thought to have insatiable sexual appetites when compared with the mild or nonexistent feelings of their female counterparts. Marie Stopes, author of the wildly popular 1918 book, *Married Love* and the subsequent primer, *Enduring Passions*, explained that female sexuality was determined by an underlying "pulse,"[32] of which women themselves were largely unaware. The loving husband was directed to uncover and attune himself to this mysterious feminine rhythm. Later, the Dutch gynecologist Van de Velde advised husbands to initiate their wives in sexual technique as teachers schooled pupils; he wrote that sexual intercourse with women on top was unhealthy, as it imposed upon men an unnatural state of passivity.[33]

While presenting sex as the glue that held marriage and families together, early sex manuals treated the male drive as a physiological constant and female longing as faint and intermittent. They also viewed "single" women as aberrant. Steady sexual activity within a marital framework was now the norm, and advisors accordingly considered unmarried women to be a tragic unfortunates who would become mentally and physically stunted by their (presumed) celibacy.[34] The female orgasm within marriage had become the gateway to mental health—the path to feminine fulfillment. Freudians like Wilhelm Stekel posited that only lesbians, who were afraid to assume the inherently passive female stance, refused to reach orgasm with men.[35] In Freudian doctrine such women were frigid, unfit mothers who would instill homosexuality in their children. According to the experts young girls who did not receive the appropriate sexual indoctrination and marry early enough—before the age of thirty—would join the man-hating ranks of the lesbians and suffragists; women who dared to demand a voice in politics through access to the voting polls.[36] The honeymoon was, accordingly, mandated as a period of all-important sexual initiation, a time at which men and women assumed their natural roles and patient restrained grooms carefully initiated trembling brides in the ways of love.

During World War Two entrepreneurs began catering specifically to honeymooners, creating the kind of gimmicks and packages still featured in today's bridal magazines. Ad campaigns, honeymoon hotels, promotional packages that included free extras, contests and sweepstakes, "Honeymooners Clubs" that awarded special certificates, and magazine accounts of celebrity honeymoons seduced brides and grooms with what had become "a single coherent honeymoon script."[37] The narrative of recreational travel, sexual initiation, marital privilege, and conjugal togetherness appealed to those in America's postwar era of heterosexual conformity, when the country enjoyed unprecedented economic prosperity, and an enormous number of men and women could, for the first time, afford the postwedding excursion. Many traveled to Niagara Falls in western New York, America's honeymoon mecca and the site that Oscar Wilde famously described as "the second greatest disappointment" in every American married woman's life.[38] Niagara Falls' local radio station featured a regular morning program, "Honeymoon in Niagara," on which honeymooners were invited to visit the studio, where they were interviewed and showered with gifts. In 1948 the falls had its first television broadcast featuring, of course, a honeymooning couple, and sentimental accounts of honeymoons at Niagara, often authored by husband a wife teams, appeared in American magazines throughout the 1950s.[39]

With marriage at the center of culture and sex at the center of marriage, much rested on the honeymoon. "I don't know what I expected, exactly, but based on what I'd read and heard, I thought it would be extraordinary," says Rita Schwartz, a retired interior designer who married in 1958 and spent her wedding night in a motel in Hastings, New York. "I mean, I had given myself orgasms before, but I thought he would do it better and differently—I thought I would feel it throughout my whole body, including my eyeballs. I thought it would be explosive. And we got to the hotel, took off our clothes, jumped in the shower . . . and, you know, that was it. A bit of a letdown!"[40] Postwar experts emphasized the wedding night as a cataclysmic sexual experience and the honeymoon as a period during which couples achieved erotic chemistry and compatibility. Psychoanalytically biased advisors applied extraordinary pressure to this interval, rendering it a period of pivotal importance and predicting that a bad series of first sexual encounters might cause lifelong impotence in men (especially those who were too close to their mothers) and "honeymoon shock" in women. "Bad honeymoons wrecked three out of five marriages, caused nervous and mental disorders, and as Canadian sex expert Alfred Tyler explained, 'More psychological damage may be done on the honeymoon than the balance of life can correct.'"[41] The notion shared by postwar culture's popular medical practitioners and advice columnists—and furthered by honeymoon advertisers—was that this trip entailed the end of sexual innocence for both groom and bride. Especially for the bride, it ushered in a new stage of sexual (and hence emotional) maturity. As a paramount experience of physical initiation that set the tone of the entire relationship, the bride and groom's first sexual encounter had to be mutually enjoyable. Bad sex could inflict psychic traumas that might stunt both partners, resulting in marital divisiveness that would, in turn, negatively affect society as a whole.

The reclusive sexualized ritual of the honeymoon continues to the present day, although it is no longer considered a period of first sexual contact. By the end of the 1960s Niagara Falls had lost its monopoly on honeymoon tourism as the horizons of middle-class brides and grooms expanded to include myriad new destinations offered by travel agents: the Poconos, California, the Florida Keys, New York City, and Europe. Newlyweds of the 1980s and 1990s, many of whom cohabitated before the wedding, no longer viewed the trip as an erotic transition. With the loosening of premarital sexual restrictions, the old postwar honeymoon resorts came to seem quaintly outdated. But according to wedding magazine surveys, the majority—98 percent—of American married couples still take honeymoons;[42] the postwar venues have been abandoned, but the idealized erotic retreat has not. Honeymoon-oriented brochures, travel agencies, and web sites proliferate; advertisers and marriage advisors alike now promote the honeymoon as a sexual marathon rather than a sexual initiation; it is an opportunity to establish one's primary emotional affinity to one's spouse rather than the time to achieve sexual balance within wedlock.

Contemporary marriage primers allude to the honeymoon rhapsodically, as a private period in which the newly married couple can experience total emotional and sexual surrender. Conventionally paid for by the groom,[43] the optimal honeymoon has the quality of a romantic whirlwind in which a woman is whisked away rather than physically abducted, romanced rather than deflowered. Mutual sexual fulfillment is still paramount, although marriage advisors no longer believe that mediocre sex can inflict permanent psychic scars. The all-important *Bride's Book of Etiquette* urges women to enhance their first night of marriage with the Gothic flourish of transportation over the threshold: "Even if you are in familiar surroundings, be carried over the threshold (as brides have been for centuries...)."[44] While this primer tells young women that the honeymoon entails "the most important sexual encounter"[45] of their lives, it also urges newlyweds not to pressure each other sexually. "Realize that this is the just the first of many nights together or the continuation of what is already a satisfying relationship."[46]

In contemporary marital advice literature the honeymoon still maintains its erotic focus. Bridal magazines stress the sexual pungency of the postwedding getaway, featuring spreads of honeymoon lingerie that urge brides to "slip into something silky and sexy," like the "Delicious halter-style top and silk tap pant in 'smoking' silver with black lace trim," or to "Go glam, starlet style, with a satin and chiffon baby doll nightie trimmed with maribou," or to "Play the part of the coquette in a sexy white lace teddy with double straps and matching full length sheer robe."[47] Models adorned in designer lingerie assume the poses of lusty brides, gazing from lavishly appointed double beds or beautifying themselves for their grooms in elegantly tiled marble bathrooms, applying makeup, toenail polish, and perfume in preparation for a mystical sexual union. Honeymoon sex is portrayed as both titillating and therapeutic. Typical honeymoon columns feature an array of sensual activities purported to relax the mind as they they bolster the libido. Herbal wraps, aromatherapy, yoga classes, mineral water soaks, meditation sessions, and "his and hers massages—complete with instructions so you can treat each other back at home"[48] are the standard features of couples resorts. Such activities are designed for the bride and groom to unwind to the point that they can lavish total physical attention on each other, gratifying each other's every erotic need as an expression of slavish mutual devotion. Honeymoon columns even couch practical advice in the language of romantic excess, urging newlyweds to dissolve their independent identities and merge as a single, blissful unit. "Get lost in each other, not in your rental car,"[49] a recent issue of *Modern Bride* magazine admonishes in a feature on how to acquire maps for honeymoons on the road. In its article on romantic cruises this same issue states, "You've found the perfect shipmate, now use this matchmaker to set you up with a dream boat."[50]

Above all today's marriage advisors emphasize conjugal solitude as a happy relief afforded by the modern honeymoon. *Modern Bride* urges newlyweds to visit the Caribbean island of Grenada, where they can, "Find the enchanted garden," explaining, "the Bay Gardens are so cleverly terraced and planted that you'll feel as though you're deep in an exotic forest,"[51] and adding that on Grenada's La Segresse nature center couples feel that they've arrived "at the end of the edge of the world."[52] Michael R. Perry's *The Groom's Survival Manual* tells the anecdote of an allegedly real couple identified as Rick and Marilyn. During their prewedding months this couple was deluged with invitations to parties and events, and Rick became exhausted by the demands being placed on his time and frustrated with his fiancée's new sociability; he yearned for the early days of their courtship when they would bask solely in each other's company. When Rick confronted Marilyn with her irritating habit of devoting time to others, she shocked him by admitting that she too disliked social gatherings: "To his surprise, Marilyn laughed, and shouted, 'I wish we could skip all these things too! I hate 'em,'"[53] and admitted, "'I wish we could pick up our backpacks, go way out in the woods by a stream, and sit on a rock. Like for a week. No phone, no cars, and no people—except you.'"[54] The archetypal "shrewd groom,"[55] Rick made his fiancée's dream a reality by orchestrating a honeymoon in a Minnesota campsite, where the two castaways roughed it together, far from the reaches of intrusive friends and relatives and out of bounds of civilization itself.

The relationship industry also offers prescriptions on how to extend the honeymoon's period of conjugal isolation and sexual bliss into the life of the marriage itself. In discussing the optimal length of honeymoons in his *What the Hell Is a Groom and What's He Supposed to Do?*, John Mitchell quips, "determine how long you want your honeymoon to last (forever and ever, every day is our honeymoon...my wife made me say that),"[56] but a chorus of marriage advisors now seriously demand that the American honeymoon last approximately fifty years. In order to help couples achieve the elusive goal of a thrilling marital romance, these experts offer programs for sexual longevity and concoct bromides for erotically stalled marriages. Their ideal is one that those living prior to the twentieth century would have considered preposterous: lifelong sexual ecstasy with a single partner.

One such cheerleader for erotic marriage is Ellen Kreidman, a high-profile relationship consultant who runs a regular six-week workshop entitled "Light His Fire." A middle-aged suburbanite with frosted hair and a ferocious smile, Kreidman sums up her own philosophy with the claim that, "We have all the answers within us."[57] Like most in the relationship industry, she has contempt for received bodies of knowledge, and she scoffs at the disciplines. "I have degrees in psychology and education," she explains, "but that doesn't really matter. More important is that I have been married twenty-three years to the same man and I have three happy, well-adjusted children."[58] Kreidman singles out wives whose marriages have lost their luster. She shares the dating advisor's belief in the intractable power of the self. In her view, the female self is the locus of all authority—the catalyst for change and improvement. Through sheer self-will, the American wife can transform her humdrum marriage into a passionate love affair. Armed with determination and a positive demeanor, she can effect miracles, and the natural focal point of her energy should be marital healing. Kreidman, who holds women accountable for male philandering, claims that male ego is naturally fragile and that husbands stray, not because they're sexually restless but because the average American wife is a scold, a harpie, and a nag. She urges her female readers to stop berating their husbands and instead shower them with compliments followed by kinky erotic advances. By continually bolstering her man's self-esteem—flattering him with attention and praise and taking the lead sexually—the average wife can transform her henpecked husband into a swaggering Romeo and sexually jump-start her marriage.

Like many relationship shamans, Kreidman offers herself as a role model, presenting a conversion narrative in which she hit bottom before finding the truth in a sudden epiphanic moment. She wrote (so to speak) her 1989 primer *Light His Fire* after suffering a matrimonial ordeal. Kreidman reveals that her early domestic life was idyllic. Happily married for many years to an affluent man, she was a pampered upper-class wife with full-time, live-in help and no troublesome extramarital commitments. When she was pregnant with her third child, her husband lost his job, the domestic bubble burst, and Kreidman, having no vocation or income of her own, plunged into a severe depression. One day, en route from the supermarket in her car, she collapsed and began sobbing, but an internal voice suddenly came to her, instructing, "For things to change, *you* have to change."[59]

This Augustinian moment led to Kreidman's proactive philosophy and the development of her marital healing program. Facing an economic and personal crisis, this marriage propagandist did not evaluate her decision to live her adult life as the dependent of another person. She did not pursue a professional degree or an academic course of study but rather redoubled her efforts to strengthen what she believed to be her most important role, that of wife. Kreidman claims that she threw herself full-time into enriching her marriage and salvaged the floundering relationship. Her program, which involves perceiving the marriage as an abstract entity separate from both husband and wife, and repairing this sacred organism with loving care, emerged from this period:

> Perhaps I didn't feel like a walk on the beach, but the marriage *required* a walk on the beach. I certainly didn't feel like a weekend alone with my husband, but the marriage *required* a weekend alone together. A call just to say I was thinking about him and loved him was very hard to make, but the marriage *required* that call. A candle-light dinner was very difficult to plan, but the marriage *required* that kind of atmosphere. Making love was the furthest thing from our minds, but the touching and healing that comes from that union was *required* by the marriage.[60]

Kreidman advises the American wife to ignite her marriage with unwavering attention, complimenting her husband, pampering him, lavishing physical affection upon him, and listening to him with total absorption. Her list of ways to keep a man's "fire" eternally "lit" includes buying him flowers or balloons, throwing him a surprise party, giving him a manicure, tying him up during sex, leaving a post-it on the bottom of the toilet seat that reads, "Take care of my favorite part of your body,"[61] preparing the marriage bed for love by filling it with rose petals, and serving an elaborate dinner with no silverware. "Tell him you have to feed each other with your hands."[62] Her list of suggested pet names for the American husband include Tiger Lover, Hunky Punky, Dr. Nude, Big Kahuna, Stud Dumpling, Love Bucket, Butter Butt, Pudding Pie, and Peaches.[63] With lascivious tricks and mawkish nicknames the American wife can maintain her position of centrality in her husband's emotional life and secure permanent fidelity. Kreidman promises that the result of her readers' steadfast efforts will be lifelong matrimonial bliss. By offering constant emotional support and sexual stimulation, modern American woman can perpetuate a long-term, erotically charged honeymoon. "I still light my husband's fire,"[64] Kreidman asserts proudly.

According to pundits like Kreidman, the American wife must function schizophrenically, combining the roles of psychotherapist and call girl. She must stand by her man, intuiting his emotions, offering unconditional love and support, steadying his nerves. She must also constantly reinvent herself sexually, perking up her home life with an array of erotic costumes, gimmicks, routines, and props. Marriage, in this perspective, is and should be a full time job, with all other professional and personal obligations accorded secondary status. Most of Kreidman's colleagues in the relationship industry concur, and most share her belief that sexual adventurousness is essential to long-term romance. In her manual, *How to Stay Lovers for Life*, social worker Sharyn Wolf offers women a list of "Guerrilla Mating Tactics," hardcore strategies for keeping sexual tension alive. This spiky-haired redhead promises that marriage can indeed be permanent honeymoon:

> There are honeymoon weekends when you make special plans to go away alone together.... There are honeymoon days, which may sometimes go unrecognized because they happen while you are going about your usual routines. And there are honeymoon moments when you are sitting the couch together, the light catches his face a certain way, and all you can think is, "This is great. I'm sitting next to the greatest person in the world."[65]

But Wolf warns that couples must work at maintaining sexual voltage within marriage. After setting some ground rules for issues like shared housework, husbands and wives must habitually lavish sexual attention on each other. These demonstrations of passion should always include an element of surprise, and, for women, a component of naughtiness. Wolf advises the female reader to astonish her husband with sexual overtures, catching him off guard and dazzling him with her inventiveness. "Bite him lightly on the back of the neck when he isn't expecting it." "Have a professional photographer take sexy shots of you in various stages of nudity and present them to your partner." "Make Marilyn Monroe lips, licking and pouting—being always careful not to cross the line into Miss Piggy." "Tell him that instead of putting perfume behind your ears, you touched your vagina, and put that scent behind your ears." "Take a scissors and, while standing in front of him, cut off your underpants, snipping them off at the sides," she suggests.[66] Having snared her man, the wife who parades around her home in crotchless panties, leaves erotic notes in her husband's briefcase, gives him coupons promising oral sex, rubs him down with almond-scented oil, and regales him with embellished stories of her previous sexual encounters, will keep him, and she will keep him in a state of rapt sexual devotion.

Dagmar O'Connor, the author of *How to Make Love to the Same Person for the Rest of Your Life and Still Love It*, concedes that sexual desire within marriage wanes over time but proffers a list of methods by which couples can fuel their faltering sex lives. She suggests relinquishing the myth of "the real thing" (e.g. intercourse in the missionary position as the most legitimate form of sexual expression) for an array of open-ended sensual experiments. She also recommends a set of meditations intended to create a state of constant sexual arousal: "Next time you pass a bedroom window with the curtains drawn, imagine what could be happening behind them." "Rediscover the lost art of mentally undressing people." "Imagine other couples making love—any couple."[67] In her program, once husband and wife are sexed up enough from constant fantasies about others, they encounter each other with volcanic energy. A humdrum marriage with little time for passion and, when time permits, only the most perfunctory sex, will quickly evolve into an explosive love affair that lasts a lifetime.

O'Connor deals with the inevitable extramarital attractions that plague long-term unions by suggesting that couple's script these attractions into the marital narrative. "Write your own x-rated movies,"[68] she advises, and suggests simulation games in which husband and wife check into a hotel under false names and pretend to be cheating on each other. Or the wife complains about her spouse *to her spouse*, who simulates the roles of sympathetic lover. Or she pretends to be a prostitute, has callous sex with her husband, and then barks, "Just leave your money on the dresser." Or the two pretend to be actors making an x-rated video.[69]

These suggestions are typical of the formula concocted by marriage advisors. They are evidence of the fact that husbands and wives fantasize about others and are confined and frustrated by the demands of institutionalized monogamy. Rather than suggesting a logical course of action—sexual release elsewhere—advisors like O'Connor combine incompatible elements, blending extramarital lust into marriage itself. "Sex, at its best, brings us closer to our 'animal' selves and further from our 'socialized' selves—it is always a 'breaking of the rules' of civilized behavior,"[70] O'Connor explains, as if allowing the most staid of married couples to play at being degenerate sexual outlaws would magically cement the union.

Because the middle-class companionate marriage ideal demands not just outward devotion but deep wells of romantic feeling, marriage advisors are unwilling to face the fact that sexual ecstasy is virtually impossible to maintain with a single person over the course of fifty years. To sidestep this difficult reality they concoct sensual game plans, erotic strategies, and elaborate scenarios for inducing lust. When these simulations do not involve impersonating figures from the underworld, such as prostitutes, pimps, and adult film stars, they entail laborious demonstrations of sensitivity. Daniel Beaver's *Beyond the Marriage Fantasy* preaches the message of marital vulnerability. Beaver attributes matrimonial alienation to the fact that men, socialized to be tough competitors, cannot let down their guards with their wives. Hypermasculinity is thus the cause of male irresponsibility within marriage. The American husband "thinks he is 'no longer a man' when he becomes vulnerable, and he has no cultural support system to tell him otherwise. It is no wonder that he panics and sometimes resorts to juvenile behavior before he finally grows up and begins to enjoy his newly found life."[71]

Offering women the reassuring fantasy that male infidelity stems from emotional stuntedness rather than sexual boredom within marriage, Beaver proceeds to recommend exercises for creating vulnerability ("the cornerstone of a good marriage"),[72] inducing trust, and enhancing sexual pleasure. He offers the traditional "blind walk," in which one partner leads the other, blindfolded, on a thirty-minute walk, as well as an "exercise to explore pleasure," in which one partner touches the other's entire naked body for an indeterminate period of time. These sensory exercises are intended to establish a more intimate union between husband and wife, taking their emotional closeness to new depths and presumably intensifying their mutual attraction. Therapists like Beaver, whose trade is based on the belief that mature sexuality occurs solely within romantic matrimony, can never consider the possibility that sexual attraction does not flow from trust, love, or intimacy. With its conflation of blissful wedlock and healthy sexual expression, the relationship industry cannot admit that lust has its own machinery that operates independently of the individual's conscious desires or plans. It is certainly true that long-term relationships—both amorous and platonic—offer a great deal. Trust, allegiance, intellectual camaraderie, and a sense of foundational support are only some of the comforts of the ongoing, time-tested relationship. But these valuable bonds, which deepen over time, do not necessarily facilitate sexual passion. That the most thrilling sexual encounters often involve no sharing and even less caring is a painfully inconvenient fact for the relationship industry's disciples of matrimony.

Self-help books are not the only venues for promoting eroticized marriage. Women's magazines are among the most prominent cultural vehicles to advertise the lifelong-honeymoon ideal. Of the many glossies available at newsstands, *Redbook* is the periodical most assiduously dedicated to the principle of keeping romance alive within wedlock. The magazine is a virtual cornucopia of advice for the married woman who is sexually frustrated or merely concerned that her husband's libido may be waning. *Redbook*'s August 1999 issue establishes the trajectory of the average, healthy American marriage. Author Francine Russo explains that marriages go through three distinct stages: fusion, which takes place in the twenties and entails blazing passion and the loss of personal identity, differentiation, which takes place in the thirties and entails rediscovery of self and distancing from one's husband, and, finally, reconnecting, which takes place in the forties and involves the establishment of a new, more mature relationship.[73] "At first you're two hearts beating as one,"[74] Russo rhapsodizes. But the glow of hot sex doesn't have to fade as the years pass. According to Russo, while the initial thrill of marriage entails searing erotic encounters, sex becomes even more pleasurable when husbands and wives establish independent identities and even more enjoyable in the final "integration" stage of marriage.

Like most marriage advisors, Russo perceives female psychological growth solely in terms of the marriage narrative. In her understanding, American women marry in their twenties, and the marital relationship becomes the focal point of their lives, the means by which emotional advancements and setbacks can be measured. Like most marriage consultants, Russo perceives the institution of wedlock as a moral and spiritual haven. She quotes Norfolk, Virginia, based "marital and family specialist" Laura Roberto Forman, who explains that this final stage of conjugal unification is essential to the individual's emotional development and sense of social identity. "By your forties, the marriage is incredibly meaningful, a formative part of yourself.... It's the place where you are most deeply known, the safe place where you build trust and continuity in a world that's more and more fragmented."[75] To maintain this sacred domestic zone, Russo suggests that long-married couples indulge in togetherness rituals. She applauds Kansas City math teacher Sara Woodward, who, after nineteen years of marriage, presented her husband, retail manager Eric Woodward, with a stack of coupons good for one breakfast a month out together. Because Eric has redeemed the coupons regularly, the pair now has a standing date at which to share and care, discussing the pressing issues in their lives. Happy with their newfound intimacy, Eric praises his relationship, explaining, "Now it's all built on trust." Russo also commends Hyde Park, Utah, contractor Don Corbridge and his wife Barbara; married for twenty years, the two have recently decided to travel to another country for a year or two to reconnect while doing "humanitarian projects."[76]

Rituals contrived to enable husbands and wives to reconnect, the reaffirmation of wedding vows after thirty years of marriage, second honeymoons, or joint retreats taken in middle age are standard fare for *Redbook*. Because it assumes wedlock to be the central relationship in each woman's life, *Redbook* advises that the marriage must be constantly worked on: adjusted, fine tuned, perfected. Frequently the special maintenance rituals are sexual in nature. The magazine's March 2000 issues provides a list of ways to make marriage "more thrilling."[77] The list of activities includes skydiving (to induce erotic fear), reenacting one's husband's marriage proposal in a public setting, shaving one's husband's face and allowing him to shave one's legs (in order to establish trust), and renting a hotel room in the middle of the day for a two-hour erotic session. *Redbook*'s June issue suggests baby talk as a means of establishing intimacy: "Just a few words in a special tone of voice can light a hot fire,"[78] explains Kenneth Garrett, coauthor of the book, *Relationship Styles & Patterns*. "Have Sex Like You're Single,"[79] entreats the magazine's August 2000 issue. Another list ensues. Journalist Miranda Davis orders her married female readers to ignite their husbands stalled libidos with a series of sexual tricks: phone sex during a business trip, pulling a "Sharon Stone" (i.e. attending a formal party with no underwear beneath one's evening gown), and pretending to be one's "injured" husband's nurse. A mother of two who's been married for ten years, Davis shares her own technique for jump-starting things at home: "So how could I possibly seduce my lover of fifteen years?"[80] she queries. With unexpected fellatio performed on a school night. "That night, after the kids were asleep, I staked out my husband, who was watching the news in the den. I muted the TV, and before he could object, I got down on my knees, undid his pants, and, reader, I blew him."[81]

There is an underlying desperation in such anecdotes. They betray women's fear of the inevitable—the waning sexual partnership, which, over the years, becomes, increasingly, a platonic relationship that resembles those presumably less important bonds. Such fear is based on the unexamined beliefs that marriage is central to female happiness and self-worth, that sex is the wellspring of marriage, and that female sexuality flourishes in a monogamous arrangement and a domestic setting. Magazines like *Redbook* never explore the possibility that the waning of sexual desire within a particular relationship might not be a tragedy. They never suggest that periods of celibacy might be spiritually or intellectually beneficial, and they never broach the possibility of occasional liaisons with other partners. Wedlock is assumed to be the center of each woman's universe and sexual contact a barometer of every marriage's health. With matrimony as her central project, the contemporary American wife must work at keeping an exclusive monopoly on her husband's libido, staging special sexual events and constantly prodding him toward the act of intercourse. *Redbook* authors assume, however, that males are a different breed, a species with a kind of natural wanderlust. They therefore urge wives to stay one step ahead of the game, titillating their husbands with erotic simulations, role-plays, and kinky surprises, orchestrating sexual encounters in new exotic settings, or donning outfits that will evoke images of the postwedding honeymoon. "Slip into something that will trigger an erotic memory,"[82] advise Mary K. Moore and Michelle Zaffino.

Through erotic massage, games of strip poker, afternoon liaisons in hotel rooms, sexy voice mail messages left at work, shared bubble baths, and sudden makeout sessions in cars stalled in deserted parking lots, the *Redbook* woman maintains a state of "passionate monogamy."[83] It is surely a sign of our culture's increasing sexualization of wedlock that a periodical that once offered home-sewing patterns and family recipes and featured articles on breast feeding and serving in the P.T.A. now tells its readers how to apply perfume erotically, use pornography as a marital aid, enjoy joint masturbation sessions, and indulge in erotic shaving rituals. With its techniques of sexual maintenance, *Redbook* purports to keep the American marriage on course. Its journalists cater to American women's most insidious fears about losing their allure and, subsequently, their husbands. Since, in this magazine's perspective, an empty conjugal bed is tantamount to a meaningless life, no amount of therapeutic physical activity is enough.

Yet, as it coaches women in the art of marital maintenance, *Redbook* also promotes the idea that married sex is the most pleasurable form of erotic activity. "Marriage makes him hot!"[84] a recent cover promises, and the article inside praises official coupledom as the state in which men are most content, in which "the thrills keep coming."[85] According to journalist Wendy Hubbert such thrills include late-night pillow talk, shared housework, and a constant antidote to the dreaded state of solitude on a Saturday night: matrimonial togetherness. They also include pride in simply being a couple: "There's a definite feeling of accomplishment that married people feel with each anniversary that passes, knowing you've stared down the ever-looming 50 percent divorce rate and come out on the winning side. Aside from being a commitment, an expression of love, and a worldwide institution, being married is a real achievement."[86] Marriage, in the fictionalized world of the women's magazine, is a seamless totality that blends all that is good and meaningful. Only in sanctioned, male-female coupledom do human beings achieve the deepest and most loyal form of friendship, the most profound type of self-knowledge, the most socially beneficial living situation, and the most delicious uninhibited sex.

This distinctly modern, American fantasy of marriage as a perpetual honeymoon is the joke at the heart of director Sam Mendes' 1999 cinematic satire, *American Beauty*. The film is narrated by a corpse named Lester Burnham (Kevin Spacey), a former advertising writer and suburbanite in an unspecified region of the country that resembles many parts of Southern California. After a long period of emotional numbness, Lester comes to life emotionally at the age of forty-two before his untimely shooting at the hands of a troubled neighbor. His account of the last year of his life, when he impulsively quit his job, took a position flipping burgers in a local fast-food restaurant, began enjoying marijuana and exercising regularly, and developed a sexual obsession with his daughter's best friend Angela (Mena Suvari), constitutes the film's narrative. "I feel like I've been in a coma for about twenty years, and I'm just now waking up," muses Lester. He recounts the brief period of his emotional awakening in voice-over, and we see his life, and the lives of those around him unfold. His voice from beyond the grave is a death knell to the American family, just as Billy Wilder's 1950 *Sunset Boulevard*, narrated by the disembodied voice of a deceased screenwriter, was a death knell to the era of silent films. But that film betrayed a certain nostalgia for once-great artists of an age that had passed into obscurity with the invention of sound film. The compelling idea of *American Beauty* is that sentimental nostalgia for the family is itself a destructive pathology.

American Beauty is about realizing, with a sudden jolt, that one's life is circumscribed by convention. America's overarching social convention is marriage, and the film's central victim (and purveyor) of marriage ideology is Lester's wife Carolyn (Annette Bening), an efficient, well-dressed real estate agent who has worn her perky professional mask for so long that her face has grown into it. Disappointed in her lackluster husband and sullen daughter Jane (Thora Birch), Carolyn is nevertheless an energetic whirlwind. Her vitality is almost retaliatory; Lester and Jane are so quietly alienated that their silence seems to suck all sound out of the air of the Burnham home. Carolyn, as if compensating for their negativity, is full of verve. Always active, she is first viewed in the early morning, tending the roses in her front yard. ("See the way the handle on those pruning shears matches her gardening clogs? That's not an accident," observes Lester's voice-over.) Carolyn keeps her home neutrally decorated with bland reproduction furniture, in immaculate order. She repeats the mantras of self-help tapes and videos—slogans that teach the unlimited power of positive thinking and the untrammeled power of the self. Standing in the living room of a tacky prefab home with an oppressively ugly interior, she repeats to herself, "I will sell this house today." As she cleans the house before potential buyers arrive and then stands in front of a mirror and applies lipstick, this phrase assumes the quality of a chant: "I will sell this house today. I will sell this house today. I will sell this house today." Leading a skeptical couple through the kitchen of the house, she explains, "It's a dream come true for any cook. Just filled with positive energy, huh?"

With her determination to live a life "filled with positive energy," Carolyn has become, in her husband's words, "joyless." She has inhaled the philosophy of America's new age corporate gurus who urge their clients to succeed through focused cheeriness. Annette Bening's tightly controlled performance conveys the horror of a person of such ferocious optimism that she makes life a prison for those around her. Carolyn's dedication to positivity is chilling, because it is wedded so totally to the gospel of American success—the doctrine of capitalism that enshrines financial autonomy, cheering each individual's untrammeled economic ascent and attributing weakness, lack of discipline, and a bad attitude to those who fail. An industrious go-getter, Carolyn equates happiness with success in business, and she believes that anyone determined, hardworking, and cheerful enough will succeed. Her life is a prolonged effort to be upbeat. She listens to Lawrence Welk, whose music expresses her feelings; to alleviate stress she fires a gun at the local shooting range. In one sequence she drives alone in her Mercedes Benz-ML320 listening to Bobby Darrin's song, "Don't Rain on My Parade;" she sings along with the voice on the tape deck, looking increasingly defiant and confident. In another sequence she again sits behind the wheel listening to a motivational tape, which instructs, "... disinvesting problems of their power and removing their ability to make us afraid. This is the secret to centered living. Only by taking full responsibility for your problems—*and* their solutions—will you ever be able to break free from the constant cycle of victimhood. Remember, you are only a victim if you choose to be." Carolyn speaks along with the tape, intoning, "I refuse to be a victim."

Part of exuding confidence is exuding normality; marriage in *American Beauty* is, as Lester Burnham explains, "a commercial," for normality. Because he acknowledges this fact, and because he tries to alter the script of the commercial, he dies. Carolyn, on the other hand, emits only positive conventionality, which means displaying a unified lusty marriage whenever she is in public, despite the fact that she and Lester have long stopped touching each other. As the two enter a professional cocktail party, Carolyn reminds Lester that they must appear to be blissfully married. "Now listen to me, this is an important business function. As you know, my business is selling an image. And part of my job is to live that image." Her husband makes a mockery of her plan by exposing it and publicly ridiculing her devotion to the adages of popular psychology. In the presence of Carolyn's idol, the local "Real Estate King" Buddy Kane (Peter Gallagher), Lester kisses Carolyn passionately and then grins, exclaiming, "We have a very healthy relationship." "I see," Buddy replies, looking mystified. But Carolyn finds a mentor, lover, and soul mate in Buddy, another frighteningly positive, lone entrepreneur who tells her, at their first date, "Call me crazy, but it is my philosophy that in order to be successful, one must project an image of success." The film shows that these two self-starters, whose lives are a round of networking activities, business engagements, and professional workshops, speak the same language—the language of success-oriented self-improvement. When Lester catches Carolyn and Buddy kissing in her Mercedes, she looks crestfallen and can only explain, lamely, "We were at a seminar."

Lester and Carolyn's marriage-gone-bad is the American honeymoon turned inside out. Their relationship lacks the two ingredients insisted upon by marriage counselors: eroticism, and open communication. We first glimpse Lester masturbating in the shower. ("This will be the high point of my day.") His act of physical self-gratification is not arbitrary; it is a sign that he and his wife are no longer married lovers who woo and tantalize each other physically. Presented graphically in the film's opening scenes, the relationship's erotic breakdown deflates the American marital romance ideal. We see the gaping chasm between marriage advisors' mythic view of conjugal sex and the Burnhams' revulsion for each other. The Burnhams are in many ways a regular couple; Kevin Spacey plays an average-looking guy with a median middle-class income working at a middle management job and living in a suburb that is neither shabby nor upscale. Carolyn is a fit, put together version of many women in their early forties rejoining the work force after a period at home raising children. Her position as a real estate agent requires no particular brilliance or educational background, and it yields profits that are adequate but not lavish. The Burnham's home, their lawn, and their street are all deliberately nondescript, as if to suggest that this couple is an emblematic American family, middle-of-the road, typical in its degree of dysfunction.

Lester's frequent masturbation and his infatuation with a high school student demonstrate how the cultural ideal of eroticized marriage is unworkable. As the years pass, married partners lose physical interest in each other. They become attracted to others, and these others are, frequently, wildly inappropriate love objects. Sexual desire cannot be internally regulated and made wholesome in accordance with the ideals of middle-class conjugality. Its nature is to be unpredictable, unstable, slightly out of our control. This does not mean that the world is our sexual playground, and it does not license adults to behave as predators with adolescents. Screenwriter Alan Ball humanizes his protagonist; in a key final scene, when the teenage wet dream Angela offers herself to Lester, he suddenly perceives her, not as a carnal fantasy but as a frightened child. Presented with that which he most desires, he controls himself and declines her offer. But *American Beauty* illustrates the extent to which it is cruelly unrealistic to demand lifelong erotic intensity between partners.

Carolyn, a modern American woman of the 1990s and a devotee of self-help manuals and motivational tapes, insists on appearing to have a healthy marriage, because amorous failure would render her, in her own eyes, a failed human being. The pressure she places on the marriage drives her and her husband farther apart. With his flat immobile face and eyes that flicker with despair and amusement, Kevin Spacey offers a brilliant rendition of a man who has come to perceive his wife as a cultural cartoon. Rituals of family unity, such as the Burnhams' nightly meals at the beautifully appointed, candle lit dining room table, are filmed with the principals at a physical distance from each other. Lester and Carolyn sit on opposite ends of the table, staring at each other, antagonists with nothing to say. In between them is their miserable uncomfortable daughter. The atmosphere is not one of togetherness but of *institutionalized* togetherness—isolation made more painful by the insistence upon regular family activities. It would be easier and more humane for these three people to admit that they don't especially like each other and go their separate ways, but reverence for the marriage-based family renders this taboo. Carolyn is the standard bearer for contemporary marriage and the emotional tyrant who imposes a template of domestic conventionality upon the members of the household. But her attempt to project a happy, bourgeois marital image does not fool the more clever people who pass through the Burnhams' lives. "I think he and your mother have not had sex in a long time," decrees young Angela after initially meeting her friend's father.

A different kind of emotional tyranny exists in the home of the Burnhams' new next door neighbors, a marine colonel named Fitts (Chris Cooper) and his wife Barbara (Allison Janney) and son Ricky (Wes Bentley). They adhere to an earlier model of the American family—a military marriage in which the husband's authority is absolute. Colonel Fitts, whose secret is another one of this film's horrifying and delicious black jokes, rules his home with an iron hand. He lavishes no affection upon his wife and son. He is of an earlier, preenligthened era; the period of the pragmatic, morally upright American family that did not require openness or sensitivity between its members and did not mandate sexual devotion between married partners. When he sits at home in his den watching the television program *Hogan's Heroes* on cable television, he chuckles at the show's presentation of life in the army without appearing to notice his wife, sitting at a distance from him on the couch, looking depressed and lost. When his son Ricky violates one of the many rules of the house, the colonel does not communicate by expressing his feelings of disappointment. He does not articulate concern for Ricky or arrange a meeting with a family therapist to open channels of communication. He barges into his son's room, punches Ricky in the face repeatedly, and demands, "Fight back, you little pussy!" This domestic tyrant's philosophy of childrearing centers on discipline—

breaking the will of his son and beating him into emotional submission for his own good.

Ricky, a cool, emotionally and financially resourceful drug dealer, responds by mimicking his father's military rhetoric. "Discipline. Yes, sir, thank you for trying to teach me. Don't give up on me, Dad," he pleads in mock desperation, and the colonel isn't bright enough to catch the joke. Ricky, who possesses an array of expensive audiovisual equipment, is something of an amateur filmmaker. His bedroom shelves are lined with videotapes—tapes of neighbors and fellow students whom he captures on film, generally without their permission. Much of *American Beauty* is filtered through Ricky's perspective; we see the Burnhams through the lens of his Digicam, as he tapes them from his bedroom window. As we watch Lester and Jane in their kitchen, attempting to converse, we cannot hear their words, and their isolation from each other is excruciating. With his Buddha-like placidity, Ricky views these people as if they're specimens under a microscope whose disturbances he's observing and documenting for science. To survive his father's emotional abuse and his mother's quiet anguish, he's had to retreat to his own plateau, and from this plane he views those around him with superior detached fascination. His videotaping demonstrates the spatial isolation of the suburbs, showing how in a world in which each home is its own fortress, people lose the ability to reach out and instead peer in, gazing at each other voyeuristically. Ricky's camera also, of course reveals the ways in which middle-class men and women view each other in terms of images and roles. Without their voices—with only gestures and facial expressions— Lester and Carolyn see each other, not as individuals, but as husband and wife. Jane sees them as parents, they perceive her as daughter, and Ricky distances everyone with his lens until he forges an alliance with Jane, and they decide to leave their biological families behind forever.

The stiflingly intimate, honeymoonlike conditions of family life and the solitary privacy of the suburban household has rendered communication between individuals impossible. The characters in *American Beauty* stare at each other, wanting to speak but possessing no vocabulary adequate for their emotions and also knowing that if they articulated their thoughts, the social framework in which they live would be shattered. When Lester starts cracking up, it's not in the funny, kooky sense in which film protagonists often let loose; it's an act of rebellion against an unfeasible marriage ideal that has compressed his emotions into a vice. Ironically, the only couple thriving in this environment of intense conjugal seclusion consists of two gay men. The Burnhams' other next door neighbors are a friendly tax attorney and his anesthesiologist partner. Amusingly named Jim and Jim, these two, beaming robust professionals played by Scott Bakula and Sam Robards, dress alike and even resemble each other physically. Mendes and Ball suggest that the male lovers are indistinguishable from each other and from the myriad, gay men living openly homosexual lives who paired off and set up households throughout the 1990s. Most importantly, they are indistinguishable from the straight couples on their block. These two enmeshed partners are virtual clones of heterosexual man and wife. They keep the domestic shrine of their home in order, trading gardening tips and compliments with Carolyn. They jog together each morning and give Lester pointers on fitness. Upon his arrival in the neighborhood they visit the bewildered Colonel Fitts with a welcome basket filled with flowers and vegetables from their backyard and gourmet pasta. ("It's unbelievably fresh. You just drop it in the water and it's done.") Their life is a commercial for a different kind of normality—the virtuous, gay long-term relationship.

Jim and Jim are what Daniel Harris calls a "good gay" couple. Walking emblems of the recent gay fetish for heteronormativity, they are as far removed from the once decadent, urban gay nightlife as Lester and Carolyn are. In Harris' words, such relationships have "the appearance of corporate mergers between two gym-toned yuppies who open joint bank accounts, set up housekeeping in gentrified 'fix-its,' entertain lavishly, and embroider their hyphenated monograms on 'his and his' towels."[87] An endless commercial for the wholesomeness of homosexuality, Jim and Jim's life is a round of domestic and community-oriented activities. They crave (and assume) the insider status of the married, carrying themselves with the straight married homeowner's confident sense of entitlement and self-worth. Caricatures of gay marriage-mania, their presence on the block rounds out *American Beauty*'s dark parable of American family life. The film's heterosexual plot demonstrates that, although they don't know it yet, the model Jim and Jim imitate is fundamentally flawed. Although their companionate marriage seems happy and their life does appear to be the kind of honeymoon prescribed by the relationship industry, viewers finally cannot know for sure. Marriage — especially marriage that demands lifelong romance—is an elaborate and tiring performance.

II. Glad-to-be-Married Propaganda:
The Celebrity Marriage as a Neverending Honeymoon

The June 22, 1998, issue of *People* magazine features a photograph of the rangy Australian actress Nicole Kidman wearing a strapless gown and diamond choker, her strawberry blonde hair cascading around her face in ringlets, her arms wrapped around her comparatively diminutive husband, film actor Tom Cruise. "Nicole & Tom: 'We will be on our honeymoon the rest of our lives,'" the copy reads.[88] "Nicole Kidman bares all—about her daring Broadway debut, marriage to Tom Cruise, and their fight for privacy,"[89] declares another 1998 headline; wearing another strapless number, her arms crossed, her hair flattened into a straight curtain, Kidman stares defiantly, angrily, from the cover of *Newsweek*, as if ready to pounce on any potential intruders who would dare to violate the boundaries of her conjugal privacy.

The ideal of keeping marital romance alive—of wedlock as a neverending honeymoon of erotic delight, emotional disclosure, and deepening loyalty—rests on the fantasy of a world hostile to marriage. In article after article, interview after interview, marriage propagandists imagine an antagonism between the safe haven of the nuclear family home and the ominous, foreboding outside world where any number of threatening strangers lurk who could divide members of the couple: separating them by making demands on their time and attention, tempting them with nonmarital activities, distracting them from their primary and most fulfilling roles as husband and wife.

Any number of high-profile celebrity couples perpetuate this fantasy, displaying their conjugal piety in magazine and television interviews. Of these, the most conspicuous, until their recent separation, were Kidman and Cruise, who were regularly photographed hand-in-hand at awards shows and premieres and were the frequent subject of photo spreads and television and magazine interviews in which they declared their undying love for each other and attested to the erotic health of their ten-year marriage. *People* magazine characterizes the couple as one whose "passion seems eternal"[90] and reports that the two were seen at the April 1998 annual Artist's Rights Foundation dinner kissing in between courses and massaging each other's shoulders. These conspicuous displays are accompanied by hyperbolic proclamations of devotion. Cruise depicts his marriage as a balance of erotic fire and boundless confidence. "My first reaction to her was lust. Then I got to know her and it was trust. Lust and trust, that was it."[91] Kidman and Cruise express the celebrity couple's popular belief that marital happiness demands symbiosis, and journalists applaud the brand of institutionalized togetherness summed up by Cruise who exclaimed in a 1996 interview with *Vanity Fair* magazine, "I go where she goes or she goes where I go," adding, "My best friend is Nic."[92] In a recent interview with *Talk* magazine Kidman declared proudly that in ten years of marriage she and Cruise have never been separated for more than thirteen days,[93] comparing their attachment to that of musician Paul McCartney and his wife Linda, who boasted only one night apart in twenty-nine years of marriage.

What do these conjoined stars do with with their time? Apparently they engage in strenuous athletics, hiking through Nepal, mountain-climbing, scuba diving, and skydiving. "She had a bad jump one time, but we did one more jump, and we came together in the air and kissed,"[94] says Cruise. Journalistic accounts focus on Kidman's athletic adventurousness, stressing her ability to keep up with her husband in his regular round of strenuous, dangerous physical activities. "You're never going to harness her," says producer Jerry Bruckheimer.[95] These comments again demonstrate the new aesthetic of romance, which relies not on traditional female delicacy but on the image of the couple as tough physical competitors. When applied to the celebrity couple, the physical equity in which husbands and wives lift weights in the gym, run marathons, practice martial arts, and French kiss while jumping out of planes ensures absolute togetherness. Men no longer retreat into the male sanctum of the locker room, the basketball court, or the boxing ring, so that the homosocial bond that such activities once provided has eroded. In the new iconography of the couple, husbands and wives are mandated to visit these sports arenas in pairs, stuck together like Siamese twins.

While journalists and fans emphasize Nicole Kidman's strength and feisty independence, she stresses her own sense of wifely and maternal obligation. She claims to be fierce about protecting her two adopted children, Isabella and Connor: "We don't take them to premieres—we don't take them to anything."[96] She admits to doing far more work around the house than her husband and alludes to this inequity as the happily married woman's lot. Women, after all are the domestic bedrock of the family: "You're organizing all of their lives. I was cleaning out Bella's closet today. Would Tom be cleaning out Bella's closet? Would he know what's in her closet? Probably not." But Kidman presents herself as a paradigm of marital virtue who has her priorities in order. "It's tough being a woman and having kids and working.... I only work now if I feel it's worth it. And I have to say no to things I really love because it's just not the right time. Sure, you could try to do it all and try to take all the roles you want, but you wouldn't know your kids and you wouldn't have your marriage.... Distance destroys relationships."[97] Kidman admits that she has willingly allowed her career to take a back seat to her husband's: "That's my choice."[98] The final reward for this wifely and maternal sacrifice, in her view, is conjugal permanence: "I see myself as an old woman and he's an old man and we're married."[99]

In devastatingly conventional account after account, a marriage-obsessed media portrays glamorous, high-powered couples who live in a state of blissfully unequal, connubial fusion. While studio-controlled actors and actresses were once urged to conceal their private lives, appearing before the public in staged publicity shots and limiting the contents of their interviews to sound bites for their latest films, today's celebrity couples reveal the most intimate details of their lives, discussing their traumatic childhoods, rocky adolescences, struggles with drug addiction, eating disorders, failed romances, and successful relationships. They also share the details of their courtships, romantic impasses, couple's counseling sessions, sexual practices, emotional breakthroughs, cohabitations, marriage proposals, weddings, fertility treatments, miscarriages, pregnancies, Lamaze classes, at-home childbirths, episiotomies, breast feeding techniques, and childrearing philosophies. With the breakdown of privacy between celebrities and their public, today's famous couples have become paradigmatic models for marital bliss.

They gather under the single banner of the nuclear family, assuring fans that despite their success and fabulous wealth, they put spouses and children above all else. Celebrity couples proclaim, univocally, that the privileges afforded by their staggering incomes are trivial—unimportant in comparison with the "real" values provided by their cozy family lives. They coach their followers in the art of conjugal intimacy, urging fans to consider marriage as the sole index of life's meaning.

The celebrity wife in particular now considers herself to be a high priestess of wisdom, an expert on marriage and marriage-related topics and a source of advice on how to keep romance alive. Journalists generally depict her as a fierce lioness protecting her brood and describe her commitment to marital privacy as both a moral triumph and an ongoing battle. A December 1999 issue of *People* magazine features a photograph of actress Meg Ryan on its cover. "After a messy childhood, *You've Got Mail's* MEG RYAN fights a daily battle to keep her own family first,"[100] the cover copy explains. The feature article describes Ryan's dedication to her nuclear family enhanced by photographs of her holding her six-year-old son, Jack, and standing arm in arm with her husband, actor Dennis Quaid. The article quotes friends speaking rhapsodically about the (since defunct) marriage of Ryan and Quaid as a quasi-mystical union in which the boundaries between the principal's individual identities blur. "When Meg talks about Dennis there is a kind of wonderment in it,"[101] explains director Nora Ephron. "I have always been touched by the fact that whenever you ask her what she is doing, she automatically tells you what Dennis is doing. They have a very strong bond,"[102] says director Griffin Dunne.

Celebratory accounts of celebrity marriages rest on this notion of fusion buttressed by the ludicrous fiction that the world is somehow hostile to couples. Hollywood, in particular, is presented as the natural antagonist to marriage and family values; its agents, producers, directors, and publicists are not viewed as professional assets to the actor or actress but as coldhearted parasites determined to tear each bride and groom from each other's arms. But fame itself is presented as the ultimate villain. "Fame won't wreck my marriage,"[103] declares actress Debra Messing, who beams from the cover of the November 2000 issue *Glamour* magazine in a blue sequined dress. Christine Spines' article,

"Amazing Grace," describes the actress admiringly as "a lovestruck new-lywed" who blushes when speaking of her husband and who "values close relationships—none more than the eight-year romance she had shared with actor-screenwriter Daniel Zelman. Spines praises Messing as a woman with two feet planted firmly on the ground who has relin-quished career opportunities for marriage. "The couple's lengthy engagement, coupled with Messing's determination not to let her career impinge on marital happiness, will undoubtedly help keep them together. In fact, during her hiatus this year, she says, 'I turned down amazing opportunities, because I truly believe the most important thing is the happiness and solid-rootedness of your home life.'"[104] While she feels morally empowered in extolling marriage above friendship and career, Messing describes her husband as a foundational support—the individual who has made her professional success possible: "He's my cor-nerstone.... I don't know how I would have pursued my Hollywood career if I had been single."[105]

In the myopic self-admiring universe of the celebrity wife, the "sin-gle" woman is indeed disadvantaged; a shallow, self-absorbed careerist whose life lacks emotional depth. Trivializing "single" women is essential to the married star's self-presentation. She tends to cast an image of her-self as someone who has outgrown "single" life and matured into marital commitment. "She's starred in everything from horror films to goofy comedies," declares a headline in *McCalls* of actress Jamie Lee Curtis. "But as she hits the big four-oh, the sexy actress is putting her career on hold. The reasons? Annie, eleven, and Tom, two."[106] Photographs of Curtis standing alongside her husband, actor Christopher Guest, and holding her son, decorate an article that affirms marriage and mother-hood as the actress' best role and depicts Curtis as a woman who tries to "keep it real," living without live-in help in a Spanish-style home in Los Angeles, where she prepares three meals a day for her brood. While she has her priorities in order, gladly performing domestic tasks, eschewing professional opportunities, and never demanding that her husband make similar sacrifices, the celebrity wife can feel smugly superior to her "single" counterpart. Adrift in the cold hollow world of the unmarried, lacking a foothold in the sacrosanct realm of sanctioned domesticity, "single" girls would seem to lack all life's bounty.

An October issue of *Us* magazine declares that the Los Angeles home actress Kyra Sedgwick shares with her husband, actor Kevin Bacon, is "hallowed ground."[107] In a black-and-white photograph, the wiry blonde actress stares soberly at the reader. Wearing a sleeveless black shirt, her hands planted firmly on her hips, she seems to be challenging outsiders to intrude upon the sacred space of her domicile. Like many celebrity couples who profess terror of separation and assert that distance and solitude dissolve relationships, Sedgwick and Bacon have an institutionalized togetherness pact, an agreement that they will never spend more than two weeks apart. But the actress makes it clear that conjugal enmeshment hasn't dulled the relationship's sexual edge: "I think he's the hottest guy I've ever seen in my life," gushes Sedgwick proudly. "He and Marlon Brando in *Streetcar*, and that's it."[108]

It is peculiar that so many contemporary female performers who have garnered wealth and critical acclaim working in exciting, creative facets of the entertainment business, continually express alienation from their own industry, exalting amorous seclusion. To an extent, this has always been the case. Hollywood actresses have long preached the gospel of married togetherness and maternal wholesomness to their fans. But glad-to-be-married propaganda has become an ironclad rule among the entertainment industry's elite, and there are now few, if any, exceptions to this rule. The perception of an ever-intensifying marriage mystique first struck me in fact, when, a few years ago, I was watching television in what was then my Manhattan apartment. Flicking through channels with the remote control, I came to a cable special on actress Bette Davis. The documentary covered Davis' fifty years in film, combining excerpts from her movies with interviews with friends and conversations with the star herself. In one late interview the steely indefatigable Davis addressed the issue of what constitutes a worthwhile female life. She explained her feeling that work, more than anything else, had made her life happy and meaningful. She added that in her own philosophy, women must have work apart from the unpaid domestic tasks they may perform at home, apart from those they care for, apart from their primary relationships. I remember being struck dumb by the simple truth of these claims. I was equally impressed by the fact that this remarkable woman, whose career peaked in the 1930s and 1940s made them without apology or qualification.

It is impossible for me to imagine an actress or female musical performer making such bold statements today. While women as a whole may have achieved greater independence, the female celebrity of the 1990s and early millennium must downplay her own ambition and disparage the business that has enriched her. The estrangement she expresses from her own work does not appear to me to be genuine; rather it is the false mask of conjugal piety that she wears in order to mollify her fans. The celebrity wife must assure her public that the success she has worked so hard to achieve is in fact accidental—that the focal point of her energy is really her marriage and its offspring. She must soften herself in accordance with cultural demands for marital femininity, asserting that she is not really a driven professional or a focused artist but rather a devoted wife. Country singer Faith Hill, often photographed smooching with her husband, singer Tim McGraw, is a premiere example of the self-admiringly married celebrity spouse. With a platinum single and five Academy of Country Music Awards, "Hill points to her marriage to fellow country star Tim McGraw as her greatest accomplishment."[109] Her vow never to spend more than three days apart from him stems from her belief that marriage, unlike friendship or work, provides "that stability."[110]

A standard-bearer for modern marriage, the celebrity wife expresses an almost hysterical fear of being alone and a fervent belief in matrimonial fusion. Her rhetoric affirms romantic symbiosis; she never considers the fact that such terror of solitude does not demonstrate a healthy relationship—quite the contrary. With their absurd togetherness pacts, their commitment to amorous seclusion, and their primary allegiance to each other, today's high-profile husbands and wives represent the companionate marriage ideal taken to a cartoonish extreme. The female partner almost always serves as the relationship's spokesperson. Model Kirsty Hume, for instance, praises the rural isolation she now enjoys in the Woodstock, New York, "Love Shack" she shares with her husband, musician Donovan Leitch. "When Dono and I met it was a period in our lives where you go out all the time. But I got sick of living that way. Now, even if we wanted to go out, there would be nowhere to go. The things we do now are more conducive to our marriage."[111] Describing her "finely tuned partnership"[112] with actor Arnold

Schwarzenegger to *Good Housekeeping* magazine, television journalist Maria Shriver explains, "If he's going to be away on location I'll stay at home. I never leave. If I have to go somewhere, I take all my kids with me."[113] "Work inevitably takes the couple in different directions at times. When that happens, Shriver assumes a more traditional role,"[114] explains journalist Joanna Powell approvingly. Like many celebrity wives, Shriver perceives the longevity of her twelve-year marriage as a moral victory. She proudly attributes it to her own early marriage mania, explaining that she always intended to emulate her parents' rock solid partnership and that she continues to approach wedlock with fierce determination. "I got married with the idea that I was going to make it work, and that I would do my utmost to make it work.... When I meet people who have been married forty-five or fifty years, I sit right down and start asking questions: 'What do you do? How do you do it?'"[115]

Among the many peculiar cultural dogmas expressed by the celebrity wife is the conviction that marital longevity is a moral triumph. Rather than perceiving wedlock as an ordinary act of sexual conformity that yields many material and emotional rewards, the married movie star presents it as an act of uncommon courage and self-sacrifice. Rather than acknowledging that in a conjugally organized society that panders to couples, being in a couple is the easiest way to live, the celebrity wife extols her romance as a courageous choice. Popular journalists encourage this fiction: the issue of *People* magazine featuring Nicole Kidman and Tom Cruise as perpetual honeymooners includes an article celebrating long-term celebrity marriages, star couples who "prove lasting love can be more than a Hollywood fantasy."[116] The article offers "a showbiz sampling," extolling the "tin" (over ten years) marriage of actors Tom Hanks and Rita Wilson, the crystal (over fifteen years) union of actress Valerie Bertinelli and rock musician Eddie Van Halen, the "china" (over twenty years) relationship of actress Meryl Streep and sculptor Don Gummer, the "silver" (over twenty-five years) romance of actors Michael Tucker and Jill Eikenberry, the "pearl" (over thirty years) liaison of singers Johnny Cash and June Carter, the "ruby" (over forty years) coupling of actors Paul Newman and Joanne Woodward, the "sapphire" (over forty-five years) love affair of former President Ronald Reagan and former first lady Nancy Reagan, the "gold" (over fifty years) relationship of actors Eli Wallach and Anne Jackson, and the "diamond" (over sixty years) marriage of comedian Bob Hope and singer Dolores Hope. Studded with photographs of celebrity couples kissing, embracing, strolling hand-in-hand, and grinning lasciviously at each other, this piece provides the standard recipes for matrimonial longevity. The couples themselves offer piercingly original observations, such as the claim that marriage takes "a lot of hard work and a lot of love,"[117] the assertion that trust is essential to a healthy relationship, and the belief that it's important to let one's partner be him or herself. The underlying message of the article is not contained in its hackneyed advice or its montage of beaming airbrushed couples, but in its underlying assumption that those who have maintained lengthy monogamous relationships have somehow emerged as moral victors. The unstated and dangerous belief is that those lacking an amorous "other" or those with serial lovers or those with multiple partners or those who devote themselves to their friends are morally dubious, fragmentary beings.

For the celebrity wife, characterizing her marriage as an ethical and personal triumph involves distancing herself from her premarriage persona and expressing the belief that matrimony has brought her spiritual tranquility and self-knowledge. "Before I had a family, making movies was my family," explains actress Michelle Pfeiffer in a recent interview with *Premiere* magazine. "It was so much how I defined myself. I still love making movies, and I take pride in them, but I take more pride in my role as mother and wife."[118] Pfeiffer often appears in print these days, extolling her marriage to television writer/producer David E. Kelley and marveling over the foibles of their two children, Claudia and John. She presents herself, not as a glamorous film diva, but as a happy *hausfrau* who's most content doing the simple things: picking up the children from school, helping them with homework, fixing their lunches. Celebrity wives like Pfeiffer, who claims to be in a state of semiretirement in order to manage her domestic affairs, indulge in a politically retrograde form of self-presentation. They draw a sharp dividing line between their former "single" lives, when they were putatively self-absorbed, social, career oriented, and always on-the-move, and the stable centeredness of married existence. The benchmark of this narrative is "starting" a family—acquiescing to the marriage proposal, donning the white dress, striding up the aisle, sequestering oneself on the honeymoon, and pro-creating. The unstated premise of this self-congratulatory fairy tale is that family is something one *starts* and not something one builds over time, beginning with friendships in childhood. According to the modern celebrity's propaganda, the community of friends, teachers, mentors, lovers, exlovers, that each one of us tends to accumulate—the people whom we love, the people who make us angry, the people who pull us through—don't count. The closed nuclear family is primary; it is the source of our morality as well as our hopes and dreams, and it must therefore remain the focal point of our attention.

The common narrative that emerges is often one of rediscovering values—coming through a difficult time—a period of depression, finan-cial trouble, illness, unhappy love affairs, or experimentation with drugs—to find the light at the end of the tunnel—a marriage-based fam-ily. A September 2000 issue of *Us* magazine shows color photographs of that most shamelessly exhibitionistic celebrity couple, Michael Douglas and Catherine Zeta-Jones, posing with their infant son, Dylan. On the cover Zeta-Jones snoozes peacefully on Douglas' chest, wearing what appears to be a white silk negligee, as he cradles their naked son with his left arm and gazes tranquilly into space. The photographs inside the magazine, that accompany an article entitled, "Family Ties," show a top-less Zeta-Jones caressing their son and depict the couple holding him as they prepare for a sensual kiss. Interested readers learn how the two stars met, rapidly conceived a child and viewed the fetus on sonograms, and how Douglas cut the cord at his son's birth. They also learn that Douglas, after a rocky personal life, is finally "happy and content,"[119] and that this new serenity comes from a blissful home life that admits few intruders. "We're both homebodies...and loners in many ways. We spend a lot of time together. An inordinate amount,"[120] Douglas explains, and his spouse happily concurs: "Sometimes we feel we should really make an effort to try and get out and see some people. But we're quite happy to be in!"[121] (An earlier issue of *Us* ecstatically reported that since their initial courtship in 1999 the two have only spent two nights apart.)[122]

The nudity in this photo spread is of course suggestive of constant erotic activity in the Douglas household. The celebrity's narrative of marital self-improvement is generally combined with another fiction, the story of the couple meant to be together who met, fell in love, married, and entered a lifelong sexual trance. According to Hollywood's publicity machine, the lives of married stars consist of constant sexual acrobatics; magazine accounts inevitably run photographs of stars engaging in just the kind of sybaritic activities that people enjoy on their honeymoons: athletics, sightseeing, upscale dining, and passionate sex. The celebrity marriage does not merely exist, it "cooks," "simmers," "sizzles," "smokes," and "burns." More an erotic barbecue than a relationship, it is a vehicle through which its principals display their lusty appetites, pawing each other in front of television and tabloid cameras as they hypocritically bemoan their lack of privacy. While it is purported to be a moral center, the Hollywood household is also presented as a grotto of steamy sensual delights. Celebrities take pride in their sexual athletics—as long as those marathons are contained within wedlock. Explaining her recipe for a successful marriage, actress Rita Wilson decrees, "You gotta talk, you gotta listen, you gotta laugh. And—now we're getting into Trudie-and-Sting territory—you gotta have lots of tantric-yoga sex."[123] When she is not contorting herself into positions from the *Kama Sutra* with husband Tom Hanks, Wilson is doting on their two sons, Chester and Truman. A full-time wife and mother, she proudly asserts that she places family above career. "Everybody has their needs and requirements, and mine is that my family stays together."[124] Her sexual role models, the middle-aged English rock star, Sting, and his actress wife, Trudie Styler, are, likewise, often photographed embroiled in passionate makeout sessions or shown elongating their muscular bodies into yoga poses, seemingly in preparation for lengthy sessions of conjugal love. Sting has in fact informed the press that sexual interludes with his wife typically last seven hours and include dinner and a movie.[125]

Journalists applaud such mutual physical adulation. Magazine articles that admiringly describe actors Michael Tucker and Jill Eikenberry levitating above their bed in sexual ecstasy[126] or that detail director Mike Nichols and his wife, anchorwoman Diane Sawyer's favorite bedroom game—"Captain Baby," in which one spouse does the other's bidding without question—[127] express clear approbation for these couples' kinky stamina. An August 2000 issue of *Us* magazine featuring celebrity couples ("Finding Happiness: Are Fame and Wealth Enough or Is It All

About Love?")[128] reports that married actors Billy Bob Thornton and Angelina Jolie have purchased a four-million-dollar home that comes with a kitchen in the master bedroom: "If we stock it right, we won't have to leave the bedroom for weeks," gloats Jolie, who is often photographed flashing the tattoo of her husband's first and middle name she has imprinted on her left arm.[129] Often contemporary celebrities declare their physical devotion to their spouses through body art. Actress Melanie Griffith, who recently informed *Redbook* magazine that she and her husband, actor Antonio Banderas, make love every night, tattooed Banderas' first name on her right arm as an anniversary present. ("People think movie stars are different. But I face the same problems that all other women do,"[130] Griffith pledges. To share her marital bromides with the world at large she has created a website that includes such "transformational guides" as excerpts from her private journals and Banderas' paella recipe.) The English actor Jude Law, who "prides himself on putting family first,"[131] has the Beatles lyric, "You Came Along and Turned Everything On, Sexy Sadie," tattooed on his arm, in honor of his wife, actress Sadie Frost. Twenty years after Beatle John Lennon, that most exhibitionistic of celebrity husbands, appeared in *Rolling Stone* magazine naked, astride his wife, performance artist Yoko Ono, a generation of famous couples continue to take his cue and flaunt their carnality at the public. Encoded in their public sexual bravado is the belief that passionate married sex is tantamount to psychological normality and therefore requisite to popularity—every celebrity's ultimate goal. Angus McLaren explains that, "In past generations, if one's sex life was not all that one might have wished, the failing could be dismissed as only another of life's many minor disappointments. In the early twentieth century, as increasing numbers of commentators claimed that any normal person had to experience sensual bliss, the pursuit of sexual satisfaction took on an unprecedented importance."[132]

How a small group of famous wealthy performers chooses to present itself to its public may appear unimportant. It is not. In a society that lacks a formal aristocracy, movie stars, musicians, and television personalities have become our royalty. The successes and failures of their films, television programs, and records are carefully tracked by the media. But reporters also publicize such personal information as celebrities' clothing, interior design choices, diets, fitness routines, romantic liaisons, and life philosophies. Celebrity wives who present themselves as lusty icons of domesticity—beaming homebodies who have wisely stepped off the career track to happily perform domestic chores for their husbands and children—exert a powerful influence on the popular imagination. Their advice forms a kind of feedback loop. They deliberately appeal to a large segment of the American public, and their self-presentation is shrewdly designed to valorize the lives of their fans. Actresses, rock stars, and television anchorwomen who glowingly detail their domestic lives do so to assure women throughout the country that their cinematic idols are just plain folks—married gals who cook, car pool, change diapers, quarrel with their husbands, and then make up again, but who understand, through it all, the primacy of family life. Given her dazzling array of choices, the celebrity wife assures her admirers that she still chooses the kind of grinding domestic work that is imposed upon them within marriage and motherhood. And in stressing her matrimonial priorities, the celebrity emphasizes the common bond she has with the women who view her films, purchase her albums, or tune in to watch her on television. Despite physical distance and a clear socioeconomic divider, the Beverly Hills actress asserts that she is really no different from the Iowa housewife; both define family biologically, both put family first, both love their husbands, and both are dedicated to keeping marital romance alive. Most importantly, neither is "single." In attempting to downplay her extraordinary privilege the celebrity wife powerfully reinforces the idea of wedlock as the ultimate female aspiration. Flattering her fans by upholding domestic isolation and marital enmeshment as virtuous achievements, today's famous bride enhances the marriage mystique.

The celebrity wife is our culture's most conspicuous cheerleader for wedlock, but she is only one of many voices for marriage propaganda. As we have seen, such propaganda comes in many forms. It is transmitted through ritual and popular entertainment, through commerce and advice from trained "experts." It is reinforced by reactionary promarriage legislation; several states have recently enacted governmental initiatives to deter divorce and enhance the quality of individual unions. Oklahoma has earmarked 10 million dollars for premarriage classes and training classes for parents and an annual Governor and First Lady's Conference on Marriage. Arkansas governor Mike Huckabee has declared a "marital emergency" in his state and announced a series of efforts intended to reduce the divorce rate. Florida has a Look-Before-You-Leap law, which discounts marriage certificates for couples who take a premarital preparation course. In Utah, a commission on marriage has been formed to make policy recommendations to Governor Michael Leavitt. Couples marrying in Louisiana may sign a contract stating that, should their marriages fail, they will undergo couples counseling instead of requesting a no-fault divorce and agree to a twelve-to- eighteen-month waiting period before divorce is granted.[133] In June 2000, a coalition of one hundred scholars, judges, social workers, theologians, therapists, and attorneys signed a Statement of Principles for the marriage movement in which they "vowed to keep marriage on the public agenda, promote its joys, and find ways to mend marriages in trouble."[134] The misguided notions that marriage is tantamount to virtue and that wedlock fosters endless erotic and personal pleasure are stronger than they have ever been. These beliefs impose an oppressive template upon both women and men, but their effects on women are especially harmful. I think these effects finally create a lackluster commitment to intellectual and professional life accompanied by the sense that one's ultimate albeit unstated goal is state-sanctioned sexual partnership.

This has never been more true than it is today, when the professions are open to women, "men only" signs have generally disappeared from the public domain, and yet marriage—patriarchy's deepest structure— remains entrenched. This dangerous situation presents women with nothing overt against which to organize; the most destructively sexist force in our midst has been sentimentalized to the point of apparent harmlessness. Even the most spirited, highly educated, self-proclaimed feminists pursue marriage ardently and tend not to perceive their own behavior in political terms. It is now common to hear pathfinding American women of the 1960s and 1970s express frustration with the complacence of the younger generation. In her recent book, *Sex and Power*, author and law professor Susan Estrich writes that most of her female students believe that they no longer face discrimination. The young women she teaches typically express ambivalence about the whole subject of career advancement. Estrich writes, "When you point out how few women there are at the top, they shrug and say, 'Who wants to be there?' In the first five minutes, a female law review president will tell you that she doesn't want to live like a man or like the hard-driving women of my generation. She's not planning to make partner. Two years, and then pregnancy, and then who knows? I have never, ever heard a male law review president talk like that."[135] Estrich's anecdotes are telling, but her solution to the dilemma of female apathy—a workplace that includes childcare—is superficial. For women to internalize seriously and mean-ingfully the project of our own actualization, we must first perceive our-selves outside of the marital economy. We must dispense with the marriage mystique.

In the course of writing this book I have enjoyed many spirited dis-cussions with friends about my research and analysis. Married friends and colleagues have often asked me, as a sort of parlor game, to propose an alternative to marriage. The truth is, I have no alternative to suggest, no five-stage plan that would pave the way for social equity, no utopian model for sexual relationships between men and women. The very idea that a uniform model for all sexual relationships is desirable seems to me to be rooted in marriage culture and stained with the biases of conjugal ideol-ogy. In an optimal future, no single model of relationship would enjoy privileged status. Some people would naturally gravitate toward lifelong, monogamous sexual partnerships, others toward a series of such partner-ships, other toward celibacy, others toward multiple sexual relationships. Some might choose to live with their lovers, others to live with biological relatives, others to live alone, still others to live communally with friends. Law and social custom would respect and reward all models equally.

In 1963 Betty Friedan wrote of "the happy housewife heroine," explaining how the idealization of female domesticity is tied to a process of cultural mythmaking that Friedan termed "the feminine mystique." "The feminine mystique says that the highest value and the only commit-ment for women is the fulfillment of their own femininity. It says that the great mistake of western culture, through most of its history, has been the undervaluation of this femininity. It says this femininity is mysterious and intuitive and close to creation and origin of life that man-made sci-ence may never understand it."[136] These same qualities of magical think-ing contribute to our own culture's marriage mystique. As powerful as

HERE COMES THE BRIDE

the notion of gender difference has been throughout the twentieth century, the enshrinement of conjugality has been no less destructive. The idea that romance-based marriage is the highest human aspiration and the ultimate female good pervades American culture. It is bolstered by the notion that individuals—especially women—find ultimate fulfillment in a sanctioned, monogamous, sexual partnership and that those without spouses are fragmentary "single" beings whose lives are in error. A romance-obsessed media, bolstered by myriad psychological theorists, offers model after model of complementary heterosexual partnership, warning those who undervalue such partnership and eschew "commitment" that they are ignoring life's central purpose. The sense of the couple as a unit so basic, so intrinsic, and so mystical that it defies analysis, is everywhere. The belief that all other forms of attachment are of lesser importance is so deeply ingrained that it generally requires no defense.

To achieve real social equity, women—and men—must dispense with the stories they tell themselves about wedlock: fairy tales about personal choice, unique, private love, individualism, and self-expression. A more honest and comprehensive account of what wedlock is and what it is not is necessary to neutralize the marriage mystique. Marriage is a social institution firmly anchored in the notion of male dominance, and, in its every scripted ritual and gesture, the big white wedding reifies this tradition. Marriage is not a set of universal essential impulses. Current romance-tinged wedlock is another chapter in this institution's history. It does not represent the replacement of old, nasty, sexist customs with new, friendly, enlightened ones. Companionate marriage does not signal untrammeled progress over the past, and its participants should not justify their choices with the celebratory claim that, in the twentieth century, antiquated myths about love, sex, and gender have been magically eclipsed by conjugal egalitarianism. For American men and women, domestic life is far from equal, and today's middle-class marriage ideal is just the packaging of another set of prejudices: the exaltation of amorous love over all other relationships and the belief that monogamous heterosexual partnership should garner lavish emotional and material rewards. As the pages of this book have shown, the notion of matrimony as destiny for women is as deeply entrenched in our own culture as it has been in any past era. I hope for a future in which this is no longer the case.

Notes

Introduction

1 Adrienne Rich, "When We Dead Awaken: Writing as Re-Vision," in *Criticism: The Major Statements*, ed. Charles Kaplan (New York: St. Martin's, 1986), 524.

2 See Paula Hyman's "The Jewish Family: Searching for a Usable Past," in *On Being a Jewish Feminist: A Reader*, ed. Susannah Heschel (New York: Schocken, 1983), 19–26.

3 Lawrence Stone, *The Family, Sex, and Marriage in England: 1500–1800* (New York: Harper Torchbooks, 1977), 22.

4 Ian Watt, *The Rise of the Novel: Studies in Defoe, Richardson, and Fielding* (Berkeley: University of California Press, 1957), 187.

5 Gerda Lerner, *The Creation of Patriarchy* (New York: Oxford University Press, 1986), 74–75.

6 Virginia Woolf, *A Room of One's Own* (San Diego: Harcourt Brace Jovanovich, 1929), 110.

7 Lerner, *Creation of Patriarchy*, 75.

8 Simone de Beauvoir, *The Second Sex*, trans. and ed. H.M. Parshley (Toronto: Bantam, 1961), 424.

9 For an excellent account of the faulty studies of this sort that circulated in the 1980's, fanning the flames of marriage hysteria among American women, see Susan Faludi's *Backlash: The Undeclared War Against American Women* (New York: Crown Publishers, 1981), 3–19.

10 Chrys Ingraham, *White Weddings: Romancing Heterosexuality in Popular Culture* (New York: Routledge, 1999), 79–80.

11 Virginia Woolf, *Jacob's Room* (San Diego: Harcourt Brace & Company, 1922), 8.

12 Jane Austen, *Pride and Prejudice* (London: Penguin Books, 1996), 103.

Chapter One

1 John Boswell, *Same Sex Unions in Premodern Europe* (New York: Villard Books, 1994), xix. Boswell quotes Lou Phillips' 1959 hit, "Sea of Love" and Wayne Fontana's 1965 "The Game of Love."

2 Gerda Lerner, *Why History Matters: Life and Thought* (New York: Oxford University Press, 1997), 123.

3 Simone de Beauvoir, *The Second Sex*, trans. H.M. Parshley (New York: Bantam, 1970), xix.

4 Olwen Hufton, "Women, Work, and the Family," in *A History of Women in the West: Renaissance and Enlightenment Paradoxes*, ed. George Duby and Michelle Perrot (Cambridge: Harvard University Press, 1993), 29–30.

5 Gerda Lerner, *The Creation of Patriarchy* (New York: Oxford University Press), 121.

6 *The Oxford Companion to Classical Civilization*, ed. Simon Hornblower and Anthony Spawforth (Oxford: Oxford University Press, 1998), 446. Marilyn Yalom writes that Greek marriage was probably traumatic for the fourteen- and fifteen-year-old girls systematically obliged to leave their homes and take up residence with their husbands' families, who might or might not treat them decently. *A History of the Wife* (New York: HarperCollins, 2001), 20–21.

7 Boswell, *Same Sex Unions*, 40.

8 Frances and Joseph Gies, *Marrriage and the Family in the Middle Ages* (New York: Harper & Row Publishers: 1987), 23.

9 Ibid., 50.

10 Paul Veyne, "The Roman Empire," in *A History of Private Life: From Pagan Rome to Byzantium*, trans. Arthur Goldhammer, ed. Paul Veyne (Cambridge: Harvard University Press, 1987), 39.

11 Gies, *Marriage and the Family*, 33–4.

12 Ibid., 54.

13 Ibid., 91.

14 Ibid., 113–114.

15 C. Warren Hollister, *Medieval Europe: A Short History* (New York: John Wiley & Sons, 1964), 139. Georges Duby, *The Knight, the Lady, and the Priest:The Making of Marriage in Medieval France*, trans. Barbara Bray (New York: Pantheon, 1983), 90.

16 Gies, *Marriage and the Family*, 169.

17 Duby, *The Knight, the Lady*, 104–105.

18 Christopher N. L. Brooke, *The Medieval Idea of Marriage* (Oxford: Oxford University Press, 1989), 120.

19 Ibid., 263.

20 Duby, *TheKnight, the Lady*, 24.

21 Brooke, *Medieval Ideal of Marriage*, 50.

22 *Encyclopedia of the Renaissance*, Paul F. Grandler, Editor in Chief (New York: Charles Scribner's Sons, 1999), 51–2.

23 Elisja Schulte Van Kessel, "Virgins and Mothers Between Heaven and Earth," in *A History of Women in the West:Renaissance and Enlightenment Paradoxes*, trans. Arthur Goldhammer, ed. Paul Veyne (Cambridge: Harvard University Press, 1993), 149.

24 *The Oxford Encyclopedia of the Reformation*, Vol. 3, ed. Hans J. Hillerbrand (New York: Oxford University Press, 1996), 18–23. Yalom, *History of the Wife*, 99.

25 Lawrence Stone, *The Family Sex and Marriage in England: 1500–1800* (New York: Harper& Row, 1977) 109–145.

26 Ibid., 145.

27 James Trager, *A Woman's Chronology* (New York: Henry Holt, 1994), 190.

28 Kathleen Nulton Kemmerer, *"A neutral being between the sexes:" Samuel Johnson's Sexual Politics* (Lewisburg, Bucknell University Press, 1998), 32–3. Maureen Waller, *1700: Scenes from London Life* (New York: Four Walls Eight Windows, 2000), 31–32.

29 Bonnie S. Anderson and Judith P. Zinser, *A History of Their Own: Women in Europe from Prehistory to the Present*, Vol. II (New York: Harper & Row, 1988), 149.

30 The poet was Coventry Patmore. At a speech to the London National Society for Women's Service in January, 1931, Virginia Woolf spoke of the necessity of

metaphorically killing the angel in the house as a necessary prelude to the act of writing; this speech became the basis of her famed essay "Professions for Women." Michele Barrett, ed., *Virginia Woolf: Women and Writing* (San Diego: Harcourt Brace & Company, 1942), 58–60.

31 Walter E. Houghton, *The Victorian Frame of Mind, 1830–1870* (New Haven: Yale University Press, 1957), 352.

32 John R. Gillis, *For Better, For Worse: British Marriages 1600 to the Present* (New York: Oxford University Press, 1985), 285–6.

33 Joan Perkin, *Victorian Women* (New York: New York University Press, 1993), 88.

34 Ibid., 75.

35 Lawrence Stone, *Road to Divorce: A History of the Making and Breaking of Marriage in England* (Oxford; Oxford University Press, 1995), 375–6.

36 An important exception is the women who have distinguished themselves in religious life as mystics, itinerant preachers, and the leaders of devotional communities. See Gerda Lerner's, *The Creation of Feminist Consciousness: From the Middle Ages to Eighteen Seventy* (New York: Oxford University Press, 1993), 46–115.

37 Carolyn B. Ramsey, "Sex and the Social Order: The Selective Enforcement of Colonial American Adultery Laws in the English Context," *Yale Journal of Law & the Humanities* 10:1 (Winter 1998), 191–228.

38 Phyllis Coleman, "Who's Been Sleeping in My Bed? You and Me and the State Makes Three," *Indiana Law Review* 24:1 (1991), 399–416.

39 Chrys Ingraham, *White Weddings : Romancing Heterosexuality in Popular Culture* (New York: Routledge, 1999), 167–8.

40 Ibid., 168–9.

41 For an excellent analysis of the plethora of damning media images of Ms. Lewinsky, see chapter 3 of Leora Tannenbaum's *SLUT: Growing Up Female With a Bad Reputation* (New York: Seven Stories Press, 1999), 95–9.

42 *People* Oct. 2000:65.

43 Ibid., 64.

44 "Politically Incorrect," ABC, 24 June 1999.

45 Ingraham, *White Weddings*, 169–70.

46 Writing in 1997 the *Americanist* Gerda Lerner claimed, "In 1890 the divorce rate was 3.5 percent of all marriages, today it is nearly 50 percent." [sic] *Why History Matters*, 97. Divorce rates doubled between the mid 1960s and the mid 1970s; by 1973 one out of three American marriages ended in divorce. A more accepting attitude toward divorce accompanied these numbers. In 1970 California became the first state to develop a "no-fault" divorce system; by the end of the decade 35 states had enacted similar provisions. Rochelle Gatlin, *American Women Since 1945* (Jackson: University Press of Mississippi, 1987), 65, 144, 146.

47 Sarah Bernard, "Early to Wed," *New York* Jun. 1997: 41.

48 Ibid., 43.

49 Ibid., 43.

50 Ibid., 41.

51 Ibid.

52 Ibid., 40.

53 Ibid., 41.

54 Lois Smith Brody, "Brides are my Beat," *Glamour* Sep. 1998: 322.

55 Brooke, *Medieval Idea of Marriage*, 64.
56 Iyanla Vanzant, *In the Meantime: Finding Yourself and the Love You Want* (New York: Simon & Schuster, 1998), 157–8.
57 Ibid., 326.
58 Ibid., 77.
69 Ibid., 90.
60 Ibid., 121.
61 Ibid., 226–7.
62 Ibid., 141.
63 Ibid., 326.
64 Ibid., dedication page.
65 Ellen Fein and Sherrie Schneider, *The Rules: Time-tested Secrets for Capturing the Heart of Mr. Right* (New York, Warner Books, 1995), 68.
66 Ibid., 175.
67 Ibid., 9.
68 Ibid., 23.
69 Ibid., 36.
70 Barbara De Angelis, Ph.D., *The Real Rules: How to Fnd the Right Man for the Real You* (New York, Dell Publishing, 1997).
71 Ibid., 128.
72 Ibid., 131.
73 Ibid., 52.
74 Ibid., 47.
75 Ibid., 14.
76 Ibid., 141.
77 Ibid., 156.
78 Bradley Gerstman, Esq., Christopher Pizzo, C.P.A., and Rich Seldes, M.D., *What Men Want* (New York: HarperPaperbacks, 1998), 259.
79 Ibid., 259.
80 Ibid., 137.
81 Ibid., 125.
82 Ibid., 98.
83 Steven Carter and Julia Sokol, *Men Who Can't Love* (New York: Berkley Books, 1987), 67–8.
84 Ibid., 67.
85 *Mode* Aug. 1999: 71.
86 Suzanne Murray, "Is He Relationship Ready," *Cosmopolitan* Nov. 2000:220–22.
87 Peter Jon Lindberg, "Lost in 'I Need Space,'" *Glamour* Nov. 2000:168.
88 Ibid.
89 Murray, "Is He Relationship Ready," 222.
90 Marisa Cohen, "Hit by the Mack Truck of Love!", *Glamour* Jul. 1999:155.
91 Ibid., 155.
92 *Mademoiselle* Jan. 2000:89.
93 Ibid., 89.
94 *Mademoiselle* Aug. 1999:107.
95 Ibid., 107
96 Nancy Miller, "How to Get a Man to Marry You," *Marie Claire* Nov. 1999: 106–9.

97 *Cosmopolitan* May 1999:229.

98 *Cosmopolitan* Nov. 2000:182.

99 Ibid., 184.

100 Ibid., 183–4.

101 *Glamour* Dec. 2000:98.

102 *Cosmopolitan* Jul. 1999: 51.

103 Ibid., 51.

104 *New Yorker* Jan. 2001: 66.

105 Lerner, *Why History Matters*, 97.

106 Helen Gurley Brown, *Sex and the Single Girl* (New York: Pocket Books, 1962), 1.

107 Esther Crain, "The Best Man-Meeting Methods (You've *Never* Tried)" *Cosmopolitan* Sep. 1999:214–19.

108 Megan Fitzmorris McCafferty, "How Deep Is His Love?" *Cosmopolitan* Mar. 2000:205.

109 Ibid., 206.

110 *Cosmopolitan* Sep. 1999: 211.

111 Nicole Beland, "Play *Cosmo's* Love Tarot and Learn Your Romantic Destiny," *Cosmopolitan* Aug. 1999: 204.

112 *Cosmopolitan* Sep.1999:332.

113 Laura Gilbert, "Size Up Any Guy By His Looks," *Cosmopolitan* Sep. 1999: 261–3

114 J.D. Heiman, "How She Hooked Me," *Cosmopolitan* Sep. 1999:82.

115 Steve Johnson, "The Right Things to Say (and Do) After Sex," *Cosmopolitan* Aug. 1999, 152.

116 *Cosmopolitan* Jul. 2000: 124.

117 *Cosmopolitan* Oct. 2000: 170.

118 Megan Fitzmorris McCafferty, "When Should You Marry?", *Cosmopolitan* Aug. 1999: 238–40.

119 *Cosmopolitan* Aug. 2000: 124.

120 Ibid., 126.

121 Tamala M. Edwards, "Flying Solo," *Time* Aug 2000: 49.

122 Ibid., 48.

123 Such novels include Helen Fielding's *New York Times* bestseller *Bridget Jones' Diary*, Melissa Bank's *The Girls' Guide to Hunting and Fishing*, Amy Sohn's *Run Catch Kiss*, and Kate Christenson's *In the Drink*. *New York* magazine recently quoted Grove/ Atlantic publisher Morgan Entrekin as stating that, because the number of never-married women has tripled in the past two decades, "Without question, 30–45 year-old women are currently the core readers of the fiction market." Sarah Bernard, "Success and the Single Girl," *New York* Apr. 1999: 34–6.

124 *Time* Aug. 2000: cover.

125 *Newsweek* Aug. 1999: 60.

126 *Talk* Sep. 2000: 70.

127 "Fox 5 10:00 News," Fox, 8 November 2000.

128 Karen Lindsey, "Friends as Family" in *Reading America: Cultural Contexts for Critical Thinking and Writing*, ed. Gary Colombo, Robert Cullen, and Bonnie Lisle (Boston: St. Martin's Press, 1989), 472.

129 Lisa DePaulo, "Woman On Top," *New York* October 2000:36.

130 *Cosmopolitan* Jun. 1999:48.

131 DePaulo, "Woman on Top," 36.

132 Ibid., 37.

133 Ibid., 117.

134 *People* Oct. 2000: 121.

135 Ibid., 121.

136 Ibid., 121.

137 *People* Oct. 2000: cover.

138 Ibid., 116.

139 Ibid., 119.

140 Ibid., 122.

141 Ibid., 122.

142 Ibid., 119.

143 Edwards, "Flying Solo," 52.

144 Ibid., 52.

145 Edwards, "Flying Solo," 47.

146 Ibid., 50.

147 Rebecca Johnson, "Picky, Picky, Picky: the Dilemma of the New Single Woman," *Talk* Sep. 2000: 104.

148 Ibid., 104.

149 Wdwars, "FLying Solo," 53.

150 *The Letters of Heloise and Abelard,* trans. Betty Radice (London: Penguin, 1974), 113.

151 Brooke, *Medieval Idea of Marriage,* 91.

152 Ibid., 23–27.

153 Henry James, *The Bostonians* , ed. Charles R. Anderson (London: Penguin, 1986), 47.

154 *The Oxford English Dictionary,* second edition, volume XVI (Oxford:Clarendon Press, 1989), 243.

155 Ian Watt, *The Rise of the Novel : Studies in Defoe, Richardson, and Fielding* (Berkeley: University of California Press 1957), 144–146. Watt quotes the eighteenth-century journalist Richard Steele.

156 James, *The Bostonians,* 64.

157 Isadora Duncan, *My Life* (New York: Liveright, 1927), 17.

158 Ibid., 18.

159 See Betty Friedan, *The Feminine Mystique* (New York:Dell Publishing Company, 1974), 28–61.

160 Rochelle Gatlin, *American Women Since 1945* (Jackson: University Press of Mississippi), 16–18.

161 Mark Caldwell, *A Short History of Rudeness* (New York: Picador USA, 1999), 101–4.

162 Ingraham, *White Weddings,* 43.

163 Ibid., 49.

164 Caldwell, *History of Rudeness,* 108.

165 Jean L. Backus, ed., *Letters from Amelia: 1901–1937* (Boston: Beacon Press, 1982), 104–5.

166 *Us Weekly* Sep. 2000:47. On September 3, 2000, at the age of 66, Steinem married entrepreneur David Bale in a ceremony held near Stilwell, Oklahoma.

167 Judy Brady, "I Want a Wife." Reprinted in *The Winchester Reader,* ed. Robert Atwan and Donald McQuade (Boston: St. Martin's Press, 1990), 486.

168 Ibid., 487.

Chapter Two

1 See Erich Auerbach's *Mimesis: The Representation of Reality in Western Literature*, trans. Willard R. Trask (Princeton: Princeton University Press, 1953) and Joaquin Martínez-Pizarro's *A Rhetoric of the Scene: Dramatic Narrative in the Early Middle Ages* (Toronto: University of Toronto Press, 1989).

2 Henry James, *The Portrait of a Lady* (London: Penguin Books, 1984), 116.

3 Virginia Woolf, *A Room of One's Own* (San Diego: Harcourt, Brace Jovanovich, Publishers, 1929), 44.

4 Joseph Allen Boone, *Tradition Counter Tradition: Love and the Form of Fiction* (Chicago: University of Chicago Press, 1987), 34–43.

5 Pauline Kael, *5001 Nights at the Movies* (New York: Henry Holt & Company, 1991), 496.

6 John Mitchell, *What the Hell is a Groom and What is He Supposed to Do?* (Kansas City: Andrews McMeel Publishing, 1999), 22–5.

7 Michael Perry, *The Groom's Survival Manual* (New York: Pocket Books, 1991), 2–3.

8 Scott Omelianuk and Ted Allen, *Esquire's Things a Man Should Know About Marriage* (New York: Riverhead Books, 1999), 5.

9 Ibid., 6.

10 Glen Freyer, "Popping the Question: How Seriously do Men Take the Moment?" *Glamour.* October, 1999:122.

11 Paul Reiser, *Couplehood* (New York: Bantam Books, 1994), 147–48.

12 Ibid., 147.

13 Ibid., 147.

14 Arlene Hamilton Stewart, *A Bride's Book of Wedding Traditions* (New York: Hearst Books), 48.

15 Sigmund Freud, *New Introductory Lectures on Psycho-Analysis,* ed. and trans. James Strachey (New York: W.W. Norton & Company, 1965), 107–8, 160–1.

16 ———. *Civilization and Its Discontents,* ed. and trans. James Strachey (New York: W.W. Norton & Company, 1961), 53, 87–9, 94.

17 Adrienne Rich, *Of Woman Born: Motherhood as Experience and Institution* (New York: W.W. Norton & Company, 1986), 196.

18 Sigmund Freud, *Totem and Taboo: Some Points of Agreement Between the Mental Life of Savages and Neurotics*, ed. and trans. James Strachey (New York: W.W. Norton & Company, 1950), 178.

19 Jaclyn C. Barrett-Hirschhaut, *1000 Questions About Your Wedding* (Arlington, Texas: The Summit Publishing Group, 1997), 3.

20 Freyer, "Popping the Question," 220.

21 *Martha Stewart's Weddings* Winter 2000:cover.

22 "Will You Marry Me?" Day, advertisement, *Bride's* February/March 2000:102–3.

23 *Modern Bride* April/May 1999:72.

24 Gregory Godek, *1001 Ways to be Romantic* (Naperville, Illinois: Casablanca Press, 2000), 225.

25 *In Style* February 1999:234.

26 "What is it about the way we frame manhood that, even today, it still depends so on 'feminine' dependence for its survival? A little-noted finding by the Yankelovich Monitor survey, a large, nationwide poll that has tracked social attitudes for the last two decades, takes us a good way toward a possible answer. For twenty years, the Monitor's pollsters have asked its subjects to define masculinity. And for twenty

years, the leading definition, ahead by a huge margin, has never changed. It isn't being a leader, athlete, lothario, decision maker, or even just being 'born male.' It is simply this: being a 'good provider for his family.'" Susan Faludi, *Backlash: The Undeclared War Against American Women* (New York: Crown Publishers, 1991), 65.

27 *People*: July 5, 1999:89.

28 Ibid., 96.

29 Ibid., 115.

30 Freyer, "Popping the Question," 220.

31 *For the Bride* Summer 1998:119.

32 Sally Killbridge and Mallory Samson, *Real Weddings: A Celebration of Personal Style* (New York: Clarkson Potter, 1999), 54.

33 *Bride's* February/March 2000:74.

34 Ibid., 6.

35 Daniel Harris, "The Romantic," *Salmagundi* 123 (Summer 1999):71–2.

36 Judith Martin, *Miss Manners on Weddings* (New York: Crown, 1995), 57.

37 Ibid., 57–8.

38 Nancy F. Cott, *The Bonds of Womanhood: "Woman's Sphere" in New England, 1780–1835* (New Haven: Yale University Press, 1977), 5, 77–8.

39 Harris, "Romantic," 76.

40 Scott Kay Platinum, advertisement, *Bride's* Feb./Mar. 2000:6–7.

41 De Beers, advertisement, *Bride's* Feb./Mar. 2000:21.

42 Kilbridge and Samson, *Real Weddings*, 110.

43 *In Style* Feb. 2001: 317.

44 Harris, "Romantic," 68.

45 Keepsake Diamond Jewelry, advertisement, *Bride's* Feb./Mar. 2000:29.

46 De Beers, advertisement, *Modern Bride* Jun./Jul. 1999:11.

47 Christian Bauer, advertisement, *Modern Bride* Jun./Jul. 1999:25.

48 Gottlieb & Sons, advertisement, *Bride's* Feb./Mar. 2000:137.

49 Antonio Bonnano and Antoinette L. Matlins, *Engagement and Wedding Rings* (Woodstock, Vermont: Gemstone Press, 1999), 7–14.

50 Ibid., 14.

51 Perry, *Groom's Survival Manual*, 11.

52 Mitchell, *What the Hell is a Groom*, 21–1.

53 Suzanne Finnamore, "Otherwise Engaged," *Modern Bride* Jun./Jul. 1999: 335.

54 Ibid., 338.

55 Marg Stark, *What No One Tells the Bride* (New York: Hyperion, 1988), 5.

56 Ibid., 43.

57 Barrett-Hirschhaut, *1000 Questions*, 2.

58 Ibid., 3.

59 Cele Goldsmith Lalli, *Modern Bride Guide to Etiquette* (New York: John Wiley & Son, Inc.1993), 1.

60 Stark, *What No One Tells*, 44.

61 Diane Ackerman, *A Natural History of Love* (New York: Random House, 1994), 268.

62 Martin, *Miss Manners*, 59.

63 Mitchell, *What the Hell is a Groom?*, 30.

64 Ibid., 29.

65 Mitchell, *What the Hell is a Groom?*, 28.

Chapter Three

1 Lawrence Stone, *Road to Divorce: A History of the Making and Breaking of Marriage in Modern England* (Oxford: Oxford University Press, 1995), 51. Stone's point is not that timeless marital customs have shifted but that twentieth-century conjugal procedures have loosened up and come to resemble the more fluid and haphazard arrangements characteristic of early modern life.

2 Editors of *Variety, Variety Portable Movie Guide* (New York: Berkley Boulevard Books, 1999), 107.

3 Susan Faludi, *Backlash: The Undeclared War Against American Women* (New York: Crown Publishers Inc., 1991).

4 Faludi's research in this area uncovers three basic points: the significance of paid professional work to female self-esteem as emphasized by American women themselves as far back as the 1950s, the 40–60 per cent improvement in the mental health of American women as the woman's movement's strides have given them access to better employment, expanding their sense of their own potential, and the fact that married women experience more anxiety and depression than their "single" counterparts. Ibid., 35–9.

5 Editors of *Bride's* magazine, *Bride's Book of Etiquette* (New York: Perigree, 1999), 3.

6 *The Engagement Journal: A Book to Hold Your Memories* (New York: Ziff-Davis Publishing Company, 1984), 8–9.

7 *Bride's Book of Etiquette*, 1.

8 Ibid., 2.

9 Carley Roney, *The Knot's Complete Guide to Weddings in the Real World* (New York: Broadway Books, 1998), 2.

10 Adrienne Rich, *Of Woman Born: Motherhood as Experience and Institution* (New York: W.W. Norton & Company, 1986), 61.

11 *Town and Country*: November, 1999:258–62.

12 Faludi, *Backlash*, xiv.

13 Ibid., xiii.

14 Gerda Lerner, *Why History Matters: Life and Thought* (New York: Oxford University Press, 1997), 99–100. I feel compelled to point out that, given the fact that women do most of the world's unpaid and low paying labor, the right to terminate a pregnancy and opt against the fulltime job of motherhood is, literally, the right to a 12-hour work day instead of a 24-hour work day.

15 Michael A. Messner, *Politics of Masculinities: Men in Movements* (London: Sage Publications, 1997), 46.

16 Ibid., 46.

17 Arlene Hamilton Stewart, *A Bride's Book of Wedding Traditions* (New York: Hearst Books), 156.

18 Editors of *Bride's Magazine, Bride's Book of Etiquette*, 177.

19 "Wedding Countdown," *Wedding Bells* Spring/Summer 1999:54.

20 Hamilton Stewart, *Bride's Book*, 10–11.

21 Ibid., 2.

22 Gerda Lerner, *The Creation of Patriarchy* (New York: Oxford University Press, 1986), 101–22.

23 Anti-abortion activist John Willke has objected to pro-choice women who "remove the right of a husband to protect the life of the child he has fathered in his wife's

womb." The anti-choice priest Father Michael Carey has said, "God didn't create women independently." Operation Rescue founder Randall Terry, who wishes to ban birth control and eliminate premarital sex, has stated, "Radical feminism gave birth to child killing" and that "Radical feminism, of course,... hates motherhood, hates children for the most part, promotes lesbian activity." He has called Planned Parenthood founder Margaret Sanger a "whore" and claimed "She was an adulteress, and slept all over the place, all over the world, with all kinds of people." Faludi, *Backlash*, 402, 408. Right to Life Minister Jerry Falwell has described his constituency as "citizens who are pro family, pro moral, pro life, and pro American..." Colin Francome, *Abortion Freedom: A Worldwide Movement* (London: George Allen& Unwin, 1984), 11. Faye Ginsburg's 1980s case study of anti-choice women in Fargo, North Dakota concluded that many of its subjects saw abortion as a threat to the "link between sex and marriage upon which women's security depends." Linda Gordon, *Woman's Body, Woman's Right: Birth Control in America* (New York: Penguin Books, 1990), 409.

24 Lerner, *Creation of Patriarchy*, 110–11.

25 Rachel Adler, *Engendering Judaism: An Inclusive Theology and Ethics* (Boston: Beacon Press, 1988), 170–71.

26 *The Torah: A Modern Commentary* (New York:Union of American Hebrew Congregations, 1981), Genesis 29:19.

27 Ibid., Deuteronomy 22:16–17.

28 John Boswell, *Same Sex Unions in Premodern Europe* (New York: Villard Books, 1994), 40.

29 Frances and Joseph Gies, *Marriage and the Family in the Early Middle Ages* (New York: Harper & Row Publishers, 1987), 54.

30 Georges Duby, Dominique Barthelemy, and Charles de La Ronciere, "Portraits," *A History of Private Life*, trans. Arthur Goldhammer and ed. Georges Duby (Cambridge: Harvard University Press, 1988), 290–1.

31 Mary P. Ryan, *Womanhood in America: From Colonial Times to the Present* (New York: Franklin Watts, 1975), 20.

32 Georges Duby, *The Knight, the Priest, and the Lady: the Making of Modern Marriage in Medieval France* , trans. Barbara Bray (New York: Pantheon Books, 1983), 170–1.

33 Eileen Livers, *The Unofficial Guide to Planning Your Own Wedding* (USA: MacMillan, 1999), 4.

34 Shu Shu Costa, *Wild Geese and Tea: An Asian American Wedding Planner* (New York: Riverhead Books, 1997), 23.

35 Harriette Cole, *Jumping the Broom: The African American Wedding Planner* (New York: Henry Holt and Company, 1995), 36.

36 Editors of *Signature Bride Magazine, Going to the Chapel* (New York: G.P. Putnam's Sons, 1997), 21.

37 Ibid., 21.

38 Ruth Muzzy and R. Kent Hughes, *The Christian Wedding Planner* (Wheaton, Illinois: Tyndale House Publishers, Incorporated, 1991), 6.

39 John Mitchell, *What the Hell is the Groom Supposed to Do?* (Kansas City: Andrews McMeel Publishing, 1999), 30–1.

40 *Talk* Sep. 2000:100.

41 Elizabeth L. Post, *Emily Post on Second Weddings* (New York: HarperPerennial, 1991), 3.

42 *Modern Bride* March 1999:562.

43 Chrys Ingraham estimates that the average American couple spends $19,104 on its wedding. *White Weddings: Romancing Heterosexuality in Popular Culture* (New York: Routledge, 1999), 4.

44 Rich, *Of Woman Born*, 42.

45 Daniel B. Syme, *The Jewish Home: A Guide for Jewish Living* (Northvale, NJ: Jason Aaronson Inc., 1988), 77.

46 *Catechism of the Catholic Church* (New York: Doubleday, 1995), 456.

47 *Plato's Republic*, trans.G.M.A. Grube (Indianapolis: Hackett Publishing Company, 1974), Bk. VII.

48 Faludi, *Backlash*, 58.

49 Ibid., 58.

50 Ibid., 58.

Chapter Four

1 Formal engagement announcements in newspapers are increasingly rare, perhaps because the small town newspaper seems an antiquated vehicle for communication in the electronic age, or perhaps because such publications now charge a nominal fee. Where it lingers on, the newspaper announcement, like all aspects of wedding protocol, is governed by strict rules of etiquette. Wedding experts instruct couples to contact their hometown papers six to one month prior to the wedding day, providing the following information: the names of the bride and groom, the names of both sets of parents, the schools the bride and groom have attended with degrees received, their current job titles and employers, and the location of the wedding. As primary players in the marital drama, the bride's gleeful parents—never the groom's mother and father—often make the formal announcement. Jaclyn C. Barrett-Hirschhaut, *1001 Questions About Your Wedding* (Arlington, Texas: The Summit Publishing Group, 1997), 23.

2 Invitations by Dawn, advertisement, (Invitations by Dawn Catalog, 1999–2000), 4.

3 Rexcraft, advertisement, (Rexcraft Catalog, 1999–2000), 3.

4 Ibid., 2.

5 Ibid., 3.

6 Arlene Hamilton Stewart, *A Bride's Book of Wedding Traditions* (New York: Hearst Books), 85 87.

7 John Gillis, *For Better, For Worse: British Marriages 1600 to the Present* (New York: Oxford University Press, 1985), 285–286.

8 Hamilton Stewart, *Bride's Book*, 88.

9 Linda Otto Lipsett, *To Love and Cherish: Brides Remembered* (Lincolnwood, Illinois: NTC Publishing Group, 1997).

10 Robin Fox, *Kinship & Marriage: An Anthropoligical Perspective* (London: Cambridge University Press, 1967), 31.

11 Jack Goody, *Production and Reproduction: A Comparative Study of the Domestic Domain* (London:Cambridge University Press, 1976).

12 *The Bride's Book of Ettiquette* (New York: Perigree, 1999), 73–74.

13 Yetta Gruen, *Weddiquette* (New York: Penguin, 1995).

14 Beverly Clark, *Weddings: A Celebration* (Carpinteria, California: 1996), 70.

15 Perigree, *Bride's Book,* 72.

16 Sally Kilbridge and Mallory Samson, *Real Weddings: A Celebration of Personal Style* (New York: Clarkson Potter, 1999), 113.

17 Ibid., 39.

18 Ibid., 92.

19 Madeline Barillo, *The Wedding Source Book* (Lowell House, 1996), 181.

20 Don Altman, *201 Ways to Make Your Wedding Special* (Los Angeles, Moon Lake Media, 1994), 61.

21 Ibid., 60.

22 Richard Mitzer, *The Longest Aisle: An Offbeat Guide to Planning Your Wedding* (Citadel Press, 1994).

23 I do not mean to imply that Victorians unanimously and happily accepted a common marital experience. Clearly, the nineteenth-century's notion of rigidly gendered marriage, in which women were mandated to live as selfless, domestic angels, was an oppressive experience for many. This is evidenced by the fact that the West's first waves of organized feminism took place at the end of the Victorian era in response to these very social conditions. I merely point out that the period's marital ideal, as expressed in its conduct literature, was univocal and powerful.

24 Daphne Rose Kingma, *Weddings from the Heart: Contemporary and Traditional Ceremonies for an Unforgettable Wedding* (Berkeley:Conari Press, 1991), 27–28.

25 *Modern Bride* Feb./Mar. 1999: 288.

26 Creations by Elaine, advertisement. *Modern Bride,* Jun./Jul. 1999: 143.

27 Now and Forever, advertisement, *Modern Bride,* Jun./Jul. 1999:171.

28 Heart Thoughts, advertisement, *Modern Bride,* Jun./Jul. 1999:185.

29 Renaissance Writings, advertisement, *Martha Stewart Living,* Summer/Fall 1998: 315.

30 Invitations by Dawn, 35.

31 Beverly Clark, *Planning A Wedding to Remember* (1986).

32 Altman, *201 Ways,* 60.

33 Daniel Harris, "Zaniness," *Salmagundi* 104–105 (Fall 1994/Winter 1995): 206–217.

34 *People* : Jul. 5, 1999:80.

35 Rexcraft, 97.

36 Judith Martin, *Miss Manners On Weddings* (Crown, 1995), 81.

37 Mitzer, *Longest Aisle.*

38 "Modern Traditions," *Wedding Bells,* Spring/Summer 1999: 26.

39 Shu Shu Costa, *Wild Geese and Tea: An Asian American Wedding Planner* (New York: Riverhead Books, 1997), 35.

40 Harriette Cole, *Jumping the Broom: The African American Wedding Planner* (New York: Henry Holt and Company, 1993), 79.

41 Ibid., 80.

42 *In Style* Feb. 2001: 307.

43 Gillis, *For Better, For Worse,* 5.

Chapter Five

1 Steinem republished the essay under the title "I Was a Playboy Bunny" in *Outrageous Acts and Everyday Rebellions* (New York: Holt, Rinehart and Winston, 1983), 29–69.

2 Lawrence Otis Graham, "Invisible Man" in *The Best American Essays 1993* , ed. Robert Atwan and Joseph Epstein (New York: Ticknor & Fields, 1993), 114–130.

3 Nancy Armstrong, *Desire and Domestic Fiction: A Political History of the Novel* (New York: Oxford University Press, 1987), 59.

4 Bloomingdale's, *Inspirations: The Bloomingdale's Home Planner* (1997), 79.

5 Ibid., no page number.

6 Ibid., no page number.

7 Ibid., no page number.

8 Armstrong, *Desire and Domestic Fiction*, 73.

9 *Bloomingdale's Home Planner*, 14.

10 Ibid., 18.

11 Ibid., 24.

12 Ibid., 132.

13 Ibid., 143.

14 Ibid., 140.

15 Ibid., no page number.

16 Ibid., 6.

17 Ibid., 88.

18 Ibid., no page number.

19 Ibid., 32.

20 Ibid., 63.

21 Ibid., 76.

22 Ibid., 52.

23 Ibid., 15.

24 Ibid., 88.

25 Ibid., 107.

26 Ibid., 104.

27 Ibid., 112.

28 Virginia Woolf, *To the Lighthouse* (New York: Harcourt, Brace & World, Inc., 1927), 77.

29 Lerner, *Creation of Patriarchy*, 54–75 and 101–122.

30 Ibid., 9.

31 John Boswell, *Christianity, Social Tolerance, and Homosexuality: Gay People in Western Europe from the Beginning of the Christian Era to the Fourteenth Century* (Chicago: University of Chicago Press, 1980), 10.

32 See Charles Kaiser's *The Gay Metropolis* (San Diego: Harcourt Brace & Company, 1997), 88–104.

33 The Wedding Registry at Chelsea Passage, Barney's New York, advertisement, *Wedding Bells New York* Spring/Summer 1999:23.

34 The Service Merchandise Gift Registry, advertisement, *Wedding Bells New York* Spring/Summer:14–15.

35 Noritake Dinnerware, advertisement, *Wedding Bells New York* Spring/Summer 1999:9.

36 Christian Bauer, advertisement, *Modern Bride* Jun./Jul. 1999:27.

37 Superclubs, advertisement, *Modern Bride* Jun./Jul. 1999:419.

38 Amy Bloom, "We Few, We Happy Few," *Mirabella* Jan.1999: 84.

39 Pundits throughout our century have championed the "naturalness" of wedlock. It is interesting to note the extent to which a contemporary female therapist like Bloom echoes the male sociologist Ernest R. Groves whose study *The Marriage Crisis* (New York: Longmans, Green, & Co., 1928) opens with the sweeping statement, "No desire is more universal nor more strongly felt among young people than the wish to be happily married. It may perhaps be too much to say that all young men and women hope to achieve marriage happiness, but so few are without this yearning that one can safely say that normal youth usually looks forward to being some day happily married."

40 Bloom, "We Few," 87.

41 Lerner, *Creation of Patriarchy*, 106–8

42 James Trager, *The Women's Chronology* (New York: Henry Holt and Company, 1994), 14. Marilyn Yalom, *A History of the Wife* (New York: HarperCollins, 2001), 20.

43 Daniel B. Syme, *The Jewish Home: A Guide for Jewish Living* (Northvale, New Jersey: Jason Aronson Inc., 1988), 77–78.

44 Paul Veyne, "The Roman Empire" in *A History of Private Life: From Pagan Rome to Byzantium* , trans. Arthur Goldhammer and ed. Paul Veyne (Cambridge: Harvard University Press, 1987), 38.

45 Frances and Joseph Gies, *Marriage and the Family in the Middle Ages* (New York: Harper & Row, 1987), 33.

46 Bonnie S. Anderson and Judith P. Zinser, *A History of Their Own: Women in Europe from Prehistory to the Present* , vol. I, (New York: Harper & Row, 1988), 394–402.

47 Lawrence Stone, *The Family, Sex, and Marriage in England: 1500-1800* (New York: Harper & Row, 1977), 232.

48 Vern L. Bullough, Brenda Shelton, and Sarah Slavin, *The Subordinated Sex : A History of Attitudes Toward Women* (Athens, Georgia: The University of Georgia Press, 1988), 261.

49 Laurel Thatcher Ulrich, *Good Wives: Image and Reality in the Lives of Women in Northern New England, 1650-1750* (New York: Random House, 1980), preface.

50 John Gillis' history *For Better, For Worse: British Marriages 1600 to the Present* (New York: Oxford University Press, 1985) includes the text of the following 1847 bidding announcement: "As we intend to enter the matrimonial State on Tuesday, the 25th day of May inst., we are encouraged by our Friends to make a BIDDING on the occasion of the same day, at the Young Woman's Father's House called Penrose Cottage; when and where the favour of your good and agreeable company is humbly solicited, and whatever donation you may be pleased to confer on us then well be thankfully received, warmly acknowledged, and cheerfully repaied whenever called for on a similar occasion."

51 *In Style* Spring 2001:98.

52 *Wedding Bells New York*: Spring/Summer 1999: 59.

53 Adrienne Rich, *Of Woman Born: Motherhood as Experience and Institution* (New York: W.W. Norton & Company, 1986), 235.

54 Cicero, *On the Good Life* , trans. Michael Grant (London: Penguin, 1971), 187.

55 Ibid., 204.

Chapter Six

1 For an overview of recent prochastity initiatives including governmental repudiation of comprehensive sex education curricula , the promotion of factually inaccurate abstinence-only programs, and evangelical organizations that preach virginity to teenagers, see Leora Tannenbaum's *Slut:Growing Up Female with a Bad Reputation* (New York: Seven Stories Press, 1999), 241–7.

2 Ibid., 45–86.

3 Jaclyn C. Barrett-Hirschhaut, *1000 Questions About Your Wedding* (Arlington, Texas: The Summit Publishing Group), 322.

4 Arlene Hamilton Stewart, *A Bride's Book of Wedding Traditions* (New York: Hearst Books), 18.

5 Janet Anastasio, *The Wedding Shower Book* (Holbrook, Massachusetts: Adams Publishing, 1992), 9.

6 The Editors of *Signature Bride* magazine, *Going to the Chapel* (New York: G.P. Putnam's Sons, 1997), 183.

7 Helen Latner, *The Everything Jewish Wedding Book* (Holbrook, Massachusetts: Adams Media Corporation, 1998), 19.

8 John Gillis, *For Better, For Worse: British Marriages, 1600 to the Present* (New York: Oxford University Press, 1985), 223.

9 Ibid., 7, Lawrence Stone, *The Family Sex and Marriage in England:1500–1800* (New York: Harper & Row, 1979), 101–2.

10 Betty Friedan, *The Feminine Mystique* (New York: Dell, 1974), back cover.

11 *For the Bride:*Summer 1998: cover.

12 Anthony Storr, *Solitude: A Return to the Self* (New York:Ballantine Books, 1988), 8.

13 Ibid., 13.

14 Barrett-Hirschhaut, *1000 Questions*, 321–22.

15 *For the Bride:*Jul./Aug.:32.

16 Anastasio, *Wedding Shower Book*, 55.

17 *In Style:* Spring 2000:149–50

18 Judith Martin, *Miss Manners on Weddings* (New York: Crown Publishers, Inc., 1995), 67.

19 Ibid., 67.

20 Ibid., 68–9.

21 Ibid., 69.

22 Mary Wollstonecraft, *Vindication of the Rights of Woman* (London: Penguin Books, 1975), 113.

23 Michael R. Perry, *The Couple's Wedding Survival Manual* (New York: Pocketbooks, 1999), 55.

24 The Editors of *Bride's* magazine, *Bride's Book of Etiquette* (New York: Perigreee,1999), 35.

25 Ibid., 36.

26 Barrett-Hirschhaut, *1000 Questions*, 323.

27 *Bridal Guide:* Jul./Aug.: 32.

28 Diane Warner, *Complete Book of Wedding Showers* (Franklin Lanes, New Jersey: Career Press, 1998), 19.

29 Ibid., 21.

30 Anastasio, *Wedding Shower Book*, 49.

31 The Editors of *Bride's* magazine, *Bride's Book*, 36–7.

32 *Bridal Guide*, 32.

33 Daniel Harris, "The Romantic," *Salmagundi* 123(Summer 1999):70.

34 *Us*: Feb. 2000:60.

35 Ibid., 60.

36 Harris, "Romantic," 71.

37 *In Style*: Feb. 1999:242.

38 Ibid., 242.

39 *Bride's* Feb./Mar. 2000:108.

40 Anastasio, *Wedding Shower Book*, 61.

41 Hamilton Stewart, *Bride's Book*, 18.

42 *Modern Bride*:Feb./March 1999:456.

43 Editors of *Bride's* magazine, *Bride's Book*, 28.

44 Anastasio, *Wedding Shower Book*, 125.

45 Warner, *Complete Book*, 40–1.

46 Ibid., 40.

47 *Bride's* 244.

48 Becky Long, *Something Old, Something New: 101 Creative Ways to Personalize Your Wedding* (New York: Meadowbrook Press, 1997), dedication page.

49 Ibid., 80.

50 Courtney Cook, *The Best Wedding Shower Book* (New York: Simon & Schuster, 1987), 13–36.

51 *In Style*: Feb. 1999: 229.

52 Ibid., 229.

53 *In Style*: Spring:2000:76.

54 Don Altman, *201 Ways to Make Your Wedding Special* (Los Angeles: Moon Lake Media, 1994), 18

55 Ibid., 21.

56 Ibid., 21.

57 Ibid., 22–3.

58 Ibid., 17.

59 Ibid., 20.

60 Ibid., 21.

61 Virginia Woolf, "Professions for Women" in *Virginia Woolf: Women and Writing*, ed. Michele Barrett (New York: Harcourt, Brace & Company, 1942), 59.

62 Ibid., 59.

63 Ibid., 59.

64 Hamilton Stewart, *Bride's Book*, 19.

65 Ibid., 19. Diane Ackerman, *A Natural History of Love* (New York: Random House, 1994), 270–1.

66 Hamilton Stewart, *Bride's Book*, 19–20.

67 Cathy Luchetti, *"I Do!" Courtship, Love, and Marriage on American Frontier* (New York: Crown Trade Paperbacks, 1996), 15.

68 Ibid., 18.

69 Ibid., 24–5.

70 Ibid.

71 Ibid., 27–8.

72 Ibid., 149.

73 Ibid., 123.

74 Ibid., 122.

75 Ibid., 9.

76 Ibid., 19–20.

77 Anita Diamant, *The New Jewish Wedding* (New York: Fireside, 1985), 143.

78 Ibid., 145.

79 *The Oxford Study Bible*, ed. M. Jack Suggs, Katherine Doob Sakenfield, and James R. Meuller (New York: Oxford University Press, 1992), Leviticus 18:19.

80 Ibid., Leviticus 15:19–24.

81 Haviva Ner David has pointed out that the seminal eleventh and twelfth-century commentator, Rashi,believed a woman's bladder to be connected to her uterus by a tube. He also thought menstrual blood and urine emit from a single opening and concluded erroneously that urine could back up into a woman's uterus and mix with her menstrual blood. The twelfth-and thirteenth century rabbi, Nachmanides, based his important rulings on the laws of ritual purity upon the faulty premise that a woman's menstrual cycle lasts for eighteen days. *Life on the Fringes: A Feminist Journey Toward Traditional Rabbinic Ordination* (Needham, Massachusetts: JFL Books, 2000), 156.

82 For an account of the depression endemic to American housewives in the postwar years see Friedan's The *Feminine Mystique*, 11–94.

83 The editors of *Signature Bride* magazine, *Going to the Chapel*, 182.

84 Ibid., 183.

85 *Us*, 56.

86 *In Style:*Spring 2000: 42.

87 *Bride's*, 6.

88 Ibid., back cover.

89 Ibid., 106.

90 James Grace, *The Best Man's Handbook: A Guy's Guide to the Big Event* (Philadelphia: Running Press, 1999), 41.

91 Ibid., 46.

92 Ibid., 56.

93 Michael R. Perry, *The Groom's Survival Manual* (New York: Pocket Books, 1991), 144.

94 Ibid., 144.

95 Carley Roncy, *The Knot's Complete Guide to Weddings in the Real World* (New York: Broadway Books, 1998), 69.

96 Ibid., 69.

97 *Bride's*, 162.

98 Ibid., 162.

99 *Modern Bride*: Jun./Jul. 1999:100.

100 Ibid., 100.

101 Wollstonecraft, *Vindication*, 100.

102 Simone de Beauvoir, *The Second Sex*, trans. and ed. H.M. Parshley (New York: Bantam Books, 1961), 165.

103 Ibid., 442.

104 Germaine Greer, *The Female Eunich* (New York: Bantam Books, 1970),239.

105 Harriette Cole, *Jumping the Broom: The African American Wedding Planner* (New York: Henry Holt and Company, 1993), 52.

106 Victor J. Seidler, "Rejection, Vulnerability, and Friendship" in *Men's Friendships*, ed. Peter M. Nardi (London: Sage Publications, 1992), 20.

107 Theodore F. Cohen, "Men's Families, Men's Friends: A Structural Analysis of the Constraints on Men's Social Ties" in *Men's Friendships*, ed. Peter M. Nardi (London: Sage Publications, 1992), 115–30.

108 Ibid., 115.

109 Seidler, "Rejection, Vulnerability," 16.

110 Ibid., 15.

111 Ibid., 16.

112 Cohen, "Men's Families," 119.

113 Ibid., 119–20.

114 Grace, *Best Man's Handbook*, 31.

115 Ibid., 31.

116 Ibid., 31.

117 Ibid., 43.

118 Janet Maslin, *The New York Times Guide to the Best 1,000 Movies Ever Made* (New York: Times Books, 1999), 906.

119 Lois M. Tamir, Ph.D., *Men in Their Forties: The Transition to Middle Age* (New York: Springer Publishing Company, 1982), 112.

120 John Mitchell, *What the Hell is a Groom and What's He Supposed to Do?* (Kansas City: Andrews McMeel Publishing, 1999), 64.

121 Ibid., 64.

122 Roney, *Knot's Complete Guide*, 70–1.

123 The editors of Bride's magazine, *Bride's Book*, 38.

124 Donna A. Bankhead and Lynette Blas, *Last Minute Weddings* (Franklin Lakes, New Jersey: Career Press, 1999), 63.

125 Angela Lansbury, *Wedding Speeches and Toasts* (London: Ward Lock, 1994), 35.

126 Ibid., 35–6.

Chapter Seven

1 *In Style* Feb. 2001:212.

2 Ibid., 213.

3 Ibid., 216.

4 Ibid., 216.

5 Ibid., 216.

6 John Gillis, *For Better, For Worse: British Marriages 1600 to the Present* (New York: Oxford University Press, 1989), 294.

7 Yetta Fisher Gruen, *Weddiquette* (New York: Penguin Books, 1986), 183.

8 Editors of Bride's magazine, *Bride's Book of Etiquette* (New York: Perigree, 1999), 111

9 Editor's of Bride's magazine, *Bride's Book*, 112–14.

10 *In Style* Spring 2000: 183.

11 Ibid., 184–5.

12 Ibid., 439–40.

13 *Modern Bride* Apr./May 1999:41.

14 Ibid., 41.

15 Sally Kilbridge and Mallory Samson, *Real Weddings: A Celebration of Personal Style* (New York: Clarkson Potter Publishers,1999), 138.

16 Ibid., 138.

17 Ibid., 138.

18 Alan and Denise Fields, *1999 Bridal Guide* (Boulder: Windsor Peak Press, 1999),75.

19 Ibid. 75.

20 Superstars of the fashion world such as Cindy Crawford, Christy Turlington, and Claudia Schiffer earn approximately ten million dollars a year for their modeling. Daniel Harris, *Cute, Quaint, Hungry, and Romantic: The Aesthetics of Consumerism* (New York: Basic Books, 2000), 223.

21 Diane Ackerman, *A Natural History of Love* (New York: Random House, 1994), 271. Ingraham, *White Weddings*, 29.

22 Arlene Hamilton Stewart, *A Bride's Book of Wedding Traditions* (New York: Hearst Books), 120.

23 Joan Perkin, *Victorian Women* (New York: New York University Press, 1993), 74.

24 Ibid., 64.

25 *Bridal Guide* Jul./Aug.1999: 308.

26 Ibid., 310.

27 Ibid., 313.

28 *In Style* Feb. 1999: 165.

29 Ibid., 165.

30 Harris, *Cute, Quaint, Hungry*, 214.

31 Mon Cheri, advertisement, *Modern Bride* Feb./Mar. 1999:35.

32 *Modern Bride* Feb./Mar. 1999:34.

33 Vera Wang Bridal Collection, advertisement, *Martha Stewart Weddings* Winter 2001: 29.

34 Ibid., 26.

35 The company Badgley Mischka outdoes Wang, venturing into outre, outlandish fashion. Its bridal couture advertisements feature glassy-eyed models with hairdos that look like topiary sculptures. Their heads are askew, these "brides" wear skintight gowns offset by enormous powdered wigs sprouting plastic leaves and carry white fur stoles that drag on the ground. Sometimes the models are blindfolded. As an alternative to white gloves, their arms are affixed with rhinestones or spray-painted white up to the elbow.

36 Cocoe Voci, advertisement, *Martha Stewart Weddings* Winter 2001:351.

37 *Bridal Guide* Jul./Aug. 1999:301.

38 Ibid., 303.

39 Impression, advertisement, *Modern Bride* Jun./Jul.1999:123.

40 Ibid., 309.

41 Ibid., 311.

42 David's Bridal, advertisement, (David's Bridal Catalog, 1999), 21.

43 Jaclyn C. Barrett-Hirschhaut, *Elegant Bride's 1001 Questions About Your Wedding* (Arlington, Texas: Summit Publishing Group, 1970), 73–6.

44 Ellen Willis, *No More Nice Girls: Countercultural Essays* (Hanover and London: Wesleyan University Press, 1992), 52.

45 Ibid., 52.

46 Ibid., 52.

47 Ibid., 53.

48 Ibid., 54.

49 Ibid., 55.

50 Wolfson's article, "Why We Should Fight for the Right to Marry" was originally published in the *Journal of Gay, Lesbian, and Bisexual Identity* in 1996. It was reprinted in Andrew Sullivan's anthology, *Same-Sex Marriage Pro and Con: A Reader* (New York: Random House, 1997), 128–32, 129.

51 Ibid., 223.

52 Published in the April–June issue of the journal *Ultimate Issues* and reprinted in Andrew Sullivan's *Same-Sex Marriage Pro and Con: A Reader* (New York: Random House, 1997), 61–6, Prager's article "Homosexuality, the Bible, and Us—A Jewish Perspective," is truly peculiar. It argues that in order to become fully human, men and women must merge into couples and states that the Hebrew Bible codifies a laudable ideal of marital sex which should remain the norm to the present day. It does not take into account the fact that biblical marriage was polygamous; the patriarchs and Israelite kings took many wives and copulated as well with servants and concubines. Prager seems to view sexuality in the ancient near east as a mirror image of modern, suburban marriage among the American middle class.

53 "The Life and Trials of Ally McBeal," Fox, 17 January, 2000.

54 Ibid.

55 Ibid.

56 Ibid.

57 Ibid.

58 *Mademoiselle* Dec. 2000: cover.

59 Wendy Bristow, "Could You Snag This Prince?", *Mademoiselle* Dec. 2000:106.

60 Ibid., 107.

61 Ibid., 107.

62 Ibid., 108.

63 Letitia Baldridge, *Legendary Brides* (New York: HarperCollins Publishers, 2000), 118.

64 Ingraham, *White Weddings*, 31.

65 Baldridge, *Legendary Brides*, 125.

66 Victoria Houseman, *Made in Heaven:Unscrambling the Marriages and Children of Hollywood Stars* (Illinois: Bonus Books, 1991), 168.

67 Baldridge, *Legendary Brides*, 102.

68 Jay Mulvaney, "The Kennedy Family Wedding Album," *Ladies' Home Journal* Oct. 1999:207.

69 Ibid., 207.

70 Sarah Bradford, *America's Queen: The Life of Jacqueline Kennedy Onassis* (New York: Viking, 2000).

71 Mark Shaw, *The John F. Kennedy's* (New York: Rizzoli, 2000).

72 Bradford, *America's Queen*, 37.

73 Bradford, *America's Queen*, 73.

74 Baldridge, *Legendary Brides*, 105.

75 Bradford, *America's Queen*, 71.

76 Baldridge, *Legendary Brides*, 138. "Earl Spencer's emotional denunciation of the press in his funeral oration turned him briefly into the 'People's Earl', until press reports of his divorce later revealed him as a serial adulterer who had driven his bulemic wife into a nursing home." *Diana, the Making of a Media Saint,* ed. Jeffrey Richards, Scott Wilson, and Linda Woodhead (London: I.B. Tauris Publishers, 1999), 9.

77 Introduction, *Diana, the Making of a Media Saint,* ed. Jeffrey Richards, Scott Wilson, and Linda Woodhead (London: I.B. Tauris Publishers, 1999), 1.

78 Sally Bedel Smith, *Diana in Search of Herself: Portrait of a Troubled Princess* (New York: Signet, 1999), 68.

79 Ibid.,20, 66.

80 Paul Heelas, "Diana's Self and the Quest Within," in *Diana: The Making of a Media Saint,*ed. Jeffrey Richards, Scott Wilson, and Linda Woodhead (London: I.B. Tauris Publishers, 1999), 102.

81 Jeffrey Richards, "The Hollywoodization of Diana," in *Diana: The Making of a Media Saint,*ed. Jeffrey Richards, Scott Wilson, and Linda Woodhead (London: I.B. Tauris Publishers, 1999), 65. *In Style* Spring 2000:46.

82 Baldridge, *Legendary Brides,* 138.

83 Ibid., 140.

84 *People* Jul. 1999:71.

85 Baldridge, *Legendary Brides,* 140.

86 *People* Jul. 1999:71.

87 In 1976 the anthropologist Mary Leakey found three trails of fossilized hominid footprints at Laetoli and claimed that they proved that human ancestors walked upright 3.6 million years ago. In 1977 Doctor Roslyn S. Yalow shared the Nobel Prize for Medicine with two male colleagues. She had pioneered a new method of radioummunoassay to measure the blood levels of hormones, enzymes, and drugs. It showed that diabetics have high blood insulin levels and was used to detect potential hepatitis in blood donors. President Ronald Reagan appointed Arizona judge Sandra Day O'Connor to the Supreme Court in 1981. The second female justice was Washington D.C. circuit judge Ruth Bader-Ginsburg, appointed by President Bill Clinton and confirmed in 1993. The first woman to walk in space was Soviet cosmonaut Svetlana Savitskaya, in 1984. American biologist Katherine Sullivan followed suit in the same year, as a member of the seven-member *Challenger* crew. James Trager, *The Women's Chronology* (New York: Henry Holt & Company, 1994), 645, 651, 570, 670, 717, 683. Despite these remarkable achievements, the public has not been saturated with images of any of these women and none have had stamps issued in their name.

Chapter Eight

1 Diane Ackerman, *A Natural History of Love* (New York: Random House, 1994), 36–37.

2 Homer H. Clark, *The Law of Domestic Relations in the United States* (St. Paul: West Publishing, 1987), 68.

3 Ackerman, *History of Love,* 268.

4 Frances and Joseph Gies, *Marriage and the Family in the Middle Ages* (New York: Harper & Row, 1987), 106.

5 Christopher N. L. Brooke, *The Medieval Idea of Marriage* (Oxford: Oxford University Press, 1989), 248.

6 Gies, *Marriage and the Family,* 243. The Jewish communities scattered throughout Europe had their own wedding rituals, which, from the twelfth century on, entailed

the groom's formal acquisition of the bride, the reading of a marriage contract, the blessing of a shared goblet of wine, and the recitation of a series of nuptial benedictions. But Jews were influenced by the Christian majority, as evidenced by the late medieval Ashkenazic acceptance of monogamy as a marital norm. Marilyn Yalom, *A History of the Wife* (New York: HarperCollins, 2001), 55.

7 John Gillis, *For Better, For Worse: British Marriages, 1600 to the Present* (New York: Oxford University Press, 1985),34.

8 Ibid., 57–62.

9 Ibid., 64.

10 In Jewish ceremonies the groom as well as the bride is escorted to the *huppah*. Traditionally the groom is attended by his father and future father-in-law and the bride accompanied by her mother and future mother-in-law, in keeping with the gender segregation of orthodox Jewish ritual. "Marriage," in *Encyclopedia Judaica* (Keter Publishing House Ltd., 1971), 1036–1037. In most modern Jewish weddings the principals are now escorted by their individual sets of biological parents, reflecting the relaxation of gender restrictions in conservative, reform, and reconstructionist Judaism.

11 Gillis, *For Better, For Worse*, 135–145.

12 Ibid., 135–136. Marriage is one of the central concerns of eighteenth-century English fiction. Novels of the period often investigate the question of a woman's freedom of choice in selecting a marriage partner, presenting various perspectives on the traditional idea of arranged unions based on parental authority. In both Samuel Richardson's 1747–9 Clarissa and Henry Fielding's 1749 *Tom Jones*, a heroine is forced to receive the addresses of a loathed suitor chosen by her parents. In the former work the tragic protagonist flees her parents' home, is raped, and dies. In the latter novel the heroine marries the man of her dreams, ultimately, with her father's consent. The late eighteenth century witnesses the full development of the romantic novel, whose main theme is the struggle of romantic love and personal autonomy against parental control. In Fanny Burney's 1778 *Evelina*, for instance, the sheltered female protagonist enters the London marriage market, rejects her grandmother's marriage scheme, and finally weds an aristocratic figure of benevolent paternalism with whom she falls in love. Most twentieth-century readers are familiar with the early nineteenth-century's novelistic marriage plot from the works of Jane Austen —or from film versions of her novels, which often fail to capture this author's ironic view of courtship. In fictions like Austen's 1811 *Sense and Sensibility* and her 1818 *Northanger Abbey*, provincial young girls travel to Bath and London, where they are taken to chaperoned balls and social gatherings and mingle with various suitors. Despite their naivete and financial disadvantages, these heroines ultimately do find husbands. For more on the marriage plot see Jane Spencer's *The Rise of the Woman Novelist: From Aphra Behn to Jane Austen* (Oxford: Basil Blackwell, 1986) and Joseph Allen Boone's *Tradition Counter Tradition: Love and the Form of Fiction* (Chicago: University of Chicago Press, 1987).

13 "The Queen is most anxious to enlist every one who can speak or write to join in checking this mad, wicked folly of 'Women's Rights,' with all its attendant horrors, on which her poor feeble sex is bent, forgetting every sense of womanly feeling and propriety," wrote Queen Victoria in 1870, after England's parliament had passed the Married Women's Property Act, a piece of legislation authored by Richard Marsden Pankhurst which allowed married women to retain their earnings. Similar legisla-

tion had been passed in the United States: first, in 1839, in Mississippi, and later in New York and Massachusetts. James Trager, *A Woman's Chronology* (New York: Henry Holt and Company, 1994), 293, 239, 251, 263.

14 *Wedding Bells* Fall/Winter 2000: 7.

15 Ackerman, *Natural History*, 272.

16 *The Oxford Study Bible,* ed. M. Jack Suggs, Katherine Doob Sakenfield, and James R. Meuller, (New York: Oxford University Press, 1992).

17 Ibid., Gen. 2:1.

18 Ibid., Gen. 2:23.

19 Ibid., Gen. 2:24.

20 Ibid., Gen. 3:1–16.

21 Gerda Lerner, *The Creation of Patriarchy* (New York: Oxford University Press, 1986), 96.

22 *Oxford Study Bible.*

23 Ibid., Gen. 17:7.

24 Ibid., Gen. 17:9–14.

25 Anita Daimant, *The New Jewish Wedding* (New York: Simon & Schuster, 1985), 27.

26 Philip and Hanna Goodman, *The Jewish Marriage Anthology* (Philadelphia: Jewish Publication Society of America, 1965), 44. (Zohar 1:89a).

27 *Catechism of the Catholic Church* (New York: Doubleday, 1995), 446.

28 *Catechism,* 448.

29 Gertrud Meuller Nelson and Christopher Witt, *Sacred Threshold: Rituals and Readings for a Wedding With Spirit* (New York: Doubleday, 19998), 126.

30 Michael MacFarlane, *Wedding Vows: Finding the Right Words* (New York: Sterling Publishing Co., Inc., 1992), 33.

31 Rachel Adler, *Engendering Judaism* (Boston: Beacon Press, 1998), 181.

32 Diamant, *New Jewish Wedding,* 191.

33 Chris Aridas, *Your Catholic Wedding* (New York: the Crossroad Publishing Company, 1982), 60.

34 Yetta Fisher Gruen, *Your Wedding:Making it Perfect* (New York: Penguin, 1986), 252.

35 Gruen, *Your Wedding,* 254

36 David C. and Esther R. Gross, *Under the Wedding Canopy: Love and Marriage in Judaism* (New York: Hippocrene Books, 1996), 65.

37 Gross, *Love and Marriage in Judaism,* 65.

38 Pope Pious XI, "Christian Marriage," in *Catholicism,* ed. George Brantl (New York: George Braziller, 1961), 210.

39 Ibid., 211.

40 Ibid., 210.

41 Aridas, *Your Catholic Wedding,* 103.

42 Diamant, *New Jewish Wedding,* 177.

43 Ibid., 177.

44 Harriete Cole, *Jumping the Broom: the African American Wedding Planner* (New York: Henry Holt and Company, 1993), 123.

45 Roger Fritts, *For As Long As We Both Shall Live* (New York: Avon Books, 1993), 12.

46 Ibid., 11.

47 Etiquette now permits friends to officiate at wedding ceremonies in states like California and Massachusetts, where virtually anyone can be licensed for a day by either a county clerk or the secretary of state. *In Style* magazine suggests having "a

loved one or someone special" perform the ceremony as a way of personalizing it. *In Style* Spring 2000:207.

48 Daphne Rose Kingma, *Weddings from the Heart:Contemporary and Traditional Ceremonies for an Unforgettable Wedding* (Berkeley: Conari Press, 1991), 112.

49 Ibid., 112.

50 Ibid., 113.

51 Ibid., 59.

52 *In Style* February 1999: 222.

53 *People* Jul.1999:83.

54 Ibid., 224.

55 *People* , 83.

56 Fritts, *For as Long*, 13.

57 Ibid., 13.

58 Ibid., 28.

59 Sally Kilbridge and Mallory Sampson, *Real Weddings: A Celebration of Personal Style* (New York: Clarkson Potter Publishers, 1999), 88.

60 Ibid., 97.

61 Ibid., 92.

62 Kingma, *Weddings from the Heart*, 131.

63 *In Style* Spring 2000:215.

64 Fritts, *For As Long As We Both Shall Live*, 31.

65 *Us* Feb. 2000: 58.

66 Ibid., 93.

67 Kingma, *Weddings from the Heart*, 124.

68 Michael MacFarlane, *Wedding Vows: Finding the Perfect Words* (New York: Sterling Publishing Co., Inc., 1992), 86.

69 Fritts, *For As Long As We Both Shall Live*, 47.

70 Ibid., 45.

71 Ibid., 48.

72 *People* Jul. 1999:98.

73 *People* Aug. 2000:118.

74 Fritts, *For As Long As We Both Shall Live*, 7.

75 Ibid., 52.

76 Ibid., 24.

77 Ibid., 65.

78 Barbara Eklof, *With These Words I Thee Wed: Contemporary Vows for Today's Couples* (Holbrook, Massachusetts: Adams Publishing, 1989), 25.

79 Ibid., 27.

80 Ibid., 38.

81 Ibid., 79.

82 Fritts, *For As Long As We Both Shall Live*, 53.

83 Kingma, *Weddings from the Heart*, 176.

84 *In Style* Spring 2000:209.

85 *Modern Bride* Jun./Jul. 1999:118.

86 Charriol, advertisement, *Modern Bride* Apr./May 1999: 113.

87 *Wedding Bells* Spring/Summer 1999, 66.

88 Ibid., 66.

89 *In Style* Spring 2000: 208.

90 *For the Bride* Summer 1998:32.

91 *In Style* Spring 2000: 209.

92 Diamant, *New Jewish Wedding*, 176.

93 Fritts, *For As Long As We Both Shall Live*, 60.

94 Ibid., 64.

95 MacFarlane, *Wedding Vows*, 34.

96 Fritts, *For As Long As We Both Shall Live*, 81.

97 Kingma, 151.

98 Rabbi Debra Orenstein, *Lifecycles: Jewish Women on Life Passages and Personal Milestones* (Woodstock, Vermont: JewishLights Publishing, 1994), 157.

99 Ibid., 157.

100 The *Yihud* has been featured in many recent bridal magazines. A special feature in *Wedding Bells*, for instance, celebrates the ritual's therapeutic qualities: "During many traditional Jewish wedding ceremonies, just after the couple is officially married, the bride and groom will leave the *huppah*... and spend 10 to 15 minutes alone in *yichud* (seclusion), within a specially designated private area, perhaps the rabbi's study, the temple library, or the bride's changing room...The private time helps to let what's just happened sink in and to let the couple truly enjoy and appreciate the moment. Any couple wanting a brief retreat could plan to make a stop at a park, lookout point, or other secluded, beautiful spot during the trip from the ceremony to the reception." *Wedding Bells* Spring/Summer 1999:26.

101 Orenstein, *Lifecycles*, 178.

102 Ibid., 178–179.

103 Ibid., 179.

104 Ibid., 180.

105 Ibid., 180.

106 Rachel Biale, *Women and Jewish Law. The Essential Texts, Their History, and Their Relevance for Today* (New York: Schocken Books, 1984), 229–30.

107 Orenstein, *Lifecycles*, 158.

108 Janet Maslin, Vincent Canby , et al., *The New York Times Guide to the Best 1,000 Movies Ever Made*, ed. Peter M. Nichols. (Random House, 1999), 17.

109 Brooke, *Medieval Idea of Marriage*, 104.

110 Arranged marriages persist, of course, in other parts of the world. Journalist Sherry Amatenstein reports reports that in India an estimated 90 per cent of marriages are arranged, and in Bangladesh rural women are commonly married against their will and urban women subjected to arranged marriages. In Pakistan arranged marriage is very much the norm. Amatenstein depicts how female children of parents who have emigrated to the United States from these countries must contend with the imposition of old world marital norms. "American Women Forced Into Arranged Marriages," *Marie Claire*. April, 1999: 40–46. I myself have encountered this phenomenon in my dealings with two extremely distressed Pakistani-born female undergraduates I taught recently at New York University, both of whom confided to me that their parents were arranging to betroth them to significantly older men — whom they had never met—from their country of origin.

111 Gerda Lerner, *The Creation of Feminist Consciousness* (New York: Oxford University Press, 1993), 283.

Chapter Nine

1 Optimum Care, advertisement. *Essence* May 1999: 11.

2 Ibid., 11.

3 Ibid., 11.

4 Mitchell, *What the Hell Is a Groom?*, 56.

5 Kilbridge and Samson, *Real Weddings*, 140.

6 Jean T. Barrett, *Colin Cowie Weddings* (Boston: Little, Brown and Company, 1998), 158.

7 Arlene Hamilton Stewart, *A Bride's Book of Wedding Traditions* (New York: Hearst Books), 177.

8 Diane Ackerman, *A Natural History of Love* (New York: Random House: 1994), 271.

9 Hamilton Stewart, *Bride's Book*, 201.

10 Jean T. Barrett, *Colin Cowie Weddings*, 79.

11 Ibid., 189.

12 *Martha Stewart Weddings* Winter 2000: 96.

13 Ibid., 154.

14 *Martha Stewart Weddings* Summer/Fall 1998:76.

15 *Martha Stewart Weddings* Winter 2001:192.

16 Ibid., 76.

17 *People* Jul.1999: 133.

18 *In Style* Nov. 1999:441.

19 Ibid., 445.

20 Ibid., 445.

21 Ibid., 445.

22 *In Style* Feb. 1999:226–230.

23 Ibid. 240.

24 Ibid., 240.

25 *In Style* Spring 2000:223.

26 Ibid., 218–23.

27 *Us Weekly* Dec. 2000:49.

28 Ibid., 48.

29 Ibid., 48.

30 *In Style* Feb. 2001:307.

31 *Us Weekly* Dec. 2000: 49.

32 *In Style* Feb. 2001:322.

33 Ibid., 321–2.

34 *In Style* Feb. 1999:212.

35 Ibid., 212.

36 Ibid., 210.

37 *People* Aug. 2000:120.

38 Ibid., 120.

39 Ibid., 117.

40 Kilbridge and Samson, *Real Weddings*, 22.

41 Ibid., 26.

42 Ibid., 31.

43 *Modern Bride* Jun./Jul.1999:279.

44 Julia Chaplin, "Here Comes the Bride, and Her Sponsors," *New York Times* 24 Sep. 2000: 9:1.

45 *People* Aug.2000:120.

46 Constance C.R. White, "The Price a Woman Pays to Say 'I Do,'" *New York Times* 29 Jun. 1997: E5.

47 Chapin, "Here Comes the Bride," 9:4.

48 Barbara Ehrenreich, *The Hearts of Men: American Dreams and the Flight from Commitment* (Garden City, New York: Anchor/Doubleday, 1983), 121.

49 William J. Goode, *World Changes in Divorce Patterns* (New Haven: Yale University Press, 1993), 164–177.

50 Rochelle Gatlin, *American Women Since 1945* (Jackson and London:University Press of Mississippi, 1987), 189.

51 Greg J. Duncan and Saul D. Hoffman, "What Are the Economic Consequences of Divorce?", *Demography* 25:4 (November, 1988): 641. Atlee L. Stroup and Gene E. Pollock, "Economic Consequences of Marital Dissolution," in *The Economics of Divorce: The Effects on Parents and Children*, ed. Craig A. Everett (New York: The Haworth Press, Inc., 1994), 47. While they concede that women are more economically vulnerable in the divorce process, Stroup and Pollock claim that the male standard of living also declines post-divorce—ten as opposed to thirty per cent.

52 Judith Harris, *The Nurture Assumption:Why Children Turn Out the Way They Do* (New York: Simon & Schuster, 1998), 303.

53 Rhona Mahoney, *Kidding Ourselves: Breadwinning, Babies, and Bargaining Power* (New York: HarperCollins, 1995),19.

54 Ibid., 18.

55 Feminist manifestos of the 1960s and 1970s often express the touchingly naive assumption that marriage will fade away as a cultural institution as women become more empowered. Originally published in 1970, Germaine Greer's *The Female Eunich* is one such work. Greer concludes her chapter, "The Middle Class Myth of Love and Marriage," by totally dismissing the ideal of romantic wedlock; "But it isn't true and it never was, and now for sure it never will be" (Toronto: Bantam Books, 1970), 231. With such total confidence in matrimony's imminent demise, social critics of this period must have felt no need to analyze the wedding industry. Recent feminist critiques like Chris Ingraham's *White Weddings: Romancing Heterosexuality in Popular Culture* (New York:Routledge, 1999) provide useful facts on the purchasing habits of middle class Americans but offer a disappointingly simplistic, Marxist analysis of the wedding industry. In renditions like Ingraham's innocent American women are misled and exploited by rapacious corporate C.E.O.s who cynically sell the marriage ideal at the expense of female liberation. Such accounts misrepresent a complicated process in which female fantasies of self-aggrandizement in wedlock intersect with business interests, fueling marital consumerism.

56 For a typical critique of the beauty industry see Susan Douglas' "Narcissism as Liberation" in *Ways of Reading: An Anthology for Writers*, ed. David Bartholmae and Anthony Petrosky (Boston: St. Martin's Press, 1996), 115–136. Attacks on pornography include Susan Brownmiller's *Against Our Will: Men, Women, and Rape* (New York: Fawcett Columbine, 1975), 392–6, Andrea Dworkin's *Pornography: Men Possessing Women* (New York:Putnam, 1981), and Gloria Steinem's "Erotica vs. Pornography" in *Transforming a Rape Culture*, ed. Emilie Buchwald, Pamela R. Fletcher, and Martha Roth (Minneapolis: Milkweed Editions, 1993), 31–6.

57 Respondents to a survey that I recently conducted of 20 working women between the ages of 27 and 40 indicate that my own spending habits are pretty typical. None of these women spends more than 20 dollars on pornography in a given year, and each admitted to spending between 50 and 300 dollars on beauty products per year.

58 White, "The Price a Woman Pays," E5. "Although not as 'epidemic' as some social critics would lead us to believe, there has been a persistent and steady increase in the number of divorces from the 1960s through the mid-1980s. Estimates in the likelihood of divorce vary by age and cohort, and a number of methodological problems make precise estimates difficult to obtain. In general, about 45% to 50% of all marriages end in divorce (Clark & Wilson, 1994, Bumpuss, Sweet, & Cherlin, 1991)." Kris Bulcroft, Linda Smeins, and Richard Bulcroft, *Romancing the Honeymoon: Consummating Marriages in Modern Society* (Thousand Oaks, California: Sage Publications, 1999), 30.

59 Harris, *The Nurture Assumption*, 50–1.

60 Lionel Tiger, "Omnigamy: A New Kinship System" in *The Little, Brown Reader*, ed. Marcia Stubbs and Sylvan Barnett (Boston: Little, Brown, & Company, 1986), 19.

61 Ibid., "Omnigamy," 20.

62 Ibid., 20.

63 Hamilton Stewart, *A Bride's Book of Wedding Traditions*, 222.

64 John R. Gillis, *For Better, For Worse: British Marriages 1600 to the Present* (New York:Oxford University Press, 1985), 74.

65 Hamilton Stewart, *Bride's Book*, 224.

66 Editors of *Bride's* Magazine, *The Bride's Book of Etiquette* (New York: Perigree, 1999), 207.

67 *In Style* Spring 2000:150.

68 *Glamour* Dec. 1999:146.

69 Ibid., 146.

70 *Cosmopolitan* May 1999:164.

71 Ibid., 164–6.

72 *In Style* Spring 2001: 78.

73 *People* Jun. 1998:102–8.

74 Editors of *Bride's* Magazine, *Bride's* Book, 215.

75 *Bride's* Feb./Mar. 2000:170.

76 *In Style* Spring 2001: 246.

77 James Grace, *The Best Man's Handbook* (Philadelphia: Running Press, 1999), 121.

78 Ibid., 110.

79 Ibid., 118.

80 Ibid., 119.

81 Ibid., 124.

82 Ibid., 128.

83 Angela Lansbury, *Wedding Speeches and Toasts* (London: Ward Lock, 1994), 76.

84 Barbara Jefferey, *Wedding Speeches and Toasts* (London: Foulsham, 1998), 58–63.

85 Michael R. Perry, *The Groom's Survival Manual* (New York: Pocket Books, 1991), 195.

86 John Mitchell, *What the Hell is a Groom and What's He Supposed to Do?* (Kansas City: Andrew McMeel Publishing, 1999), 106.

87 *The Letters of Abelard and Heloise*, trans. Betty Radice (London:Penguin, 1974), 114.

88 Lansbury, *Wedding Speeches*, 42.

89 *Wedding Bells* Spring/Summer 1999:150.

90 Jefferey, *Wedding Speeches*, 18.

91 *Martha Stewart Weddings* Winter 2001:310.

92 Editors of *Bride's* Magazine, *Bride's Book*, 214.

93 Van Horn-Hayward, advertisement, *Martha Stewart Weddings* winter 2001: 380.

94 Ibid.

95 *Modern Bride* Apr./May 1999:267.

96 Kilbridge and Samson, *Real Weddings*, 48.

97 Diane Ackerman, *A Natural History of Love* (New York: Random House, 1994), 273.

98 Simon R. Charsley, *Wedding Cakes and Cultural History* (London and New York: Routledge, 1992),39–40.

99 Ibid., 46.

100 Ackerman, *Natural History*, 273.

101 Charsley, *Wedding Cakes*, 57–8.

102 Ibid., 72.

103 Craig Claiborne, Pierre Franey, and the Editors of Time-Life Books, *Classic French Cooking* (New York: Time Life Books, 1970), 73–7.

104 Charsley, *Wedding Cakes*, 76.

105 Ibid., 84–5.

106 Jaclyn C. Barrett-Hirschhaut, *Elegant Bride's 1000 Questions About Your Wedding* (Arlington, Texas: Summit Publishing Group, 1997), 377

107 *People* Jul.1999:113.

108 *People* Jun. 1998:89.

109 Charsley, *Wedding Cakes*, 138.

110 Ibid., 14–15.

111 Ibid., 24.

112 *Martha Stewart Weddings* Winter 2000:318.

113 Ibid., 330.

114 *Bridal Guide* Jul. 1999:149.

115 *Martha Stewart Weddings* Winter 2000: 322.

116 Barrett, *Cowie Weddings*, 181.

117 Kilbridge and Samson, *Real Weddings*, 22.

118 *In Style* Spring 2000: 108–13.

119 Roland Barthes, "Ornamental Cookery," in *Mythologies*, trans. Annette Lavers (New York: Farrar, Straus, and Giroux, 1957), 78–80.

120 Don Altman, *201 Unique Ways to Make Your Wedding Special* (Los Angeles: Moon Lake Media, 1994), 27.

121 *In Style* Spring 2000:229.

122 Daniel Harris, *Cute, Quaint Hungry and Romantic: The Aesthetics of Consumerism* (New York: Basic Books, 2000), 153–78.

123 Susan Sontag, "Notes on 'Camp,'" in *Against Interpretation* (New York: Farrar, Straus, & Giroux, 1961), 275–92.

124 Ibid., 280.

Chapter Ten

1 Advertisement, *modern Bride* Apr./May 1999:535.

2 Air Pacific, advertisement, *Modern Bride* Apr./May 1999: 566.

3 Allegro Resorts, advertisement, *Bridal Guide* Jul./Aug. 1999:395.

4 Beaches, advertisement, *Modern Bride* Apr./May 1999:555.

5 Kea Lani Hotel, advertisement, *Modern Bride* Apr./May 1999:583.

6 The Westin Resort, advertisement, *Modern Bride* Jun./Jul. 1999:447.

7 Breezes, advertisement, *Modern Bride* Feb./Mar. 1999:819.

8 Advertisement, *Bride's* Feb./Mar. 2000:1205.

9 Swept Away Resort, advertisement, *For the Bride by Demetrios* Summer 1998:265.

10 SuperClubs, *Modern Bride* Feb./Mar. 1999:861.

11 Karmina Palace, advertisement, *Bride's* Feb./Mar. 1999: 1153.

12 Advertisement, *Modern Bride* Feb./Mar. 1999: 846.

13 Elbow Beach Bermuda, advertisement, *Bride's* Feb./Mar. 1999:1145.

14 Swept Away Resort, advertisement, *For the Bride by Demetrios* Summer 1998:265.

15 Sheraton Hotel & Resorts, Hawaii, advertisement, *Bride 's* Feb. /Mar. 2000:1195.

16 Ibid., 1195.

17 Sol Melia, advertisement, *Bride's* Feb./Mar. 2000:1230.

18 Advertisement, *Modern Bride* Jun./Jul. 1999:422.

19 John Boswell, *Same Sex Unions in Premodern Europe* (New York: Villard Books, 1994), 34–5.

20 Kris Bulcroft, Linda Smeins, and Richard Bulcroft, *Romancing the Honeymoon: Consummating Marriage in Modern Society* (Thousand Oaks, California: Sage Publications, 1999), xiii.

21 Ibid., xiii.

22 Lawrence Stone, *The Family, Sex, and Marriage in England: 1500–1800* (New York: Haper & Row, 1977), 223.

23 Karen Dubinsky, *The Second Greatest Disappointment: Honeymooning and Tourism at Niagara Falls* (New Brunswick, New Jersey: Rutgers University Press, 1999), 20.

24 Stone, *Family, Sex, and Marriage*, 224.

25 Arlene Hamilton Stewart, *A Bride's Book of Wedding Traditions* (New York: Hearst Books), 247–54.

26 Dubinsky, *Second Greatest Disappointment*, 20.

27 Ibid., 21.

28 Ibid., 22.

29 Jonathan Katz, *The Invention of Heterosexuality* (New York: Dutton, 1995), 85.

30 Angus McLaren, *Twentieth-Century Sexuality: A History* (Oxford: Blackwell Publishers, 1999), 47.

31 Dubinsky, *Second Greatest Disappointment*, 160.

32 Marie Stopes, *Married Love* (London: Fifield, 1918), 43–4

33 McLaren, *Twentieth -Century Sexuality*, 57–8.

34 W.F. Robie, *Rational Sex Ethics* (Boston: Richard C. Badger, 1916), 114.

35 Wilhelm Stekel, "Frigidity in Mothers," in *The New Generations: the Intimate Problems of Modern Parents and Children*, ed. V.F. Calverton and Samuel D. Calverton (London: Allen and Unwin, 1930), 247–60.

36 McLaren, *Twentieth-Century Sexuality*, 59. For a stringent corrective to the confused, biased representations of female sexuality in early sex manuals see the first five

chapters of Barbara Seaman's *Free and Female* (Greenwich, Connecticut: Fawcett Crest, 1972).

37 Dubinsky, *Second Greatest Disappointment*, 168.

38 This is actually a paraphrase. Upon returning to England from Niagara Falls in 1882 Wilde allegedly described the waterfalls as follows: "Every American bride is taken there, and the sight of the stupendous waterfall must be one of the earliest, if not the keenest disappointments in American married life." Lloyd Lewis and Henry Justin Smith, *Oscar Wilde Discovers America* (New York, Benjamin Bloom, 1967), 163.

39 Dubinsky, *Second Greatest Disappointment*, 232.

40 Rita Schwartz, personal interview, 22 September, 2000.

41 Dubinsky, *Second Greatest Disappointment*, 216.

42 Ibid., 244.

43 Although modern etiquette dictates that the groom and his biological family cover honeymoon costs, increasingly, communities have begun shouldering the expenses of honeymoons. Marital entitlement has expanded to include a relatively new institution: honeymoon registries, to which friends send gift checks to subsidize the getaway. *Modern Bride* Feb./Mar. 1999: 814.

44 Editors of *Bride's* magazine, *The Bride's Book of Etiquette* (New York: Perigree, 1999), 282.

45 Ibid., 282.

46 Ibid., 282.

47 *Modern Bride* Feb./Mar. 1999:785–6.

48 Ibid., 840.

49 Ibid., 820.

50 Ibid., 812.

51 Ibid., 840.

52 Ibid., 840.

53 Michael R. Perry, *The Groom's Survival Manual* (New York: Pocket Books, 1991), 164.

54 Ibid., 164.

55 Ibid., 165.

56 John Mitchell, *What the Hell is a Groom and What's He Supposed to Do?* (Kansas City: Andrews McMeel Publishing, 1999), 90.

57 Ellen Kreidman, *Light His Fire* (New York: Dell, 1989), 4.

58 Ibid., 8.

59 Ibid., 3.

60 Ibid., 5.

61 Ibid., 119.

62 Ibid., 121.

63 Ibid., 196.

64 Ibid., 8.

65 Sharyn Wolf C.S.W., *How to Stay Lovers for the Rest of Your Life* (New York: Dutton, 1997), xi.

66 Ibid., 271.

67 Dagmar O'Connor, *How to Make Love to the Same Person for the Rest of Your Life and Still Love it* (New York: Bantam Books, 1985), 152.

68 Ibid., 206.

69 Ibid., 206–8.

70 Ibid., 203.

71 Daniel Beaver, *Beyond the Marriage Fantasy* (New York:HarperPaperbacks, 1983), 89.

72 Ibid., 93.

73 Francine Russo, "Keep Your Marriage Strong at 25, 35, 45," *Redbook* Aug.1999: 94, 119–22.

74 Ibid., 94.

75 Ibid., 123.

76 Ibid., 123.

77 "18 Ways to Make Your Marriage More Thrilling," *Redbook* Mar. 2000:143–44, 161.

78 *Redbook* Jun. 1999: 50.

79 Miranda Davis, "Have Sex Like You're Single," *Redbook* Aug. 2000: 84–9.

80 Ibid., 85.

81 Ibid., 86.

82 Mary K. Moore and Michelle Zaffino, "In the Mood in 4 Minutes," *Redbook* Sep. 1999:62.

83 "Passionate Monogamy," *Redbook* Jun. 1999:57.

84 *Redbook* Nov. 2000: cover.

85 Ibid., 146.

86 Ibid. ,163.

87 Daniel Harris, *The Rise and Fall of Gay Culture* (New York: Hyperion, 1997), 53.

88 *People* Jun. 1998: cover.

89 *Newsweek* Dec. 1998: cover.

90 *People* Jun. 1998:113

91 Newsweek Dec. 1998: 71.

92 *People* Jun. 1998: 115.

93 *Talk* Sep. 2000:184.

94 Ibid., 74.

95 Ibid., 71.

96 *Talk* Sep. 2000:184.

97 Ibid., 184.

98 Ibid., 184.

99 *Newsweek* Jun. 1998:70.

100 *People* Dec. 1999: cover.

101 Ibid., 108.

102 Ibid., 110.

103 *Glamour* Nov. 2000: cover.

104 Ibid., 276.

105 Ibid., 292.

106 *McCall's* Oct. 1998: 22.

107 *Us* Oct. 20:00.

108 Ibid., 70.

109 *People* Jul.1999:96.

110 Ibid., 96.

111 *Talk,* Sep. 2000:100.

112 *Good Housekeeping* Mar. 1999: 106.

113 Ibid. 107.

114 Ibid., 107.

115 Ibid., 107.

116 *People* Jun. 1998: 115.

117 Ibid., 117.

118 *Premiere* Sep. 1999:74.

119 Martin Townsend, "Family Ties," *Us* Sep. 2000:70.

120 Ibid., 70.

121 Ibid., 70.

122 *Us* Aug. 2000:57.

123 *Us* Feb. 2000: 88.

124 *People* Jun. 1998: 118.

125 *Cosmopolitan* May 2000: 243.

126 Ibid., 43.

127 *Ladies' Home Journal* Oct. 1999: 199.

128 *Us* Aug 2000:61.

129 Ibid., 61.

130 Jeanne Wolf, "Melanie Bounces Back," *Redbook* Feb. 2001:89.

131 *Us.* Feb. 2000: 80.

132 Angus McLaren, *Twentieth-Century Sexuality: A History* (Oxford: Blackwell Publishers, 1999), 111.

133 *Redbook* Feb. 2001:56–8.

134 Ibid., 58.

135 Susan Estrich, *Sex and Power* (New York: Riverhead Books, 2000), 13.

136 Betty Friedan, *The Feminine Mystique* (New York: Dell, 1974), 37.

Index